# Must We Mean What We Say?

Reissued with a new preface to sit alongside the volume on Stanley Cavell in the Contemporary Philosophy in Focus series, this famous collection of essays covers a remarkably wide range of philosophical issues (there are essays on Wittgenstein, Austin, Kierkegaard, and the philosophy of language) and extends beyond philosophy into discussions of music and drama.

"This book changed philosophy. When it was originally published it was both exhilarating and astonishing—for its daring disregard of disciplinary boundaries, as Cavell linked his beautiful essays on Lear and Beckett to ruminations about Wittgenstein and the relationship between knowing and acknowledging; for its disregard of the artificial distinction between the analytic and the continental, as it linked Kierkegaard to Austin; and, above all, for its insistence on speaking in a human voice, in a discipline that was largely in flight from the human. Unfortunately, although the book did change philosophy, giving permission to many young people to follow their philosophical passion in strange directions, its challenge, thirty years later, remains as urgent and radical as ever. No reader of Cavell should be surprised to observe that, now as then, new forms of reductionism, scientism, and sheer flight prove appealing to those for whom a complex human understanding is more than their hearts can bear."—Martha Nussbaum, author of *Upheavals of Thought*

"This book is still the best introduction to the wide-ranging thoughts and the powerful imagination of one of America's most distinguished men of letters. In it, Cavell weaves together Wittgenstein's reactions to philosophical skepticism with Shakespeare's descriptions of human needs, and J. L. Austin's appeals to 'the ordinary' with reflections on how art lets us see familiar objects anew. No one since William James has been so successful at re-humanizing philosophy—at rescuing that academic discipline from hyperprofessionalized self-absorption."—Richard Rorty, author of *Contingency, Irony and Solidarity*

Stanley Cavell is the Walter M. Cabot Professor of Aesthetics and the Theory of Value at Harvard University, Emeritus.

# Must We Mean What We Say?

## A Book of Essays

### Updated edition

STANLEY CAVELL
*Harvard University*

PUBLISHED BY THE PRESS SYNDICATE OF THE UNIVERSITY OF CAMBRIDGE
The Pitt Building, Trumpington Street, Cambridge, United Kingdom

CAMBRIDGE UNIVERSITY PRESS
The Edinburgh Building, Cambridge CB2 2RU, UK
40 West 20th Street, New York, NY 10011-4211, USA
477 Williamstown Road, Port Melbourne, VIC 3207, Australia
Ruiz de Alarcón 13, 28014 Madrid, Spain
Dock House, The Waterfront, Cape Town 8001, South Africa

http://www.cambridge.org

First published 2002

Printed in the United States of America

*Typeface* Baskerville 10/13 pt.      *System* QuarkXPress [BTS]

*A catalog record for this book is available from the British Library.*

*Library of Congress Cataloging in Publication Data*

Cavell, Stanley, 1926–
  Must we mean what we say? / Stanley Cavell. – Updated ed.
    p.   cm.
  Includes bibliographical references and indexes.
  ISBN 0-521-82188-6 – ISBN 0-521-52919-0 (pb.)
    1. Philosophy, Modern.   I. Title.
  B945 .C271 2003
    190–dc21        2002071642

ISBN   0 521 82188 6   hardback
ISBN   0 521 52919 0   paperback

*To Cathy and Rachel*

# Contents

# Permissions

# Acknowledgments

Four of the ten essays in this volume are published here for the first time:

The reading of *Endgame* was written in the summer and fall of 1964 and I have used some selection of its material each spring since then in the Humanities course which the Department of Philosophy at Harvard offers in the General Education program of the college. Similar selections were the basis for lectures given at Western Reserve University and the Case Institute, at the University of Saskatchewan, and at the University of North Carolina.

"Kierkegaard's *On Authority and Revelation*" was prepared for a colloquium on that book held at the University of Minnesota by its Department of Philosophy in January 1966.

"Knowing and Acknowledging" is an expansion of my contribution to a colloquium held at the University of Rochester in May 1966. Its original version was written as a set of comments on a paper presented at that Colloquium by Professor Norman Malcolm; that is the paper of his, subsequently published with minor revisions, which is cited in this essay.

Part I of the reading of *King Lear* was written in the summer of 1966, partly as preparation for, partly out of dissatisfaction with, my lectures in the Humanities course mentioned previously. Part II was written in the summer and fall of 1967, during a period in which a sabbatical term was generously granted early by Harvard University in order that I might bring this book to a finish.

Nothing like it would have been started apart from Harvard's Society of Fellows, in which I was a Junior Fellow from 1953–1956. The highest praise of the Society, and all it asks, is expressed in the work produced by the years of freedom it provides. In my case, the most precious benefit of those years was the chance to keep quiet, in particular to postpone the Ph.D., until there was something I wanted, and felt readier, to say.

The six essays which have already been published have been brought into uniform stylistic format; otherwise they appear here without, or with trivial, alterations. I might mention here one stylistic habit of mine which, in addition to irritation, may cause confusion. I use dots of omission in the usual way within quoted material, but I also use them apart from quotations in place of marks such as "etc." or "and so on" or "and the like." My little justifications for this are (1) that since in this use they often indicate omissions of the end of lists of examples or possibilities which I have earlier introduced, I am in effect quoting myself (with, therefore, welcome abbreviation); and (2) that marks such as "and the like," when needed frequently, seem to me at least as irritating as recurrent dots may be, and in addition are false (because if the list is an interesting one, its members are not in any obvious way "like" one another). I also use these dots, and again at the end of lists, as something like dots of suspension; not, however, because I suppose this device to dramatize the mind at work (generally, the opposite is truer) but because I wish to indicate that the mind might well do some work to produce further relevant examples. I can hardly excuse my use of list dots, any more than other of my habits which may annoy (e.g., a certain craving for parentheses, whose visual clarity seems to me to outweigh their oddity); for if I had found better devices for helping out my meaning, there would be no excuse for not having employed them. A further idiosyncracy is especially noticeable in the later essays, the use of a dash before sentences. Initial recourse to this device was as a way of avoiding the change of topic (and the necessity for trumped up transitions) which a paragraph break would announce, while registering a significant shift of attitude or voice toward the topic at hand. The plainest use of the device is an explicit return to its old-fashioned employment to mark dialogue.— But there are so many justifications for not writing well.

My editors at Scribners have evidently had a mixed lot to contend with in helping to order this work. I am grateful for their indulgences, as well as for tact in drawing lines.

For permission to reprint I am grateful to the original publishers:

"Must We Mean What We Say?" is a greatly expanded version of a paper read as part of a symposium at a meeting of the American Philosophical Association, Pacific Coast Division, on December 19, 1957. The first part of that symposium was "On the Verification of Statements About Ordinary Language," by Professor Benson Mates. These papers were first published together in *Inquiry*, Vol. 1 (1958) and both are reprinted in V. C. Chappell, ed., *Ordinary Language* (Englewood Cliffs: Prentice-Hall, Inc., 1964). The page references to Professor Mates' paper are according to its occurrence in the Chappell collection.

"The Availability of Wittgenstein's Later Philosophy" was first published in *The Philosophical Review*, LXXI (1962), and reprinted in George Pitcher, ed., *Wittgenstein: The Philosophical Investigations* (Garden City, New York: Doubleday and Company, Inc., 1966). Material for this paper was prepared during a period in which I received a grant from the Henry P. Kendall Foundation, to which I wish to express my gratitude.

"Aesthetic Problems of Modern Philosophy" was prepared for a volume of original essays by younger American philosophers, edited by Max Black, *Philosophy in America* (London; George Allen & Unwin Ltd., 1965; Ithaca: Cornell University Press, 1965). Approximately the first half of this paper was presented to a meeting of the American Society for Aesthetics in October 1962. It was written during the year 1962–63 in which I was in residence at the Institute for Advanced Study at Princeton, as was a longer study from which the Austin paper, listed immediately below, was extracted. These are fragments of the continuing profit that year remains for me.

"Austin at Criticism" was published first in *The Philosophical Review*, LXXIV (1965), and reprinted in Richard Rorty, ed., *The Linguistic Turn* (Chicago and London: The University of Chicago Press, 1967).

"Music Discomposed" was read as the opening paper of a symposium held at the sixth annual Oberlin Colloquium in Philosophy in April 1965 and was published, together with the comments on it by Professor Monroe Beardsley and by Professor Joseph Margolis, as part of the Proceedings of that Colloquium, in Capitan and Merrill, eds., *Art, Mind, and Religion* (Pittsburgh: University of Pittsburgh Press, 1967). Most of the material in sections V, VI, and VII of this essay was presented as part of a symposium called "Composition, Improvisation and Chance," held at a joint meeting of the American Musicological Society, the Society for Ethnomusicology, and the College Music Society, at the University of California, Berkeley, December 1960. The title of the symposium, as well as my participation in it, were both the work of its moderator, Joseph Kerman. I am grateful to him also for suggestions about the initial material I presented at Berkeley and about an earlier draft of the present paper.

"A Matter of Meaning It" constitutes my rejoinders to Beardsley and Margolis; while not read at the Oberlin Colloquium, it is included in its Proceedings.

The few personal acknowledgments which are scattered through these essays scarcely suggest the debts I have accumulated in the writing of them. Because the largest of these are debts of friendship as much as of instruction, I must hope that they were partly discharged in the course of incurring them, for certainly the essays alone are insufficient repayment. I am thinking of conversations with Thomas Kuhn (especially during 1956–58, our first two years of teaching at Berkeley) about the nature of history and, in particular, about the relations between the histories of science and of philosophy; of the countless occasions on which I have learned about continental philosophy and literature from Kurt Fischer, in everything from isolated remarks to the course of lectures he gave to his graduate seminar at Berkeley on Nietzsche's *Zarathustra*; of the years during which Thompson Clarke taught me to understand the power of traditional epistemology, and in particular of skepticism. My debt to Clarke is systematic, because it was through him, together with a study of Wittgenstein's *Philosophical Investigations* (on which we gave a joint seminar in 1959–60), that I came to see that everything I had said (in "Must We Mean What We Say?") in defense of the appeal to ordinary language could also be said in defense, rather than in criticism, of the claims of traditional philosophy; this idea grew for me into an ideal of criticism, and it is central to all my work in philosophy since then. Its most explicit statement, in the work which appears here, is given in the opening pages of "Knowing and Acknowledging." It is a guiding motivation of my Ph.D. dissertation. *The Claim to Rationality* (submitted to Harvard University in 1961, now soon to be published), a fact I mention here because ideas and formulations of that book (in particular, the view it develops of Wittgenstein's later philosophy) appear throughout the essays collected here, and I am uneasy about the possibility that from time to time I am relying on it as backing for claims which in the space of an essay are not developed enough to stand by themselves. This creates obvious risks of delusion.

The piece on Kierkegaard, the two on music, and that on Lear— that is to say, the bulk of the latest work—were written during periods in which their controlling ideas were recurrent topics of conversation with Michael Fried and John Harbison; the reservations and the satisfactions they expressed were always guiding for me. Their wives, Ruth Fried and Rose Mary Harbison, were frequently very much a part of those conversations, as they are part of those friendships; if what I owe to them is less specific, it is no less real. To say, in addition, that I owe to Michael Fried's instruction any understanding I have come to about modernist painting and sculpture, scarcely describes the importance that access of experience has had for me over the past three or four years. Its confirmation and correction and extension of my thoughts about the arts and about modernism is suggested by the writings of his to which I refer in various of the later essays; but conversations with him about those topics, and about history and criticism, and about poetry and theater, are equally, if silently, present in them.

First books tend to over-ambitiousness, and nowhere more than in the bulk of debts they imagine themselves able to answer for.

I cannot forgo the pleasure of thanking my teachers of philosophy—Henry David Aiken, Abraham Kaplan, and Morton White— especially for their encouragement to think of, or to remember, philosophy as something more than the preoccupation of specialists. To the late J. L. Austin I owe, beyond what I hope is plain in my work, whatever is owed the teacher who shows one a way to do relevantly and fruitfully the thing one had almost given up hope of doing. And because all the pieces of this book were written after I had begun to teach, the responses of my students are often guiding in the way I have written, in everything from the specific choice of an example or allusion to a general tendency to swing between dialogue and harangue. Here I single out Allen Graubard and John McNees and Timothy Gould, whose intellectual companionship and whose acts of friendship since I came back to Cambridge to teach, are unforgettable.

That since that time I have enjoyed the friendship of Rogers Albritton, and therewith the power of his intelligence and sensibility, is a fortune which only those who know him can begin to appreciate.

My mother and father have waited for, and supported, these first fruits in the peculiar patience, and impatience, known only to parents. My uncle, Mendel Segal, began his avuncularity by supporting my infancy on his shoulders, and continued it, through my years in graduate school and my first years of teaching, with brotherly advice which usually cost him money. My wife, Cathleen Cohen Cavell, beyond the moments of timely editing and encouragement, kept in balance the sabbatical months in which the final stages of composition were accomplished. And now my daughter Rachel can see what it was I was doing as I inexplicably scribbled away those hundred afternoons and evenings.

That I am alone liable for the opacities and the crudities which defeat what I wanted to say, is a miserably simple fact. What is problematic is the expense borne by those who have tried to correct them, and to comfort the pain of correcting them.

S.C.

*31 December 1968*
*Cambridge, Massachusetts*

# Preface to Updated Edition of
# *Must We Mean What We Say?*

Friends have repeatedly remarked to me that some later preoccupation of mine can be found foreshadowed in passages of *Must We Mean What We Say?* This quality of previewing might be understood merely as a consequence of the book's history, that although it is my first book, and although its title essay was written in 1957, it collects work from the ensuing dozen years and was not published until I was into my fourth decade, when my interests may be thought to have been fairly developed. But I understand the presence of notable, surprising anticipations to suggest something more specific about the way, or space within which, I work, which I can put negatively as occurring within the knowledge that I never get things right, or let's rather say, see them through, the first time, causing my efforts perpetually to leave things so that they can be, and ask to be, returned to. Put positively, it is the knowledge that philosophical ideas reveal their good only in stages, and it is not clear whether a later stage will seem to be going forward or turning around or stopping, learning to find oneself at a loss.

I received my first copy of the book from its publisher on the day of what I recall as the most tortured of the emergency faculty meetings following the massive arrest of students occupying the main administration building of Harvard College, in April of 1969, so that my initial joy, or its expression, in perceiving the book's existence in the world, was largely put aside, whether as a relief from isolation or as a source of refuge it was hard to tell. But each of the ten essays making up the book has its own history, as does its Foreword, and a way of introducing this new edition of them is to give a little of the history in each case.

For some years, the only essays in the book that were discussed in print, or reprinted from it, were the opening two, sometimes as a pair; and those discussions were responses to their original appearance in philosophy journals, and, I believe, subsided after their collection into the book. The context of their companion essays in *Must We Mean What We Say?* would have, perhaps, made it plainer to their readers (as they made it plainer to me) that in their declarations of indebtedness to the work of J. L. Austin and of Wittgenstein's *Philosophical Investigations*, my motivating question was less how we know what we say and mean (which was the point on which criticism of those two papers were centered) than it was the question of what it betokens about our relation to the world, and others, and myself, that I do in fact, to an unknown extent, inescapably know (barring physical or psychic trauma), and that I chronically do not know or cannot say what I mean, and that I can know further by bethinking myself of what I would rather or might or must or could say, or not say, or rather not. Few philosophers would now, I believe, deny that the ability to speak a language carries with it the ability to perform these linguistic feats, but I assume most do not attach the importance I continue to do to the bearing of this ability on the questions of self-knowledge and of skepticism. Controversy over the importance of the ordinary is more likely now to arise in the form of a question not of the epistemological but of the political bearing of the ordinary, say upon whether the appeal to the ordinary is a mode of conforming to the state of one's society or of criticizing it.

The opening essay, "Must We Mean What We Say?," was undertaken as the result not so much of an invitation as of an assignment. Near the end of my first year of teaching at Berkeley, in the spring of 1957, I was told that a panel on ordinary language philosophy was being scheduled at the coming Christmas meetings of the Pacific Division of the American Philosophical Association, in which I would have a chance, let's say an obligation, to defend in public the views I had been advancing all year concerning the ground-breaking philosophical importance of the work of Austin, in the form of a response to a paper to be presented by my senior colleague Benson Mates. I had, as a result of Austin's visiting Harvard my last semester there, thrown away what may have been a partially written Ph.D. dissertation, and consequently arrived in Berkeley to take up the position of Assistant Professor there not only without a degree but with no concrete idea for a dissertation (an unthinkable circumstance after my generation in graduate school). The imposition of the obligation was fair enough. It was time that I get into the open some formulation of what had seemed so enlivening in my encounters with Austin, or else suffer the humiliation of finding that it was not, at my hands, defensible in grown-up discussion.

Reading the essay now, I still sense in it the initial exhilaration in finding ways to mean everything I was saying, and to say a larger fraction of what I had philosophically to say, than I had ever experienced. The elation was an experience as of escaping from what I had inarticulately felt in my philosophical education, and remaining in much of philosophy's dispensation as I began my life of teaching philosophy, as prohibitions on, or suspicions of, everyday speech, quite in the absence of patient attention to the individual utterance. I am struck by a double anticipation in a formulation from the last page of "Must We Mean What We Say?" which speaks of Socrates "coax[ing] the mind down from self-assertion—subjective assertion and private definition—and leading it back, through the community, home." First, the sense of the philosopher as responding to one lost will become thematic for me as my understanding of Wittgenstein's *Investigations* becomes less primitive than it was; second, the literary or allegorical mode of the formulation is something I recognized early as a way of mine of keeping an assertion tentative, that is, as marking it as a thought to be returned to. The implication that philosophical lostness requires something like guidance of a therapeutic sort may or may not be clear to others in these words, but they were ones in which at that period of my life I associated with the work of psychoanalysis. (The formulation "back, through the community, home" seems ambiguous as between meaning leading the mind back to its home in the community, or rather back, beyond this, to itself. Ambiguity was perhaps the best I could do then with the idea of philosophy's ancient therapeutic ambition, before I had gotten into questions of the fantasy of a private language, of skepticism's power to repudiate ordinary language, and of philosophy's arrogance in its calling to speak for humanity, for "us.")

I suppose that the idea of the philosopher as guide was formed in me in resistance to the still current idea of the philosopher as guard. So I should perhaps add that at no period of my life has it occurred to me that philosophical problems are unreal, that is, that they could be cured and philosophy thus ended, as if left behind. The problems I was concerned with are better expressed as about the all but unappeasable craving for unreality; Kant's diagnosis of such perplexities was as Transcendental Illusions.

I had in "Must We Mean What We Say?" already suggested understanding the philosophical appeal to the ordinary in relation to Kant's transcendental logic (*Must We Mean . . . ?* p. 13), namely as the sense of uncovering the necessary conditions of the shared world; but not until the second essay of the book, "The Availability of Wittgenstein's Later Philosophy," was I able to give a certain textuality to this relation to Kant, at the point at which Wittgenstein in the *Investigations* announces that "Our investigation . . . is directed not toward phenomena, but, as one might say, toward the 'possibilities' of phenomena" (*ibid.* p. 65). And it would not be until after completing *The Claim of Reason* that I would feel I had secured some significant progress in assessing the difference it makes that Wittgenstein sees illusions of meaning as something to which the finite creature is subject chronically, diurnally, as if in every word beyond the reach of philosophical system. The idea that there is no absolute escape from (the threat of) illusions and the desires constructed from them, say there is no therapy for this, in the sense of a cure for it—or rather the pervasiveness and hence invisibility of the idea that there might be some such escape—was evidently something that captured my fascination, halfway through *Must We Mean What We Say?*, with Samuel Beckett's *Endgame,* in effect a study of the circumstance that "You're on earth, there's no cure for that" (*ibid.* p. 129).

"The Availability of Wittgenstein's Later Philosophy" was written in answer to the invitation to prepare a review-essay of the publication of Wittgenstein's *The Blue and Brown Books* together with David Pole's *The Later Philosophy of Wittgenstein,* the first book (to my knowledge, in English) on its subject. My writing in this essay is from time to time marked by exasperation, even anger, always philosophically suspicious. No doubt the emotion was a response to encountering in Pole's book a dismissive treatment of work that had changed my sense of philosophy's possibilities (and rather encouraged my sense of intellectual isolation), a dismay exacerbated by the book's uniformly receiving praise, in my hearing, for its efforts. Nevertheless, I am not pleased to see my declaration that "none of [Wittgenstein's] thought is to be found" in Pole's book; I remember once changing that accusation to read "little of Wittgenstein's thought . . . etc." and finding the change to be evasive and condescending. A more interesting reason for my review's moments of extreme impatience was my beginning to learn how difficult it was going to be, difficult in some way unprecedented in my experience, to say in some undisappointing way what my sense of the importance of Wittgenstein's work turned upon. Hence my impatience, not surprisingly, was in large part impatience with myself.

Accepting the invitation had in effect meant committing myself to reading Wittgenstein's *Preliminary Studies for the "Philosophical Investigations"* (the over-title of *The Blue and Brown Books*) with a seriousness I knew I had not begun to give to the *Investigations* itself. No deadline for my essay was set or imagined, and I waited until the end of the academic year to allow the project uninterruptedly to take all summer if necessary. In fact what took all summer was just reading through Wittgenstein's two (preliminary) texts, which initiated notes and elaborations on my part larger in bulk than the bulk of Wittgenstein's texts. Along with finding my way to the excitement of accompanying the intensity of thought expressed in these pages, I was discovering about the ordinary what I missed in Austin, namely, that if, as Wittgenstein puts the matter, "What we do is lead words back from their metaphysical to their everyday use," then to understand how this happens we must understand how we have drifted, or been driven, *away* from the everyday, living as it were in exile from our words, not in a sure position from which to mean what we say. In short I discovered that skepticism, which metaphysics is apt to undertake to defeat, is a renewed threat in Wittgenstein, whereas Austin rather imagines that both skepticism and metaphysics can fairly readily be put aside, with the attentiveness and good will appealed to by his methods, as if the strength of ordinary language were more characteristic of it than its vulnerability. I note three passages, or formulations, from the essay, beyond the thematic matters, for example, of rules and of our knowledge of our language, that recurrently motivate later work of mine.

Take first the paragraph in "The Availability of Wittgenstein's Later Philosophy" that runs: "We learn and teach words in certain contexts, and then we are expected, and expect others, to be able to project them into further contexts. . . . Nothing insures that we will make . . . the same projections. That on the whole we do is a matter of our sharing routes of interest and feeling . . . senses of humor and of significance . . . , of what is outrageous, of what is similar to what else . . . all the whirl of organism Wittgenstein calls 'forms of life'. . . . It is a vision as simple as it is difficult and as difficult as it is (and because it is) terrifying" (p. 52). In recent years this passage has been receiving increasing attention. The "vision" I speak of in the passage becomes further worked out ten years later as Chapter VII of *The Claim of Reason*, entitled "Wittgenstein's Vision of Language," where the idea in *Must We Mean . . . ?* of the communicative power of language as requiring nothing beyond (behind, beneath) our sharing, and maintaining, our human forms of life to ensure its success, is expressed in *The Claim of Reason* as there being "no reason" (p. 178) for our sharing them. (Such a requirement— for, let's say, a metaphysical grounding of our ability to communicate—would amount to requiring that we have a reason for caring about one another in general, for attaching any significance to the fact that some things on earth manifest forms of life, and that some of these, to speak so, have souls. I also say there that these possibilities and necessities of our forms of life are nothing more and nothing less than natural (having two chapters earlier gone to some lengths to show that the distinction between the natural and the conventional is unstable).

Second, the characterization of the style of *Philosophical Investigations* as, among other matters, a crossing of the genres of Dogmatics and Confession and Dialogue served, even in the space of a brief concluding section, to establish for me the issue of Wittgenstein's writing as one to which I have never stopped turning my thoughts.

Third, the formulation, "Belief is not enough [in reacting, for example, to Wittgenstein's extraordinary remark, 'If a lion could talk we could not understand him']. Either the suggestion penetrates past assessment and becomes part of the sensibility from which assessment proceeds, or it is philosophically useless" (p. 71) prepares the way for, years later, in Part Four (the final, longest part) of *The Claim of Reason*, my recognition that at some stage in that part, the role of the *Investigations* is no longer one of being interpreted (cp. *The Claim of Reason*, p. xv). I would say now that this recognition was one of finding that an object of interpretation has become a means of interpretation, and the one because of the other. This became true of Austin for me earlier than of Wittgenstein, and it seems to me true in varying degrees of every writer (of what person or object not?) that I have ever taken with seriousness. Some of course prove to be more fruitful, or fateful, than others.

But while I had gained, from writing "The Availability of Wittgenstein's Later Philosophy," what I felt was a usable sense of the depth of *Philosophical Investigations*, I was still far from seeing how to articulate this sense with the details of that text. I had, however, enough confidence now to make a beginning of a new dissertation that had been forming in my mind and in my notes on the relation between epistemology and ethics, or knowledge and the justification of confrontation, call it the articulation of the standing from which to question conduct and character, of oneself and of another, in differentiation from the standing to confront claims to knowledge. The main courses I offered in 1959–60, on Wittgenstein and on moral philosophy, were conscious preparations for the writing out of the ideas of the dissertation, so that when I began the consecutive writing, in the fall of 1960, even though I was still teaching full time, the dissertation was completed seven months later, namely before the remaining essays in *Must We Mean What We Say?* were written.

I mark this moment by citing a formulation, out of sequence, that I find related to those from "The Availability . . .," namely from the Foreword to *Must We Mean What We Say?*, the piece of the book that still seems to me to speak for itself, written as its last, in 1968, within the opening phase of the decades of intellectual turmoil throughout the humanities and their related social sciences, that fill much of the remaining years of the twentieth century. In that phase, the students' call for "relevance" in their studies was at its rawest and most relentless, and the formulation I have in mind is more or less obviously a response to that cry: "If philosophy is esoteric, that is not because a few men guard its knowledge but because most men guard themselves against it" (*Must We Mean . . . ?*, p. xxvii). It is at the same time a good instance of my manner of invoking an arresting concept, one that has halted me, like esotericism, whose pertinence I felt strongly in connection with ordinary language practice (how could we become alienated from the words closest to us?—but then again, from what others?), but which I would not be able to speak about with much consequence until years later. Of course there seems no way of telling in the moment of such a formulation whether it is intellectually evasive or whether it is understandably to be trusted. What justifies creating junctures at which readers are asked to make such wagers one way or the other?

The academic year 1962–63, in transition to returning to teach at Harvard, was spent on sabbatical leave, and its first fruits were represented by the third essay, "Aesthetic Problems of Modern Philosophy," one of a number invited from younger American philosophers to appear in a volume called *Philosophy in America.* I chose the topic both to identify myself with the arts, which somehow joined in forming my interest in a life in philosophy (perhaps helped by my only once in six years of teaching at Berkeley having taught a course in aesthetics, and then not satisfyingly, and not again, it turned out, for twenty years), and more immediately prompted by the idea of continuing the issue of my relation to my language by relating it to Kant's idea of my capacity to give objectivity to aesthetic judgments, that is, to trace their distinctive source of necessity and universality. This was meant to open a new path in the continuing effort to illuminate the question whether my judgments of what I mean in speaking (or generally in conducting myself) are a priori or a posteriori. I had nothing further substantial to say about this until my interpretation of criteria in the opening chapters of *The Claim of Reason*, where my relation to my (ordinary) speech is in effect pictured as my chronic expatriation from it, the result of philosophy's uncontrolled search for, let's say, purity—as if what philosophy is compelled, like revolted Coriolanus, to say to Rome is, "I banish you."

Only in stages have I come to see that each of my ventures in and from philosophy bears on ways of understanding the extent to which my relation to myself is figured in my relation to my words. This establishes from the beginning my sense that in appealing from philosophy to, for example, literature, I am not seeking illustrations for truths philosophy already knows, but illumination of philosophical pertinence that philosophy alone has not surely grasped—as though an essential part of its task must work behind its back. I do not understand such appeals as "going outside" philosophy.

I point to three formulations in "Aesthetic Problems of Modern Philosophy" that have recurred often in my thoughts and that are characteristic of something I can recognize as my manner, namely to introduce a remark in a guise (calling attention to itself) meant to mark an intuition which I find guiding, or whose obscurity or incompleteness is meant to be undisguised, intended to remind myself in public, as it were, that I find significance here that I have not earned, to which accordingly I know I owe a return. One such formulation is meant to characterize a task of philosophy I find proposed in *Philosophical Investigations*, one I call "undo[ing] the psychologizing of psychology" ("Aesthetic Problems...," p. 91). This thought will be taken further two years later in the essay on Kierkegaard (the sixth of *Must We Mean...?*). The formulation helped me in my ongoing bouts of revising my dissertation, *The Claim to Rationality*, into what became *The Claim of Reason*. It is specifically a way of thinking about what Wittgensteinian criteria and grammar do.

I point, second, to the formulation "Ordinary language philosophy is about whatever ordinary language is about" (p. 95), which expresses a desire of mine for philosophy, that it invites me to reason about anything in my experience, anything I find of interest, from philosophy's wish to inhibit or discount certain interests (say in the arts) or to reform or escape or limit to a minimum of distinct points its recourse to the ordinary, to Beckett's finding the extraordinary ordinary and Chekhov's finding the ordinary extraordinary.

A third formulation is "Nothing is more human than to deny them [viz., human necessities]" (p. 96). The human drive to the inhuman, tempting philosophy to the monstrous, is as reasonable and uncompromised a statement of the subject of Part Four of *The Claim of Reason*, as any other I have found. That part is in effect a small book, reflecting on the larger book to which, as it were, it is irreversibly bound, and lies in the background of much of the work I have done since then.

"Austin At Criticism," the fourth essay of *Must We Mean What We Say?*, was the result of an invitation for a review-essay of Austin's

*Philosophical Papers,* published in 1962, two years after Austin's death at the age of forty-eight; the essay does not disguise a concluding tone fitting a memorial address. My wish to articulate my undiminished, life-changing gratitude for Austin's innovations seemed to require articulating my sense of Austin's refusal (as it struck me) to draw consequences from those innovations that did justice to their radicality. What I found lacking is suggested in the essay's idea of "terms of criticism," meant to show that Austin's charges or images of philosophers as lazy, wily, drunk with arrogance, etc. cannot, on his own grounds, be taken with philosophical seriousness. On the contrary, they encourage the sense that the appeal to the ordinary is trivial, or eccentric, directed against at most marginal errors in philosophical practice. In *The Claim of Reason,* my charge against Austin is centered on his misconceived claim that his work defeated what I came to call the threat of skepticism. So I want to add here that Austin's work has in recent years taken on renewed significance for me, in various ways: as I came to appreciate more deeply than I had in the past his work on the performative utterance I wished to protect it somewhat from Derrida's distinct but limited admiration of it (in "Signature, Event, Context") and somewhat from its subsequent reception in what in Cultural Studies is called performance theory, where Austin's work plays a more explicit role than for the moment it plays in professional philosophy (where his name is less often mentioned than his work is assumed—his memory lives under what is for me a puzzling grudge); and more recently I have broached the issue of the relation of Austin's treatment of what he calls "slips," in his great essay "Excuses," with what Freud calls slips in *The Psychopathology of Everyday Life,* both thinkers seeing the condition of the human as immersed in a sea of responsibility, Austin wishing to limit responsibility in a way that allows civilized discourse and conduct to continue, Freud to expand it so radically as to require a new vision of the human, of its inevitable turnings from itself that threaten civilized intercourse, as well as of its powers to reason, in unexpected forms, with these threats, to turn back.

I postpone for a moment considering the fifth essay, on Beckett, to mention the three philosophical essays that follow it, the sixth on Kierkegaard, and the seventh and eighth on music. The concluding paragraph of the Kierkegaard essay now reads to me as a response to various issues of meaning what we say, from the sense of Wittgenstein's perception of us as, in philosophizing (hence when not?), estranged from our words, to Heidegger's identification of the everyday as caught up in inauthentic speech, what he (and Kierkegaard, and Nietzsche) calls something like "chatter." The main purpose of the pair on music is to lay out explicitly some issues of the modern, a concept, or perhaps it is hardly more than a recurrent experience of the world and the philosophy it calls for (and the art, and what institution not?) as having decisively but not yet intelligibly changed, as having become strange, that keeps making its appearance throughout the essays of *Must We Mean What We Say?* Why, although I seem to recall reading music before I could read words, I have not written about music again until fairly recently, and increasingly, is something I am beginning to write about.

The ninth essay, "Knowing and Acknowledging," written in response to an invitation to respond to Norman Malcolm's essay "The Privacy of Experience," represents a decisive step in the line of philosophical work represented by what precedes it. Malcolm's philosophical honesty and his admiration for Wittgenstein's achievements prompted from me reaffirmations simultaneously of my roots in analytical philosophy as well as of my conviction in Wittgenstein's criticism of that mode of philosophizing. Acknowledgment became a recurrent theme of my work from the time of its isolation for attention in "Knowing and Acknowledging" and provides, together with the essay that follows it, on *King Lear* ("The Avoidance of Love") the title of Part Four of *The Claim of Reason* ("Between Acknowledgment and Avoidance"). Its formulation of the skeptic's plight as one which in mortality, let's call it, presents itself as sort of limitation, "a metaphysical finitude as an intellectual lack" (p. 262), is one I invoke periodically in later work where I speak of "the threat of skepticism" as a sort of human compulsion to over-intellectuality (not simply a Faustian desire to know everything but a demonic will to measure every relation against that of knowing), as it were a natural weakness (to say the least) of the creature enamored of its intelligence.

The *Lear* essay, the tenth and last of the book, together with the essay on Beckett's *Endgame*, "Ending the Waiting Game"—the two essays, whatever degree of philosophicality they are granted, distinguished from the rest and linked by their constituting readings of incontestably literary works—make up almost two-fifths of the pages of *Must We Mean What We Say?* They were not invited by any field, indeed it was after the Beckett essay had been praised and turned down for publishing by several literary/cultural journals (with requests either to shorten it for an article or lengthen it for a book) that I recognized it would have to help me make its own home. At some point in composing the *Lear* material I felt I saw what this home was going to be. Both of these essays originated in lectures on their respective plays that I had assigned in the large lecture course that the Harvard Department of Philosophy offered in what was called, from 1945 to 1979, General Education; from that time it was replaced in stages by a differently conceived Core Curriculum. Both programs were sophisticated versions of a "distribution requirement" and meant to shape a measure of intellectual community among the undergraduate body at large. I thought of my contribution as a course in reading, a skill prior to the ability to distinguish among fields of study, and of its mission as providing an introduction to philosophy for those who may or may not go (or have gone) on to a career in the profession of philosophy. But these intentions do not in themselves warrant calling these somewhat unplaceable essays philosophical.

My sense that they are to be understood so arose negatively from the realization that they fit into no standing idea of a literary essay, a sense confirmed explicitly in recent years by several literary scholars and critics of Shakespeare who have reported their experience of strangeness upon encountering the *Lear* piece when it first appeared. Positively, it would not be until completing *The Claim of Reason* that I could claim explicitly of a Shakespearean tragic hero that his fate is bound up with a process philosophy calls skepticism. And not until writing the Introduction to the collection of my essays on six plays of Shakespeare, *Disowning Knowledge*, in the mid-1980s, would I find that I could fully articulate the fact and the way that the principal concepts that govern my reading of *Othello*, which closes *The Claim of Reason*, though they are not marked as technical, had been developed with increasing pertinence across the pages of the book that precede it, in characterizing the process, or call it the problematic, of skepticism with respect to the existence of others.

That the concepts which in my writing do the work of theory are not distinguished as technical, or given technical restrictions, may be expressed as saying that for philosophy, as I care about it most, ordinary language is no less or more an object of interpretation than a means of interpretation, and the one because of the other.

It could, I think, also justly be said of the texture and progress of the *Lear* essay, which closes *Must We Mean What We Say?*, that it works out, in terms developed in sketching the idea of acknowledgment in the essay that precedes it, the consequences, which prove tragic, of the avoidance of acknowledgment, work which as it were completes the analysis of acknowledgment as philosophy had come upon it. But that evidently was not something the author of *Must We Mean What We Say?* was capable then of saying. In that sense he can be said not to have known what he was doing.

What I did seem to know about what I was doing, namely, that I was glad to have reached the point of entrusting a book to the world (something my teacher Austin had never done, something a number of philosophers I admired in my generation working in relation to analytical philosophy had never done, have until now, I believe, not done), I indicated in the Foreword to *Must We Mean What We Say?*, where my tone of, let me say, anxious elation, as of finding myself roughly intact, dreams evidently alive after many chances to disparage them, seems to have found responsive chords in others who have also had to be patient longer than they had figured to begin to see their attraction to philosophy manifest itself in work of their own, in however unpredictable forms. This unpredictability may be linked with my impression, mentioned near the beginning of this new Preface, that with the appearance of *Must We Mean What We Say?* even the public discussion of its opening two papers subsided—as if I had put together a book in such a way that it asked to be accepted or rejected as a whole. While I cannot deny such an impulse in myself, I must add that it also makes me happy to learn that the individual parts of it continue to find acceptance sufficient to warrant the reissuing of the whole.

I did discover something further a year after completing the book, on a fellowship at Wesleyan's Humanities Center, about the effect on myself of putting the book behind me, or perhaps I should say, of having it to stand behind. Its independence of me freed me for I suppose the most productive, or palpably so, nine months of my life, in which I recast the salvageable and necessary material of my Ph.D. dissertation as the opening three parts of what would become *The Claim of Reason* and completed small books on film (*The*

*World Viewed*) and Thoreau (*The Senses of Walden*). I consider those small books to form a trio with *Must We Mean What We Say?*, different paths leading from the same desire for philosophy. I think of *Must We Mean . . . ?* as a lucky book, not because, as in other instances, it came so quickly, or else with so much difficulty that it is easy to imagine its never coming to pass. I call it, on its title page, a Book of Essays, having found that the interaction of the essays, despite the differences of their causes, have the feel of a sequence of chapters as much as a collection of independent texts. It is a texture I am glad of and feel lucky to have managed, supposing it is there; but lucky most distinctly in not having had, for institutional or professional reasons, to rush a book into print before I had one I felt lucky in having. (It would have been nice for me if this had all happened years earlier than it did; but that would have required a different life, nicer or not.)

My gratitude to the book in hand, associated with this surprise at its existence, is somehow expressed in a fact I learned of some years after hearing little about any consequences its publication may have had, namely, that two large libraries, one on each coast, had listed the book among those that had been repeatedly stolen, and consequently were no longer to be reordered for their catalogues. Moved as I am by the fantasm of students too poor to buy the book but too attached to it to overcome the desire to possess it, I nevertheless hope that the present printing allows for its freer circulation.

*Cambridge/Brookline*
*September 1, 2001*

# Foreword: An Audience for Philosophy

If the essays which follow do not compose a book, collecting resonance from one another, nothing I can say in introducing them will alter that fact. The relations among them are no less complex than the complexities I have sought to trace within the essays themselves; and any concept I would wish to use in characterizing their relations is either itself already at work within the essays, so far as I have been able to put it to work, or else it would require the working of another essay to do what I would want with it. The surface thematic overlappings among the essays are, I think, sometimes surprising, or surprisingly numerous. Because it would be tiresome to list them here, I have made an index of the themes I find, and found as I wrote, to be of guiding importance. Certainly I do not by this mean to suggest that I have fully treated any one of these themes; a number of them are just glanced at. But I have in each case wished that the place I have made for a theme's appearance provides data for further investigation of it.

Although various portions or drafts of separate essays were being written during essentially the same period, I have as far as possible arranged them chronologically according to their date of completion. It will be said that two of them—those on *Endgame* and on *King Lear*—are pieces of literary criticism, or at best applications of philosophy, while the remainder are (at least closer to being) straight philosophy. I wish to deny this, but to deny it I would have to use the notions of philosophy and of literature and of criticism, and the denial would be empty so far as those notions are themselves unexamined and so far as the impulse to assert such distinctions, which in certain moods I share, remains unaccounted for. Its account must include the obvious fact that these subjects, as I conceive of them, do resemble one another. One line of resemblance is marked where, in the essay on *King Lear*, I suggest a sense in which that play could be called "philosophical drama" and where I characterize a "philosophical criticism"; another line is projected at the points at which I note that each philosophy will produce "terms of criticism" directed against other philosophies, or against common sense, which are specific to that philosophy, and hence defining for it. In wishing to deny that some of these essays are philosophical and others not, I do not deny that there are differences among them, and differences between philosophy and literature or between philosophy and literary criticism; I am suggesting that we do not understand these differences. At various moments I am led to *emphasize* distinctions between philosophy and various of its competitors, various interests and commitments and tastes with which, at various moments in history, philosophy was confusible—e.g., between philosophy and science, and art, and theology, and logic.

If I deny a distinction, it is the still fashionable distinction between philosophy and meta-philosophy, the philosophy of philosophy. The remarks I make *about* philosophy (for example, about certain of its differences from other subjects) are, where accurate and useful, nothing more or less than philosophical remarks, on a par with remarks I make about acknowledgment or about mistakes or about metaphor. I would regard this fact—that philosophy is one of its own normal topics—as in turn defining for the subject, for what I wish philosophy to do. But someone who thinks philosophy is a form of science may not accept that definition, because his picture is of a difference between, say, speaking about physics and doing physics. And this may be not only a special view of philosophy, it may be a partial view of science; because certain ways in which certain persons talk about a science are a part of the teaching of the science, and the ways in which the science is taught and learned may be taken as essential to an understanding of what that science is.

I do assert a distinction throughout these essays which, because it may seem either controversial or trivial, I want to call attention to from the beginning—a distinction between the modern and the traditional, in philosophy and out. My claim is not that all contemporary philosophy which is good is modern; but the various discussions about the modern I am led to in the course of these essays are the best I can offer in explanation of the way I have written, or the way I would wish to write. The essential fact of (what I refer to as) the modern lies in the relation between the present practice of an enterprise and the history of that enterprise, in the fact that this relation has become problematic. Innovation in philosophy has characteristically gone together with a repudiation—a specifically cast repudiation—of most of the history of the subject. But in the later Wittgenstein (and, I would now add, in Heidegger's *Being and Time*) the repudiation of the past has a transformed significance, as though containing the consciousness that history will not go away, except through our perfect acknowledgment of it (in particular, our acknowledgment that it is not past), and that one's own practice and ambition can be identified only against the continuous experience of the past. (This new significance in philosophical repudiation itself has a history. Its most obvious precursor is Hegel, but it begins, I believe, in Kant. For it is in Kant that one finds an explicit recognition that the terms in which the past is criticized are specific to one's own position, and require justification from within that position. A clear instance of such a Kantian term of criticism is his characterization of an opposed "Idealism" as making the world "empirically ideal and transcendentally real"; another is his diagnosis of "dialectical illusion.") But "the past" does not in this context refer simply to the historical past; it refers to one's own past, to what is past, or what has passed, within oneself. One could say that in a modernist situation "past" loses its temporal accent and means anything "not present." Meaning what one says becomes a matter of making one's sense present to oneself. This is the way I understand Wittgenstein's having described his later philosophy as an effort to "bring words *back*" to their everyday use (*Philosophical Investigations*, §116; my emphasis), as though the words we use in philosophy, in any reflection about our concerns, are *away*. This is why Wittgenstein's interlocutors, when he writes well, when he is philosophically just, express thoughts which strike us as at once familiar and foreign, like temptations. (Heidegger's consciousness that our deepest task, as philosophers and as men, is one of *getting back* to a sense of words and world from which we are now away, is an intimate point of similarity with Wittgenstein.)

These reflections will perhaps seem uncongenial to many of my professional colleagues, but they are meant to collect data which most of us, I believe, have noticed, but perhaps have not connected, or not taken to be potentially philosophical. Take, for example, the fact that the isolated analytical article is the common form of philosophical expression now, in the English speaking world of philosophy; something reflected in the fact that the common, and best, form of philosophy textbook is the assemblage of articles around individual topics. This is often interpreted as symptomatic of philosophy's withdrawal from its cultural responsibilities. The trouble with such an idea is that it occurs to a person who imagines himself certain of his culture's needs, and certain of his capacity to supply them on demand, and ignorant of our cultural situation—in which each major form of expression (say painting and music and philosophy) has, where serious, taken upon itself the characteristic cultural responsibility of preserving itself against its culture, against its own past accomplishments, which have helped to inform, and to distort, present culture; past accomplishments which are used as names by those incapable of contributing to the present, against those who would take those accomplishments as setting the tasks of the present, or setting the terms in which present activity has its meaning and acquires its standards.

Analytical philosophy can, alternatively, be interpreted as symptomatic of philosophy's finally coming of age, or accepting its age, assimilating itself to the form in which original scientific results are made known. The trouble with this idea is that these articles are not *accepted* the way scientific papers are; they are not felt to embody results which every member of the profession can then build from. On the contrary, it seems to me commonly assumed among the serious philosophers I know that when they look into a new article they will find not merely a number of more or less annoying errors, but that they will find the whole effort fundamentally wrong, in sensibility or method or claim. Even when it is good—that is, when it contains one interesting or useful idea—the interest or usefulness cannot simply be taken over as it stands into one's own thought, but will require independent development or justification from within one's own procedures. It often happens that what makes an article or passage famous is its enunciation of a thesis which the profession is fully prepared to annihilate. The refuting of Mill on "desirable," or Moore on "indefinable," or Wittgenstein on "private language," have become minor industries, established more than one living. These can be disheartening facts, especially among the young who are entering the profession and still deciding whether it can support life—as though the profession as a whole has forgotten how to praise, or forgotten its value. (In emphasizing that criticism has been the life of philosophy from its beginning, I do not wish to camouflage what is genuinely disheartening about its present. I mean merely to remember that criticism *need* not be uncomprehending, nor always entered out of enmity.) It is hard to convey, to anyone who has not experienced it, how pervasive this *malaise* has become. For it controls one's response to one's own past work as well as to the work of others, and it applies not merely to chunky articles, but to each assertion one hears or makes.

The figure of Socrates now haunts contemporary philosophical practice and conscience more poignantly than ever—the pure figure motivated to philosophy only by the assertions of others, himself making none; the philosopher who did not need to write. I should think every philosopher now has at least one philosophical companion whose philosophical ability *and accomplishment* he has the highest regard for, who seems unable to write philosophy. Were such a person content with silence he would merely be the latest instance of a figure always possible within philosophy, possible indeed nowhere else. (It would make no sense to speak of someone as a gifted novelist who had never written a novel; nor of someone as a scientist who had made no contribution to science. In the case of the scientist, the contribution need not be his *own* writing; but one could say that he must affect what his *field* writes. His contribution, that is, may be oral, but it must affect a tradition which is essentially not oral; this suggests that such contributions must be exceptional. It indicates further that *writing* plays differing roles in different enterprises, even that "writing" means something different, or has a different inflection, in contexts like "writing a novel," "writing a fugue," "writing a report," "writing (up) an experiment," "writing (down) a proof." If silence is always a threat in philosophy, it is also

its highest promise.) But one finds instead various contraries of con-
tentment, perhaps a tendency, more or less contained, to cynicism
or to despair about the value of writing or of philosophy altogether—discontents often not sufficiently unambiguous, or not
showing early enough, to force or to permit a break with the field.
Philosophy inspires much unhappy love.

If these are facts of philosophical practice now, they must have
a sociological-historical explanation; and what needs to be explained
is what these facts point to, that the writing of philosophy is *difficult*
in a new way. It is the difficulty modern philosophy shares with the
modern arts (and, for that matter, with modern theology; and, for
all I know, with modern physics), a difficulty broached, or reflected,
in the nineteenth-century's radical breaking of tradition within the
several arts; a moment epitomized in Marx's remark that "...
the criticism of religion is in the main complete ..." and that "...
the task of history, once the world beyond the truth has disappeared,
is to establish the truth of this world ..." (*Contribution to the Critique
of Hegel's Philosophy of Right*, Introduction). This is the beginning of
what I have called the modern, characterizing it as a moment in
which history and its conventions can no longer be taken for
granted; the time in which music and painting and poetry (like
nations) have to define themselves against their pasts; the beginning
of the moment in which each of the arts becomes its own subject,
as if its immediate artistic task is to establish its own existence. The
new difficulty which comes to light in the modernist situation is that
of maintaining one's belief in one's own enterprise, for the past and
the present become problematic together. I believe that philosophy
shares the modernist difficulty now everywhere evident in the major
arts, the difficulty of making one's present effort become a part of
the present history of the enterprise to which one has committed
one's mind, such as it is. (Modernizers, bent merely on newness, do
not have history as a problem, that is, as a commitment. The conflict between modernizers and modernists is the immediate topic of
the two essays on music—numbers VII and VIII.) I might express my
particular sense of indebtedness to the teaching of Austin and to the
practice of Wittgenstein by saying that it is from them that I learned
of the possibility of making my difficulties about philosophy into
topics within philosophy itself—so that, for example, my doubts
about the relevance of philosophy now, its apparent irrelevance to
the motives which brought me to the subject in the first place, were

no longer simply obstacles to the philosophical impulse which had to be removed *before* philosophy could begin, hence motives for withdrawing from the enterprise. It was now possible to investigate philosophically the very topic of irrelevance, and therewith the subject of philosophy itself: it is characteristic of philosophy that from time to time it appear—that from time to time it be—irrelevant to one's concerns, or incredible in itself; just as it is characteristic that from time to time it be inescapable. No doubt there is a danger of evasion in this spiralling self-consciousness; perhaps one should indeed search for more congenial work. Just as there is the danger of excusing poor writing in insisting upon the complexities of consciousness one is at each moment attempting to record, or to acknowledge. —Am I talking only about a condition within America? If so, it is said in the spirit in which a certain kind of American has usually spoken of his country's release from the past: out of a sense of disappointment in struggle with vistas of peculiar promise. And as usual, it is the expression of shock in finding that one's mind is not, and is, European; which in practice means (and in philosophical practice means emphatically) English or German. —If others do not share these doubts, or find these dangers, I certainly have no wish to implicate them.

✳ ✳

The topics of the modern, of the philosophy of philosophy, and of the form of philosophical writing, come together in the question: What is the audience of philosophy? For the answer to this question will contribute to the answer to the questions: What is philosophy? How is it to be written? In case a philosopher pretends indifference to this question, or not recognize that he has an answer to it, I should note that this question intersects the question: What is the teaching of philosophy? Not, of course, that *this* question is likely to seem more attractive to those responsible for teaching it. On the contrary, like their pressed colleagues in other fields, professors of philosophy are likely to regard their teaching obligations as burdens, certainly as distant seconds in importance to their own work. Whatever the reason for this state of affairs, it has a particular pertinence for the philosopher. A teacher of literature is, say, a professor of English, and he can say so; a professor of anthropology is an anthropologist, and he can say so. But is a professor of philosophy a philosopher? And to whom can he say so? One often says instead, asked what it is one does, that one teaches philosophy. And that is the problem. *Does* one teach philosophy? And when one is gripped by that question, one is really asking: Can philosophy be taught? Who is in a position to speak for philosophy? Such questions express that difficulty I referred to a moment ago as one of maintaining one's belief in one's own enterprise. (Hegel, I am told, said that he was the last professor of philosophy. I think I know what he would have meant—that he was the last man to feel that he could speak evenly about every way in which the philosophical impulse has found expression, the last with the natural conviction that his own work was the living present of philosophy's history, able to take that history for granted. And that would mean that philosophy, as it has been known, is past. The mention of Hegel here reminds me that the sorts of problems I have spoken of in connection with the teaching of philosophy more familiarly arise in thinking about the history of philosophy, about whether anyone but a philosopher can write or know its history, and about whether a philosopher could allow himself to do so.)

When, in "Austin at Criticism" (Essay IV), I complain that Austin never described his procedures accurately and circumstantially, I am in effect complaining simultaneously of a lack in his philosophizing and of a failure in his teaching. These complaints have their proper weight only against the recognition of how powerful a teacher he was; for it was in part because Austin was devoted to teaching, according to a particular picture of what teaching can be, or should be, that he avoided certain ranges of what the teaching of philosophy perhaps must be—the *personal* assault upon intellectual complacency, the private evaluation of intellectual conscience. (This range of teaching is not confined to philosophy, though its proportions and placement will vary from subject to subject. This is what I am talking about in the opening of the essay on *King Lear*, in pointing to the New Critics' concentration on the *teachable* aspects of poetry.) A major motive for wishing to leave the field of philosophy, for wishing relief from it, from one's periodic revulsions from it, would be to find something which could be taught more conveniently, a field in which it was not part of one's task to *vie* with one's students, nor to risk misleading them so profoundly. Wittgenstein, though he swiftly resigned his appointment as Professor, was, as I read him, unofficially readier for these requirements, and like every great teacher he would have distrusted his right, or the necessity, to impose them. (The great teacher invariably claims not to want followers, i.e., imitators. His problem is that he is never more seductive than at those moments of rejection.) I find that his *Philosophical Investigations* often fails to make clear the particular way in which his examples and precepts are to lead to particular, concrete exercises and answers, for all his emphasis upon this aspect of philosophy. At the same time, his book is one of the great works about *instruction*—the equal, in this regard, of Rousseau's *Émile* and of Kierkegaard's *Philosophical Fragments*.

Because such writing as Wittgenstein's and such practice as Austin's strike certain minds as conservative, and because such minds are as apt as any to be over-confident in the faith that contrasts, like conservative vs. liberal, and liberal vs. radical, helpfully explain the behavior of the world and clear the mind for steady action, it is worth noting that these teachers thought of their work as revolutionary—not merely because what they did was new (something which can be overrated or overprized) but because they also thought it plain enough and immediately fruitful enough to establish a new common practice in thinking, and open to talent regardless of its standing within the old intellectual orders. This is another guise of the issue of the modern. I mention it again here because those of us who share, or credit, Wittgenstein's and Austin's sense of their revolutionary tasks are responding (as part of the experience of their work in making problematic the relation of philosophy to its tradition) to the concern and implication of their work for correct instruction. (There is no revolutionary social vision which does not include a new vision of education; and contrariwise.) This, together with the fact that their philosophical procedures are designed to bring us to a *consciousness* of the words we must have, and hence of the lives we have, represents for me a recognizable version of the wish "to establish the truth of this world." But then wherever there really is a love of wisdom—or call it the passion for truth—it is inherently, if usually ineffectively, revolutionary; because it is the same as a hatred of the falseness in one's character and of the needless and unnatural compromises in one's institutions.

When, in what follows, I feel pressed by the question of my right to speak for philosophy, I sometimes suggest that I am merely speaking for *myself*, and sometimes I suggest that philosophy is not *mine* at all—its results are true for every man or else they are worthless.

Are these suggestions both right, or are they evasions? They express an ambivalence about the relevance or importance of philosophy—one might say, about its possession—which is also one of philosophy's characteristic features. I have recently noticed a bit of philosophical literary practice which seems to betray this ambivalence. On half a dozen occasions over a period of a few months I found one philosopher or another referring to something called "Horatio's philosophy" or "Horatio's view of philosophy," as though Hamlet's strangely welcomed discovery that

> There are more things in heaven and earth, Horatio,
> Than are dreamt of in your philosophy.

constitutes a crack at Horatio rather than a manic release from philosophy (and from reasonableness) as a whole. (The generalizing non-possessive "your" is common enough in Hamlet's way of speaking, and there is no evidence that Horatio's view of the world is distinctive.) Perhaps the reason for this misreading is that philosophers have become threatened by an idea that philosophy has its limitations or impotencies. But I think it also expresses a legitimate confusion about the source or possession of philosophy altogether, as though half believing and half fearing that its natural state is one of private persuasion. I call this confusion legitimate because it isn't as though the philosopher had some automatic or special assurance that his words are those of and for other men, nor even that any particular arrival of his words ought to be accepted by others. His examples and interpretations have, and are meant to have, the weight an ordinary man will give them; and he is himself speaking as an ordinary man, so that if he is wrong in his claims he must allow himself to be convinced in the ways any man thinking will be, or will not be. —Who is to say whether a man speaks for all men?

Why are we so bullied by such a question? Do we imagine that if it has a sound answer the answer must be obvious or immediate? But it is no easier to say who speaks for all men than it is to speak for all men. And why should that be easier than knowing whether a man speaks for me? It is no easier than knowing oneself, and no less subject to distortion and spiritlessness. If philosophy is esoteric, that is not because a few men guard its knowledge, but because most men guard themselves against it.

It is tautological that art has, is made to have, an audience, however small or special. The ways in which it sometimes hides from its audience, or baffles it, only confirms this. It could be said of science, on the other hand, that it has no audience at all. No one can share its significance who does not produce work of the same kind. The standards of performance are institutionalized; it is not up to the individual listener to decide whether, when the work meets the canons of the institution, he will accept it—unless he undertakes to alter those canons themselves. This suggests why science can be "popularized" and art not (or not in that way), and why there can be people called critics of art but none called critics of science. I might summarize this by saying that academic art is (with notable exceptions) bad art, whereas academic science is—just science. (It is hardly an accident that creative scientists are on the whole at home in a university and that creative artists on the whole are not.) Now, what is academic philosophy? It seems significant that this question has no obvious answer. In the way it is significant that the questions, "What is the audience of philosophy? Must it have one? If so, what is it to gain from it?", have no obvious answers.

When you wish to make serious art popular what you are wishing is to widen the audience for the genuine article. Is this what someone wants who wants to widen the audience for philosophy by writing summaries or descriptions of philosophical works? Or is he, as in the case of popular science, providing simplifications which are more or less useful and faithful substitutes for the original work? Neither of these ideas makes good sense of philosophy. I think someone who believes in popular, or in popularizing, philosophy (as differentiated from someone in an open business venture who finds profit in excerpting and outlining anything in demand) believes that the ordinary man stands in relation to serious philosophy as, say, the ordinary believer stands in relation to serious theology—that he cannot understand it in its own terms but that it is nevertheless good for him to know its results, in some form or other. What reason is there to believe this? There is every reason to believe, on the contrary, that this is the late version of one of philosophy's most ancient betrayals—the effort to use philosophy's name to put a front on beliefs rather than to face the source of assumption, or of emptiness, which actually maintains them. Those who guard themselves from philosophy show a healthier respect for it than those who are certain they know its results and know to whom they apply. For when philosophy is called for one cannot know beforehand where it will end. That is why Plato, as is familiar, at the beginning of the *Republic* allows the good old man to leave ("to see to the sacrifice") before Socrates releases his doubts; and why, recalling that moment, Nietzsche's Zarathustra leaves the old man ("the old saint") he first encounters on his descent back to man, without relating his sickening tidings. Philosophy must be useful or it is harmful. These old men have no need of it, not necessarily because they are old, but because their passion for their lives is at one with their lives; either, as in the case of Cephalus, because his private passion is well spent and he is without rancor, or because, as in the case of the old forest creature, his passion remains in control of his old God, who was worthy of it. The advantage of their age is that their sincerity is backed by the faithfulness of a long life. Otherwise, where sincerity asserts itself, it calls for testing. I do not say that everyone has the passion or the knack or the agility to subject himself to philosophical test; I say merely that someone can *call* himself a philosopher, and his book philosophical, who has not subjected himself to it.

My purpose is to make such facts into opportunities for investigation rather than causes for despair. The question of philosophy's audience is born with philosophy itself. When Socrates learned that the Oracle had said no man is wiser than Socrates, he interpreted this to mean, we are told, that he knew that he did not know. And we are likely to take this as a bit of faded irony or as a stuffy humility. What I take Socrates to have seen is that, about the questions which were causing him wonder and hope and confusion and pain, he knew that he did not know what no man can know, and that any man could learn what he wanted to learn. No man is in any better position for knowing it than any other man—unless *wanting* to know is a special position. And this discovery about himself is the same as the discovery of philosophy, when it is the effort to find answers, and permit questions, which nobody knows the way to nor the answer to any better than you yourself. Then what makes it relevant to know, worth knowing? But relevance and worth may not be the point. The effort is irrelevant and worthless until it becomes necessary to you to know such things. There is the audience of philosophy; but there also, while it lasts, is its performance.

# I

# Must We Mean What We Say?

That what we ordinarily say and mean may have a direct and deep control over what we can philosophically say and mean is an idea which many philosophers find oppressive. It might be argued that in part the oppression results from misunderstanding, that the new philosophy which proceeds from ordinary language is not *that* different from traditional methods of philosophizing, and that the frequent attacks upon it are misdirected. But I shall not attempt to be conciliatory, both because I think the new philosophy at Oxford is critically different from traditional philosophy, and because I think it is worth trying to bring out their differences as fully as possible. There *is*, after all, something oppressive about a philosophy which seems to have uncanny information about our most personal philosophical assumptions (those, for example, about whether we can ever know for certain of the existence of the external world, or of other minds; and those we make about favorite distinctions between "the descriptive and the normative," or between matters of fact and matters of language) and which inveterately nags us about them. Particularly oppressive when that philosophy seems so often *merely* to nag and to

Since writing the relevant portions of this paper, I have seen three articles which make points or employ arguments similar to those I am concerned with: R. M. Hare, "Are Discoveries About the Uses of Words Empirical?" *Journal of Philosophy*, Vol. LIV (1957); G. E. M. Anscombe, "On Brute Facts," *Analysis*, Vol. XVIII (1957–1958); S. Hampshire and H. L. A. Hart, "Decision, Intention and Certainty," *Mind*, Vol. LXVII (1958). But it would have lengthened an already lengthy paper to have tried to bring out more specifically than will be obvious to anyone reading them their relevance to what I have said.

try no special answers to the questions which possess us—unless it be to suggest that we sit quietly in a room. Eventually, I suppose, we will have to look at that sense of oppression itself: such feelings can come from a truth about ourselves which we are holding off.

My hopes here are modest. I shall want to say why, in my opinion, some of the arguments Professor Mates brings against the Oxford philosophers he mentions are on the whole irrelevant to their main concerns. And this will require me to say something about what I take to be the significance of proceeding, in one's philosophizing, from what we ordinarily say and mean. That will not be an easy thing to do without appearing alternately trivial and dogmatic. Perhaps that is only to be expected, given the depth and the intimacy of conflict between this way of proceeding in philosophy and the way I take Mates to be following. These ways of philosophy seem, like friends who have quarreled, to be able neither to tolerate nor to ignore one another. I shall frequently be saying something one could not fail to know; and that will appear trivial. I shall also be suggesting that something we know is being overemphasized and something else not taken seriously enough; and that will appear dogmatic. But since I am committed to this dialogue, the time is past for worrying about appearances.

✳ ✳

Professor Mates is less concerned to dispute specific results of the Oxford philosophers than he is to question the procedures which have led these philosophers to claim them. In particular, he doubts that they have assembled the sort of evidence which their "statements about ordinary language" require. As a basis for his skepticism, Mates produces a disagreement between two major figures of the school over the interpretation of an expression of ordinary language—a disagreement which he regards as symptomatic of the shallowness of their methods.[1] On Mates' account of it, the conflict is not likely to be settled successfully by further discussion. We are faced with two professors (of philosophy, it happens) each arguing (claiming, rather) that

---

[1] I am too conscious of differences in the practices of Oxford philosophers to be happy about referring, in this general way, to a school. But nothing in my remarks depends on the existence of such a school—beyond the fact that certain problems are common to the philosophers mentioned, and that similar questions enter into their attempts to deal with them. It is with these questions (I mean, of course, with what I understand them to be) that I am concerned.

the way he talks is the right way and that what he intuits about language is the truth about it. But if this is what their claims amount to, it hardly seems worth a philosopher's time to try to collect evidence for them.

To evaluate the disagreement between Austin and Ryle, we may distinguish among the statements they make about ordinary language, three types:[2] (1) There are statements which produce *instances* of what is said in a language ("We do say . . . but we don't say—"; "We ask whether . . . but we do not ask whether—"). (2) Sometimes these instances are accompanied by *explications*—statements which make explicit what is implied when we say what statements of the first type instance us as saying ("When we say . . . we imply (suggest, say)—"; "We don't say . . . unless we mean—"). Such statements are checked by reference to statements of the first type. (3) Finally, there are *generalizations,* to be tested by reference to statements of the first two types. Since there is no special problem here about the testing of generalizations, we will be concerned primarily with the justification of statements of the first two types, and especially with the second.

Even without attempting to be more precise about these differences, the nature of the clash between Ryle and Austin becomes somewhat clearer. Notice, first of all, that the statement Mates quotes from Austin is of the first type: "Take 'voluntarily' . . . : we may . . . make a gift voluntarily . . ."—which I take to be material mode for, "We say, 'The gift was made voluntarily.'" (The significance of this shift of "mode" will be discussed.) Only one of the many statements Mates quotes from Ryle is of this type, viz., "It makes sense . . . to ask whether a boy was responsible for breaking a window, but not whether he was responsible for finishing his homework in good time. . . ." The statements of Ryle's which clash with Austin's are different: "In their most ordinary employment 'voluntary' and 'involuntary' are used . . . as adjectives applying to actions which ought not to be done. We discuss whether someone's action was voluntary or not only when the action seems to have been his fault . . . etc." These do not produce *instances* of what we say (the way "We say 'The boy was responsible for breaking the window'" does); they are

---

[2] Perhaps I should say "ideal" types. The statements do not come labeled in the discourse of such philosophers, but I am going to have to trust that my placing of statements into these types will not seem to distort them.

generalizations—as the phrases "actions which" and "only when" show—to be tested by producing such instances.

It is true that the instance quoted from Austin does go counter to Ryle's generalization: making a gift is not always something which ought not to be done, or something which is always someone's fault. There is clearly a clash here. But is our only intelligent course *at this point* to take a poll? Would it be dogmatic or unempirical of us to conclude simply that Ryle is wrong about this, that he has settled upon a generalization to which an obvious counterinstance has been produced? It is, moreover, an instance which Ryle himself may well be expected to acknowledge as counter to his generalization; indeed, one which he might have produced for himself. The fact that he did not need indicate only that he was too quick to accept a generalization, not that he is without (good) evidence for it. One of Mates' objections to Ryle can be put this way: Ryle *is* without evidence— anyway, without very good evidence—because he is not entitled to a statement of the first type (one which presents an *instance* of what we say) in the absence of experimental studies which demonstrate its occurrence in the language.

To see that this objection, taken in the general sense in which Mates urges it, is groundless, we must bear in mind the fact that these statements—statements that something is said in English—are being made by native speakers of English. Such speakers do not, in *general*, need evidence for what is said in the language; they are the source of such evidence. It is from them that the descriptive linguist takes the corpus of utterances on the basis of which he will construct a grammar of that language. To answer *some* kinds of specific questions, we will have to engage in that "laborious questioning" Mates insists upon, and count noses; but in general, to tell what is and isn't English, and to tell whether what is said is properly used, the native speaker can rely on his own nose; if not, there would be nothing to count. No one speaker will say everything, so it may be profitable to seek out others; and sometimes you (as a native speaker) may be unsure that a form of utterance is as you say it is, or is used as you say it is used, and in that case you will have to check with another native speaker. And because attending so hard to what you say may itself make you unsure more often than is normal, it is a good policy to check more often. A good policy, but not a methodological necessity. The philosopher who proceeds from ordinary language, in his use of himself as subject in his collection of data, may be more informal than the descriptive linguist (though not more than the linguistic theorist using examples from his native speech); but there is nothing in that to make the data, in some general way, suspect.

Nor does this imply a reliance on that "intuition or memory" which Mates (p. 68)[3] finds so objectionable. In claiming to know, in general, whether we do or do not use a given expression, I am not claiming to have an infallible memory for what we say, any more than I am claiming to remember the hour when I tell you what time we have dinner on Sundays. A normal person may forget and remember certain words, or what certain words mean, in his native language, but (assuming that he has used it continuously) he does not remember the *language*. There is a world of difference between a person who speaks a language natively and one who knows the language fairly well. If I lived in Munich and knew German fairly well, I might try to intuit or guess what the German expression for a particular phenomenon is. Or I might ask my landlady; and that would probably be the extent of the laborious questioning the problem demanded. Nor does the making of either of the sorts of statement about ordinary language I have distinguished rely on a claim that "[we have] already amassed . . . a tremendous amount of empirical information about the use of [our] native language" (Mates, ibid.). That would be true if we were, say, making statements about the history of the language, or about its sound system, or about the housewife's understanding of political slogans, or about a special form in the morphology of some dialect. But for a native speaker to say what, in ordinary circumstances, is said when, no such special information is needed or claimed. All that is needed is the truth of the proposition that a natural language is what native speakers of that language speak.

Ryle's generalization, however, requires more than simple, first level statements of instances; it also requires statements of the second type, those which contain first level statements together with an "explication" of them. When Ryle claims that ". . . we raise questions

[3] Page references to Mates' paper, "On the Verification of Statements About Ordinary Language," throughout this essay are according to its occurrence in the collection entitled *Ordinary Language*, V. C. Chappell, ed. (Englewood Cliffs, N.J.: Prentice-Hall, Inc., 1964).

of responsibility only when someone is charged, justly or unjustly, with an offence," he is claiming both, "We say 'The boy was responsible for breaking a window,' but we do not say 'The boy was responsible for finishing his homework in good time,' " and also claiming, "When we say 'The boy was responsible for (some action)' we imply that the action was an offence, one that ought not to have been done, one that was his fault." I want to argue that Ryle is, in general, as entitled to statements of this second type as he is to statements of the first type; although it is just here that the particular generalization in question misses. We know Austin's example counters Ryle's claims because we know that the statement (of the second type), "When we say, 'The gift was made voluntarily' we imply that the action of making the gift was one which ought not to be done, or was someone's fault" is false. This is clearly knowledge which Mates was relying on when he produced the clash between them. I will take up statements of the second type in a moment.

Before proceeding to that, let us look at that clash a bit longer: its importance has altered considerably. What Austin says does not go fully counter to Ryle's story. It is fundamental to Austin's account to emphasize that we cannot *always* say of actions that they were voluntary, even when they obviously were not involuntary either. Although we can (sometimes) say, "The gift was made voluntarily," it is specifically not something we can say about ordinary, unremarkable cases of making gifts. Only when the action (or circumstances) of making the gift is in some way unusual (instead of his usual Christmas bottle, you give the neighborhood policeman a check for $1000), or extraordinary (you leave your heirs penniless and bequeath your house to your cat), or untoward (you give your rocking horse to your new friend, but the next morning you cry to have it back), can the question whether it was voluntary intelligibly arise. Ryle has not completely neglected this: his "actions which ought not be done" and his "action [which] seems to have been . . . [someone's] fault" are clearly examples of actions which are abnormal, untoward, questionable; so he is right in saying that about these we (sometimes) raise the question whether they were voluntary. His error lies in characterizing these actions incompletely, and in wrongly characterizing those about which the question *cannot* arise. Normally, it is true, the question whether satisfactory, correct, or admirable performances are voluntary does not arise; but this is because there is usually nothing about such actions to question; nothing has gone wrong.

Not seeing that the condition for applying the term "voluntary" holds quite generally—viz., the condition that there be something (real or imagined) fishy about any performance intelligibly so characterized—Ryle construes the condition too narrowly, supposes that there must be something *morally* fishy about the performance. He had indeed sensed trouble where trouble was: the philosophical use of "voluntary" stretches the idea of volition out of shape, beyond recognition. And his diagnosis of the trouble was sound: philosophers imagine, because of a distorted picture of the mind, that the term "voluntary" must apply to all actions which are not involuntary (or unintentional), whereas it is only applicable where there is some specific reason to raise the question. The fact that Ryle fails to specify its applicability precisely enough no more vitiates his entire enterprise than does the fact that he indulges a mild form of the same vice he describes: he frees himself of the philosophical tic of stretching what is true of definite segments of what we do to cover *everything* we do (as epistemologists stretch doubt to cover everything we say), but not from the habit of identifying linguistic antitheses with logical contradictories:[4] in particular, he takes the question, "Voluntary or not?" to mean, "Voluntary or involuntary?" and seems to suppose that (responsible) actions which are not contemptible must be admirable, and that whatever I (responsibly) do either is my fault or else is to my credit. These antitheses miss exactly those actions about which the question "Voluntary or not?" really has no sense, viz., those ordinary, unremarkable, natural things we do which make up most of our conduct and which are neither admirable nor contemptible; which, indeed, could only erroneously be said to go on, in general, in *any* special way.[5] Lacking sureness here, it is not surprising that

[4] The harmfulness of this habit is brought out in Austin's "A Plea for Excuses," reprinted in his *Philosophical Papers*, J. O. Urmson and G. J. Warnock, eds. (Oxford: The Clarendon Press, 1961). Pages 130ff. of his paper contain an elaborate defense of (anyway Austin's version of) "ordinary language philosophy." No one concerned with the general subject of the present symposium (or, in particular, with the possibility of budging the subject of moral philosophy) should ( = will) neglect its study.

[5] Austin's discovery (for our time and place, anyway) of normal action is, I think, important enough to bear the philosophical weight he puts upon it—holding the clue to the riddle of Freedom. (See Chappell, op. cit., p. 45.) A case can also be made out that it was failure to recognize such action which produced some of the notorious

Ryle's treatment leaves the subject a bit wobbly. Feeling how *enormously* wrong it is to remove "voluntary" from a *specific* function, he fails to sense the slighter error of his own specification.[6]

I have said that the ordinary language philosopher is also and equally entitled to statements of the second type I distinguished, which means that he is entitled not merely to say what (words) we say, but equally to say what we should mean in (by) saying them. Let us turn to statements of this type and ask what the relation is between what you explicitly say and what you imply; or, to avoid begging the question, ask how we are to account for the fact (supposing it to be a fact) that we only say or ask A ("X is voluntary," or "Is X voluntary?") where B is the case (something is, or seems, fishy about X).[7] The philosophical problem about this arises in the following way: Philosophers who proceed from ordinary language are likely to insist that if you say A where B is not the case, you will be misusing A, or distorting its meaning. But another philosopher will not want to allow that, because it makes the relation between A and B appear to be a logical one (If A then B; and if not-B then not-A); whereas logical relations hold only between statements, not between a statement and the world: *that* relation is "merely" conventional (or, even, causal?). So the occasion on which we (happen to?) *use* a statement cannot be considered part of its meaning or logic. The solution is then to call the latter the semantics of the expression and the former its pragmatics.

But if we can forget for a moment that the relation between A

paradoxes of classical Utilitarianism: what neither the Utilitarians nor their critics seem to have seen clearly and constantly is that about unquestionable (normal, natural) action no question is (can be) raised; in particular not the question whether the action ought or ought not to have been done. The point is a logical one: to raise a question about an action is to put the action in question. It is partly the failure to appreciate this which makes the classical moralists (appear?) so moralistic, allows them to suppose that the moral question is *always* appropriate—except, of course, where the action is unfree (caused?). But this is no better than the assumption that the moral question is *never* appropriate (because we are never *really* free). Such mechanical moralism has got all the punishment it deserves in the recent mechanical antimoralism, which it must have helped inspire.

[6] At the same time, Ryle leaves "involuntary" as stretched as ever when he allows himself to speak of "the involuntariness of [someone's] late arrival," *The Concept of Mind* (London: Hutchinson and Co., Ltd., 1949), p. 72.

[7] I realize that the point is controversial and that in putting so much emphasis on it I may be doing some injustice to the point of view I am trying to defend. There may be considerations which would lead one to be more temperate in making the point; but against the point of view Mates is adopting, it seems to me to demand all the attention it can get.

and B *cannot* be a logical one, we may come to feel how implausible it is to *say* that it is not logical; or rather, to say that nothing *follows* about B from the utterance of A. It is implausible because we do not accept a question like "Did you do that voluntarily?" as appropriate about any and every action. If a person asks you whether you dress the way you do voluntarily, you will not understand him to be curious merely about your psychological processes (whether your wearing them "proceeds from free choice . . ."); you will understand him to be implying or suggesting that your manner of dress is in some way peculiar. If it be replied to this that "voluntary" does not *mean* "peculiar" (or "special" or "fishy") and hence that the implication or suggestion is part merely of the pragmatics of the expression, not part of its *meaning* (semantics), my rejoinder is this: that reply is relevant to a different claim from the one urged here; it is worth saying *here* only if you are able to account for the *relation* between the pragmatics and the semantics of the expression. In the absence of such an account, the reply is empty. For consider: If we use Mates' formula for computing the pragmatic value of an expression—"He wouldn't say that unless he . . ."—then in the described situation we will complete it with something like ". . . unless he thought that my way of dressing is peculiar." Call this implication of the utterance "pragmatic"; the fact remains that he wouldn't (couldn't) say what he did without implying what he did: he MUST MEAN that my clothes are peculiar. I am less interested now in the "mean" than I am in the "must." (After all, there is bound to be some reason why a number of philosophers are tempted to call a relation logical; "must" is logical.) But on this, the "pragmatic" formula throws no light whatever.

What this shows is that the formula does not help us account for the element of necessity ("must") in statements whose implication we understand. But it is equally unhelpful in trying to explain the implication of a statement whose use we do *not* understand (the context in which the formula enters Mates' discussion). Imagine that I am sitting in my countinghouse counting up my money. Someone who knows that I do that at this hour every day passes by and says, "You ought to do that." What should we say about his statement? That he does not know what "ought" means (what the dictionary says)? That he does not know how to use the word? That he does not know what obligation is? Applying the formula, we compute: "He wouldn't say that unless he asks himself whenever he sees anyone doing anything, 'Ought that person to be doing that or ought he not?' " This may indeed account for his otherwise puzzling remark; but it does so by telling us something we did not know about *him;* it tells us nothing whatever we did not know about the words he used. Here it is *because* we know the meaning and use of "ought" that we are forced to account in the way Mates suggests for its extraordinary occurrence. I take Mates' formula, then, to be expandable into: "Since I understand the meaning and use of his expression, he wouldn't say that unless he . . ." . Perhaps Mates would consider this a distortion and take a different expansion to be appropriate: "He wouldn't say that unless he was using his words in a special way." But now "say that" has a very different force. The expanded form now means, "I know what his expression would ordinarily be used to say, but he can't wish to say that: I don't understand what he is saying." In neither of its expansions, then, does the formula throw any light on the way an expression is being used: in the one case we already know, in the other we have yet to learn. (Another expansion may be: "He wouldn't say that unless he was using X to mean Y." But here again, it is the semantics and pragmatics of Y which are relevant to understanding what is said, and the formula presupposes that we already understand Y.)

Our alternatives seem to be these: Either (1) we deny that there is any rational (logical, grammatical) constraint over the "pragmatic implications" of what we say—or perhaps deny that there *are* any *implications,* on the ground that the relation in question is not deductive—so that unless what I say is flatly false or unless I explicitly contradict myself, it is pointless to suggest that what I say is wrong or that I must mean something other than I say; or else (2) we admit the constraint and say either (a) since all necessity is logical, the "pragmatic implications" of our utterance are (quasi-)logical implications; with or without adding (b) since the "pragmatic implications" cannot be construed in terms of deductive (or inductive) logic, there must be some "third sort" of logic; or we say (c) some necessity is not logical. None of these alternatives is without its obscurities, but they are clear enough for us to see that Mates is taking alternative (1),[8]

---

[8] As is most clearly shown where he says (p. 72) ". . . When I say 'I may be wrong' I do not *imply* that I have no confidence in what I have previously asserted; I only indicate it." Why "only"? Were he willing to say ". . . but I do (inevitably) indicate it," there may be no argument.

whereas the philosopher who proceeds from ordinary language is likely to feel the need of some form of (2). Alternative (2a) brings out part of the reason behind the Oxford philosopher's insistence that he is talking logic, while (2b) makes explicit the reason other philosophers are perplexed at that claim.[9]

The difference between alternatives (1) and (2) is fundamental; so fundamental, that it is very difficult to argue. When Mates says, "Perhaps it is true that ordinarily I wouldn't say 'I know it' unless I felt great confidence in what I was asserting . . . ," what he says is not, if you like, *strictly* wrong; but it is wrong—or, what it implies is wrong. It implies that whether I confine the formula "I know . . ." to statements about which I feel great confidence is *up to me* (*rightly* up to me); so that if I say "I know . . ." in the absence of confidence, I have not misused language, and in particular I have not stretched the *meaning* of the word "know." And yet, if a child were to say "I know . . ." when you know the child does not *know* (is in no position to say he knows) you may reply, "You don't really mean (N.B.) you *know*, you only mean you believe"; or you may say, "You oughtn't to say you *know* when you only *think* so."

There are occasions on which it would be useful to have the "semantic-pragmatic" distinction at hand. If, for example, a philosopher tells me that the statement, "You ought to do so-and-so" expresses private emotion and is hortatory and hence not, strictly speaking, meaningful, then it may be worth replying that nothing follows about the meaning (semantics) of a statement from the way it is used (pragmatics); and this reply may spare our having to make up special brands of meaning. But the time for that argument is, presumably, past.[10] What needs to be argued now is that something *does* follow from the fact that a term is used in its usual way: it entitles you (or, using the term, you entitle others) to make certain inferences, draw certain conclusions. (This is part of what you say when you say that you are talking about the *logic* of ordinary language.) *Learning what these implications are is part of learning the language;* no less a part

---

[9] Alternative (2b) has been taken—for different, but not unrelated, reasons—in the writings of John Wisdom, e.g., "Gods," in *Logic and Language*, 1st series, Antony Flew, ed. Oxford: Basil Blackwell & Mott, Ltd., 1951), p. 196; in S. Toulmin, *The Place of Reason in Ethics* (London: Cambridge University Press, 1950), p. 83; and in S. Hampshire, "Fallacies in Moral Philosophy," *Mind*, Vol. LVIII (1949), 470f.

[10] It was essentially the argument with which the pragmatists attempted to subdue emotive "meaning." See John Dewey, "Ethical Subject-Matter and Language," *Journal of Philosophy*, Vol. XLII (1945), 701ff.

than learning its syntax, or learning what it is to which terms apply: they are an essential part of what we communicate when we talk. Intimate understanding is understanding which is implicit. Nor *could* everything we say (mean to communicate), in normal communication, be said explicitly[11]—otherwise the only threat to communication would be acoustical. We are, therefore, exactly as responsible for the specific implications of our utterances as we are for their explicit factual claims. And there can no more be some general procedure for securing that what one implies is appropriate than there can be for determining that what one says is true. Misnaming and misdescribing are not the only mistakes we can make in talking. Nor is lying its only immorality.

✳ ✳

I am prepared to conclude that the philosopher who proceeds from ordinary language is entitled, without special empirical investigation, to assertions of the second sort we distinguished, viz., assertions like, "We do not say 'I know . . .' unless we mean that we have great confidence . . . ," and like "When we ask whether an action is voluntary we imply that the action is fishy" (call this S). But I do not think that I have *shown* that he is entitled to them, because I have not shown what kind of assertions they are; I have not shown when such assertions should be said, and by whom, and what should be meant in saying them. It is worth trying to indicate certain complexities of the assertions, because they are easy to over-

---

[11] I think of this as a law of communication; but it would be important and instructive to look for apparent counterinstances. When *couldn't* what is said be misunderstood? My suggestion is, only when nothing is implied, i.e., when everything you say is said explicitly. (Shoùld we add: or when all of the implications of what is asserted can be made explicit *in a certain way*, e.g., by the methods of formal logic? It may be along such lines that utterances in logical form come to seem the ideal of understandable utterances, that here you can communicate *only* what you say, or else *more* than you say without endangering understanding. But we might think of formal logic not as the guarantor of understanding but as a substitute for it. Cf. W. V. O. Quine, "Mr. Strawson on Logical Theory," *Mind*, Vol. LXII (1953), 444f. Then we can express this "law of communication" this way: What needs understanding can be misunderstood.) But when *is* everything said explicitly? When the statement is about sense-data rather than "physical" objects? When it is about the (physical) movements I make rather than the (nonphysical?) actions I perform? Perhaps the opponents of the Quest for Certainty (whose passion seems to have atrophied into a fear of the word "certain") have embarked upon a Quest for Explicitness. Strawson's notion of *presupposing* is relevant here, since explicitness and presupposition vary inversely. See "On Referring," *Mind*, Vol. LIX (1950); reprinted in *Essays in Conceptual Analysis*, Antony Flew, ed. (London: Macmillan & Co., Ltd., 1956).

look. Something important will be learned if we realize that we do *not* know what kind of assertion S is.

When (if) you feel that S is necessarily true, that it is a priori, you will have to explain how a statement which is obviously not analytic *can* be true a priori. That S is not analytic is what (is all that) is shown by Mates' arguments about the "semantic-pragmatic" confusion; it is perfectly true that "voluntary" does not *mean* (you will not find set beside it in a dictionary) "fishy." When I am impressed with the necessity of statements like S, I am tempted to say that they are categorial—about the concept of an action *überhaupt*. (A normal action is neither voluntary nor involuntary, neither careful nor careless, neither expected nor unexpected, neither right nor wrong. . . .) This would account for our feeling of their necessity: they are instances (not of Formal, but) of Transcendental Logic. But this is really no explanation until we make clearer the need for the concept of an action in general.

However difficult it is to make out a case for the necessity of S, it is important that the temptation to call it a priori not be ignored; otherwise we will acquiesce in calling it synthetic, which would be badly misleading. Misleading (wrong) because we know what would count as a disproof of statements which are synthetic (to indicate the willingness to entertain such disproof is the point of calling a statement synthetic), but it is not clear what would count as a disproof of S. The feeling that S must be synthetic comes, of course, partly from the fact that it obviously is not (likely to be taken as) analytic. But it comes also from the ease with which S may be mistaken for the statement, " 'Is X voluntary?' implies that X is fishy" (T), which does seem obviously synthetic. But S and T, though they are true together and false together, are not everywhere interchangeable; the identical state of affairs is described by both, but a person who may be entitled to say T, may not be entitled to say S. Only a native speaker of English is entitled to the statement S, whereas a linguist describing English may, though he is not a native speaker of English, be entitled to T. What entitles him to T is his having gathered a certain amount and kind of evidence in its favor. But the person entitled to S is not entitled to *that* statement for the same reason. He *needs* no evidence for it. It would be misleading to say that he *has* evidence for S, for that would suggest that he has done the sort of investigation the linguist has done, only less systematically, and this would make it seem that his claim to know S is very weakly based. And it would be equally misleading to say that he does *not* have evidence for S, because that would make it appear that there is something he still needs, and suggests that he is not yet entitled to S. But there is nothing he needs, and there is no evidence (which it makes sense, in *general*, to say) he has: the question of evidence is irrelevant.

An examination of what does entitle a person to the statement S would be required in any full account of such statements. Such an examination is out of the question here. But since I will want to claim that Mates' "two methods" for gathering evidence in support of "statements about ordinary language" like S are irrelevant to what entitles a person to S, and since this obviously rests on the claim that the concept of evidence is, in general, irrelevant to them altogether, let me say just this: The clue to understanding the sort of statement S is lies in appreciating the fact that "we," while plural, is first person. First person *singular* forms have recently come in for a great deal of attention, and they have been shown to have very significant logical-epistemological properties. The plural form has similar, and equally significant, properties; but it has been, so far as I know, neglected. The claim that in general we do not require evidence for statements in the first person plural does not rest upon a claim that we cannot be wrong about what we are doing or about what we say, but only that it would be extraordinary if we were (often). My point about such statements, then, is that they are sensibly questioned only where there is some special reason for supposing what I say about what I (we) say to be wrong; only here is the request for evidence competent. If I am wrong about what he does (they do), that may be no great surprise; but if I am wrong about what I (we) do, that is liable, where it is not comic, to be tragic.

Statements like T have their own complexities, and it would be unwise even of them to say simply that they are synthetic. Let us take another of Mates' examples: " 'I know it' is not (ordinarily) said unless the speaker has great confidence in it" (T'). Mates takes this as patently synthetic, a statement about matters of fact (and there is no necessary connection among matters of fact). And so it might be, said by a Scandinavian linguist as part of his description of English. But if that linguist, or if a native speaker (i.e., a speaker entitled to say, "We do not say 'I know it' unless . . .") uses T' in teaching someone to speak English, or to remind a native speaker of something he knows but is not bearing in mind, T′ sounds less like a descriptive statement than like a rule.

Because of what seems to be the widespread idea that rules always sort with commands and must therefore be represented as imperatives, this complementarity of rule and statement may come as something of a shock. But that such complementarity exists can be seen in writings which set out the rules for games or ceremonies or languages. In *Hoyle's Rules of Games* we find statements like, "The opponent at declarer's left makes the opening lead . . . Declarer's partner then lays his whole hand face up on the table, with his trumps if any on the right. The hand so exposed is the *dummy*. . . . The object of play is solely to win tricks, in order to fulfill or defeat the contract"; in *Robert's Rules of Order*, the rules take the form, "The privileged motion to adjourn takes precedence of all others, except the privileged motion 'to fix the time to which to adjourn,' to which it yields" (in Section 17, headed "To Adjourn"); taking a grammar at random we find, "Mute stems form the nominative singular by the addition of -s in the case of masculines and feminines. . . . Before -s of the nominative singular, a labial mute (p, b) remains unchanged." These are all statements in the indicative, not the imperative, mood. (Some expressions in each of these books tell us what we *must* do; others that we *may*. I will suggest later a reason for this shift.) In one light, they appear to be descriptions; in another to be rules. Why should this be so? What is its significance?

The explanation of the complementarity has to do with the fact that its topic is actions. When we say how an action is done (how to act) what we say may report or describe the way we *in fact* do it (if we are entitled to say how "we" do it, i.e., to say what we do, or say what we say) but it may also lay out a way of doing or saying something which is to be *followed*. Whether remarks like T′—remarks "about" ordinary language, and equally about ordinary actions—are statements or rules depends upon how they are taken: if they are taken to state facts and are supposed to be believed, they are statements; if they are taken as guides and supposed to be followed, they are rules. Such expressions are no more "in themselves" rules or (synthetic) statements than other expressions are, in themselves, postulates or conclusions or definitions or replies. We might put the relation between the two contexts of T′ this way: Statements which describe a language (or a game or an institution) are rules (are binding) if you want to speak that language (play that game, accept that institution); or, rather, *when* you are speaking that language, playing that game, etc. *If it is* TRUE *to say " 'I know it' is not used unless you have great confidence in it," then, when you are speaking English, it is* WRONG *(a misuse) to say "I know it" unless you have great confidence in it.* Now the philosopher who proceeds from ordinary language assumes that he and his interlocutors are speaking from within the language, so that the question of whether you want to speak that language is pointless. Worse than pointless, because strictly the ordinary language philosopher does not, in general, *assume* that he and his interlocutors are speaking from within a given (their native) language—any more than they speak their native language, in general, *intentionally.* The only condition relevant to such philosophizing is that you speak (not this or that language, but) period.

At this point the argument has become aporetic. "Statements about ordinary language" like S, T and T′ are not analytic, *and* they are not (it would be misleading to call them) synthetic (just like that).[12] Nor do we know whether to say they are a priori, or whether to account for their air of necessity as a dialectical illusion, due more to the motion of our argument than to their own nature. Given our current alternatives, there is no way to classify such statements; we do not yet know what they are.

✳ ✳

Before searching for new ways into these problems, I should perhaps justify my very heavy reliance on the idea of *context,* because

---

[12] If it still seems that statements like S and T *must* be synthetic, perhaps it will help to realize that anyway they are not *just some more* synthetic statements about voluntary action, on a par with a statement to the effect that somebody does (indeed) dress the way he does voluntarily. It may be true that if the world were different *enough,* the statements would be false; but that amounts to saying that if "voluntary" meant something other than it does, the statements would not mean what they do—which is not surprising. The statements in question are more closely related to such a statement as "The future will resemble the past": this is not a (not just another) prediction, on a par with statements about whether it will rain. Russell's chicken (who was fed every day throughout its life but ultimately had its neck wrung) was so well fed that he neglected to consider what was happening to other chickens. Even if he had considered this, he would doubtless still have had his neck wrung; but at least he wouldn't have been outsmarted. He could have avoided *that* indignity because he was wrong only about one thing; as Russell very properly says, ". . . in spite of frequent repetitions there sometimes is a failure at the last," *The Problems of Philosophy* (London: Oxford University Press, 1912), p. 102. But if the future were not (in the *general* sense needed) "like" the past, this would not be *a* failure. The future may wring our minds, but by that very act it would have given up trying to outsmart us.

on Mates' description of what a statement of context involves, it should be impossible ever to make one. Let me recall his remarks: "We have all heard the wearying platitude that 'you can't separate' the meaning of a word from the entire context in which it occurs, including not only the actual linguistic context, but also the aims, feelings, beliefs, and hopes of the speaker, the same for the listener and any bystanders, the social situation, the physical surroundings, the historical background, the rules of the game, and so on ad infinitum" (p. 71). Isn't this another of those apostrophes to the infinite which prevents philosophers from getting down to cases? [13] Of course if I have to go on about the context of "voluntary" ad infinitum, I would not get very far with it. But I would claim to have characterized the context sufficiently (for the purpose at hand) by the statement that something is, or is supposed to be, fishy about the action. Giving directions for using a word is no more prodigious and unending a task than giving directions for anything else. The context in which I make a martini with vodka is no less complex than the context in which I make a statement with "voluntary." Say, if you like, that these actions take place in infinitely complex contexts; but then remember that you can be given directions for doing either. It may be wearying always to be asked for a story within which a puzzling remark can seriously be imagined to function; but I know no better way of maintaining that relevance, or sense of reality, which each philosopher claims for himself and claims to find lacking in another philosophy. At least it would spare us the surrealism of worries like " 'What time is it?' asserts nothing, and hence is neither true nor false; *yet* we all know what it means *well enough* to answer it";[14] or like "If we told a person to close the door, and received the reply, 'Prove it!' should we not, to speak mildly, grow somewhat impatient?" [15]

In recommending that we ignore context in order to make "provisional divisions" of a subject and get an investigation started, Mates is recommending the wrong thing for the right reason. It is

[13] A complaint Austin voiced in the course of his William James Lectures, on Performatives, at Harvard in the Spring term of 1955; published as *How to Do Things with Words* (Cambridge, Harvard University Press, 1962); also Galaxy Books edition (New York: Oxford University Press, Inc., 1965).

[14] John Hospers, *An Introduction to Philosophical Analysis* (Englewood Cliffs, N.J.: Prentice-Hall, Inc., 1953), p. 69. My emphasis.

[15] Charles Stevenson, *Ethics and Language* (New Haven: Yale University Press, 1944), p. 26.

true that we cannot say everything at once and that for some problems some distinction of the sort Mates has in mind may be of service. My discontent with it is that it has come to deflect investigation— I mean from questions on which Oxford philosophy trains itself. Where your concern is one of constructing artificial languages, you may explain that you mean to be considering only the syntax (and perhaps semantics) of a language, and not its pragmatics. Or where it becomes important to emphasize a distinction between (where there has come to be a distinction between) scientific and metaphysical assertion, or between factual report and moral rule, you may set out a "theory" of scientific or factual utterance. In these cases you will be restricting concern in order to deal with certain properties of formal systems, certain problems of meaning, and to defeat certain forms of nonsense. Flat contradiction, metaphysical assertion masquerading as scientific hypothesis, mere whim under the posture of an ethical or aesthetic (or psychological or legal) judgment—these perhaps need hounding out. But the philosopher who proceeds from ordinary language is concerned less to avenge sensational crimes against the intellect than to redress its civil wrongs; to steady any imbalance, the tiniest usurpation, in the mind. This inevitably requires reintroducing ideas which have become tyrannical (e.g., existence, obligation, certainty, identity, reality, truth . . .) into the specific contexts in which they function naturally. This is not a question of cutting big ideas down to size, but of giving them the exact space in which they can move without corrupting. Nor does our wish to rehabilitate rather than to deny or expel such ideas (by such sentences as, "We can never know for certain . . ."; "The table is not real (really solid)"; "To tell me what I ought to do is always to tell me what you want me to do . . .") come from a sentimental altruism. It is a question of self-preservation: for who is it that the philosopher punishes when it is the mind itself which assaults the mind?

✳ ✳

I want now to turn to two other, related, questions on which Mates finds himself at issue with the Oxford philosophers. The first concerns their tendency to introduce statements of the first sort I distinguished not with "We do say . . ." but with "We *can* say . . ." and "We *can't* say . . .". The second question concerns, at last directly, reasons for saying that we "must" mean by our words what those words *ordinarily* mean.

Let me begin by fulfilling my promise to expand upon my remark that Austin's saying, "We may make a gift voluntarily" is "material mode" for "We can say, 'The gift was made voluntarily.'" The shift from talking about language to talking about the world occurs almost imperceptibly in the statement of Austin's which Mates quotes—almost as though he thought it did not much matter *which* he talked about. Let me recall the passage from Austin: ". . . take 'voluntarily' and 'involuntarily': we may join the army or make a gift voluntarily, we may hiccough or make a small gesture involuntarily." He begins here by mentioning a pair of words, and goes on to tell us what we may in fact do. With what right? Why is it assumed that we find out what voluntary and involuntary actions *are* (and equally, of course, what inadvertent and automatic and pious, etc., actions are) by asking when we should *say* of an action that it is voluntary or inadvertent or pious, etc.?

But what is troubling about this? If you feel that finding out what something is must entail investigation of the world rather than of language, perhaps you are imagining a situation like finding out what somebody's name and address are, or what the contents of a will or a bottle are, or whether frogs eat butterflies. But now imagine that you are in your armchair reading a book of reminiscences and come across the word "umiak." You reach for your dictionary and look it up. Now what did you do? Find out what "umiak" means, or find out what an umiak is? But how could we have discovered something about the world by hunting in the dictionary? If this seems surprising, perhaps it is because we forget that we learn language and learn the world *together*, that they become elaborated and distorted together, and in the same places. We may also be forgetting how elaborate a process the learning is. We tend to take what a native speaker does when he looks up a noun in a dictionary as the characteristic process of learning language. (As, in what has become a less forgivable tendency, we take naming as the fundamental source of meaning.) But it is merely the end point in the process of learning the word. When we turned to the dictionary for "umiak" we already knew everything about the word, as it were, but its combination: we knew what a noun is and how to name an object and how to look up a word and what boats are and what an Eskimo is. We were all prepared for that umiak. What seemed like finding the world in a dictionary was really a case of bringing the world to the dictionary. We had the world with us all the time, in that armchair; but we felt the weight of it only when we felt a lack in it. Sometimes we will need to bring the dictionary to the world. That will happen when (say) we run across a small boat in Alaska of a sort we have never seen and wonder—what? What it is, or what it is called? In either case, the learning is a question of aligning language and the world.[16] What you need to learn will depend on what specifically it is you want to know; and how you can find out will depend specifically on what you already command. How we answer the question, "What is X?" will depend, therefore, on the specific case of ignorance and of knowledge.

It sometimes happens that we know everything there is to know about a situation—what all of the words in question mean, what all of the relevant facts are; and everything is in front of our eyes. And yet we feel we don't know something, don't understand something. In this situation, the question "What is X?" is very puzzling, in exactly the way philosophy is very puzzling. We feel we want to ask the question, and yet we feel we already have the answer. (One might say we have all the *elements* of an answer.) Socrates says that in such a situation we need to remind ourselves of something. So does the philosopher who proceeds from ordinary language: we need to remind ourselves of *what we should say when*.[17] But what is the point of reminding ourselves of that? When the philosopher asks, "What should we say here?", what is meant is, "What would be the normal thing to say here?", or perhaps, "What is the most natural thing we could say here?" And the point of the question is this: answering

---

[16] For modern instruction in the complexities of this question, see Austin's and P. F. Strawson's contributions to the symposium, "Truth," *Proceedings of the Aristotelian Society*, Suppl. Vol. XXIV (1950); D. F. Pears, "Universals" and "Incompatibilities of Colours," both in *Logic and Language*, 2nd series, Antony Flew, ed. (Oxford: Basil Blackwell & Mott, Ltd., 1953); W. V. O. Quine, "Two Dogmas of Empiricism," *Philosophical Review*, Vol. LX (1951); reprinted in *From a Logical Point of View* (Cambridge, Mass.: Harvard University Press, 1953); and John Wisdom, papers collected in *Philosophy and Psycho-Analysis* (Oxford: Basil Blackwell & Mott, Ltd., 1953), especially "Philosophical Perplexity," "Metaphysics and Verification," and "Philosophy, Metaphysics and Psycho-Analysis."

[17] The emphasized formula is Austin's. Notice that the "should" cannot simply be replaced by "ought to," nor yet, I believe, simply replaced by "would." It will not, that is, yield its secrets to the question, "Descriptive or normative?" (See "A Plea for Excuses," op. cit., p. 129.)

it is sometimes the only way to tell—tell others and tell for ourselves —what the situation *is*.

Sometimes the only way to tell. But when? The nature of the Oxford philosopher's question, and the nature of his conception of philosophy, can be brought out if we turn the question upon itself, and thus remind ourselves of when it is we need to remind ourselves of what we should say when. Our question then becomes: When should we ask ourselves when we should (and should not) say "The x is F" in order to find out what an F(x) is? (For "The x is F" read "The action is voluntary (or pious)," or "The statement is vague (or false)," or "The question is misleading.") The answer suggested is: When you have to. When you have more facts than you know what to make of, or when you do not know what new facts would show. When, that is, you need a clear view of what you already know. When you need to do philosophy.[18] Euthyphro does not need to learn any new facts, yet he needs to learn something: you can say either that in the *Euthyphro* Socrates was finding out what "piety" means or finding out what piety is.

* *

When the philosopher who proceeds from ordinary language tells us, "You can't say such-and-such," what he means is that you cannot say that *here* and communicate *this* situation to others, or understand it for yourself.[19] This is sometimes what he means by calling certain expressions "misuses" of language, and also makes clear the consequences of such expressions: they break our understanding. The normativeness which Mates felt, and which is certainly present, does not lie in the ordinary language philosopher's assertions *about* ordinary use; what is normative is exactly ordinary use itself.

The way philosophers have practiced with the word "normative"

[18] This is part of the view of philosophy most consistently represented in and by the writings of John Wisdom. It derives from Wittgenstein.

[19] Of course you can *say* (the words), "When I ask whether an action is voluntary I do not imply that I think something is special about the action." You can say this, but then you may have difficulty showing the relevance of *this* "voluntary" to what people are worrying about when they ask whether a person's action was voluntary or whether our actions are ever voluntary. We might regard the Oxford philosopher's insistence upon ordinary language as an attempt to overcome (what has become) the self-imposed irrelevance of so much philosophy. In this they are continuing—while at the same time their results are undermining—the tradition of British Empiricism: being gifted pupils, they seem to accept and to assassinate with the same gesture.

in recent years seems to me lamentable. But it is too late to avoid the word, so even though we cannot now embark on a diagnosis of the ills which caused its current use, or those which it has produced, it may be worth forewarning ourselves against the confusions most likely to distract us. The main confusions about the problem of "normativeness" I want to mention here are these: the idea (1) that descriptive utterances are opposed to normative utterances; and (2) that prescriptive utterances are (typical) instances of normative utterances.

We have touched upon these ideas in talking about rule-statement complementarity; here we touch them at a different point. In saying here that it is a confusion to speak of some general opposition between descriptive and normative utterances, I am not thinking primarily of the plain fact that rules have counterpart (descriptive) statements, but rather of the significance of that fact, viz., that what such statements describe are *actions* (and not, e.g., the *movements* of bodies, animate or inanimate). The most characteristic fact about actions is that they can—in various specific ways—go wrong, that they can be performed incorrectly. This is not, in any restricted sense, a moral assertion, though it points the moral of intelligent activity. And it is as true of describing as it is of calculating or of promising or plotting or warning or asserting or defining. . . . These are actions which we perform, and our successful performance of them depends upon our adopting and following the ways in which the action in question is done, upon what is normative for it. Descriptive statements, then, are not opposed to ones which are normative, but in fact presuppose them: we could not do the thing we call describing if language did not provide (we had not been taught) ways normative for describing.

The other point I wish to emphasize is this: if a normative utterance is one used to create or institute rules or standards, then prescriptive utterances are not examples of normative utterances. Establishing a norm is not telling us how we *ought* to perform an action, but telling us how the action *is* done, or how it is *to be* done.[20] Contrariwise, telling us what we ought to do is not instituting a norm

<hr />

[20] This latter distinction appears in two senses of the expression "establishing a rule or standard." In one it means finding what is in fact standard in certain instances. In the other it means founding what is to be standard for certain instances. "Settle" and "determine" have senses comparable to those of "establish."

to cover the case, but rather presupposes the existence of such a norm, i.e., presupposes that there is something to do which it would be correct to do here. Telling us what we ought to do may involve *appeal* to a pre-existent rule or standard, but it cannot constitute the establishment of that rule or standard. We may expect the retort here that it is just the *appeal* which is the sensitive normative spot, for what we are really doing when we appeal to a rule or standard is telling somebody that they ought to adhere to it. Perhaps this will be followed by the query "And suppose they don't accept the rule or standard to which you appeal, what then?" The retort is simply false. And to the query one may reply that this will not be the first time we have been tactless; nor can we, to avoid overstepping the bounds of relationship, follow every statement by ". . . if you accept the facts and the logic I do," nor every evaluation by ". . . if you accept the standards I do." Such cautions will finally suggest appending to everything we say ". . . if you mean by your words what I mean by mine." Here the pantomime of caution concludes. It is true that we sometimes appeal to standards which our interlocutor does not accept; but this does not in the least show that what we are there really doing is attempting to institute a standard (of our own). Nor does it in the least show that we are (merely) expressing our own opinion or feeling on the matter. We of course *may* express our private opinion or feeling—we normally do so where it is not clear what (or that any) rule or standard fits the case at hand and where we are therefore not willing or able to appeal to any.

The practice of appealing to a norm can be abused, as can any other of our practices. Sometimes people appeal to a rule when we deserve more intimate attention from them. Just as sometimes people tell us what we ought to do when all they mean is that they want us to. But this is as much an abuse where the context is moral as it is where the context is musical ("You ought to accent the appoggiatura"), or scientific ("You ought to use a control group here"), or athletic ("You ought to save your wind on the first two laps"). Private persuasion (or personal appeal) is not the paradigm of ethical utterance, but represents the breakdown (or the transcending) of moral interaction. We can, too obviously, become morally inaccessible to one another; but to tell us that these are the moments which really constitute the moral life will only add confusion to pain.

If not, then, by saying what actions *ought* to be performed, how *do* we establish (or justify or modify or drop) rules or standards? What general answer can there be to this general question other than "In various ways, depending on the context"? Philosophers who have imagined that the question has one answer for all cases must be trying to assimilate the members of Football Commissions, of Child Development Research Teams, of University Committees on Entrance Requirements, of Bar Association Committees to Alter Legal Procedures, of Departments of Agriculture, of Bureaus of Standards, and of Essene Sects, all to one "sort" of person, doing one "sort" of thing, viz., establishing (or changing) rules and standards. Whereas the fact is that there are, in each case, different ways normative for accomplishing the particular normative tasks in question. It has in recent years been emphasized past acknowledgment that even justifications require justification. What now needs emphasizing is that (successfully) justifying a statement or an action is not (cannot be) justifying its justification.[21] The assumption that the appeal to a rule or standard is only justified where that rule or standard is simultaneously established or justified can only serve to make such appeal seem hypocritical (or anyway shaky) and the attempts at such establishment or justification seem tyrannical (or anyway arbitrary).

It would be important to understand why we have been able to overlook the complementarity of rule and statement and to be content always to sort rules with imperatives. Part of the reason for this comes from a philosophically inadequate (not to say disastrous) conception of action; but this inadequacy itself will demand an elaborate accounting. There is another sort of reason for our assumption that what is binding upon us must be an imperative; one which has to do with our familiar sense of alienation from established systems of morality, perhaps accompanied by a sense of distance from God. Kant tells us that a perfectly rational being does in fact (necessarily) con-

---

[21] It is perfectly possible to maintain that *any* "justifications" we offer for our conduct are now so obviously empty and grotesquely inappropriate that nothing we used to call a justification is any longer acceptable, and that the *immediate* questions which face us concern the ultimate ground of justification itself. We have heard about, if we have not seen, the breaking down of convention, the fission of traditional values. But it is not a Continental dread at the realization that our standards have no ultimate justification which lends to so much British and American moral philosophizing its hysterical quality. (Such philosophy has been able to take the death of God in its stride.) That quality comes, rather, from the assumption that the question of justifying cases is on a par with (appropriate in the same context as) the question of justifying norms.

form to "the supreme principle of morality," but that we imperfectly rational creatures are necessitated *by* it, so that for us it is (always appears as) an imperative. But if I understand the difference Kant sees here, it is one *within* the conduct of rational animals. So far as Kant is talking about (the logic of) action, his Categorical Imperative can be put as a Categorial Declarative (description-rule), i.e., description of what it *is* to act morally: When we (you) act morally, we act in a way we would regard as justified universally, justified no matter who had done it. (This categorial formulation does not tell us how to determine *what was done;* neither does Kant's categorical formulation, although, by speaking of "the" maxim of an action, it pretends to, or anyway makes it seem less problematical than it is.) Perhaps it is by now a little clearer why we are tempted to retort, "But suppose I don't *want* to be moral?"; and also why it would be irrelevant here. The Categorial Declarative does not tell you what you *ought* to do *if* you want to be moral (and hence is untouched by the feeling that no imperative can really be *categorical,* can bind us no matter what); it tells you (part of) what you in fact do when you *are* moral. It cannot—nothing a philosopher says can—insure that you will not act immorally; but it is entirely unaffected by what you do or do not want.

I am not saying that rules do not sometimes sort with imperatives, but only denying that they always do. In the Britannica article (eleventh edition) on chess, only one paragraph of the twenty or so which describe the game is headed "Rules," and only here are we told what we *must* do. This paragraph deals with such matters as the convention of saying "j'adoube" when you touch a piece to straighten it. Is the difference between matters of this kind and the matter of how pieces move, a difference between penalties (which are imposed for misplay) and moves (which are accepted in order to play at all)—so that we would cheerfully say that we can play (are playing) chess without the "j'adoube" convention, but less cheerfully that we can play without following the rule that "the Queen moves in any direction, square or diagonal, whether forward or backward"? This would suggest that we may think of the difference between rule and imperative as one between those actions (or "parts" of actions) which are easy (natural, normal) for us, and those we have to be encouraged to do. (What I do as a rule you may have to be made or directed to do.) We are likely to forget to say "j'adoube," so we have to be *made* (to remember) to do it; but we do not have to be *made* to move the Queen in straight, unobstructed paths.[22] This further suggests that what is thought of as "alienation" is something which occurs *within* moral systems; since these are profoundly haphazard accumulations, it is no surprise that we feel part of some regions of the system and feel apart from other regions.[23]

So the subject of responsibility, of obligation and commitment, opens into the set of questions having to do with differences between doing a thing wrongly or badly (strangely, ineptly, inexactly, partially . . .) and not doing the thing at all. These differences take us into a further region of the concept of an action: we have noted that there are many (specific) ways in which an action can go wrong (at least as many as the myriad excuses we are entitled to proffer when what we have done has resulted in some unhappiness); but it would be incorrect to suppose that we are *obligated* to see to it (to take precautions to insure), *whenever* we undertake to do anything, that none of these ways will come to pass. Our obligation is to avoid doing something at a time and place or in a way which is *likely* to result in some misfortune, or to avoid being careless where it is easy to be, or to be *especially* careful where the action is dangerous or delicate, or avoid the temptation to skip a necessary step when it seems in the moment to make little difference. If for *all* excuses there were relevant obligations, then there would be no excuses and action would become intolerable. Any *particular* excuse may be countered with a *specific* obligation; not even the best excuse will always get you off the hook (That is no excuse; you should have known that was likely

[22] Though in another context we might have. Imagine that before chess was introduced into our culture, another game—call it Quest—had been popular with us. In that game, played on a board with 64 squares, and like chess in other respects, the piece called the Damsel had a fickle way of moving: its first move, and every odd move afterwards, followed the rule for the Queen in chess; its even moves followed the rule for the Knight. It may be supposed that when people began to play chess, it often happened that a game had to be stopped upon remembering that several moves earlier a Queen was permitted a Knight's move. The rule for the Queen's move might then have been formulated in some such way as: You must move the Queen in straight, unobstructed paths. . . .

[23] Perhaps this difference provides a way of accounting for our tendency sometimes to think of laws as rules and at other times to think of them as commands. This may (in part) depend upon where we—i.e., where our normal actions—stand (or where we imagine them to stand) with respect to the law or system of laws in question. It may also be significant that when you are describing a system of laws, you are likely to think of yourself as external to the system.

to result in an accident, you ought to have paid *particular* heed here, etc.).

Without pretending to give an account of (this part of) obligation, what I think the foregoing considerations indicate is this: a statement of what we *must* do (or say) has point only in the context (against the background) of knowledge that we are in fact doing (or saying) a thing, but doing (saying) it—or running a definite risk of doing or saying it—badly, inappropriately, thoughtlessly, tactlessly, self-defeatingly, etc.; or against the background of knowledge that we are in a certain position or occupy a certain office or station, and are *behaving* or *conducting ourselves* inappropriately, thoughtlessly, self-defeatingly. . . . The same is true of statements about what we *may* do, as well as those containing other "modal auxiliaries"—e.g., about what we *should* do, or what we *are* or *have* to do, or are *supposed* to do, and about one sense of what we *can* do; these are all intelligible only against the background of what we are doing or are in a position (one sense of "able") to do. These "link verbs" share the linguistic peculiarity that while they are verb-like forms they cannot stand as the main verb of a sentence. This itself would suggest that their use is not one of prescribing some new action to us, but of setting an action which is antecedently relevant to what we are doing or to what we are—setting it relevantly into the larger context of what we are doing or of what we are.[24] "You must (are supposed, obliged, required to) move the Queen in straight paths . . ." or "You may (can, are allowed or permitted to) move the Queen in straight paths . . ." say (assert) no more than "You (do, in fact, always) move the Queen in straight paths . . ."; which of them you say on a given occasion depends not on any special motive or design of yours, nor upon any special mode of argument. There is no question of *going from* "is" to "must," but only of appreciating which of them should be said when; i.e., of appreciating the position or circumstances of the person to whom you are speaking. Whatever makes one of the statements true makes them all true, though not all appropriate.

To tell me what I must do is not the same as to tell me what I

---

[24] But this requires a great deal of work. We must have a better description of the "class" and the function of "modal auxiliaries," and we need an understanding of what makes something we do "another" action and what makes it "part" of an action in progress.

ought to do. I must move the Queen in straight paths (in case I am absent-minded and continue moving it like the Damsel; cf. n. 22). What would it mean to tell me that I *ought* to move the Queen in straight paths? "Ought," unlike "must," implies that there is an alternative; "ought" implies that you can, if you choose, do otherwise. This does *not* mean merely that there is something else to do which is in your *power* ("I *can* move the Queen like the Knight; just watch!") but that there is one within your *rights*. But if I say truly and appropriately, "You must . . ." then in a perfectly good sense nothing you then do can prove me wrong. You CAN *push the little object called the Queen* in many ways, as you can *lift* it or *throw* it across the room; not all of these will be *moving the Queen*. You CAN ask, "Was your action voluntary?" and say to yourself, "All I mean to ask is whether he had a sensation of effort just before he moved," but that will not be finding out whether the action was voluntary. Again, if I have borrowed money then I *must* (under normal circumstances) pay it back (even though it is rather painful).[25] It makes sense to tell me I *ought* to pay it back only if there is a specific reason to suppose, say, that the person from whom I got the money *meant to give* it to me rather than merely *lend* it (nevertheless he needs it badly, worse than I know), or if there is a reason to pay it back tomorrow instead of next week, when the debt falls due (I'll save interest; I'll only spend it and have to make another loan). The difference here resembles that between doing a thing and doing the thing well (thoughtfully, tactfully, sensibly, graciously . . .).

This difference may be made clearer by considering one way principles differ from rules. Rules tell you what to do when you do the thing at all; principles tell you how to do the thing well, with skill

---

[25] "Must" retains its logical force here. Kant may not have provided an analysis sufficient to sustain his saying that "a deposit of money must be handed back because if the recipient appropriated it, it would no longer be a deposit"; but Bergson too hastily concludes that Kant's explanation of this in terms of "logical contradiction" is "obviously juggling with words." See Bergson's *The Two Sources of Morality and Religion* (New York: Holt, Rinehart & Winston, Inc., 1935), p. 77. The difference between your *depositing* and simply *handing over* some money has in part to do with what you mean or intend to be doing—and with what you *can* mean or intend by doing what you do in the way you do it in that particular historical context. We may, following a suggestion of H. P. Grice's ("Meaning," *The Philosophical Review*, Vol. LXVI, 1957), think of the actions of depositing and of accepting a deposit as complicated "utterances": you intend that what you do shall be understood. Then it will not seem so extraordinary to say that a later "utterance" (viz., appropriating the entrusted money) contradicts a former one (viz., accepting a deposit).

or understanding. In competitive games, acting well amounts to doing the sort of thing that will win, so the principles of games recommend strategy. "No raise should [N.B.] be given to partner's suit without at least Q-x-x, J-10-x, K-x-x, A-x-x, or any four trumps. . . ." But you could fail to adopt this and still play bridge, even play well. It is a principle of strategy in Culbertson's system;[26] but another expert may have a different understanding of the game and develop principles of strategy which are equally successful. Principles go with understanding. (Having an understanding of a game is not knowing the rules; you might find a book called Principles of Economics or Psychology, but none called Rules of Economics, etc.) Understanding a principle involves knowing how and where to apply it. But some moves seem so immediately to be called for by the principles of strategy, that their formulations come to be thought of as rules: Should we say, "The third hand plays high . . ." or "The third hand should play high . . ."? You may, strictly speaking, be playing bridge if you flout this, but you won't be doing the sort of thing which will win (and therefore not really playing? When is not doing a thing well not really doing the thing?). All players employ maxims (which may be thought of as formulating strategies as though they were moves) in order to facilitate their play; like everything habitual or summary, maxims have their advantages and their dangers. Both the rules which constitute playing the game, and the "rules" or maxims which contribute to playing the game well have their analogues in ordinary moral conduct.

I think it is sometimes felt that drawing an analogy between moral conduct and games makes moral conduct seem misleadingly simple (or trivial?), because there are no rules in moral conduct corresponding to the rules about how the Queen moves in chess.[27] But this

---

[26] Cited in Hoyle Up-to-Date, A. H. Morehead and G. Mott-Smith, eds. (New York: Grosset & Dunlap, Inc., 1950).

[27] Some philosophers who employ the notion of a rule have given the impression that there are. What I am suggesting is that even if there aren't, the analogy is still a good one. One of the claims made for the concept of a rule is that it illuminates the notion of justification; and critics of the concept argue that it fails in this and that therefore the concept is unilluminating in the attempt to understand moral conduct. I think both of these claims are improper, resulting in part from the failure to appreciate differences (1) between rules and principles, and (2) between performing an action and making some movements. The concept of rule does illuminate the concept of *action*, but not that of *justified action*. Where there is a question about what I do and I cite a rule in my favor, what I do is to *explain* my action, make clear *what* I was doing, not to justify it, say that what I did was well or rightly done. Where my action

misses the point of the analogy, which is that moves and actions have to be done *correctly;* not just any movement you make will be a move, or a promise, a payment, a request. This does not mean that promising *is* (just) following rules. Yet if someone is tempted not to fulfill a promise, you may say "Promises are kept," or "We keep our promises (that is the sort of thing a promise is)," thus employing a rule-description—what I have called a categorial declarative. You may say "You must keep this promise" (you are underestimating its importance; last time you forgot). This is not the same as "You ought to keep this promise," which is only sensible where you have a reason for breaking it strong enough to allow you to do so without blame (there is a real alternative), but where you are being enjoined to make a *special* effort or sacrifice. (This is partly why "You ought to keep promises" is so queer. It suggests that we not only always want badly to get out of fulfilling promises, but that we always have some good (anyway, prima facie) reason for not keeping them (perhaps our own severe discomfort) and that therefore we are acting *well* when we do fulfill. But we aren't, normally; neither well nor ill.) "Ought" is like "must" in requiring a background of action or position into which the action in question is set; and, like "must," it does not form a command, a pure imperative. All of which shows the hopelessness of speaking, in a *general* way, about the "normativeness" of expressions. The Britannica "rules" tell us what we *must* do *in playing* chess, not what we ought to do *if* we want to play. You (must) mean (imply), in speaking English, that something about an action is fishy when you say "The action is voluntary"; you (must) mean, when you ask a person "Ought you to do that?" that there is some *specific* way in which what he is doing might be done more tactfully, carefully, etc. . . . Are these imperatives? Are they categorical or hypothetical? Have you in no way contradicted yourself if you flout them? (Cf. n. 25.)

That "modal imperatives" ("must," "supposed to," "are to," "have to" . . .) require the recognition of a background action or

is in accord with the relevant rules, it needs no justification. Nor can it receive any: I cannot *justify* moving the Queen in straight, unobstructed paths. See John Rawls' study of this subject, "Two Concepts of Rules," *The Philosophical Review*, Vol. LXIV (1955). My unhappiness with the way in which the analogy is drawn does not diminish my respect for this paper. For a criticism (based, I think, on a misunderstanding) of the view, see H. J. McCloskey, "An Examination of Restricted Utilitarianism," *The Philosophical Review*, Vol. LXVI (1957).

position into which the relevant action is placed indicates a portentous difference between these forms of expression and pure imperatives, commands. Whether I can command depends only upon
whether I have power or authority, and the only characteristics I
must recognize in the object of the command are those which tell me
that the object is subject to my power or authority. Employing a
modal "imperative," however, requires that I recognize the object as
a *person* (someone doing something or in a certain position) to whose
reasonableness (reason) I appeal in using the second person. (Compare "Open, Sesame!" with "You must open, Sesame.") This is one
reason that commands, pure imperatives, are not paradigms of moral
utterance, but represent an alternative to such utterance.

✳ ✳

Without pretending that my argument for it has been nearly full
or clear enough, let me, by way of summary, flatly state what it is I
have tried to argue about the relation between what you say and what
you (must) mean, i.e., between what you (explicitly) say and what saying it implies or suggests: If "what A (an utterance) means" is to be
understood in terms of (or even as directly related to) "what is (must
be) meant in (by) saying A," [28] then the meaning of A will not be
given by its analytic or definitional equivalents, nor by its deductive
implications. Intension is not a substitute for intention. Although
we would not call the statement "When we say we know something
we imply (mean) that we have confidence, that we are in a position to
say we know . . ." analytic, yet if the statement is true it is necessarily true in just this sense: if it is true, then when you ask what the
statement supposes you to ask, you (must) mean what the statement
says you (must) mean. Necessary and not analytic: it was—apart from
the parody of Kant—to summarize, and partly explain, this peculiarity that I called such statements categorial declaratives: declarative, because something is (authoritatively) made known; categorial,
because in telling us what we (must) mean by asserting that (or questioning whether) x is F, they tell us what it is for an x to be F (an

---

[28] Such an understanding of meaning is provided in Grice (op cit.), but I do
not think he would be happy about the use I wish to put it to. A conversation we had
was too brief for me to be sure about this, but not too brief for me to have added,
as a result of it, one or two qualifications or clarifications of what I had said, e.g., the
third point of note 31, note 32, and the independent clause to which the present note
is attached.

action to be moral, a statement claiming knowledge to be a statement expressing knowledge, a movement to be a move).[29] Shall we say that such statements formulate the rules or the principles of grammar—the moves or the strategies of talking? And is this, perhaps, to be thought of as a difference between grammar and rhetoric? But becoming clearer about this will require us to see more clearly the difference between not doing a thing well (here, saying something) and not doing the thing; and between doing a thing badly and not doing the thing. The significance of categorial declaratives lies in their teaching or reminding us that the "pragmatic implications" of our utterances are (or, if we are feeling perverse, or tempted to speak carelessly, or chafing under an effort of honesty, let us say *must be*) *meant;* that they are an essential part of what we mean when we say something, of what it is to mean something. And what we mean (intend) to say, like what we mean (intend) to do, is something we are responsible for.

Even with this slight rehabilitation of the notion of normativeness, we can begin to see the special sense in which the philosopher who proceeds from ordinary language is "establishing a norm" in employing his second type of statement. He is certainly not *instituting* norms, nor is he *ascertaining* norms (see n. 20); but he may be thought of as *confirming* or *proving* the existence of norms when he reports or describes how we (how to) talk, i.e., when he says (in statements of the second type) what is normative for utterances instanced by statements of the first type. Confirming and proving are other regions of establishing. I have suggested that there are ways normative for instituting and for ascertaining norms; and so are there for confirming or proving or reporting them, i.e., for employing locutions like "We can say . . . ," or "When we say . . . we imply—." The swift use made of them by the philosopher serves to remind mature speakers of a language of something they know; but they would erroneously be employed in trying to report a special usage of one's own, and (not unrelated to this) could not be used to change the meaning of an expression. Since saying something is never *merely* saying something, but is saying something with a certain tune and at

[29] If truth consists in saying of what is that it is, then (*this* sense or source of) necessary truth consists in saying of what is *what* it is. The question, "Are these matters of language or matters of fact?" would betray the obsession I have tried to calm. I do not claim that this explanation of necessity holds for all statements which seem to us necessary and not analytic, but at best for those whose topic is actions and which therefore display a rule-description complementarity.

a proper cue and while executing the appropriate business, the sounded utterance is only a salience of what is going on when we talk (or the unsounded when we think); so a statement of "what we say" will give us only a feature of what we need to remember. But a native speaker will normally know the rest; learning it was part of learning the language.

Let me warn against two tempting ways to avoid the significance of this. (1) It is perfectly true that English might have developed differently than it has and therefore have imposed different categories on the world than it does; and if so, it would have enabled us to assert, describe, question, define, promise, appeal, etc., in ways other than we do. But using English now—to converse with others in the language, or to understand the world, or to think by ourselves— means knowing which forms in what contexts are normative for performing the activities we perform by using the language. (2) It is no escape to say: "Still I can say what I like; I needn't always use normal forms in saying what I say; I can speak in extraordinary ways, and you will perfectly well understand me." What this calls attention to is the fact that language provides us with ways for (contains forms which are normative for) speaking in special ways, e.g., for changing the meaning of a word, or for speaking, *on particular occasions*, loosely or personally, or paradoxically, cryptically, metaphorically. . . . Do you wish to claim that you can speak strangely yet intelligibly—and this of course means intelligibly to yourself as well —in ways not provided in the language for speaking strangely?

It may be felt that I have not yet touched one of Mates' fundamental criticisms. Suppose you grant all that has been said about an ordinary use being normative for what anyone says. Will you still wish to ask: "Does it follow that the ordinary uses which are normative for what professors say are the same as the ordinary uses which are normative for what butchers and bakers say?" Or perhaps: "Is an ordinary use for a professor an *ordin·ry* ordinary use?" Is that a sensible question?

To determine whether it is, we must appreciate what it is to talk together. The philosopher, understandably, often takes the isolated man bent silently over a book as his model for what using language is. But the primary fact of natural language is that it is something spoken, spoken together. Talking together is acting together, not making motions and noises at one another, nor transferring unspeakable messages or essences from the inside of one closed chamber to the inside of another. The difficulties of talking together are, rather, *real* ones: the activities we engage in by talking are intricate and intricately related to one another. I suppose it will be granted that the professor and the baker can talk together. Consider the most obvious complexities of cooperative activity in which they engage: there is commenting ("Nice day"); commending, persuading, recommending, enumerating, comparing ("The pumpernickel is good, but the whole wheat and the rye even better"); grading, choosing, pointing ("I'll have the darker loaf there"); counting, making change, thanking; warning ("Careful of the step"); promising ("Be back next week") . . . ; all this in addition to the whole nest or combination of actions which comprise the machinery of talking: asserting, referring, conjoining, denying, . . . Now it may be clearer why I wish to say: if the professors and the baker did not understand each other, the professors would not understand one another either.

You may still want to ask: "Does this mean that the professor and baker use particular words like 'voluntary' and 'involuntary,' or 'inadvertently' and 'automatically' the same way? The baker may never have used these words at all." But the question has *now* become, since it is about *specific* expressions, straightforwardly empirical. Here Mates' "two methods" (pp. 69ff.) at last become relevant. But I am at the moment less interested in determining what empirical methods would be appropriate to investigate the matter than I am in posing the following questions: What should we say if it turned out, as it certainly might, that they in fact do use the words differently? Should we, for example, say that therefore we never have a right to say that people use words in the same way without undertaking an empirical investigation; or perhaps say that therefore they speak different languages? What should make us say that they do not speak the same language? Do we really know what it would be like to embark upon an empirical investigation of the *general* question whether we (ordinarily, ever) use language the way other people do?

There is too much here to try to unravel. But here are some of the threads: The words "inadvertently" and "automatically," however recondite, are ordinary; there are ordinary contexts (nontechnical, nonpolitical, nonphilosophical contexts) which are normative for their use. It may be that half the speakers of English do not know (or cannot say, which is not the same) what these contexts are. Some native speakers may even use them interchangeably. Suppose the baker is able to convince us that he does. Should we then say: "So the professor has no right to say how '*we* use' 'inadvertently,' or to say that when *we* use the one word we say something different from what we say when we use the other"? Before accepting that conclusion, I should hope that the following consideration would be taken seriously: When "inadvertently" and "automatically" seem to be used indifferently in recounting what someone did, this may not at all show that they are being used synonymously, but only that what each of them says is separately true of the person's action. The decanter is broken and you did it. You may say (and it may be important to consider that you are already embarrassed and flustered) either: "I did it inadvertently" or "I did it automatically." Are you saying the same thing? Well, you automatically *grabbed the cigarette* which had fallen on the table, and inadvertently *knocked over the decanter*. Naming actions is a sensitive occupation.[30] It is easy to overlook the distinction because the two adverbs often go together in describing actions in which a sudden movement results in some mishap.

Suppose the baker does not accept this explanation, but replies: "I use 'automatically' and 'inadvertently' in exactly the same way. I could just as well have said: 'I grabbed the cigarette inadvertently and knocked over the decanter automatically.'" Don't we feel the temptation to reply: "You may *say* this, but you can't say it and describe the same situation; you can't mean what you would mean if you said the other"? But suppose the baker insists he can? Will we then be prepared to say: "Well you can't say the one and mean what *I* mean by the other"? Great care would be needed in claiming this, for it may look like I am saying, "I know what I mean and I say they are different." But why is the baker not entitled to this argument? What I must not say is: "I know what words mean in *my* language." Here the argument would have pushed me to madness. It *may* turn out (depending upon just what the dialogue has been and where it was stopped) that we should say to the baker: "If you cooked the way you talk, you would forgo special implements for different jobs, and peel, core, scrape, slice, carve, chop, and saw, all with one knife. The

---

[30] Austin's work on Excuses provides a way of coming to master this immensely important idea. The way I have put the point here is due directly to it.

distinction is there, in the language (as implements are there to be had), and you just impoverish what you say by neglecting it. And there is something you aren't noticing about the world." [31]

But to a philosopher who refuses to acknowledge the distinction we should say something more: not merely that he impoverishes what he can say about actions, but that he is a poor theorist of what it is to do something. The philosopher who asks about everything we do, "Voluntary or not?" has a poor view of action (as the philosopher who asks of everything we say, "True or false?" or "Analytic or synthetic?" has a poor view of communication), in something like the way a man who asks the cook about every piece of food, "Was it cut or not?" has a poor view of preparing food. The cook with only one knife is in much better condition than the philosopher with only "Voluntary or involuntary?" to use in dividing actions, or "True or false?" to use in hacking out meaningful statements. The cook can get on with the preparation of the meal even if he must improvise a method here and there, and makes more of a mess than he would with more appropriate implements. But the philosopher can scarcely *begin* to do his work; there is no job the philosopher has to get on with; nothing ulterior he must do with actions (e.g., explain or predict them), or with statements (e.g., verify them). What he wants to know is what they are, what it is to do something and to say something. To the extent that he improvises a way of getting past the description and division of an action or a statement, or leaves a mess in his account—to that extent he leaves his own job undone. If the philosopher is trying to get clear about what preparing a meal is and asks the cook, "Do you cut the apple or not?", the cook may say, "Watch me!" and then core and peel it. "Watch me!" is what we should reply to the philosopher who asks of our normal, ordinary actions, "Volun-

---

[31] Three points about this conclusion need emphasizing. (1) It was reached where the difference concerned isolated *words*; where, that is, the shared *language* was left intact. (2) The tasks to be performed (scraping, chopping, excusing a familiar and not very serious mishap) were such as to allow execution, if more or less crude, with a general or common implement. (3) The question was over the meaning of a word in general, not over its meaning (what it was used to mean) on a particular occasion; there was, I am assuming, no reason to treat the word's use on this occasion as a special one.

Wittgenstein's role in combatting the idea of privacy (whether of the meaning of what is said or what is done), and in emphasizing the *functions* and *contexts* of language, scarcely needs to be mentioned. It might be worth pointing out that these teachings are fundamental to American pragmatism; but then we must keep in mind how different their arguments sound, and admit that in philosophy it is the sound which makes all the difference.

tary or not?" and who asks of our ethical and aesthetic judgments, "True or false?" Few speakers of a language utilize the full range of perception which the language provides, just as they do without so much of the rest of their cultural heritage. Not even the philosopher will come to possess all of his past, but to neglect it deliberately is foolhardy. The consequence of such neglect is that our philosophical memory and perception become fixated upon a few accidents of intellectual history.

*  *

    I have suggested that the question of "[verifying] an assertion that a given person uses a *word* in a given way or with a given sense" (Mates, ibid., my emphasis) is not the same as verifying assertions that "We say . . ." or that "When we say . . . we imply—." This means that I do not take the "two basic approaches" which Mates offers in the latter part of his paper to be directed to the same question as the one represented in the title he gives to his paper (at least on my interpretation of that question). The questions are designed to elicit different types of information; they are relevant (have point) at different junctures of investigation. Sometimes a question is settled by asking others (or ourselves) what we say here, or whether we ever say such-and-such; on the basis of these data we can make statements like " 'Voluntary' is used of an action only where there is something (real or imagined) fishy about it." I take this to be a "statement about ordinary language" (and equally, about voluntary action). But surely it is not, under ordinary circumstances, an assertion about how a word is used by *me* (or "some given person"); it is a statement about how the word is used in English. Questions about how a given person is using some *word* can sensibly arise only where there is some specific reason to suppose that he is using the word in an unusual way. This point can be put the other way around: the statement "I (or some given person) use (used) the word X in such-and-such a way" implies (depending on the situation) that you intend (intended) to be using it in a special way, or that someone else is unthinkingly misusing it, or using it misleadingly, and so on. This is another instance of the principle that actions which are normal will not tolerate any special description. In a *particular* case you may realize that words are not to be taken normally, that some want or fear or special intention of the speaker is causing an aberration in the drift of his words. A little girl who says to her brother, "You can have half my candy" may mean, "Don't take any!"; the husband who screams in fury, "Still no buttons!" may really be saying, "If I were honest, I'd do what Gauguin did." A knave or a critic or an heiress may say, "X is good" and mean, "I want or expect or command you to like (or approve of) X"; and we, even without a special burden of malice, or of taste, or of money, may sometimes find ourselves imitating them.

Mates interprets Ryle's assertion that the ordinary use of "voluntary" applies to actions which are disapproved to mean that "the ordinary man applies the word only to actions of which he disapproves" (p. 72); this apparently involves a reference to that man's personal "aims, feelings, beliefs, and hopes"; and these, in turn, are supposedly part merely of the pragmatics (not the semantics) of a word. It is therefore a mistake, Mates concludes, to claim that the philosopher is using the word in a "stretched, extraordinary *sense*" (ibid., my emphasis) merely on the ground that he may not happen to feel disapproving about an action he calls voluntary. The mistake, however, is to suppose that the ordinary use of a word is a function of the internal state of the speaker. (It is sometimes to emphasize that your remarks about "use" are not remarks about such states that you want to say you are talking about the *logic* of ordinary language.) Another reason for the tenacity of the idea that a statement of what we mean when we say so-and-so (a statement of the second type) must be synthetic is that we suppose it to be *describing* the mental processes of the person talking. To gain perspective on that idea, it may be of help to consider that instead of saying to the child who said he *knew* (when we knew he had no right to say so), "You mean you *think* so," we might have said, "You *don't* know (or, That is not what it is to know something); you just think so." This says neither more nor less than the formulation about what he *means*, and neither of them is a description of what is going on inside the child. They are both statements which teach him what he has a *right* to say, what knowledge is.

Mates tells us (ibid.) that his "intensional approach" is meant, in part, "to do justice to the notions (1) that what an individual means by a word depends at least in part upon what he wants to mean by that word, and (2) that he may have to think awhile before he discovers what he 'really' means by a given word." With respect to the first notion, I should urge that we do justice to the fact that an individual's intentions or wishes can no more produce the general mean-ing for a word than they can produce horses for beggars, or home runs from pop flies, or successful poems out of unsuccessful poems.[32] This may be made clearer by noticing, with respect to the second notion, that often when an individual is thinking "what he 'really' means" (in the sense of having second thoughts about something), he is not thinking what he really means by a given *word*. You have second thoughts in such cases just because you cannot make words mean what you wish (*by* wishing); it is for that reason that what you say on a given occasion may not be what you really mean. To say what you really mean you will have to say something different, change the words; or, as a special case of this, change the meaning of a word. Changing the meaning is not wishing it were different. This is fur-ther confirmed by comparing the locutions "X means YZ" and "I mean by X, YZ." The former holds or fails to hold, whatever I wish to mean. And the latter, where meaning does depend on me, is per-formative;[33] something I am doing to the word X, not something I am wishing about it.

What these remarks come to is this: it is not clear what such an activity as my-finding-out-what-I-mean-by-a-word would be. But there obviously is finding-out-what-a-word-means. You do this by consult-ing a dictionary or a native speaker who happens to know. There is also something we may call finding-out-what-a-word-really-means. This is done when you already know what the dictionary can teach you; when, for some reason or other, you are forced into philoso-phizing. Then you begin by recollecting the various things we should say were such-and-such the case. Socrates gets his antagonists to with-draw their definitions not because they do not know what their words mean, but because they do know what they (their words) mean, and therefore know that Socrates has led them into paradox. (How could

---

[32] I am not, of course, denying that what you *say* depends upon what you intend to be saying. I am, rather, denying that intending is to be understood as a wanting or wishing. And I am suggesting that you could not mean one thing rather than another (= you could not mean anything) by a given word on a given occasion without relying on a (general) meaning of that word which is independent of your intention on that occasion (unless what you are doing is *giving* the word a special meaning). For an analysis of meaning in terms of intention, see Grice, op. cit.

[33] Or else it is a *special* report, like the one on p. 37, lines 29f; but it is still not a description of my wishes or intentions. The best place to find out what a "performative" is is Austin's *How to Do Things with Words* (Cambridge, Mass.: Harvard University Press, 1962). See also "Other Minds," *Logic and Language*, 2nd series, pp. 142ff.

I be led into a paradox if I could mean what I wished by my words? Because I must be consistent? But how could I *be inconsistent* if words would mean what I wanted them to mean?) What they had not realized was what they were saying, or, what they were *really* saying, and so had not known *what they meant*. To this extent, they had not known themselves, and not known the world. I mean, of course, the ordinary world. That may not be all there is, but it is important enough: morality is in that world, and so are force and love; so is art and a part of knowledge (the part which is about that world); and so is religion (wherever God is). Some mathematics and science, no doubt, are not. This is why you will not find out what "number" or "neurosis" or "mass" or "mass society" mean if you only listen for our ordinary uses of these terms.[34] But you will never find out what voluntary action is if you fail to see when we should say of an action that it is voluntary.

One may still feel the need to say: "Some actions *are* voluntary and some are involuntary. It would be convenient (for what?) to call all actions voluntary which are not involuntary. Surely I can call them anything I like? Surely what I *call* them doesn't affect what they *are?*" Now: How will you tell me what "they" are? [35] What we need to ask ourselves here is: In what sort of situations does it make no difference what I call a thing? or: At what point in a dialogue does it become natural or proper for me to say, "I (you) can call it what I (you) like"? At this point it may be safe to say that the question is (has become) verbal.[36] If you really have a way of telling just what is denoted by "all actions which are not involuntary," then you can call them anything you like.

✳ ✳

I just tried to characterize the situation in which we ordinarily ask, "What does X mean?" and to characterize the *different* situation in which we ask, "What does X really mean?" These questions nei-

---

[34] This may be summarized by saying that there is no such thing as *finding out* what a number, etc., is. This would then provide the occasion and the justification for logical construction.

[35] Cf. D. F. Pears, "Incompatibilities of Colours," *Logic and Language,* 2nd series, p. 119, n. 2.

[36] One of the best ways to get past the idea that philosophy's concern with language is a concern with words (with "verbal" matters) is to read Wisdom. Fortunately it is a pleasant way; because since the idea is one that you have to get past again and again, the way past it will have to be taken again and again.

ther conflict nor substitute for one another, though philosophers often take the second as a profound version of the first—perhaps to console themselves for their lack of progress. Isn't this part of the trouble about synonymy? "Does X *really* mean the same as Y?" is not a profound version of "Does X mean the same as Y?" It (its occasion) is, though related to the first in obvious and devious ways, different. The same goes for the pair: "What did he do?" and "What did he really (literally) *do*?"; and for the pair: "What do you see?" and "What do you *really* (immediately) *see*?"; and for the pair: "Is the table solid?" and "Is the table *really* (absolutely) solid?" Since the members of the pairs are *obviously* different, philosophers who do not see that the difference in the second members lies in their occasions, in where and when they are posed, handsomely provide special entities, new worlds, for them to be about. But this can only perpetrate—it will not penetrate—a new reality.

The profoundest as well as the most superficial questions can be understood only when they have been placed in their natural environments. (What makes a statement or a question profound is not its placing but its timing.) The philosopher is no more magically equipped to remove a question from its natural environment than he is to remove himself from any of the conditions of intelligible discourse. Or rather, he may remove himself, but his mind will not follow. This, I hope it is clear, does not mean that the philosopher will not eventually come to distinctions, and use words to mark them, at places and in ways which depart from the currently ordinary lines of thought.[37] But it does suggest that (and why) when his recommendations come too fast, with too little attention to the particular problem for which we have gone to him, we feel that instead of thoughtful advice we have been handed a form letter. Attention to the details of cases as they arise may not provide a quick path to an all-embracing system; but at least it promises genuine instead of spurious clarity.

Some philosophers will find this program too confining. Philosophy, they will feel, was not always in such straits; and it will be difficult for them to believe that the world and the mind have so terribly altered that philosophy must relinquish old excitements to science and to poetry. There, it may be claimed, new uses are still invented by profession, and while this makes the scientist and the poet harder to

[37] As Austin explicitly says. (See "A Plea for Excuses," p. 133.)

understand initially, it enables them eventually to renew and to deepen and to articulate our understanding. No wonder the philosopher will gape at such band wagons. But he must sit still. Both because, where he does not wish to invent (hopes not to invent), he is not entitled to the rewards and licenses of those who do; and because he would otherwise be running from his peculiar task—one which has become homelier perhaps, but still quite indispensable to the mind. The "unwelcome consequences" (Mates, p. 67) which may attend using words in ways which are (have become) privately extraordinary are just that our understanding should lose its grasp. Not only is it true that this can happen without our being aware of it, it is often very difficult to become aware of it—like becoming aware that we have grown pedantic or childish or slow. The meaning of words *will*, of course, stretch and shrink, and they will be stretched and be shrunk. One of the great responsibilities of the philosopher lies in appreciating the natural and the normative ways in which such things happen, so that he may make us aware of the one and capable of evaluating the other. It is a wonderful step towards understanding the abutment of language and the world when we see it to be a matter of convention. But this idea, like every other, endangers as it releases the imagination. For some will then suppose that a private meaning is not more arbitrary than one arrived at publicly, and that since language inevitably changes, there is no reason not to change it arbitrarily. Here we need to remind ourselves that ordinary language is natural language, and that its changing is natural. (It is unfortunate that artificial language has come to seem a general *alternative* to natural language;[38] it would, I suggest, be better thought of as one of its capacities.) Some philosophers, apparently, suppose that because natural language is "constantly" changing it is too unstable to support one exact thought, let alone a clear philosophy. But this Heraclitean anxiety is unnecessary: linguistic change is itself an object of respectable study. And it misses the significance of that change. It is exactly

---

[38] This sometimes appears to be the only substantive agreement between the philosophers who proceed from ordinary language and those who proceed by constructing artificial languages. But this may well be obscuring their deeper disagreements, which are, I believe, less about language than about whether the time has come to drag free of the philosophical tradition established in response to, and as part of, the "scientific revolution" of the sixteenth and seventeenth centuries. I have found instruction about this in conversations with my friend and now former colleague Thomas S. Kuhn, to whom I am also indebted for having read (and forced the rewriting of) two shorter versions of this paper.

because the language which contains a culture changes with the changes of that culture that philosophical awareness of ordinary language is illuminating; it is that which explains how the language we traverse every day can contain undiscovered treasure. To see that ordinary language is natural is to see that (perhaps even see why) it is normative for what can be said. And also to see how it is by searching definitions that Socrates can coax the mind down from self-assertion —subjective assertion and private definition—and lead it back, through the community, home. That this also renews and deepens and articulates our understanding tells us something about the mind, and provides the consolation of philosophers.

Professor Mates, at one point in his paper, puts his doubts about the significance of the claims of ordinary language this way: "Surely the point is not merely that if you use the word 'voluntary' just as the philosopher does, you may find yourself entangled in the philosophic problem of the Freedom of the Will" (p. 67). Perhaps the reason he thinks this a negligible consequence is that he hears it on analogy with the assertion, "If you use the term 'space-time' just as the physicist does, you may find yourself entangled in the philosophic problem of simultaneity." The implication is that the problem must simply be faced, not avoided. I, however, hear the remark differently: If you use alcohol just as the alcoholic does, or pleasure as the neurotic does, you may find yourself entangled in the practical problem of the freedom of the will.

# II

# The Availability of
# Wittgenstein's Later Philosophy

Epochs are in accord with themselves only if the crowd comes into these radiant confessionals which are the theatres or the arenas, and as much as possible, . . . to listen to its own confessions of cowardice and sacrifice, of hate and passion. . . . For there is no theatre which is not prophecy. Not this false divination which gives names and dates, but true prophecy, that which reveals to men these surprising truths: that the living must live, that the living must die, that autumn must follow summer, spring follow winter, that there are four elements, that there is happiness, that there are innumerable miseries, that life is a reality, that it is a dream, that man lives in peace, that man lives on blood; in short, those things they will never know.

—JEAN GIRAUDOUX

In June of 1929 Wittgenstein was awarded a Ph.D. from Cambridge University, having returned to England, and to philosophy, less than a year earlier. His examiners were Russell and Moore, and for his dissertation he had submitted his *Tractatus,* published some seven or eight years earlier, written earlier than that, and now famous. The following month, he refused to read a paper ("Some Remarks on Logical Form") which he had prepared for the joint session of the Mind Association and Aristotelian Society, and which obviously goes with the ideas he had worked out in the *Tractatus.* Years later he said to Moore "something to the effect that, when he wrote [the paper on logical form] he was getting new ideas about which he was still confused, and that he did not think it deserved any attention." [1]

[1] The biographical information in this (and in the final) paragraph comes from the first of Moore's three papers called "Wittgenstein's Lectures in 1930–33," *Mind,*

In January of 1930 he began lecturing at Cambridge about those new ideas, and in the academic session of 1933–1934 he dictated a set of notes in conjunction with his lectures; during 1934–1935 he dictated privately another manuscript, longer than the former, more continuously evolving and much closer in style to the *Philosophical Investigations*. These two sets of dictations—which came, because of the wrappers they were bound in, to be called, respectively, the *Blue Book* and the *Brown Book*—are now publicly available, bearing appropriately the over-title *Preliminary Studies for the "Philosophical Investigations."* [2] But the extent to which the ideas in these pages are available, now seven years after the publication of the *Investigations*, is a matter of some question even after the appearance of the first book on the later philosophy, for none of its thought is to be found in David Pole's *The Later Philosophy of Wittgenstein*. [3]

What I find most remarkable about this book is not the modesty of its understanding nor the pretentiousness and condescension of its criticism, but the pervasive absence of any worry that some remark of Wittgenstein's may not be utterly obvious in its meaning and implications. When, on the opening page, I read, "[Despite the fact that] he . . . has been popularly portrayed as a kind of fanatic of subtlety if not, worse, an addict of mystification . . . I shall maintain that Wittgenstein's central ideas . . . are essentially simple," I was, although skeptical, impressed: that would be a large claim to enter and support in discussing any difficult thinker, but it could be very worth trying to do. About Wittgenstein the claim is doubled up. For not only is one faced with the obvious surface difficulties of the writing, one is also met by a new philosophical concept of difficulty itself: the *difficulty* of philosophizing, and especially of the fruitful *criticism* of philosophy, is one of Wittgenstein's great themes (and, therefore, doubtless, simple, once we can grasp it). My disappointment was, accordingly, the sharper when I had to recognize that Pole was conceiving the task of steering toward a deep simplicity to be itself an easy one. Disappointment mounted to despair as I found the famous

LXIII (1954) and LXIV (1955); from R. R(hees)'s introduction to *The Blue and Brown Books*; and from a biographical sketch by G. H. von Wright, published together with Norman Malcolm's moving memoir, *Ludwig Wittgenstein* (Oxford: Oxford University Press, 1958).
    ²Ludwig Wittgenstein, *The Blue and Brown Books* (Oxford: Basil Blackwell & Mott, Ltd., 1958). Cited here as *BB*.
    ³London: The Athlone Press, 1958.

and exciting and obscure tags of the *Investigations* not only quoted without explanation, but quoted as though they *were* explanations:

> At least this much is clear, first that Wittgenstein distinguishes in some sense between the structural apparatus and the content of language; and secondly that he holds that philosophers are prone to the error of seeing the one in terms of the other. We make a picture of an independently existing reality. "We predicate of the thing what lies in the mode of presentation" (p. 37).

It would, for example, have been worth while to try to point to the relation of that idea—which is usually entered as summary of philosophical disorder—to the idea (cited by Pole, p. 54) that "grammar tells us what kind of object anything is" (§373)[4]—which hints at what philosophy might positively accomplish and at the kind of importance it might have.

Criticism is always an affront, and its only justification lies in usefulness, in making its object available to just response. Pole's work is not useful. Where he is not misdescribing with assurance, his counters may be of the "He says . . . , but I on the other hand say . . ." variety ("For Wittgenstein . . . an expression has as much meaning as we have given it. . . . Now as against this, I shall claim that there is always more meaning in an expression than we have given it" (pp. 83, 88)), as though the issues called for the actions of a prophet or a politician, as though it were *obvious* that what Wittgenstein means by "as much meaning" denies the possibility Pole envisages as "more meaning," and that the issue before us is not one of criticism but of commitment. The distortion to which Wittgenstein's thought is subjected is so continuous that no one error or misemphasis seems to call, more than others, for isolated discussion. This paper therefore takes the following form: the next two sections discuss the main concepts Pole attacks in his description and interpretation of Wittgenstein's view of language; the two sections which then follow comment on positions toward "ordinary language philosophy" which Pole shares with other critics of Wittgenstein; the

---

[4] All references preceded by "§" are to paragraph numbers in Part I of *Philosophical Investigations* (Oxford: Basil Blackwell & Mott, Ltd., 1953); references to Part II are preceded by "II."

final section suggests a way of understanding Wittgenstein's literary style which may help to make it more accessible.

## RULES

The main effort of Pole's work is to expose and discredit Wittgenstein's views about language. There is no problem about what those views are:

> Broadly the thesis is that a language . . . consists of a complex set of procedures, which may also be appealed to as rules. Normative notions—rightness, validity, and we may perhaps add truth—are significant inasmuch as there exist standards which we can appeal to and principles we can invoke. But where a new move is first made, a new development takes place, clearly no such standard can be applicable; we have moved beyond existing practice. Wittgenstein, it seems, is committed to holding that no such step can be called right or wrong; no evaluative assessment is possible (p. 56).

> . . . . . . . .

> We are to think of two factors in language; on the one hand particular moves or practices which are assessed by appeal to the rules, and on the other hand those rules themselves. Beyond these there is no further appeal; they are things we merely accept or adopt.

> . . . . . . . .

> Where there are no rules to appeal to we can only decide; and I suppose that it is primarily on this account that this step is called a decision (p. 61).

This sounds vaguely familiar. Its Manichean conception of "rules" reminds one of Carnap's distinction between "internal" and "external" questions and of the recent writing in moral philosophy which distinguishes between the assessment of individual actions and of social practices; its use of "decision" is reminiscent of, for example, Reichenbach's "volitional decisions" and of Stevenson's "choice" between rational and persuasive methods of supporting moral judgments. Were Pole's description meant to apply to these views, it would merely be crude, failing to suggest their source or to depict their power. As a description of Wittgenstein it is ironically blind; it is not merely wrong, but misses the fact that Wittgenstein's ideas form a sustained and radical criticism of such views—so of course it is "like" them.

Pole's description seems to involve these notions:

1. The correctness or incorrectness of a use of language is determined by the rules of the language, and "determined" in two senses:

   a) The rules form a complete system, in the sense that for every "move" within the language it is obvious that a rule does or does not apply.

   b) Where a rule does apply, it is obvious whether it has been followed or infringed.

2. Where no existing rules apply, you can always adopt a new rule to cover the case, but then that obviously changes the game.

This is rough enough, and what Wittgenstein says about games, rules, decisions, correctness, justification, and so forth, is difficult enough, but not sufficiently so that one must hesitate before saying that Pole has not tried to understand what Wittgenstein has most painfully wished to say about language (and meaning and understanding). For Pole's description seems, roughly, to suggest the way correctness is determined in a *constructed* language or in the simplest games of chance. That everyday language does not, in fact or in essence, depend upon such a structure and conception of rules, and yet that the absence of such a structure in no way impairs its functioning, is what the picture of language drawn in the later philosophy is about. It represents one of the major criticisms Wittgenstein enters against the *Tractatus*; it sets for him many of the great problems of the later philosophy—for example, the relations between word, sentence, and language—and forces him into new modes of investigating meaning, understanding, reference, and so forth; his new, and central, concept of "grammar" is developed in opposition to it; it is repeated dozens of times. Whether the later Wittgenstein describes language as being roughly like a calculus with fixed rules working in that way is not a question which can seriously be discussed.

Then what are we to make of the fact that Wittgenstein constantly compares moments of speech with moves in a game? Pole makes out this much:

[the] comparison . . . serves his purpose in at least two ways. It serves him first in that a game is usually a form of social activity in which different players fill different roles; secondly in that games observe rules (p. 29).

But what purpose is served by these points of comparison? Let us take the points in reverse order:

1. Where the comparison of language with games turns on their both "observing rules," Wittgenstein invokes and invents games not as contexts in which it is just clear what "observing rules" amounts to, but contexts in which that phenomenon can be *investigated*. In particular, the analogy with games helps us to see the following:

   *a*) In the various activities which may be said to proceed according to definite rules, the activity is not (and could not be) "everywhere circumscribed by rules" (§68). Does this mean that the rules are "incomplete"? It tells us something about what "being governed by rules" is like.

   *b*) "Following a rule" is an activity we learn against the background of, and in the course of, learning innumerable other activities—for example, obeying orders, taking and giving directions, repeating what is done or said, and so forth. The concept of a rule does not exhaust the concepts of correctness or justification ("right" and "wrong") and indeed the former concept would have no meaning unless these latter concepts already had. Like any of the activities to which it is related, a rule can always be misinterpreted in the course, or in the name, of "following" it.

   *c*) There is a more radical sense in which rules do not "determine" what a game is. One may explain the difference between, say, contract and auction bridge by "listing the rules"; but one cannot explain what *playing a game* is by "listing rules." Playing a game is "a part of our [that is, we humans'] natural history" (§25), and until one is an initiate of this human form of activity, the human gesture of "citing a rule" can mean nothing. And we can learn a new game without ever learning or formulating its rules (§31); not, however, without having mastered, we might say, the concept of a game.

*d*) There is no one set of characteristics—and this is the most obvious comparison—which everything we call "games" shares, hence no characteristic called "being determined by rules." Language has no essence (§66).

2. For Wittgenstein, "following a rule" is just as much a "practice" as "playing a game" is (§199). Now what are its rules? In the sense in which "playing chess" has rules, "obeying a rule" has none (except, perhaps, in a special code or calculus which sets up some order of precedence in the application of various rules); and yet it can be done correctly or incorrectly —which just means it can be done or not done. And whether or not it is done is not a matter of rules (or of opinion or feeling or wishes or intentions). It is a matter of what Wittgenstein, in the *Blue Book*, refers to as "conventions" (p. 24), and in the *Investigations* describes as "forms of life" (e.g., §23). That is always the ultimate appeal for Wittgenstein— not rules, and not decisions. It is what he is appealing to when he says such things as:

> If I have exhausted the justifications I have reached bedrock, and my spade is turned. Then I am inclined to say: "This is simply what I do" (§217; cf. §211).

> What has to be accepted, the given is—so one could say—*forms of life* (II, p. 226).

Pole hears such phrases as meaning:

> That [a given language-game] is played is no more than a matter of fact; it is always conceivable that it should not have been played. It might be said that the question raised is as to whether it ought to be played, and this formulation—one that Wittgenstein does not discuss —comes nearer, I believe, to the heart of the matter.

If your heart is on your sleeve, that is. Wittgenstein does not discuss whether language games *ought* to be played, for that would amount to discussing either (1) whether human beings ought to behave like the creatures we think of as human; or (2) whether the world ought to be different from what it is. For the "matters of fact" Wittgenstein is concerned with are what he describes in such ways as these:

> What we are supplying are really remarks on the natural history of human beings; we are not contributing curiosities however, but observations which no one has doubted, but which have escaped remark only because they are always before our eyes (§415).

> I am not saying: if such-and-such facts of nature were different people would have different concepts (in the sense of a hypothesis). But: if anyone believes that certain concepts are absolutely the correct ones, and that having different ones would mean not realizing something that we realize—then let him imagine certain *very general facts of nature* to be different from what we are used to, and the formation of concepts different from the usual ones will become intelligible to him (II, p. 230, my emphasis).

"It is always conceivable" that, for example, the game(s) we now play with the question "What did you say?" should not have been played. What are we conceiving if we conceive this? Perhaps that when we ask this of *A*, only *A*'s father is allowed to answer, or that it is answered always by repeating the next to the last remark you made, or that it is answered by saying what you wished you had said, or perhaps that we can never remember what we just said, or perhaps simply that we have no way of asking that question. What sense does it make to suggest that one or the other of these games ought or ought not to be played? The question is: What would our lives look like, what very general facts would be different, if these conceivable alternatives were in fact operative? (There would, for example, be different ways, and purposes, for lying; a different social structure; different ways of attending to what is said; different weight put on our words; and so forth.)

Even with these hints of echoes of shadows of Wittgenstein's "purpose" in investigating the concept of a rule, we can say this much: (1) It allows him to formulate one source of a distorted conception of language—one to which, in philosophizing, we are particularly susceptible, and one which helps secure distortion in philosophical theorizing:

> When we talk of language as a symbolism used in an exact calculus, that which is in our mind can be found in the sciences and in mathematics. Our ordinary use of language conforms to this standard of exactness only in rare cases. Why then do we in philosophizing constantly compare our use of words with one following exact rules? The answer is that the puzzles which we try to remove always spring from just this attitude towards language (*BB*, pp. 25–26) .

Or again:

> The man who is philosophically puzzled sees a law [=rule] in the
> way a word is used, and, trying to apply this law consistently, comes
> up against cases where it leads to paradoxical results (*BB*, p. 27).

(2) He wishes to indicate how inessential the "appeal to rules" is as
an explanation of language. For what has to be "explained" is, put
flatly and bleakly, this:

We learn and teach words in certain contexts, and then we are
expected, and expect others, to be able to project them into further
contexts.[5] Nothing insures that this projection will take place (in
particular, not the grasping of universals nor the grasping of books
of rules), just as nothing insures that we will make, and understand,
the same projections. That on the whole we do is a matter of our
sharing routes of interest and feeling, modes of response, senses of
humor and of significance and of fulfillment, of what is outrageous,
of what is similar to what else, what a rebuke, what forgiveness, of
when an utterance is an assertion, when an appeal, when an explanation—all the whirl of organism Wittgenstein calls "forms of life."
Human speech and activity, sanity and community, rest upon nothing
more, but nothing less, than this. It is a vision as simple as it is difficult, and as difficult as it is (and because it is) terrifying. To attempt
the work of *showing* its simplicity would be a real step in making
available Wittgenstein's later philosophy.


## DECISION

Having begun by miscasting the role of rules, and then taking
"decision" to be a concept complementary to the concept of a rule,
Pole will not be expected to have thrown light either on the real
weight (and it is not much) Wittgenstein places on the concept of
decision or on Wittgenstein's account of those passages of speech in
which, in Pole's words, "a new move is first made."

---

[5] What "learning" and "teaching" are here is, or ought to be, seriously problematic. We say a word and the child repeats it. What is "repeating" here? All we know
is that the child makes a sound which we accept. (How does the child recognize
acceptance? Has he learned what that is?)

The only passage Pole actually cites (on page 44, and again on page 61) to support his interpretation of "decision" is this one from the *Remarks on the Foundations of Mathematics*: "Why should I not say: in the proof I have won through to a decision?" (II, §27). What I take Wittgenstein to be concerned with here is the question: "What makes a proof convincing?" Without discussing either the motives of that question or the success of his answer to it, it is clear enough that Wittgenstein takes the conviction afforded by a proof to be a function of the way it can "be taken in," "be followed," "be used as a model," "serve as a pattern or paradigm." But what can be "taken in," and so forth, in this way is *not something we have a choice about, not something that can be decided.* Saying that "the problem we are faced with in mathematics is essentially to decide what new forms to fashion" (p. 44) is as sensible as saying that the problem we are faced with in composing a coda is to decide what will sound like a cadence, or that the problem faced in describing a new object is to decide what will count as a description.

What is wrong with Pole's interpretation of Wittgenstein as suggesting that the mathematician decides "to use a certain rule" is not that it takes "too literally what Wittgenstein says of standards or rules" (p. 60), but that it is not what Wittgenstein says. ("Deciding to use a certain rule" correctly describes a logician's decision to use, say, Universal Generalization, which involves certain liabilities but ones he considers outweighed by other advantages.) What Wittgenstein says is that "the expression, the result, of our being convinced is that we *accept a rule.*" We no more *decide* to accept a rule in this sense than we decide to be convinced. And we no more decide what will express our conviction here than we decide what will express our conviction about anything else—for example, that the road to New Orleans is the left one, that the development section is too long, and so forth.

Pole snaps at the word "decision" because he fears that it denies the rationality of choice; he despises this implication of its use in recent philosophizing (see p. 62). I share this concern about recent moral philosophy. But what is wrong in such discussions is not the use of the word "decision"; it is, rather, the implications which arise from an *unexamined* use of it, a use in which the concept of choice is disengaged from its (grammatical) connections with the concepts of commitment and of responsibility. How and why this has happened is something else.[6]

Wittgenstein does speak of forms of expression which we might think of as representing "a new move" in a shared language, to wit, those whose "grammar has yet to be explained" (*BB*, p. 10). (Adding "because there are no rules for its employment" adds nothing.) But he no more says of such expressions that in explaining them we decide to adopt the rules which confer meaning on them than he says about the concept of decision itself what Pole wishes him to say.

Some examples Wittgenstein gives of such expressions are: "I feel the visual image to be two inches behind the bridge of my nose" (*BB*, p. 9); "I feel in my hand that the water is three feet under the ground" (ibid.); "A rose has teeth in the mouth of a beast" (II, p. 222). What he says about them is this:

> We don't say that the man who tells us he feels the visual image two inches behind the bridge of his nose is telling a lie or talking nonsense. But we say that we don't understand the meaning of such a phrase. It combines well-known words but combines them in a way we don't yet understand. The grammar of [such phrases] has yet to be explained to us (*BB*, p. 10).

He does not say, and he does not mean, that there is "no right or wrong" about the use of such expressions. The question "Right or wrong?" has no application (yet) to such phrases, and so the statement that "such phrases are neither right nor wrong" itself says nothing. "Neither right nor wrong" may mean something like "unorthodox" or "not quite right and not quite wrong," but to use such critical expressions implies a clear sense of what would be orthodox or exactly right instances of the thing in question. Are the phrases in question unorthodox ways of saying something? What are they unorthodox ways of saying?

---

[6] If we asked, "In what kind of world would decision be unrelated to commitment and responsibility?" we might answer, "In a world in which morality had become politicalized." It is no secret that this has been happening to our world, and that we are perhaps incapable of what would make it stop happening. That is a personal misfortune of which we all partake. But the pain is made more exquisitely cruel when philosophers describe relations and conversations between persons as they would occur in a totally political world—a world, that is, in which relationships are no longer personal, nor even contractual—and call what goes on between such persons by the good (or bad) name of morality. That concedes our loss to have been not merely morality, but the very concept of morality as well.

Pole compounds critical confusion by taking the irrelevance of the question "Right or wrong?" to mean that "no evaluative assessment is possible." (If it did mean that, then we should have made no evaluative assessment of a poem when we have found it trite or incoherent or wanting a summary stanza, nor of a decision when we have shown it thoughtless or heartless or spineless. Pole's insistence on right and wrong as the touchstones of assessment represents another attempt to meet an academic distrust of morality by an academic moralism. The positions are made for one another.) Is it no assessment of a phrase to say that its grammar has yet to be explained? But that is a very particular assessment, a new category of criticism. And there is no suggestion from Wittgenstein that *any* explanation will be acceptable. He calls one explanation of the diviner's statement a "perfectly good" one (*BB*, p. 10).

Such phrases are not the only ones in which our failure to understand is attributable to our failure to understand grammar; they are only the most dramatic or obvious ones. Once we see that the grammar of an expression sometimes *needs* explaining, and realize that we all know how to provide perfectly good explanations, we may be more accessible to the request to investigate the grammar of an expression whose meaning seems obvious and ask ourselves how it *is* to be explained.

Such an investigation will doubtless be reminiscent of procedures which have long been part of the familiar texture of analytical philosophizing; in particular, it sounds something like asking for the verification of a statement—and indeed Pole suggests (p. 96) that it is not, at bottom, importantly different in its criticism of metaphysics; and it sounds like Russell's asking for the "real [that is, logical] form of a proposition"—and, of course, the Wittgenstein of the *Tractatus* had also asked for that. A profitable way, I think, to approach the thought of the later Wittgenstein is to see how his questions about grammar differ from these (and other) more familiar questions. The sorts of differences I have in mind may perhaps be suggested this way: (1) It is true that an explanation of the grammar of an assertion can be asked for by asking "How would you verify that?" But first, where that is what the question asks for, it is not to be assumed that the question itself makes good sense; in particular it is not sensible unless there is some doubt about how that assertion is conceived to be verified, and it therefore leads to no theory of meaning at all (cf. §353). Second, it is not the only way in which an explanation of grammar can be requested; it is equally indicative of our failure to understand the grammar of an assertion if we cannot answer such questions as: "How would you teach someone what that says?"; "How would you hint at its truth?"; "What is it like to wonder whether it is true?" (2) In the *Tractatus* Wittgenstein, if I understand, was asking: "Why is the logical form of a proposition its real form?" But in the later philosophy he answers, in effect: "It is not." And he goes on to ask: "Why do we (did I) think it was?"; and "What does tell us the real form (= grammar) of a proposition?"

It is part of the accomplishment of Pole's critical study of Wittgenstein that it omits any examination of the twin concepts of "grammar" and of "criteria." For what Wittgenstein means when he says that philosophy really is descriptive is that it is descriptive of "our grammar," of "the criteria we have" in understanding one another, knowing the world, and possessing ourselves. Grammar is what language games are meant to reveal; it is because of this that they provide new ways of investigating concepts, and of criticizing traditional philosophy. All this, it should go without saying, is difficult to be clear about (Wittgenstein's own difficulty is not willful); but it is what any effort to understand Wittgenstein must direct itself toward.

## THE RELEVANCE OF THE APPEAL TO
## EVERYDAY LANGUAGE

Two of Pole's claims seem to be shared by many philosophers whom Wittgenstein offends, and it would be of use to do something toward making them seem less matters for common cause than for joined investigation. The claims I have in mind concern these two questions: (1) In what sense, or to what extent, does an appeal to "our everyday use" of an expression represent a mode of criticizing the use of that expression in philosophical contexts? (2) What sort of knowledge is the knowledge we have (or claim) of "how we ordinarily use" an expression? The present section is concerned with the first of these questions, the following with the second.

Pole says, or implies, that Wittgenstein regards ordinary language as "sacrosanct," that he speaks in the name of nothing higher than the "status quo" and that he "has forbidden philosophers to tamper with [our ordinary expressions]" (p. 57). Other philosophers, with very different motives from Pole's, have received the same impression, and their impatience has not been stilled by Wittgenstein's having said that:

> a reform of ordinary language for particular purposes, an improvement in our terminology designed to prevent misunderstandings in practice, is perfectly possible. But these are not the cases we have to do with (§132).

for they persist in reading Wittgenstein's appeal to our everyday use of expressions as though his effort consisted in scorning the speech of his charwoman out of solicitude for that of his Nanny.

It takes two to give an impression; if this is a distortion of Wittgenstein's thought, it is a distortion of *something*. Of what? Pole's reference for his claim about what Wittgenstein "forbids" is to a passage which begins this way:

> Philosophy may in no way interfere with the actual use of language; it can in the end only describe it (§124).

There is a frame of mind in which this may appear as something intolerably confining.[7] Then one will hear Wittgenstein's statement as though it meant either that philosophy ought not to change it (in which case Wittgenstein will be accused of an intellectual, even social conservatism) or that the actual use of language may in no way be changed (in which case Wittgenstein will be accused of lacking imagination or a sufficient appreciation of scientific advance). What the statement means is that, though of course there are any number of ways of changing ordinary language, philosophizing does not change

---

[7] It is significant that Wittgenstein thought of his methods as liberating. "The real discovery is the one that makes me capable of stopping doing philosophy when I want to.—The one that gives philosophy peace, so that it is no longer tormented by questions which bring *itself* in question" (§133). The reason why methods which make us look at what we say, and bring the forms of language (hence our forms of life) to consciousness, can present themselves to one person as confining and to another as liberating is, I think, understandable in this way: recognizing what we say, in the way that is relevant in philosophizing, is like recognizing our present commitments and their implications; to one person a sense of freedom will demand an escape from them, to another it will require their more total acceptance. Is it obvious that one of those positions must, in a given case, be right?

it. That charge cannot be evaded by making it sound like a Nanny bleating "ou-ou-ought."

And yet it is a very perplexing indictment which Wittgenstein has entered. Why does Wittgenstein think it is one? Why do philosophers respond to it as though it were? Have they claimed to be, or thought of themselves as, changing or interfering with language?

The force of the indictment can best be seen in considering the ancient recognition that a philosophical thesis may, or may seem to, conflict with a "belief" which we take to be the common possession of common men, together with the equally ancient claim on the part of philosophers that in this conflict philosophy's position is superior to that common possession; that, for example, such claims as "We know that there are material objects," "We directly see them," "We know that other persons are sentient," all of which are believed by the vulgar, have been discovered by philosophers to lack rational justification.

But the *nature* of this discovery and the *kind* of conflict involved are problems as constant as epistemology itself. Their most recent guise is perhaps brought out if we can say this much: There would be no sense of such a discovery[8] unless there were a sense of conflict with "what we all formerly believed," and there would, in turn, be no sense of conflict unless the philosopher's words meant (or were used as meaning) what they ordinarily meant. And don't they?

The ordinary language philosopher will say: "They don't; the philosopher is 'misusing words' or 'changing their meanings'; the philosopher has been careless, hasty, even wily[9] in his use of language." The defender of the tradition may reply: "Of course they don't; the philosopher uses technical terms, or terms with special senses, in order to free himself from the vagueness and imprecision of ordinary language and thereby to assess the beliefs it expresses." Neither of these replies is very satisfactory. The former is, if not too unclear altogether to be taken seriously as an explanation of disorder,

---

[8] The importance and role of the sense of discovery in philosophical paradox (one of the constant themes in the philosophizing of John Wisdom), in particular the pervasive significance of the fact that this sense is not accounted for by the familiar criticisms made by ordinary language philosophers against the tradition, was brought in upon me in conversations with Thompson Clarke. He has also read this paper and done what he could to relieve its obscurities.

[9] Austin, "Other Minds," in *Logic and Language*, Antony Flew, ed. (Oxford: Basil Blackwell & Mott, Ltd., 1953), 2nd series, p. 133.

plainly incredible. I do not see how it can with good conscience be denied that ordinary language philosophers (for example, Austin and Ryle) have found and made trouble for traditional philosophy. But the understanding of the trouble, and so an assessment of its seriousness or permanence, is a project of a different order. And I know of no effort of theirs at this task which carries anything like that immediate conviction which is so large a part of the power of their remarks when they are working within an investigation of ordinary language itself.

On the other hand, someone who imagines that he is defending the tradition by maintaining its right and need to introduce technical terms (or, as Pole suggests, to invent special philosophical language games—on, for example pages 96-97) probably has in mind the philosopher's use of such terms as "sense data," "analytic," "transcendental unity of apperception," "idea," "universal," "existential quantifier"—terms which no ordinary language philosopher would criticize on the ground that they are not ordinary. But is the word "seeing" in the statement "We never directly see material objects" *meant* to be technical? Is "private" in "My sensations are private"? Are any of the words in such a statement as "We can never know what another person is experiencing"? Are such statements used in some special language game? The assumption, shared by our ordinary language critic and our defender of the tradition, that such words are not meant in their ordinary senses, destroys the point (not to say the meaning) of such statements. For on that assumption we cannot account for the way they seem to conflict with something we all (seem to, would say that we) believe; it therefore fails to account for what makes them seem to be discoveries or, we might say, fails to suggest what the hitherto unnoticed fact is which philosophy has discovered. Why would Descartes have professed "astonishment" at his "realization" that he might be dreaming if he had not meant to be denying or questioning what anyone who said "I believe, for example, that I am seated before the fire," and the like, would mean? And what cause, otherwise, would there have been for Hume to despair of his skeptical conclusions, regarding them as a "malady which can never radically be cured" (*Treatise,* I, iv, 2), were they not skeptical about (or, as he puts it, "contrary" to) "such opinions as we . . . embrace by a kind of instinct or natural impulse"?

It may be objected to this that scientific theories, however technical their language, have no trouble conflicting with common beliefs. But it is of crucial importance that neither Hume nor the Descartes of the *Meditations,* nor indeed anyone in that continuous line of classical epistemologists from Descartes and Locke to Moore and Price, seems to be conducting scientific investigations. In particular, they do not set out a collection of more or less abstruse facts and puzzling phenomena which they undertake to explain theoretically. Their method is uniformly what Hume describes as "profound and intense *reflection*" from which, he says, "skeptical doubt arises *naturally*" (op. cit.; my emphasis). They all begin from what seem to be facts of such obviousness that no one could fail to recognize them ("We all believe that there are material objects which continue to exist when they are unperceived"), employ examples of the homeliest extraction ("We should all say that I am now holding an envelope in my hand, and that we all see it") and considerations whose import anyone can grasp who can speak ("But no two of us see exactly the same thing"; "But there is much that I can doubt"). (Wittgenstein's originality does not come from his having said that philosophy's problems concern something we all already know.) That such facts and examples and considerations "naturally" lead to skepticism is the phenomenon concerning us here. What the relation may be between this way of coming into conflict with common belief, and science's way, is a fascinating question and one, so far as I know, as yet unexamined.

Perhaps this can now be said: If, in the nonscientific (skeptical) conflict with common belief, words are in some way deprived of their normal functioning, a conceptualization of this distortion will have to account for this pair of facts: that the philosopher's words must (or must seem to) be used in their normal way, otherwise they would not conflict with what should ordinarily be meant in using them; and that the philosopher's words cannot be used in (quite) their normal way, otherwise the ordinary facts, examples, and considerations he adduces would not yield a general skeptical conclusion.

It is such a pair of facts, I suggest, that Wittgenstein is responding to when he says of philosophical (he calls them "metaphysical") expressions that (roughly) they are "used apart from their normal language game," that their "grammar is misunderstood," that they "flout the common criteria used in connection with these expressions." Such assertions do not say that the philosopher has "changed the meaning of his words" (what meaning do they now have?). Nor are they met, if any truth is caught by them, by saying that the words are being used in special senses, for none of Wittgenstein's critical assertions would be true of technical terms. They represent new categories of criticism.

Wittgenstein is, then, denying that in the (apparent) conflict between philosophy and the common "beliefs" (assumptions?) of ordinary men, philosophy's position is superior. This does not mean, however, that he is defending common beliefs against philosophy. That "there are material objects" or that "other persons are sentient" are not propositions which Wittgenstein supposed to be open either to belief or to disbelief. They seem to be ordinary "beliefs" only when the philosopher undertakes to "doubt" them. I am not saying that this is obviously not real doubt, but merely suggesting that it is not obvious that it is, and that it is completely unobvious, if it is not real doubt, what kind of experience it is and why it presents itself as doubt.

Nor is Wittgenstein saying that philosophy's position is inferior to that of common men. Perhaps one could say that he wishes to show that, in its conflict with "what we all believe," the philosopher has no position at all, his conclusions are not false (and not meaningless), but, one could say, not *believable*—that is, they do not create the stability of conviction expressed in propositions which are subject (grammatically) to belief. (That was agonizingly acknowledged, as is familiar to us, by Hume, who wanted, but confessed failure in trying to find, an explanation of it. When he left his study he forgot, as he knew and hoped he would, the skeptical conclusions of his reflections. But what kind of "belief" is it whose convincingness fades as soon as we are not explicitly attending to the considerations which led us to it?) For Wittgenstein, philosophy comes to grief not in denying what we all know to be true, but in its effort to escape those human forms of life which alone provide the coherence of our expression. He wishes an acknowledgment of human limitation which does not leave us chafed by our own skin, by a sense of powerlessness to penetrate beyond the human conditions of knowledge. The limitations of knowledge are no longer barriers to a more perfect apprehension, but conditions of knowledge *überhaupt*, of anything we should call "knowledge." The resemblance to Kant is obvious, and I will say another word about it below.

## THE KNOWLEDGE OF OUR LANGUAGE

How can we come to such an acknowledgment of limitation? Wittgenstein's answer is: "What we do is to bring words back from their metaphysical to their everyday use" (§116). I have, in effect, asked: Why does that help? And my suggestion, essentially, was: It shows us that we did not know what we were saying, what we were doing to ourselves. But now I want to ask: How do we accomplish the task of bringing words back home? How do we know when we have done it?

Well, how does the logician know that (1) "Nobody is in the auditorium" must be transcribed differently from (2) "Peabody is in the auditorium"? By intuition? Careful empirical studies? Perhaps he will say: "But obviously we do not want the same sorts of inferences to be drawn from (1) as from (2), in particular not the inference that somebody is in the auditorium." But how does he know *that*? However he knows it—and he does—that is how Wittgenstein knows that the grammar of, say, "pointing to an object" is different from the grammar of "pointing to a color" (*BB*, p. 80; §33). Failing an awareness of that difference we take the obvious difference between them to be a function of some special experience which accompanies the act of pointing. How does Wittgenstein know that? The way Russell (and we) know that if you do not catch the difference in logical form between "Pegasus does not exist" and "Whirlaway does not whinny," you will take the obvious difference between them to indicate the presence of some special realm of being which accompanies the ordinary world.

But what kind of knowledge is this? What kind of knowledge is the knowledge of what we ordinarily mean in using an expression, or the knowledge of the particular circumstances in which an expression is actually used? Pole has this to say:

> Consider the great purpose of all this—this descriptive setting forth of language-games. It is to bring us to see that some particular move

which we took for a move in the game has no proper place in it. Such a move is to be shown as failing to connect with the rest of the pattern. Wittgenstein compares it to a wheel spinning idly, disengaged from the machine it should belong to. Here we have a luminous metaphor—and yet no more than a metaphor. For there can be no way of testing whether this or that linguistic wheel has failed to engage, except to grasp the pattern in each case; to arrive at some sort of insight into that unique set of relations which it professes but fails to form a part of (p. 81).

This is thought to show that if we

once allow that it might be right to reject a proposition or mode of speech because the pattern has no place for it, . . . it must follow that it must sometimes be right to accept others on the same ground —that the pattern requires them. There is no inherent difficulty in the notion. . . . Yet here we have a way of seeing language that the whole bent of Wittgenstein's thought was opposed to (p. 82).

If I understand what Pole is getting at (he gives no examples, here or elsewhere), he has been even less impressed by Wittgenstein's conception of language than we have seen. It is not the "bent" of Wittgenstein's thought that is opposed to the idea that the "requirement of the pattern" justifies the use we make of an expression, but the straight thrust of his whole teaching: "The more narrowly we examine actual language, the sharper becomes the conflict between it and our requirement. (For the crystalline purity of logic was, of (course, not a *result of investigation*: it was a requirement.)" (§107) "A *picture* [ = pattern?] held us captive. And we could not get outside it, for it lay in our language and language seemed to repeat it to us inexorably" (§115). Not only is there "no inherent difficulty in the notion" of "grasping a pattern," the difficulty is to get ourselves not to take our feelings of what is called for or what must be appropriate, at face value.

Other philosophers have taken the knowledge of everyday language, since it is obviously knowledge of "matters of fact," to be straightforwardly empirical, requiring the observations and verifications which we are told that any empirical judgment requires. Such philosophers find the appeal to what we should ordinarily say and mean, when this appeal is not backed by scientific collection of "our" utterances, archaically precious, while philosophers dependent upon that appeal will find the invitation to science at this point cheaply *moderne*. This conflict is not a side issue in the general conflict between Wittgenstein (together with, at this point, "ordinary language philosophy") and traditional philosophy; it is itself an instance, an expression, of that conflict, and one therefore which we will not suppose it will be simple to resolve. Wittgenstein does not speak very explicitly about the knowledge we have of our language, but when we see what kind of claim this knowledge involves, we realize that its investigation lies at the heart of the later philosophy as a whole. I shall try to suggest what I mean by that.

Neither Wittgenstein nor the ordinary language philosopher, when he asks "What should we say (would we call) . . . ?" is asking just any question about the use of language. He is, in particular, not predicting what will be said in certain circumstances, not, for example, asking how often a word will be used nor what the most effective slogan will be for a particular purpose. (Those questions can, of course, be asked; and their answers will indeed require ordinary empirical methods for collecting sociological data.) He is asking something which can be answered by remembering what is said and meant, or by trying out his own response to an imagined situation. Answers arrived at in such ways will not tell you everything, but why assume that they are meant to tell you what only the collection of new data can tell you? The problems of philosophy are not solved by "[hunting] out new facts; it is, rather, of the essence of our investigation that we do not seek to learn anything *new* by it. We want to *understand* something that is already in plain view. For *this* is what we seem in some sense not to understand" (§89).

What do such answers look like? They will be facts about what we call (how we conceive, what the concept is, what counts as), for example, a piece of wax, the same piece of wax, seeing something, not really seeing something, not seeing all of something, following, finding, losing, returning, choosing, intending, wishing, pointing to something, and so on. And we could say that what such answers are meant to provide us with is not more knowledge of matters of fact, but the knowledge of what would count as various "matters of fact." Is this empirical knowledge? Is it a priori? It is a knowledge of what Wittgenstein means by grammar—the knowledge Kant calls "transcendental."

> . . . here I make a remark which the reader must bear well in mind, as it extends its influence over all that follows. Not every kind of knowledge a priori should be called transcendental, but that only by which we know that—and how—certain representations (intuitions or concepts) can be employed or are possible purely a priori. The term "transcendental," that is to say, signifies such knowledge as concerns the a priori possibility of knowledge, or its a priori employment (Critique of Pure Reason, trans. by N. K. Smith, p. 96).

That is not the clearest remark ever made, but I should think that no one who lacked sympathy with the problem Kant was writing about would undertake to make sense of Wittgenstein's saying:

> Our investigation . . . is directed not towards phenomena, but, as one might say, towards the "possibilities" of phenomena (§90).

As the "transcendental clue to the discovery of all pure concepts of the understanding" (Critique, pp. 105ff.) Kant uses the idea that "there arise precisely the same number of pure concepts of the understanding in general, as . . . there have been found to be logical functions in all possible judgments" (p. 113). Wittgenstein follows the remark quoted above with the words: "We remind ourselves, that is to say, of the *kind of statement* that we make about phenomena. . . . Our investigation is therefore a grammatical one" (§90). And where Kant speaks of "transcendental illusion"—the illusion that we know what transcends the conditions of possible knowledge—Wittgenstein speaks of the illusions produced by our employing words in the absence of the (any) language game which provides their comprehensible employment (cf. §96). ("The results of philosophy are the uncovering of one or another piece of plain nonsense and of bumps that the understanding has got by running its head up against the limits of language" (§119).)

If his similarity to Kant is seen, the differences light up the nature of the problems Wittgenstein sets himself. For Wittgenstein it would be an illusion not only that we do know things-in-themselves, but equally an illusion that we do not (crudely, because the concept of "knowing something as it really is" is being used without a clear sense, apart from its ordinary language game). So problems emerge which can be articulated as: "Why do we feel we cannot know something in a situation in which there is nothing it makes sense to say we do not know?"; "What is the nature of this illusion?"; "What makes us dissatisfied with our knowledge as a whole?"; "What is the nature and power of a 'conceptualization of the world'?"; "Why do we conceptualize the world as we do?"; "What would alternative conceptualizations look like?"; "How might they be arrived at?" It was, I suggest, because he wanted answers to such questions that he said, "It did not matter whether his results were true or not: what mattered was that 'a method had been found'" (Moore, "Wittgenstein's Lectures," *Mind*, LXIV, 1955, p. 26).

And he also said: "There is not *a* philosophical method, though there are indeed methods, like different therapies" (§133). The sorts of thing he means by "methods" are, I take it, "[imagining or considering] a language-game for which [a given] account is really valid" (for example, §2, §48); "finding and inventing intermediate cases" (§122); "[inventing] fictitious natural history" (II, p. 230); investigating one expression by investigating a grammatically related expression, for example, the grammar of "meaning" by that of "explanation of the meaning" (*BB*, pp. 1, 24); and so on. But in all of these methods part of what is necessary is that we respond to questions like "What would we say if . . . ?" or "But is anyone going to call . . . ?". To suppose that what is then being asked for is a prediction of what will be said, and a prediction for which we have slim evidence, would be as sensible as responding to the request "Suppose you have three apples and I give you three more. How many will you have?" by saying, "How can I answer with confidence? I might drop one and have five, or inherit an orchard and have thousands."

What is being asked for? If it is accepted that "a language" (a natural language) is what the native speakers of a language speak, and that speaking a language is a matter of practical mastery, then such questions as "What should we say if . . . ?" or "In what circumstances would we call . . . ?" asked of someone who has mastered the language (for example, oneself) is a request for the person to say something about himself, describe what he does. So the different methods are methods for acquiring self-knowledge; as—for different (but related) purposes and in response to different (but related) problems—are the methods of "free" association, dream analysis, investigation of verbal and behavioral slips, noting and analyzing "transferred" feeling, and so forth. Perhaps more shocking, and certainly more important, than any of Freud's or Wittgenstein's particular conclusions is their discovery that knowing oneself is something for which there are methods—something, therefore, that can be taught (though not in obvious ways) and practiced.

Someone may wish to object: "But such claims as 'We say . . . ,' 'We are not going to call . . . ,' and so forth, are not merely claims about what *I* say and mean and do, but about what *others* say and mean and do as well. And how can I speak for others on the basis of knowledge about myself?" The question is: Why are some claims about myself expressed in the form *"We . . ."*? About what can I speak for others on the basis of what I have learned about myself? (This is worth comparing with the question: About what can I speak for others on the basis of what I decide to do? When you vote, you speak for yourself; when you are voted in, you speak for others.) Then suppose it is asked: "But how do I know others speak as I do?" About some things I know they do not; I have some knowledge of my idiosyncrasy. But if the question means "How do I know at all that others speak as I do?" then the answer is, I do not. I may find out that the most common concept is not used by us in the same way. And one of Wittgenstein's questions is: What would it be like to find this out? [10] At one place he says:

> One human being can be a complete enigma to another. We learn this when we come into a strange country with entirely strange traditions; and, what is more, even given a mastery of the country's language. We do not *understand* the people. (And not because of not knowing what they are saying to themselves.) We cannot find our feet with them (II, p. 223).

In German the last sentence employs an idiom which literally says: "We cannot find ourselves in them." We, who can speak for one another, find that we cannot speak for them. In part, of course, we find this out in finding out that we cannot speak *to* them. If speak-

[10] The nature and extent of this fact, and of the different methods required in meeting it, are suggested by the differences of problems presented to psychoanalysts in the cases of neurotic and of psychotic communication (verbal and nonverbal). See, e.g., Frieda Fromm-Reichmann, *Principles of Intensive Psychotherapy* (Chicago: University of Chicago Press, 1950; Phoenix Book), esp. ch. 8 and *passim*. Perhaps it is suggestive to say: The neurotic disguises the expression of particular communications (e.g., makes something fearful to him look and sound attractive), while the psychotic distorts his entire grammar. The neurotic has reason, and the strength, to keep what he means from himself; the psychotic has to keep what he knows he means from others. Wittgenstein is concerned with both of these kinds of incongruence.

ing *for* someone else seems to be a mysterious process, that may be because speaking *to* someone does not seem mysterious enough.

If the little I have said makes plausible the idea that the question "How do we know what we say (intended to say, wish to say)?" is one aspect of the general question "What is the nature of self-knowledge?" then we will realize that Wittgenstein has not first "accepted" or "adopted" a method and then accepted its results, for the nature of self-knowledge—and therewith the nature of the self—is one of the great subjects of the *Investigations* as a whole.

It is also one of the hardest regions of the *Investigations* to settle with any comfort. One reason for that, I think, is that so astonishingly little exploring of the nature of self-knowledge has been attempted in philosophical writing since Bacon and Locke and Descartes prepared the habitation of the new science. Classical epistemology has concentrated on the knowledge of objects (and, of course, of mathematics), not on the knowledge of persons. That is, surely, one of the striking facts of modern philosophy as a whole, and its history will not be understood until some accounting of that fact is rendered.[11] In a smart attack on the new philosophy, Russell suggests that its unconcern with the methods and results of modern science betrays its alienation from the original and continuing source of philosophical inspiration. "Philosophers from Thales onward have tried to understand the world" (*My Philosophical Development*, New York, 1959, p. 230). But philosophers from Socrates onward have (sometimes) also tried to understand themselves, and found in that both the method and goal of philosophizing. It is a little absurd to go on insisting that physics provides us with knowledge of the world which is of the highest excellence. Surely the problems we face now are not the same ones for which Bacon and Galileo caught their chills. Our intellectual problems (to say no more) are set by the very success of those deeds, by the plain fact that the measures which soak up knowledge of the world leave us dryly ignorant of ourselves. Our problem is not that we lack adequate methods for acquiring knowledge of nature,

[11] Bernard Williams, in a review of Stuart Hampshire's *Thought and Action* in *Encounter*, XV (Nov., 1960), 38–42, suggests one important fact about what I have, parochially, called "modern philosophy" (by which I meant the English and American academic traditions, beginning with Descartes and Locke and never domesticating Hegel and his successors) which, I think, is related to its unconcern with the knowledge of persons and in particular with self-knowledge; viz., its neglect of history as a form of human knowledge.

but that we are unable to prevent our best ideas—including our ideas about our knowledge of nature—from becoming ideologized. Our incapacity here results not from the supposed fact that ordinary language is vague; to say so is an excuse for not recognizing that (and when) we speak vaguely, imprecisely, thoughtlessly, unjustly, in the absence of feeling, and so forth.

Since Wittgenstein's investigations of self-knowledge and of the knowledge of others depend upon his concept of "criteria," it is worth noting that although Pole ventures a discussion of Wittgenstein's ideas about "inner experience" he prudently withholds any opinion about the role of "criteria" in those ideas. He does suggest that Wittgenstein supposed words to have meaning "in the complete absence of conscious feeling" (p. 88), as though Wittgenstein supposed the users of language to be anaesthetized; and he finds Wittgenstein supposing that "experiential elements play no part" in determining the way language is used (p. 88; cf. p. 86), whereas what Wittgenstein says is, in these terms, that what is experiential in the use of a word is not an element, not one identifiable recurrence whose presence insures the meaning of a word and whose absence deprives it of meaning. If that were the case, how could we ever assess our feelings, recognize them to be inappropriate to what we say? Feelings (like intentions and hopes and wishes, though not in the same way) are expressed in speech and in conduct generally; and the (actual, empirical) problem of the knowledge of oneself and of others is set by the multiple and subtle distortions of their expression. Here, what we do not know comprises not our ignorance but our alienation.

Because Wittgenstein does fuller justice to the role of feeling in speech and conduct than any other philosopher within the Anglo-American academic tradition, it is disheartening to find his thought so out of reach. Pole extends the line of those who, shocked at the way academic reasoning is embarrassed by the presence of feeling—its wish to remove feeling to the "emotive" accompaniments of discourse, out of the reach of intellectual assessment—counter by taking feelings too much at face value and so suffer the traditional penalty of the sentimentalist, that one stops taking his feelings seriously. Other philosophers, I believe, are under the impression that Wittgenstein denies that we can know what we think and feel, and even that we can know ourselves. This extraordinary idea comes, no doubt, from such remarks of Wittgenstein's as: "I can know what someone else is thinking, not what I am thinking" (II, p. 222); "It cannot be said of me at all (except perhaps as a joke) that I *know* I am in pain" (§246). But the "can" and "cannot" in these remarks are grammatical; they mean "it makes no sense to say these things" (in the way we think it does); it would, therefore, equally make no sense to say of me that I do not know what I am thinking, or that I do not know I am in pain. The implication is not that I cannot know myself, but that knowing oneself—though radically different from the way we know others—is not a matter of cognizing (classically, "intuiting") mental acts and particular sensations.

## THE STYLE OF THE *INVESTIGATIONS*

I mentioned, at the beginning of this paper, the surface difficulties one has in approaching the writings of Wittgenstein. His literary style has achieved both high praise and widespread alarm. Why does he write that way? Why doesn't he just say what he means, and draw instead of insinuate conclusions? The motives and methods of his philosophizing, as I have been sketching at them, suggest answers to these questions which I want, in conclusion, to indicate.[12]

The first thing to be said in accounting for his style is that he *writes*: he does not report, he does not write up results. Nobody would forge a style so personal who had not wanted and needed to find the right expression for his thought. The German dissertation and the British essay—our most common modern options for writing philosophy—would not work; his is not a system and he is not a spectator. My suggestion is that the problem of style is set for him by the two aspects of his work which I have primarily emphasized: the lack of existing terms of criticism, and the method of self-knowledge.[13]

In its defense of truth against sophistry, philosophy has employed the same literary genres as theology in its defense of the faith: against intellectual competition, Dogmatics; against Dogmatics, the

---

[12] Wittgenstein speaks of this as a problem in his preface to the *Investigations*.
[13] Perhaps another word will make clearer what I mean by "terms of criticism." Wittgenstein opens the *Investigations* (and the *Brown Book*) by quoting a passage from Augustine's *Confessions* in which he describes the way he learned to speak. Wittgenstein finds this important but unsatisfactory. Is there any short way of answering the question: What does Wittgenstein find wrong with it? (Does it commit a well-known fallacy? Is it a case of hasty generalization? Empirical falsehood? Unverifiable?)

Confession; in both, the Dialogue.[14] Inaccessible to the dogmatics of philosophical criticism, Wittgenstein chose confession and recast his dialogue. It contains what serious confessions must: the full acknowledgment of temptation ("I want to say . . ."; "I feel like saying . . ."; "Here the urge is strong . . .") and a willingness to correct them and give them up ("In the everyday use . . ."; "I impose a requirement which does not meet my real need"). (The voice of temptation and the voice of correctness are the antagonists in Wittgenstein's dialogues.) In confessing you do not explain or justify, but describe how it is with you. And confession, unlike dogma, is not to be believed but tested, and accepted or rejected. Nor is it the occasion for accusation, except of yourself, and by implication those who find themselves in you. There is exhortation ("Do not say: 'There *must* be something common . . . but *look* and *see* . . .' " (§66)) not to belief, but to self-scrutiny. And that is why there is virtually nothing in the *Investigations* which we should ordinarily call reasoning; Wittgenstein asserts nothing which could be proved, for what he asserts is either obvious (§126)—whether true or false—or else concerned with what conviction, whether by proof or evidence or authority, would consist in. Otherwise there are questions, jokes, parables, and propositions so striking (the way lines are in poetry) that they stun mere belief. (Are we asked to believe that "if a lion could talk we could not understand him"? (II, p. 223)) Belief is not enough. Either the suggestion penetrates past assessment and becomes part of the sensibility from which assessment proceeds, or it is philosophically useless.

Such writing has its risks: not merely the familiar ones of inconsistency, unclarity, empirical falsehood, unwarranted generalization, but also of personal confusion, with its attendant dishonesties, and of the tyranny which subjects the world to one's personal problems. The assessment of such failures will exact criticism at which we are unpracticed.

In asking for more than belief it invites discipleship, which runs

[14] The significance of the fact that writing of all kinds (not just "literature") is dependent, in structure and tone and effect, on a quite definite (though extensive) set of literary forms or genres is nowhere to my knowledge so fully made out as in Northrop Frye's *Anatomy of Criticism* (Princeton: Princeton University Press, 1957); the small use I have made of it here hardly suggests the work it should inspire. More immediately I am indebted to Philip Rieff's introduction to the Beacon Press edition of Adolf Harnack's *Outlines of the History of Dogma* (Boston: Beacon Press, 1957), and to the reference to Karl Barth's *Church Dogmatics* cited by Rieff.

its own risks of dishonesty and hostility. But I do not see that the faults of explicit discipleship are more dangerous than the faults which come from subjection to modes of thought and sensibility whose origins are unseen or unremembered and which therefore create a different blindness inaccessible in other ways to cure. Between control by the living and control by the dead there is nothing to choose.

Because the breaking of such control is a constant purpose of the later Wittgenstein, his writing is deeply practical and negative, the way Freud's is. And like Freud's therapy, it wishes to prevent understanding which is unaccompanied by inner change. Both of them are intent upon unmasking the defeat of our real need in the face of self-impositions which we have not assessed (§108), or fantasies ("pictures") which we cannot escape (§115). In both, such misfortune is betrayed in the incongruence between what is said and what is meant or expressed; for both, the self is concealed in assertion and action and revealed in temptation and wish. Both thought of their negative soundings as revolutionary extensions of our knowledge, and both were obsessed by the idea, or fact, that they would be misunderstood —partly, doubtless, because they knew the taste of self-knowledge, that it is bitter. It will be time to blame them for taking misunderstanding by their disciples as personal betrayal when we know that the ignorance of oneself is a refusal to know.

# III

# Aesthetic Problems
# of Modern Philosophy

The Spirit of the Age is not easy to place, ontologically or empirically; and it is idle to suggest that creative effort must express its age, either because that cannot fail to happen, or because a new effort can create a new age. Still, one knows what it means when an art historian says, thinking of the succession of plastic styles, "not everything is possible in every period." [1] And that is equally true for every person and every philosophy. But then one is never sure what is possible until it happens; and when it happens it may produce a sense of revolution, of the past escaped and our problems solved—even when we also know that one man's solution is another man's problem.

Wittgenstein expressed his sense both of the revolutionary break his later methods descry in philosophy, and of their relation to methods in aesthetics and ethics.[2] I have tried, in what follows, to suggest ways in which such feelings or claims can be understood, believing them to be essential in understanding Wittgenstein's later philosophy as a whole. The opening section outlines two problems in aesthetics each of which seems to yield to the possibilities of Wittgensteinian procedures, and in turn to illuminate them. The concluding section

[1] Heinrich Wölfflin, *Principles of Art History*, foreword to the 7th German edition. Quoted by E. H. Gombrich, *Art and Illusion* (New York: The Bollingen Series, Pantheon Press, 1960), p. 4.
[2] Reported by G. E. Moore, "Wittgenstein's Lectures in 1930–33," reprinted in Moore's *Philosophical Papers* (London: George Allen and Unwin, 1959), p. 315.

73

suggests resemblances between one kind of judgment recognizable as aesthetic and the characteristic claim of Wittgenstein—and of ordinary language philosophers generally—to voice "what we should ordinarily say."

What I have written, and I suppose the way I have written, grows from a sense that philosophy is in one of its periodic crises of method, heightened by a worry I am sure is not mine alone, that method dictates to content; that, for example, an intellectual commitment to analytical philosophy trains concern away from the wider, traditional problems of human culture which may have brought one to philosophy in the first place. Yet one can find oneself unable to relinquish either the method or the alien concern.

A free eclecticism of method is one obvious solution to such a problem. Another solution may be to discover further freedoms or possibilities within the method one finds closest to oneself. I lean here towards the latter of these alternatives, hoping to make philosophy yet another kind of problem for itself; in particular, to make the medium of philosophy—that is, of Wittgensteinian and, more generally, of ordinary language philosophy—a significant problem for aesthetics.

## TWO PROBLEMS OF AESTHETICS

Let us begin with a sheer matter of words—the controversy about whether a poem, or more modestly, a metaphor, can be paraphrased. Cleanth Brooks, in his *Well Wrought Urn*,[3] provided a convenient title for it in the expression "The Heresy of Paraphrase," the heresy, namely, of supposing that a "poem constitutes a 'statement' of some sort" (p. 179); a heresy in which "most of our difficulties in criticism are rooted" (p. 184).

> The truth of the matter is that all such formulations (of what a poem says) lead away from the center of the poem—not toward it; that the "prose sense" of the poem is not a rack on which the stuff of the poem is hung; that it does not represent the "inner" structure or the "essential" structure or the "real" structure of the poem (p.

[3] *The Well Wrought Urn* (New York: Harcourt, Brace & Co., 1947). All page references to Brooks are to this edition. "The Heresy of Paraphrase" is the title of the concluding chapter.

182). We can very properly use paraphrases as pointers and as short-hand references provided that we know what we are doing. But it is highly important that we know what we are doing and that we see plainly that the paraphrase is not the real core of meaning which constitutes the essence of the poem (p. 180).

We may have some trouble in seeing plainly that the paraphrase is *not* the real core, or essence, or essential structure or inner or real structure of a poem; the same trouble we should have in understanding what *is* any or all of these things, since it takes so much philosophy just to state them. It is hard to imagine that someone has just flatly given it out that the essence, core, structure, and the rest, of a poem is its paraphrase. Probably somebody has been saying that poetry uses ornaments of style, or requires special poetic words; or has been saying what a poem means, or what it ought to mean—doing something that makes someone else, in a fit of philosophy, say that this is distorting a poem's essence. Now the person who is accused in Brooks' writ is probably going to deny guilt, feel that words are being put into his mouth, and answer that he knows perfectly well that a "paraphrase, of course, is not the equivalent of a poem; a poem is more than its paraphrasable content." Those are the words of Yvor Winters, whose work Professor Brooks uses as "[furnishing] perhaps the most respectable example of the paraphrastic heresy" (p. 183).[4] And so the argument goes, and goes. It has the gait of a false issue—by which I do not mean that it will be easy to straighten out.

One clear symptom of this is Brooks' recurrent concessions that, of course, a paraphrase is all right—if you know what you're doing. Which is about like saying that of course criticism is all right, in its place; which is true enough. But how, in particular, are we to assess a critic's reading the opening stanza of Wordsworth's "Intimations" Ode and writing: ". . . the poet begins by saying that he has lost something" (Brooks, p. 116)? We can ransack that stanza and never find the expression "lost something" in it. Then the critic will be offended—rightly—and he may reply: Well, it does not actually say this, but it means it, it implies it; do you suggest that it does not mean that? And of course we do not. But then the critic has a *theory* about

[4] For Winters' position, I have relied solely on his central essay, "The Experimental School in American Poetry," from *Primitivism and Decadence*, itself republished, together with earlier of his critical works, under the title *In Defense of Reason* (Denver: Alan Swallow, 1947).

what he is doing when he says what a poem means, and so he will have to add some appendices to his readings of the poetry explaining that when he says what a poem means he does not say exactly quite just what the poem means; that is, he only points to its meaning, or rather "points to the area in which the meaning lies." But even this last does not seem to him humility enough, and he may be moved to a footnote in which he says that his own analyses are "at best crude approximations of the poem" (p. 189). By this time someone is likely to burst out with: But *of course* a paraphrase says what the poem says, and an *approximate* paraphrase is merely a bad paraphrase; with greater effort or sensibility you could have got it exactly right. To which one response would be: "Oh, I can tell you exactly what the Ode means," and then read the Ode aloud.

Is there no real way out of this air of self-defeat, no way to get *satisfying* answers? Can we discover what, in such an exchange, is causing that uneasy sense that the speakers are talking past one another? Surely each knows exactly what the other means; neither is pointing to the smallest fact that the other fails to see.

For one suggestion, look again at Brooks' temptation to say that his readings *approximate* to (the meaning of) the poem. He is not there confessing his personal ineptitude; he means that any paraphrase, the best, will be only an approximation. So he is not saying, what he was accused of saying, that his own paraphrase was, in some more or less definite way, inexact or faulty: he denies the ordinary contrast between "approximate" and "exact." And can he not do that if he wants to? Well, if I am right, he *did* do it. Although it is not clear that he *wanted* to. Perhaps he was *led* to it; and did he realize that, and would his realizing it make any difference? It may help to say: In speaking of the paraphrase as approximating to the poem (the meaning of the poem?) he himself furthers the suggestion that paraphrase and poem operate, as it were, at the same level, are the same kind of thing. (One shade of color approximates to another shade, it does not approximate, nor does it fail to approximate, to the object of which it is the color. An arrow pointing approximately north is exactly pointing somewhere. One paraphrase may be approximately the same, have approximately the same meaning, as another paraphrase.) And then he has to do everything at his philosophical disposal to keep paraphrase and poem from coinciding; in particular, speak of cores and essences and structures of the poem that are not reached by the paraphrase. It is as if someone got it into his head that really pointing to an object would require actually touching it, and then, realizing that this would make life very inconvenient, reconciled himself to common sense by saying: Of course we *can* point to objects, but we must realize what we are doing, and that most of the time this is only approximately pointing to them.

This is the sort of thing that happens with astonishing frequency in philosophy. We impose a demand for absoluteness (typically of some simple physical kind) upon a concept, and then, finding that our ordinary use of this concept does not meet our demand, we accommodate this discrepancy as nearly as possible. Take these familiar patterns: we do not really see material objects, but only see them indirectly; we cannot be certain of any empirical proposition, but only practically certain; we cannot really know what another person is feeling, but only infer it. One of Wittgenstein's greatest services, to my mind, is to show how constant a feature of philosophy this pattern is: this is something that his diagnoses are meant to explain ("We have a certain picture of how something must be"; "Language is idling; not doing work; being used apart from its ordinary language games"). Whether his diagnoses are themselves satisfying is another question. It is not very likely, because if the phenomenon is as common as he seems to have shown, its explanation will evidently have to be very much clearer and more complete than his sketches provide.

This much, however, is true: If you put such phrases as "giving the meaning," "giving a paraphrase," "saying exactly what something means (or what somebody said)," and so on, into the ordinary contexts (the "language games") in which they are used, you will not find that you are worried that you have not really *done* these things. We could say: *That* is what doing them really is. Only that serenity will last just so long as someone does not start philosophizing about it. Not that I want to stop him; only I want to know what it is he is then doing, and why he follows just those particular tracks.

We owe it to Winters to make it clear that he does not say any of the philosophical things Brooks attributes to him. His thesis, having expressed his total acquiescence in the fact that paraphrases are not poems, is that *some* poems cannot be paraphrased—in particular, poems of the chief poetic talent of the United States during the second and third decades of the twentieth century; that poems which are unparaphrasable are, in that specific way, defective; and that therefore this poetic talent was led in regrettable directions. The merit of this argument for us, whether we agree with its animus or not, and trying to keep special theories about poetic discourse at arm's length, is its recognition that paraphrasability is one definite characteristic of uses of language, a characteristic that some expressions have and some do not have. It suggests itself that uses of language can be distinguished according to whether or not they possess this characteristic, and further distinguished by the kind of paraphrase they demand. Let us pursue this suggestion with a few examples, following Wittgenstein's idea that we can find out what kind of object anything (grammatically) is (for example, a meaning) by investigating expressions which show the kind of thing said about it (for example, "explaining the meaning").

It is worth saying that the clearest case of a use of language having no paraphrase is its literal use. If I tell you, "Juliet [the girl next door] is not yet fourteen years old," and you ask me what I mean, I might do many things—ask you what *you* mean, or perhaps try to teach you the meaning of some expression you cannot yet use (which, as Wittgenstein goes to extraordinary lengths to show, is not the same thing as *telling* you what it means). Or again, if I say, "Sufficient unto the day is the evil thereof," which I take to be the literal truth, then if I need to explain my meaning to you I shall need to do other things: I shall perhaps not be surprised that you do not get my meaning and so I shall hardly ask you, in my former spirit, what you mean in asking me for it; nor shall I, unless my disappointment pricks me into offense, offer to teach you the meaning of an English expression. What I might do is to try to *put my thought another way,* and perhaps refer you, depending upon who you are, to a range of similar or identical thoughts expressed by others. What I cannot (logically) do in either the first or the second case is to *paraphrase* what I said.

Now suppose I am asked what someone means who says, "Juliet is the sun." Again my options are different, and specific. Again I am not, not in the same way, surprised that you ask; but I shall *not* try to put the thought another way—which seems to be the whole truth in the view that metaphors are unparaphrasable, that their meaning is bound up in the very words they employ. (The addition adds nothing: Where else is it imagined, in that context, that meanings are bound, or found?) I may say something like: Romeo means that Juliet is the warmth of his world; that his day begins with her; that only in her nourishment can he grow. And his declaration suggests that the moon, which other lovers use as emblems of their love, is merely her reflected light, and dead in comparison; and so on. In a word, I paraphrase it. Moreover, if I could not provide an explanation of this form, then that is a very good reason, a perfect reason, for supposing that I do not know what it means. Metaphors are paraphrasable. (And if that is true, it is tautologous.) When Croce denied the possibility of paraphrase, he at least had the grace to assert that there were no metaphors.

Two points now emerge: (1) The "and so on" which ends my example of paraphrase is significant. It registers what William Empson calls the "pregnancy" of metaphors, the burgeoning of meaning in them. Call it what you like; in this feature metaphors differ from some, but perhaps not all, literal discourse. And differ from the similar device of simile: the inclusion of "like" in an expression changes the rhetoric. If you say "Juliet is like the sun," two alterations at least seem obvious: the drive of it leads me to expect you to continue by saying in what definite respects they are like (similes are just a little bit pregnant); and, in complement, I *wait* for you to tell me what you mean, to deliver your meaning, so to speak. It is not up to me to find as much as I can in your words. The over-reading of metaphors so often complained of, no doubt justly, is a hazard they must run for their high interest.* (2) To give the paraphrase, to understand the metaphor, I must understand the ordinary or dictionary meaning of the words it contains, *and* understand that they are not there being used in their ordinary way, that the meanings they invite are not to be found opposite them in a dictionary. In this respect the words in metaphors function as they do in idioms. But idioms are, again, specifically different. "I fell flat on my face" seems an appropriate case. To explain its meaning is simply to *tell* it—one might say you don't *explain* it at all; either you know what it means or you don't; there is no richer and poorer among its explanations; you need imagine noth-

---

* [Added 1968. I should have made it more explicit that throughout this essay I am using "paraphrase" to name solely that specific form of account which suits metaphors (marked, for example, by its concluding sense of "and so on"). So when I say that stretches of literal prose "cannot be paraphrased," I mean to imply the specification ". . . in *that* way." Certainly an exercise useful in the teaching of reading can be given as "Paraphrase the following passage," where what is wanted is a resumé of the passage which shows a grasp of the difficult words and constructions in it and of its over-all sense. But in *that* context, paraphrase is explicitly not a candidate for anything likely to be taken as a *competitor* of the passage in question.]

ing special in the mind of the person using it. And you will find it in a dictionary, though in special locations; which suggests that, unlike metaphors, the number of idioms in a language is finite. In some, though not all, of these respects the procedure of "giving the meaning" of an idiom is like that in translating: one might think of it as translating from a given language into itself. Then how is it different from defining, or giving a synonym?

One final remark about the difference between idioms and metaphors. Any theory concerned to account for peculiarities of metaphor of the sort I have listed will wonder over the literal meaning its words, in that combination, have. This is a response, I take it, to the fact that a metaphorical expression (in the "*A* is *B*" form at least) sounds like an ordinary assertion, though perhaps not made by an ordinary mind. Theory aside, I want to look at the suggestion, often made, that what metaphors literally say is *false*. (This is a response to the well-marked characteristic of "psychic tension" set up in metaphors. The mark is used by Empson; I do not know the patent.) But to say that Juliet is the sun is not to say something false; it is, at best, wildly false, and that is not being just false. This is part of the fact that if we are to suggest that what the metaphor says is true, we shall have to say it is wildly true—mythically or magically or primitively true. (Romeo just may be young enough, or crazed or heretic enough, to have meant his words literally.) About some idioms, however, it is fair to say that their words literally say something that is quite false; something, that is, which could easily, though maybe comically, be imagined to be true. Someone might actually fall flat on his face, have a thorn in his side, a bee in his bonnet, a bug in his ear, or a fly in his ointment—even all at once. Then what are we to say about the literal meaning of a metaphor? That it has none? And that what it literally says is not false, *and* not true? And that it is not an assertion? But it sounds like one; and people do think it is true and people do think it is false. I am suggesting that it is such facts that will need investigating if we are to satisfy ourselves about metaphors; that we are going to keep getting philosophical theories about metaphor until such facts are investigated; and that this is not an occasion for adjudication, for the only thing we could offer now in that line would be: all the theories are right in what they say. And that seems to imply that all are wrong as well.

At this point we might be able to give more content to the idea that some modes of figurative language are such that in them what an expression means cannot be said at all, at least not in any of the more or less familiar, conventionalized ways so far noticed. Not because these modes are flatly literal—there is, as it were, room for an explanation, but we cannot enter it. About such an expression it may be right to say: I know what it means but I can't say what it means. And this would no longer suggest, as it would if said about a metaphor, that you really do not know what it means—or: it might suggest it, but you couldn't be sure.

Examples of such uses of language would, I think, characteristically occur in specific kinds of poetry, for example Symbolist, Surrealist or Imagist. Such a use seems to me present in a line like Hart Crane's "The mind is brushed by sparrow wings" (cited, among others, in the Winters essay), and in Wallace Stevens' "as a calm darkens among water-lights," from "Sunday Morning." Paraphrasing the lines, or explaining their meaning, or telling it, or putting the thought another way—all these are out of the question. One may be able to say nothing except that a feeling has been voiced by a kindred spirit and that if someone does not get it he is not in one's world, or not of one's flesh. The lines may, that is, be left as touchstones of intimacy. Or one might try *describing* more or less elaborately a particular day or evening, a certain place and mood and gesture, in whose presence the line in question comes to seem a natural expression, the only expression.

This seems to be what Winters, who profitably distinguishes several varieties of such uses of language, distrusts and dislikes in his defense of reason, as he also seems prepared for the reply that this is not a *failing* of language but a feature of a specific approach of language. At least I think it is a reply of this sort, which I believe to be right, that he wishes to repudiate by appealing to "the fallacy of expressive (or imitative) form," instanced by him at one point as "Whitman trying to express a loose America by writing loose poetry," or "Mr. Joyce [endeavoring] to express disintegration by breaking down his form." It is useful to have a name for this fallacy, which no doubt some people commit. But his remarks seem a bit quick in their notation of what Whitman and Joyce were trying to express, and in their explanation of why they had to express themselves as they did; too sure that a break with the past of the order represented in modern art was not itself necessary in order to defend reason; too sure that convention can still be attacked in conventional ways. And they suggest scorn for the position that a high task of art has become, in our bombardment of sound, to create silence. (*Being* silent for that purpose might be a good example of the fallacy of imitative form. But that would depend on the context.) The fact is that I feel I would have to forgo too much of modern art were I to take his view of it.

Before we leave him, we owe it to Brooks to acknowledge a feature of Winters' position which may be causing his antipathy to it. Having wished to save Winters from a misconstruction of paraphrase, we gave back to that notion a specificity which, it now emerges, opens him to further objection. For his claim that poems that cannot be paraphrased—or, as he also puts it, do not "rest on a formulable logic"—are therefore defective now means or implies that all poems not made essentially of metaphorical language (and/or similes, idioms, literal statements) are defective. It is certainly to be hoped that all *criticism* be rational, to be demanded that it form coherent propositions about its art. But to suppose that this requires all poetry to be "formulable," in the sense that it must, whatever its form and pressure, yield to paraphrase, the way single metaphors specifically do, is not only unreasonable past defense but incurs what we might call the fallacy of expressive criticism.

In summary: Brooks is wrong to say that poems cannot in principle be fully paraphrased, but right to be worried about the relation between paraphrase and poem; Winters is right in his perception that some poetry is "formulable" and some not, but wrong in the assurance he draws from that fact; both respond to, but fail to follow, the relation between criticism and its object. And now, I think, we can be brought more unprotectedly to face the whole question that motivates such a conflict, namely what it is we are doing when we describe or explain a work of art; what function criticism serves; whether different arts, or forms of art, require different forms of criticism; what we may expect to learn from criticism, both about a particular piece of art and about the nature of art generally.

The second problem in aesthetics must be sketched even more swiftly and crudely.

Is such music as is called "atonal" (not distinguishing that, for our purposes now, from the term "twelve-tone") really without tonality? (The little I will say could be paralleled, I think, in discussing the nature of the painting or sculpture called abstract or non-objective.)

The arguments are bitter and, to my knowledge, without issue; and many musicians have felt within themselves both an affirmative and a negative answer.[5] Against the idea that this music lacks tonality are (1) the theory that we are so trained to our perception of musical organization that we cannot help hearing it in a tonal frame of reference; and (2) the fact that one *can*, often, *say* what key a so-called "atonal" piece is in. In favor of the idea that it lacks tonality are (1) a theory of composition which says that it does, and whose point was just to escape that limitation, while yet maintaining coherence; and (2) the fact that it simply sounds so different. Without our now even glancing at the theories, let us look at the fact we recorded as "being able to say, often, what key a piece is in." Does that have the weight it seems to have? An instance which once convinced me of its decisiveness was this: in listening to a song of Schoenberg's, I had a clear sense that I could, at three points, hear it cadence (I almost said, try to resolve) in F♯ minor. Then surely it is *in* F♯ minor? Well, the Chopin *Barcarolle* is in the key of F♯ major. How do I know that? Because I can hear it try to cadence in F♯ major? Three or more times? And after that I am convinced it is, feel slightly relieved and even triumphant that I have been able to hear some F♯ major? But that is absurd. I *know* the key; everyone knows it; everyone knows it from the opening measure—well, at least before the bass figure that begins on the pitch of F♯: it does not take a brick wall to fall on us. I would not even know how to go about doubting its key or *trying* to hear it in its key. And I know it because I know that now it has moved to the subdominant of the key, and now the dominant of the key is being extended, and now it is modulating, and now it is modulating to a more distant key. And to know all this is to know the grammar of the expression "musical key." Sometimes, to be sure, a solidly tonal composer will, especially in "development sections," obliterate the sense of placement in a key; but this is here a special effect, and depends upon an undoubted establishment of key. So if I insist upon saying that atonal music is really tonal (and to be said it has to be insisted upon) I have, so far as my ear goes, to forgo the grammar of the expression "tonality" or "musical key"—or almost all of it: I can retain "almost cadences in" and "sounds like the dominant of," but not "related key," "distant key," "modulation" etc. And then I am in

---

[5] I am told, by Professor David Lewin, that this was true of Anton Webern, who was in doubt about his own music in this regard.

danger of not knowing what I am saying. Wittgenstein says that ". . . the *speaking* of language is part of an activity, or of a form of life" (*Investigations*, §23), and also "To imagine a language means to imagine a form of life" (ibid., §19). The language of tonality is part of a particular form of life, one containing the music we are most familiar with; associated with, or consisting of, particular ways of being trained to perform it and to listen to it; involving particular ways of being corrected, particular ways of responding to mistakes, to nuance, above all to recurrence and to variation and modification. No wonder we want to preserve the idea of tonality: to give all *that* up seems like giving up the idea of music altogether. I think it *is—like* it.

I shall not try to say why it is not fully that. I shall only mention that it cannot be enough to point to the obvious fact that musical instruments, with their familiar or unfamiliar powers, are employed —because *that* fact does not prevent us from asking: But is it music? Nor enough to appeal to the fact that we can point to pitches, intervals, lines and rhythm—because we probably do not for the most part know what we are pointing to with these terms. I mean we do not know *which* lines are significant (try to play the "melody" or "bass" of a piece of Webern's) and which intervals to hear as organizing. More important, I think, is the fact that we may see an undoubted musician speak about such things and behave toward them in ways similar (not, I think, more than similar) to the ways he behaves toward, say, Beethoven, and then we may sense that, though similar, it is a new world and that to understand a new world it is imperative to concentrate upon its inhabitants. (Of course there will be the usual consequences of mimicry and pretension.) Moreover, but still perhaps even more rarely, we may find ourselves *within* the experience of such compositions, following them; and then the question whether this is music and the problem of its tonal sense, will be—not answered or solved, but rather they will disappear, seem irrelevant.

That is, of course, Wittgenstein's sense of the way philosophical problems end. It is true that for him, in the *Investigations* at any rate, this happens when we have gone through a process of bringing ourselves back into our natural forms of life, putting our souls back into our bodies; whereas I had to describe the accommodation of the new music as one of naturalizing ourselves to a new form of life, a new world. That a resolution of this sort is described as the solution of a philosophical problem, and as the goal of its particular mode of criticism, represents for me the most original contribution Wittgenstein offers philosophy. I can think of no closer title for it, in an established philosophical vocabulary, than Hegel's use of the term *Aufhebung*. We cannot translate the term: "cancelling," "negating," "fulfilling" etc. are all partial, and "sublate" transfers the problem. It seems to me to capture that sense of *satisfaction* in our representation of rival positions which I was asking for when I rehearsed the problems of Brooks and Winters. Of course we are no longer very apt to suppose, with Hegel, that History will make us a present of it: we are too aware of its brilliant ironies and its aborted revolutions for that. But as an ideal of (one kind of) philosophical criticism—a criticism in which it is pointless for one side to refute the other, because its cause and topic is the self getting in its own way—it seems about right.

In the *Tractatus* Wittgenstein says: "The solution of the problem of life is seen in the vanishing of the problem" (6.521); and in the *Investigations* he says: ". . . the clarity that we are aiming at is indeed *complete* clarity. But this simply means that the philosophical problems should *completely* disappear" (§133). Yet he calls these problems *solved* (*Investigations*, ibid.); and he says that ". . . when no questions remain . . . just that is the *answer*" (*Tractatus*; 6.52, my emphasis). In the central concept of his later work, this would seem to mean that the problems of life and the problems of philosophy have related grammars, because solutions to them both have the same form: their problems are solved only when they disappear, and answers are arrived at only when there are no longer questions— when, as it were, our accounts have cancelled them.

But in the *Investigations* this turns out to be more of an answer than, left this way, it seems to be; for it more explicitly dictates and displays the ways philosophy is to proceed in investigating problems, ways leading to what he calls "perspicuous representation" (*übersichtliche Darstellung*). It is my impression that many philosophers do not like Wittgenstein's comparing what he calls his "methods" to therapies (§133); but for me part of what he means by this comparison is brought out in thinking of the progress of psychoanalytic therapy. The more one learns, so to speak, the hang of oneself, and mounts one's problems, the less one is able to *say* what one has learned; not because you have *forgotten* what it was, but because nothing you said would seem like an answer or a solution: there is no longer any question or problem which your words would match. You have reached conviction, but not about a proposition; and consistency, but not in a theory. You are different, what you recognize as problems are different, your world is different. ("The world of the happy man is a different one from that of the unhappy man" (*Tractatus*; 6.43).) And this is the sense, the only sense, in which what a work of art means cannot be *said*. Believing it is seeing it.

When Wittgenstein says that "the concept of a perspicuous representation . . . earmarks the form of account we give" (§122), I take him to be making a grammatical remark about what he calls a "grammatical investigation," which is what his *Investigations* consist in (§90): no other form of resolution will count as philosophical. He says of his "form of account" that it is "the way we look at things"; and he then asks, parenthetically, "Is this a 'Weltanschauung'?" (§122). The answer to that question is, I take it, not No. Not, perhaps, Yes; because it is not a *special*, or competing, way of looking at things. But not No; because its mark of success is that the world seem —be—different. As usual, the claim to severe philosophical advance entails a reconception of the subject, a specific sense of revolution.

## AESTHETIC JUDGMENT AND A PHILOSOPHICAL CLAIM

Another good cause for stumbling over the procedures of ordinary language philosophy lies in its characteristic appeal to what "we" say and mean, or cannot or must say or mean. A good cause, since it is a very particular, not to say peculiar appeal, and one would expect philosophers dependent upon it themselves to be concerned for its investigation. I will suggest that the aesthetic judgment models the sort of claim entered by these philosophers, and that the familiar lack of conclusiveness in aesthetic argument, rather than showing up an irrationality, shows the kind of rationality it has, and needs.

Hume is always a respectable place to begin. Near the middle of his essay "Of the Standard of Taste," he has recourse to a story from *Don Quixote* which is to illustrate that "delicacy" of taste said to be essential to those critics who are to form our standard of it.

It is with good reason, says Sancho to the squire with the great nose, that I pretend to have a judgment in wine: This is a quality hereditary in our family. Two of my kinsmen were once called in to give their opinion of a hogshead, which was supposed to be excellent, being old and of a good vintage. One of them tastes it; considers it; and after mature reflection pronounces the wine to be good, were it not for a small taste of leather, which he perceived in it. The other, after using the same precautions, gives also his verdict in favour of the wine; but with the reserve of a taste of iron, which he could easily distinguish. You cannot imagine how much they were both ridiculed for their judgment. But who laughed in the end? On emptying the hogshead, there was found at the bottom, an old key with a leathern thong tied to it.

First of all, the fine drama of this gesture is greater than its factual decisiveness—a bit quixotic, so to say: for the taste may have been present and the object not, or the object present and the taste not. Second, and more important, the gesture misrepresents the efforts of the critic and the sort of vindication to which he aspires. It dissociates the exercise of taste from the discipline of accounting for it: but *all* that makes the critic's expression of taste worth more than another man's is his ability to produce for himself the thong and key of his response; and his vindication comes not from his pointing out that it is, or was, in the barrel, but in getting us to taste it there. Sancho's ancestors, he tells us, in each case after the precautions of reflection, both pronounced in favor of the wine; but he does not tell us what those reflections were, nor whether they were vindicated in their favorable verdict. Hume's essay, I take it, undertakes to explore just such questions, but in his understandable difficulty in directing us to the genuine critic and distinguishing him from the pretender, he says about him just what he, or anyone, says about art itself: that he is valuable, that we may disagree about his merits in a particular case, and that some, in the long run, "will be acknowledged by universal sentiment to have a preference above others." But this seems to put the critic's worth at the mercy of the history of taste; whereas his value to us is that he is able to make that history a part of his data, knowing that in itself, as it stands, it proves nothing—except popularity. His value to art and culture is not that he agrees with its taste —which would make him useful for guiding one's investments in the art market—but that he sets the terms in which our tastes, whatever they happen to be, may be protected or overcome. Sancho's descendants would, by the eighteenth century, have risen to gentlemen, exercising distinction in a world which knew what was right, and not needing to make their tastes their own. But it is Quixote who is the patron saint of the critic, desperate to preserve the best of his culture against itself, and surviving any failure but that of his honesty and his expression of it.

The idea of the agreement or "reconciliation" of taste controls Hume's argument; it is agreement that the standard of taste is to provide, so far as that is attainable. Hume's descendants, catching the assumption that agreement provides the vindication of judgment, but no longer able to hope for either, have found that aesthetic (and moral and political) judgments lack something: the arguments that support them are not conclusive the way arguments in logic are, nor rational the way arguments in science are. Indeed they are not, and if they were there would be no such subject as art (or morality) and no such art as criticism. It does not follow, however, that such judgments are not conclusive and rational.

Let us turn to Kant on the subject, who is, here as elsewhere, deeper and obscurer. Universal agreement, or as he also calls it, the "harmony of sentiment" or "a common sense of mankind," makes its appearance in the *Critique of Judgment* not as an empirical problem —which is scarcely surprising about Kant's procedure—but as an a priori requirement setting the (transcendental) conditions under which such judgments as we call aesthetic could be made *überhaupt*. Kant begins by saying that aesthetic judgment is not "theoretical," not "logical," not "objective," but one "whose determining ground can be *no other than subjective.*" [6] Today, or anyway the day before yesterday, and largely under his influence, we would have said it is not cognitive; which says so little that it *might* have been harmless enough. Kant goes on immediately to distinguish two kinds of "aesthetical judgments," or, as he also calls them, judgments of taste; and here, unfortunately, his influence trickled out. The first kind he calls the taste of sense, the second the taste of reflection; the former concerns merely what we find pleasant, the latter must—logically must, some of us would say—concern and claim more than that. And it is only the second whose topic is the beautiful, whose role, that is, would be aesthetic in its more familiar sense. The something more these

---

[6] All quotations from Kant are from sections 7 and 8 of the *Critique of Judgment*.

judgments must do is to "demand" or "impute" or "claim" general validity, universal agreement with them; and when we make such judgments we go on claiming this agreement even though we know from experience that they will not receive it. (Are we, then, just willful or stupid in going on making them?) Kant also describes our feeling or belief when we make such judgments—judgments in which we demand "the assent of everyone," although we cannot "postulate" this assent as we could in making an ordinary empirical judgment—as one of "[speaking] with a universal voice." That is the sort of thing that we are likely nowadays to call a piece of psychology, which is no doubt right enough. But we would take that to mean that it marks an accidental accompaniment of such judgments; whereas Kant says about this claim to universal validity, this voice, that it "so essentially belongs to a judgment by which we describe anything as *beautiful* that, if this were not thought in it, it would never come into our thoughts to use the expression at all, but everything which pleases without a concept would be counted as pleasant." ⁷ The possibility of stupidity here is not one of continuing to demand agreement in the face of the fact that we won't attain it; but the stupidity of going on making aesthetic judgments at all (or moral or political ones) in the face of what they cost us, the difficulties of finding them for ourselves and the risk of explicit isolation.

Kant seems to be saying that apart from a certain spirit in which we make judgments we could have no concepts of the sort we think of as aesthetic.⁸ What can the basis for such a claim be? Let us look at the examples he gives of his two kinds of aesthetic judgments.

⁷ One might compare with this Wittgenstein's question: "What gives us *so much as the idea* that living beings, things, can feel?" (*Investigations*, §283).

⁸ Another way of describing this assumption or demand, this thing of speaking with a universal voice, of judging "not merely for himself, but for all men," Kant also describes as "[speaking] of beauty as if it were a property of things." Only "as if" because it cannot be an ordinary property of things: its presence or absence cannot be established in the way ordinary properties are; that is, they cannot be established publicly, and we don't know (there aren't any) causal conditions, or usable rules, for producing, or altering, or erasing, or increasing this "property." Then why not just say it *isn't* a property of an object? I suppose there would be no reason not to say this, if we could find another way of recording our conviction that it is one, anyway that what we are pointing to is *there*, in the object; and our knowledge that men make objects that create this response in us, and make them exactly with the idea that they will create it; and the fact that, while we know not everyone will agree with us when we say it is present, we think they are *missing something* if they don't.

. . . [someone] is quite contented that if he says, "Canary wine is pleasant," another man may correct his expression and remind him that he ought to say, "It is pleasant *to me*." And this is the case not only as regards the taste of the tongue, the palate, and the throat, but for whatever is pleasant to anyone's eyes and ears. . . . To strive here with the design of reproving as incorrect another man's judgment which is different from our own, as if the judgments were logically opposed, would be folly. . . .

The case is quite different with the beautiful. It would (on the contrary) be laughable if a man who imagined anything to his own taste thought to justify himself by saying: "This object (the house we see, the coat that person wears, the concert we hear, the poem submitted to our judgment) is beautiful *for me*." For he must not call it *beautiful* if it merely pleases him. . . .

What are these examples supposed to show? That using a form of expression in one context is all right, and using it in another is not all right. But what I wish to focus upon is the kind of rightness and wrongness invoked: it is not a matter of factual rectitude, nor of formal indiscretion but of saying something laughable, or which would be folly. It is such consequences that are taken to display a difference in the kind of judgment in question, in the nature of the concepts employed, and even in the nature of the reality the concepts capture. One hardly knows whether to call this a metaphysical or a logical difference. Kant called it a transcendental difference; Wittgenstein would call it a grammatical difference. And how can psychological differences like finding something laughable or foolish (which perhaps not *every* person would) be thought to betray such potent, or anyway different, differences?

Here we hit upon what is, to my mind, the most sensitive index of misunderstanding and bitterness between the positivist and the post-positivist components of analytical philosophy: the positivist grits his teeth when he hears an analysis given out as a logical one which is so painfully remote from formality, so obviously a question of how you happen to feel at the moment, so psychological; the philosopher who proceeds from everyday language stares back helplessly, asking, "Don't you feel the difference? Listen: you *must* see it." Surely, both know what the other knows, and each thinks the other is perverse, or irrelevant, or worse. (Here I must appeal to the experience of anyone who has been engaged in such encounters.) Any explanation of this is going to be hard to acquire. I offer the following guess, not because it can command much attention in itself, but as a way of suggesting the level I would expect a satisfying explanation to reach, a way of indicating why we lack as yet the concepts, even the facts, which must form a serious accommodation.

We know of the efforts of such philosophers as Frege and Husserl to undo the "psychologizing" of logic (like Kant's undoing Hume's psychologizing of knowledge): now, the shortest way I might describe such a book as the *Philosophical Investigations* is to say that it attempts to undo the psychologizing of psychology, to show the necessity controlling our application of psychological and behavioral categories; even, one could say, show the necessities in human action and passion themselves.[9] And at the same time it seems to turn all of philosophy into psychology—matters of what we call things, how we treat them, what their role is in our lives.

For one last glance, let us adapt Kant's examples to a form which is more fashionable, and think of the sort of reasons we offer for such judgments:

1. A: Canary wine is pleasant.
   B: How can you say that? It tastes like canary droppings.
   A: Well, I like it.
2. A: He plays beautifully doesn't he?
   B1: Yes; too beautifully. Beethoven is not Chopin.

Or he may answer:

B2: How can you say that? There was no line, no structure, no idea what the music was about. He's simply an impressive colorist.

Now, how will A reply? Can he now say: "Well, I liked it"? Of course he *can*; but don't we feel that here that would be a feeble rejoinder, a *retreat* to personal taste? Because B's reasons are obviously relevant

---

[9] Consider, for example, the question: "Could someone have a feeling of ardent love or hope for the space of one second—*no matter what* preceded or followed this second?" (*Investigations*, §583). We shall not wish to say that this is logically impossible, or that it can in no way be imagined. But we might say: given our world this cannot happen; it is not, in our language, what "love" or "hope" mean; necessary in our world that this is not what love and hope are. I take it that our most common philosophical understanding of such notions as necessity, contingency, synthetic and analytic statements, will not know what to make of our saying such things.

to the evaluation of performance, and because they are *arguable*, in ways that anyone who knows about such things will know how to pursue. A *doesn't have* to pursue them; but if he doesn't, there is a price he will have to pay in our estimate of him. Is that enough to show it is a different kind of judgment? We are still in the realm of the psychological. But I wish to say that the price is necessary, and specific to the sorts of judgments we call aesthetic.

Go back to my saying "he doesn't have to pursue" the discussion, and compare the following case:

A: There is a goldfinch in the garden.
B: How do you know?
A: From the color of its head.
B: But goldcrests also have heads that color.
A: Well, *I* think it's a goldfinch (it's a goldfinch to me).

This is no longer a feeble rejoinder, a retreat to personal opinion: and the price that would be paid here is not, as it would be in the former case, that he is not very articulate, or not discriminating, or has perverse tastes: the price here is that he is either mad, or doesn't know what the word "know" means, or is in some other way unintelligible to us. That is, *we rule him out* as a competent interlocutor in matters of knowledge (about birds?): whatever is going on, he *doesn't* know there is a goldfinch in the garden, whatever (else) he thinks he "knows." But we do not, at least not with the same flatness and good conscience, and not with the same consequences, rule out the person who liked the performance of the Beethoven: he still has a claim upon us, however attenuated; he *may* even have reasons for his judgment, or counters to your objections, which for some reason he can't give (perhaps because you've brow-beaten him into amnesia).

Leaving these descriptions so cruelly incomplete, I think one can now imagine the familiar response: "But you admit that arguments in the aesthetic case may go on, may perhaps never end, and that they needn't go on, perhaps can't go on in some cases, and that they may have different 'prices' (whatever that may mean), presumably depending on where they stop. How do you get logic out of that? What you cannot claim is that either party to the dispute, whether in the case Kant calls the taste of sense or the case he calls the taste of reflection, can *prove* his judgment. And would he want to, even if he could? Isn't that, indeed, what all your talk about criticism was about: The person accounts for his own feelings, and then, at best 'proves' them *to* another, shows them to whomever he wants to know them, the best way he can, the most effective way. That's scarcely logic; and how can you deny that it is psychology?"

It may help to reply to this: You call it psychology just because it so obviously is not logic, and it must be one or the other. (I do think that is the *entire* content of "psychology" in such objections. Such a person knows what he means by logic: how to do it, how to recognize it when he sees it done, what he can expect from it, etc. But who knows any of this about the "psychology" in question?) Contrariwise, I should admit that I call it "logic" mostly because it so obviously is not "psychology" in the way I think you mean it. I do not really think it is either of those activities, in the senses we attach to them now; but I cannot describe to anyone's satisfaction *what* it is. Wittgenstein called it "grammar"; others might call it "phenomenology."

Those of us who keep finding ourselves wanting to call such differences "logical" are, I think, responding to a sense of necessity we feel in them, together with a sense that necessity is, partly, a matter of the *ways* a judgment is supported, the ways in which conviction in it is produced: it is only by virtue of these recurrent patterns of support that a remark will count as—will be—aesthetic, or a mere matter of taste, or moral, propagandistic, religious, magical, scientific, philosophical. . . . It is essential to making an aesthetic judgment that at some point we be prepared to say in its support: don't you see, don't you hear, don't you dig? The best critic will know the best points. Because if you do not see *something,* without explanation, then there is nothing further to discuss. Which does not mean that the critic has no recourse: he can start training and instructing you and preaching at you—a direction in which criticism invariably will start to veer. (A critic like Ruskin can be a bit eager in seizing this direction, but it is a measure of his honesty, and his devotion to art, never to shrink from it; as it is part of the permanence of his writing to exemplify that moral passion which is a *natural* extension of the critical task.) At some point, the critic will have to say: This is what I see. Reasons—at definite points, for definite reasons, in different circumstances—come to an end. (Cf. *Investigations,* §217.)

Those who refuse the term "logic" are responding to a sense of arbitrariness in these differences, together with a sense that "logic" is a matter of arriving at conviction in such a way that anyone who can follow the argument must, unless he finds something definitely wrong with it, *accept the conclusion*, agree with it. I do not know what the gains or disadvantages would be of unfastening the term "logic" from that constant pattern of support or justification whose peculiarity is that it leads those competent at it to this kind of agreement, and extending it to patterns of justification having other purposes and peculiarities. All I am arguing for is that *pattern* and *agreement* are distinct features of the notion of logic.

If we say that the *hope* of agreement motivates our engaging in these various patterns of support, then we must also say, what I take Kant to have seen, that even were agreement in fact to emerge, our judgments, so far as aesthetic, would remain as essentially subjective, in his sense, as they ever were. Otherwise, art and the criticism of art would not have their special importance nor elicit their own forms of distrust and of gratitude. The problem of the critic, as of the artist, is not to discount his subjectivity, but to include it; not to overcome it in agreement, but to master it in exemplary ways. Then his work outlasts the fashions and arguments of a particular age. That is the beauty of it.

Kant's "universal voice" is, with perhaps a slight shift of accent, what we hear recorded in the philosopher's claims about "what we say": such claims are at least as close to what Kant calls aesthetical judgments as they are to ordinary empirical hypotheses. Though the philosopher seems to claim, or depend upon, severer agreement than is carried by the aesthetic analogue, I wish to suggest that it is a claim or dependence of the same kind.

We should immediately notice an obvious failure in the analogy between aesthetic judgments and the philosophical claim to voice what we say. The philosophical claim seems clearly open to refutation by an empirical collection of data about what people in fact say, whereas it makes no obvious sense to confirm or disconfirm such a judgment as "The *Hammerklavier* Sonata is a perverse work" by collecting data to find out whether the Sonata is in fact perverse. It is out of the question to enter into this difficult range of problems now. But I cannot forbear mentioning several points which I have tried elsewhere to suggest, with, to judge from results, evident unsuccess.[10]

1. I take it to be a phenomenological fact about philosophizing from everyday language that one feels empirical evidence about one's language to be irrelevant to one's claims. If such philosophizing is to be understood, then that fact about it must be understood. I am not saying that evidence about how (other) people speak can never make an ordinary language philosopher withdraw his typical claims; but I find it important that the most characteristic pressure against him is applied by producing or deepening an example which shows him that *he* would not say what he says "we" say.

2. The appeal to "what we should say if . . ." requires that we imagine an example or story, sometimes one more or less similar to events which may happen any day, sometimes one unlike anything we have known. Whatever the difficulties will be in trying to characterize this procedure fully and clearly, this much can be said at once: if we find we disagree about what we should say, it would make no obvious sense to attempt to confirm or disconfirm one or other of our responses by collecting data to show which of us is in fact right. What we should do is either (*a*) try to determine why we disagree (perhaps we are imagining the story differently)—just as, if we agree in response we will, when we start philosophizing about this fact, want to know why we agree, what it shows about our concepts; or (*b*) we will, if the disagreement cannot be explained, either find some explanation for *that*, or else discard the example. Disagreement is not disconfirming: it is as much a datum for philosophizing as agreement is. At this stage philosophizing has, hopefully, not yet begun.

3. Such facts perhaps only amount to saying that the philosophy of ordinary language is not about language, anyway not in any sense in which it is not also about the world. Ordinary language philosophy is about whatever ordinary language is about.

The philosopher appealing to everyday language turns to the reader not to convince him without proof but to get him to prove something, test something, against himself. He is saying: Look and

---

[10] See J. Fodor and J. Katz, "The Availability of What We Say," in the *Philosophical Review*, Vol. LXXII (1963), an attack, primarily, on my paper "Must We Mean What We Say?" which appears as the first essay in this book. [Added 1968. A paper by Professor Richard Henson ("What We Say," *American Philosophical Quarterly*, Vol. 2/No. 1, January 1965, pp. 52–62) includes specific rejoinders to a number of the points raised by Fodor and Katz.]

find out whether you can see what I see, wish to say what I wish to say. Of course he often seems to answer or beg his own question by posing it in plural form: "We say . . . ; We want to say . . . ; We can imagine . . . ; We feel as if we had to penetrate phenomena, repair a spider's web; We are under the illusion . . . ; We are dazzled . . . ; The idea now absorbs us . . . ; We are dissatisfied . . . ." But this plural is still first person: it does not, to use Kant's word, "postulate" that "we," you and I and he, say and want and imagine and feel and suffer together. If we do not, then the philosopher's remarks are irrelevant to us. Of course he doesn't think they are irrelevant, but the implication is that philosophy, like art, is, and should be, powerless to *prove* its relevance; and that says something about the kind of relevance it wishes to have. All the philosopher, this kind of philosopher, can do is to express, as fully as he can, his world, and attract our undivided attention to our own.

Kant's attention to the "universal voice" expressed in aesthetic judgment seems to me, finally, to afford some explanation of that air of dogmatism which claims about what "we" say seem to carry for critics of ordinary language procedures, and which they find repugnant and intolerant. I think that air of dogmatism is indeed present in such claims; but if that is intolerant, that is because tolerance could only mean, as in liberals it often does, that the kind of claim in question is not taken seriously. It is, after all, a claim about *our lives*; it is differences, or oppositions, of these that tolerance, if it is to be achieved, must be directed toward. About what we should say when, we do not expect to have to tolerate much difference, believing that if we could articulate it fully we would have spoken for all men, found the necessities common to us all. Philosophy has always hoped for that; so, perhaps, has science. But philosophy concerns those necessities we cannot, being human, fail to know. Except that nothing is more human than to deny them.

# IV

# Austin at Criticism

Except for the notable translation of Frege's *Foundations of Arithmetic* and whatever reviews there are, *Philosophical Papers* collects all the work Austin published during his lifetime.[1] In addition, this modest volume includes two papers which will have been heard about, but not heard, outside Oxford and Cambridge. The first is one of the two pieces written before the war ("Meaning," 1940) and shows more clearly than the one published a year earlier ("Are There A Priori Concepts?," 1939) that the characteristic philosophical turns for which Austin became famous were deep in preparation.[2] The second previously unpublished paper ("Unfair to Facts," 1954) is Austin's rejoinder to P. F. Strawson's part in their symposium on truth, a debate which, I believe, Austin is widely thought to have lost initially, and to lose finally with this rejoinder. Austin clearly did not concur in this opinion, repeating the brunt of his counter-charge at the end of the course of lectures he gave at Berkeley in 1958–1959.[3] The remaining five papers have all become part of the

---

[1] J. L. Austin, *Philosophical Papers*, ed. by J. O. Urmson and G. J. Warnock (Oxford: The Clarendon Press, 1961).

[2] Curiously, the 1940 paper is the most Wittgensteinian of Austin's writings, in presenting an explicit theory of what causes philosophical disability and in the particular theory it offers (sc., "We are using a working-model which fails to fit the facts that we really wish to talk about").

[3] These lectures, which he gave for many years at Oxford, were published posthumously under their Oxford title, *Sense and Sensibilia*, edited by G. J. Warnock (Oxford: The Clarendon Press, 1962). Austin's original paper on "Truth" (1950) is, of

canon of the philosophy produced in English during the past generation, yielding the purest version of what is called "Oxford philosophy" or "ordinary language philosophy." I will assume that anyone sharing anything like his direction from the English tradition of philosophy, and forced into his impatience with philosophy as it stands (or patience with the subject as it could become), will have found Austin's accomplishment and example inescapable.

As with any inheritance, it is often ambiguous and obscure in its effects. Two of these provide the subjects of my remarks here: the first concerns Austin's methods or purposes in philosophy; the second, related effect concerns the attitudes toward traditional philosophy which he inspires and sanctions.

I

I wish not so much to try to characterize Austin's procedures as to warn against too hasty or simple a description of them: their characterization is itself, or ought to be, as outstanding a philosophical problem as any to be ventured from within those procedures.

To go on saying that Austin attends to ordinary or everyday language is to go on saying, roughly, nothing—most simply because this fails to distinguish Austin's work from anything with which it could be confused. It does not, in the first place, distinguish his work from ordinary empirical investigations of language, a matter which has come to seem of growing importance since Austin's visits to the United States in 1955 and 1958. I do not say there is *no* relation between Austin's address to natural language and that of the descriptive linguist; he himself seems to have thought there was, or could be, a firmer intimacy than I find between them. The differences which, intuitively, seem to me critical, however, are these. In proceeding from ordinary language, so far as that is philosophically

course, reprinted in the book under review. The remaining previously published papers are: "Other Minds" (1946), "A Plea for Excuses" (1956), "Ifs and Cans" (1956), "How to Talk—Some Simple Ways" (1953), and "Pretending" (1958). All page references to these papers are cited according to their occurrence in *Philosophical Papers*. The concluding paper—"Performative Utterances"—is the transcript of a talk Austin gave for the B.B.C. in 1956; it is now superseded by the publication of the full set of lectures he used to give on this topic, and gave as the William James Lectures at Harvard in 1955, under the title *How to Do Things with Words* (Cambridge: Harvard University Press, 1962); also Galaxy Books edition (New York: Oxford University Press, Inc., 1965).

pertinent, one is in a frame of mind in which it seems (1) that one can as appropriately or truly be said to be looking at the world as looking at language; (2) that one is seeking necessary truths "about" the world (or "about" language) and therefore cannot be satisfied with anything I, at least, would recognize as a description of how people in fact talk—one might say one is seeking one kind of explanation of *why* people speak as they do; and even (3) that one is not finally interested *at all* in how "other" people talk, but in determining where and why one wishes, or hesitates, to use a particular expression oneself. What investigations pursued in such frames of mind are supposed to show, I cannot say—perhaps whatever philosophy is supposed to show. My assumption is that there is something special that philosophy is about, and that Austin's procedures, far from avoiding this oldest question of philosophy, plunge us newly into it. I emphasize therefore that Austin himself was, so far as I know, never anxious to underscore philosophy's uniqueness, in particular not its difference from science; he seemed, indeed, so far as I could tell, to like denying any such difference (except that there is as yet no *established* science—of linguistics or grammar perhaps—to which philosophy may aspire to be assimilated).

The qualification "ordinary language," secondly, does not distinguish this mode of philosophizing from any other of its modes—or, I should like to say, does not distinguish it philosophically. It does tell us enough to distinguish hawks from handsaws—Austin from Carnap, say—but not enough to start a hint about *how* ordinary language is appealed to, how one produces and uses its critical and characteristic forms of example, and why; nor about how and just where and how far this interest conflicts with that of any other temper of philosophy. The phrase "ordinary language" is, of course, of no special interest; the problem is that its use has so often quickly suggested that the answers to the fundamental questions it raises, or ought to raise, are known, whereas they are barely imagined. Austin's only positive suggestion for a title to his methods was, I believe, "linguistic phenomenology" ("Excuses," p. 130), and although he apologizes that "that is rather a mouthful" (what he was shy about, I cannot help feeling, was that it sounds rather pretentious, or anyway philosophical) he does not retract it. This title has never caught on, partly, surely, because Austin himself invests no effort in formulating the significance of the phenomenological impulses and data in his work—data, perhaps, of the sort suggested above in distinguishing his work from the work of linguistic science. (But even the bare title is suggestive: it suggests that the clarity Austin seeks in philosophy is to be achieved through mapping the fields of consciousness lit by the occasions of a word, not through analyzing or replacing a given word by others. In this sense, philosophy like his is not "analytical.")

Another characterization of Austin's procedures has impressive authority behind it. Professor Stuart Hampshire, in the memorial written for the *Proceedings of the Aristotelian Society*, Vol. LX (1959–1960) on the occasion of Austin's death, provides various kinds of consideration—personal, social, historical, philosophical—for assessing Austin's achievement in philosophy. The device he adopts in his own assessment is to "distinguish two slightly different theses that can plausibly be attributed to him: a strong and weak thesis" (p. iii). The strong thesis is this: "For every distinction of word and idiom that we find in common speech, there is a reason to be found, if we look far enough, to explain why this distinction exists. The investigation will always show that the greatest possible number of distinctions have been obtained by the most economical linguistic means" (ibid.). "The weaker, or negative, thesis is that we must first have the facts, and all the facts, accurately stated before we erect a theory upon the basis of them" (p. vi). The weaker thesis is "negative," presumably, because it counsels study of ordinary language as a preliminary to philosophical advance, whereas the stronger claims "that the multiplicity of fine distinctions, which such a study would disclose, would by itself answer philosophical questions about free-will, perception, naming and describing, conditional statements" (p. ix).

Hampshire's characterizations were quickly repudiated by Austin's literary executors (J. O. Urmson and G. J. Warnock, *Mind*, Vol. LXX, 1961, pp. 256–57), the weaker thesis on the ground that it is an "unambitious statement which cannot properly, or even plausibly, be magnified into a guiding *doctrine* . . . or recipe," the stronger on various grounds according to its various parts or formulations, but primarily on two: that Austin did sanction at least *some* new distinctions, and that he certainly did not claim that *all* philosophical questions could be answered by attention to fine distinctions. Urmson and Warnock are concerned, it emerges, to repudiate the idea that any such "large assertions" are contained or implied in Austin's writings

(or conversations). They conclude by saying: "Austin sometimes gave
. . . his own explanations. Why should they not be taken as meaning
just what they say?"

I want in Section II to take up that challenge explicitly, if
briefly. Immediately, it seems clear to me that Urmson and Warnock
have trivialized Hampshire's formulations, whatever their several
shortcomings. His weak thesis is hardly affected by being called an
"unambitious statement" rather than a doctrine or a recipe, partly
because it is not unambitious in Austin's practice, and partly because
of Austin's conviction, and suggestion, that most philosophers have
not merely proceeded in the absence of "all the facts," but in the
presence of practically *no facts at all,* or facts so poorly formulated
and randomly collected as to defy comprehension. The issue raised is
nothing less, I suggest, than the question: What is a philosophical
fact? What are the data from which philosophy may, and must, proceed? It would be presumptuous to praise Austin for having pressed
such questions to attention, but it is just the plain truth that nothing
he says in "his own explanations" begins to answer them. If such
questions strike a philosopher as fundamental to his subject, or even
as relevant, then I do not see how it can be denied that their answer
is going to entail "large assertions" for which, moreover, so far as they
concern Austin's practice, all the facts are directly at hand, viz., in
Austin's practice. To accept Austin's explanations as full and accurate guides to his practice would be not only to confuse advice (which
is about all he gave in this line) with philosophical analysis and
literary-critical description (which is what is needed), but to confer
upon Austin an unrivaled power of self-discernment. It is a mystery
to me that what a philosopher says about his methods is so commonly
taken at face value. Austin ought to be the last philosopher whose
reflexive remarks are treated with this complacency, partly because
there are so many of them, and partly because they suffer not merely
the usual hazards of self-description but the further deflections of
polemical animus. I return to this in the following section.

The strong thesis, in turn, is unaffected by switching its quantifi-
cation from "all" to "some," for the issue raised is whether attention
to fine distinctions can "by itself" answer *any* philosophical question.
At the place where Urmson and Warnock confidently assert that
*some* questions can be answered in this way—a matter they take as

"scarcely controversial"—they omit the qualification "philosophical," and offer no suggestion as to the particular way in which such
answers are effected. Part of Hampshire's suggestion is that accepted
philosophical theses and comparisons are drained, set against Austin's
distinctions, of philosophical interest (cf. p. iv). This is a familiar
enough fact of contemporary philosophizing, and it suggests to me
that one requirement of new philosophical answers is that they elicit
a new source of philosophical interest, or elicit this old interest in a
new way. Which is, perhaps, only a way of affirming that a change of
*style* in philosophy is a profound change, and itself a subject of philosophical investigation. Finally, were we to let Urmson and Warnock's deflations distract us from philosophical curiosity about Austin's procedures, that could only inflame our psychological curiosity
past composure; for the gap between Austin's unruffled advice to
philosophical modesty and his obsession, to say the least, with the fine-
ness of ordinary language and his claims to its revelation would then
widen to dreamlike proportions. His repeated disclaimer that ordinary language is certainly not the last word, "only it *is* the *first* word"
(alluded to by Urmson and Warnock), is reassuring only during
polemical enthusiasm. For the issue is why the first, or *any*, word can
have the kind of power Austin attributes to it. I share his sense that
it has, but I cannot see that he has anywhere tried to describe the
sources or domain of that power.

My excuse for butting into this controversy is that both sides
seem to me to sanction a description of Austin's concerns which is just
made to misdirect a further understanding of it and which is the
more harmful because of its obvious plausibility, or rather its partial
truth. I have in mind simply the suggestion that Austin's fundamental philosophical interest lay in drawing distinctions. Given this
description of the method, and asked to justify it, what *can* one
answer except: these are all the distinctions there are, or all that are
real or important or necessary, and so forth, against which, it cannot
be denied, Austin's own words can be leveled. Too obviously, Austin
*is* continuously concerned to draw distinctions, and the finer the
merrier, just as he often explains and justifies what he is doing by
praising the virtues of natural distinctions over homemade ones.
What I mean by saying that this interest is not philosophically fundamental is that his drawing of distinctions is always in the service of

further purposes, and in particular two. (1) *Part* of the effort of any philosopher will consist in showing up differences, and one of Austin's most furious perceptions is of the slovenliness, the grotesque crudity and fatuousness, of the usual distinctions philosophers have traditionally thrown up. Consequently, one form his investigations take is that of repudiating the distinctions lying around philosophy —dispossessing them, as it were, by showing better ones. And better not merely because finer, but because more solid, having, so to speak, a greater natural weight; appearing normal, even inevitable, when the others are luridly arbitrary; useful where the others seem twisted; real where the others are academic; fruitful where the others stop cold. This is, if you like, a negative purpose. (2) The positive purpose in Austin's distinctions resembles the art critic's purpose in comparing and distinguishing works of art, namely, that in this crosslight the capacities and salience of an individual object in question are brought to attention and focus. That it is as much a matter of *comparing* as of distinguishing is clear—and takes its importance—from the way in which examples and, most characteristically, stories set the stage for Austin's distinctions. This is plainly different from their entrance in, say, philosophers like Russell or Broad or even Moore, whose distinctions do not serve to compare and (as it were) to elicit differences but rather, one could say, to provide labels for differences previously, somehow, noticed. One sometimes has the feeling that Austin's differences penetrate the phenomena they record—a feeling from within which the traditional philosopher will be the one who seems to be talking about mere words. The differing role of examples in these philosophies is a topic whose importance cannot be exaggerated, and no amount of words about "ordinary language" or "make all the distinctions" will convey to anyone who does not have the hang of it how to produce or test such examples. Anyone who has tried to teach from such materials and methods will appreciate this lack, which makes it the more surprising that no one, to my knowledge, has tried to compose a useful set of directions or, rather, to investigate exactly the ways one wishes to describe the procedures and notice their varying effectiveness for others, or faithfulness to one's sense of one's own procedures. Perhaps what is wanted really is a matter of conveying "the hang" of something, and that is a very particular dimension of a subject to teach—familiar, for example, in conservatories of music, but also, I should guess, in learning a new game or entering any new territory or technique or apprenticing in a trade.

The comparison and distinguishing of related works will not exhaust the tasks of criticism, but they have particular and vivid roles in defining areas of significance, and in suggesting terms of description, and in locating foci of purpose and stresses of composition: other works tell what the given work is about. In Austin's hands, I am suggesting, other words, compared and distinguished, tell what a given word is about. To know why they do, to trace how these procedures function, would be to see something of what it is he wishes words to teach, and hints at an explanation for our feeling, expressed earlier, that what we learn will not be new empirical facts about the world, and yet illuminating facts about the world. It is true that he asks for the difference between doing something by mistake and doing it by accident, but what transpires is a characterization of *what a mistake is* and (as contrasted, or so far as contrasted with this) what an accident is. He asks for the difference between being sure and being certain, but what is uncovered is an initial survey of the complex and mutual alignments between mind and world that are necessary to successful knowledge. He asks for the difference between expressing belief and expressing knowledge (or between saying "I believe" and saying "I know") and what comes up is a new sense and assessment of the human limitations, or human responsibilities, of human knowledge; and so on.

As important as any of these topics or results within his investigations is the opportunity his purity of example affords for the investigation of philosophical method generally. Here we have, or could have—appearing before our eyes in terms and steps of deliberate, circumstantial obviousness—conclusions arrived at whose generality and convincingness depend, at least intuitively, upon a play of the mind characteristically philosophical, furnished with the usual armchairs and examples and distinctions and wonder. But how can such results have appeared? How can we learn something (about how we —how I—use words) which we cannot have failed to know? How can asking when we would *say* "by mistake" (or what we call "doing something by mistake") tell us what in the world a mistake *is*? How, given such obvious data, have philosophers (apparently) so long ignored it, forgetting that successful knowledge is a human affair, of human complexity, meeting human need and exacting human responsibility, bypassing it in theories of certainty which compare knowledge (unfavorably) with an inhuman ideal; or elaborated moral philosophies so abstracted from life as to leave, for example, no room for so homely, but altogether a central, moral activity as the entering of an excuse? What is philosophy that it can appear periodically so profound and so trivial, sometimes so close and sometimes so laughably remote, so wise and so stone stupid? What is philosophy that it causes those characteristic hatreds, yet mysterious intimacies, among its rivals? What kind of phenomenon is it whose past cannot be absorbed or escaped (as in the case of science) or parts of it freely admired and envied while other parts are despised and banished (as in art), but remains in standing competition, behind every closed argument waiting to haunt its living heirs?

## II

One pass to these questions is opened by picking at the particular charges Austin brings against his competitors, past and present. His terms of criticism are often radical and pervasive, but this should not blunt an awareness that they are quite particular, characteristic, and finite. And each of them, as is true of any charge, implies a specific view taken of a situation. This is, indeed, one of Austin's best discoveries, and nothing is of more value in the example of his original investigations than his perfect faithfulness to that perception: it is what his "phenomenology" turns on. That it fails him in criticizing other philosophers will have had various causes, but the productive possibility for us is that he has shown us the value of the procedure and that we are free to apply it for our better judgment.

I must limit myself to just one example of what I have in mind. Take Austin's accusing philosophers of "mistakes." It is worth noticing that the man who could inspire revelation by telling us a pair of donkey stories which lead us to take in the difference between doing something "by mistake" and doing it "by accident" ("Excuses," p. 133, n. 1) uses the term "mistake" in describing what happens when, for example, Moore is discussing the question whether someone could have done something other than what in fact he did ("Ifs and Cans"). Now in the case of shooting your donkey when I meant to shoot mine, the correctness of the term "mistake" is bound to the fact that questions like the following have definite answers: What mistake was made? (I shot your donkey.) What was mistaken for what? (Your donkey was mistaken for mine.) How can the mistake have occurred? (The donkeys look alike.) (How) could it have been prevented? (By walking closer and making sure, which a responsible man might or might not have been expected to do.) But there are no such answers to these questions asked about Moore's discussion—or perhaps we should say that the answers we would have to give would seem forced and more or less empty, a fact that ought to impress a philosopher like Austin.

What has Moore mistaken for what? Should we, for example, say that he mistakes the expression "could have" for "could have if I had chosen"? Then how and why and when can such a mistake have occurred? Was it because Moore has been hasty, thoughtless, sloppy, prejudiced . . . ? But though these are the sorts of answers we are now forced to give (explanations which certainly account for mistakes, and which Austin is free with in accounting for the disasters of other philosophers), they are fantastic in this context; because there is no plausibility to the suggestion, taken seriously, that, whatever Moore has done, he has made a mistake: these charges are thus, so far, left completely in the air. Such charges can equally account for someone's having been involved in an accident or an inadvertence or the like. But, as Austin is fond of saying, each of these requires its own story; and does either of them fit the conduct of Moore's argument any better than the term "mistake"? Then perhaps the mistake lies in Moore's thinking that "could have" *means* "could have if I had chosen." But now this suggests not that Moore *took one thing for another* but that he took a tack he should not or need not have taken. This might be better expressed, as Austin does sometimes express it, by saying that Moore *was mistaken* in this, or perhaps by saying that *it was a mistake for him to.* But to say someone is mistaken requires again its own kind of story, different from the case of doing something by mistake or from making a mistake. In particular it suggests a context in which it is obvious, not that one thing looks like another, but why one would be led to do the mistaken, unhappy thing in question. The clearest case I think of is one of poor strategy: "It is a mistake to castle at this stage." This charge depends upon there being definite answers to questions like the following: Why does it seem to be a good thing to do? Why is it nevertheless not a good thing to do? What would be a better (safer, less costly, more subtle, stronger) thing to do instead? Such questions do fit certain procedures of certain intellectual enterprises, for example, the wisdom of taking a certain term as undefined, the dangers of appealing to the natural rights or the cult emotions of a certain section of the voting population, the difficulties of employing a rhyme scheme of a particular sort. What is Moore trying to do to which such a consideration of plusses and minuses would be relevant?

One may feel: "Of course it is not a matter of better or worse. If Moore (or any philosopher) is wrong he is just wrong. What is absurd about the suggestion that he may have reasons for doing things his way is the idea that he may wish to tally up the advantages of being right over those of being wrong, where being right (that is, arriving at the truth) is the whole point. Cannot to say he has made a mistake —or, rather, to say he is mistaken—just mean that he is just wrong?" But it seems, rather, that "mistaken" requires the idea of a wrong alternative (either taking one thing for another, or taking one tack rather than another). Is such an alternative, perhaps, provided by Austin's account of "could have" (as sometimes indicative rather than subjunctive), and is Moore to be considered mistaken because he did not adopt or see Austin's line? But of course the problem of alternatives is a problem of what alternatives are open to a particular person at a particular moment: and what is "open to" a particular person at a particular moment is a matter of some delicacy to determine—nothing less than determining whether someone could have done or seen something. However this may be, we still need, if we are to say "mistaken," an account of why he took the "alternative" he did. There seem to be just two main sorts of answers to such a question: either you admit that it is an attractive or plausible or seemingly inevitable one, *and account for such facts,* or you will find nothing of attraction or plausibility or seeming inevitability in it and assign its choice to ignorance, stupidity, incompetence, prejudice, and so forth. When Austin is discussing Moore, his respect pushes him to suggest the former sort of explanation, but he is clearly impatient with the effort to arrive at one and drops it as soon as possible (see, for example, pp. 154, 157).

Calling philosophers prejudiced or thoughtless or childish is a common enough salute among classical philosophers: one thinks of

Bacon's or Descartes's or Hume's attitudes to other, especially to past, philosophers. It is time, perhaps, to start wondering why such charges should be characteristic of the way a philosophy responds to a past from which it has grown different or to a position with which it is incommensurable.

Other terms of criticism are implied in Austin's occasional recommendations of his own procedures. For example, one reason for following out the branches of "Excuses" thoroughly and separately is that "Here at last we should be able to unfreeze, to loosen up and get going on agreeing about discoveries, however small, and on agreeing about how to reach agreement." It is hard to convey to anyone who has not experienced it the rightness and relief words like these can have for students who have gone over the same distinctions, rehearsed the same fallacies, trotted out the same topics seminar after term paper, teaching assistant after lecturer, book after article. And the rightness and relief were completed in his confession that the subject of "Excuses" "has long afforded me what philosophy is so often thought, and made, barren of—the fun of discovery, the pleasure of cooperation, and the satisfaction of reaching agreements." These are real satisfactions, and I can testify that they were present throughout the hours of his seminar on this topic. It would hardly have occurred to anyone, in the initial grip of such satisfactions, to question whether they are appropriate to philosophy (as they obviously are to logic or physics or historical scholarship) any more than they are, in those ways or proportions, to politics or religion or art; to wonder whether their striking presence in our work now did not suggest that we had changed our subject.

The implied terms of criticism in this recommendation are, of course, that we are frozen, tied up, stopped. Granted a shared sense that this describes our position, one wants to know how we arrived at it. Sometimes Austin attributes this to our distended respect for the great figures of the past (see, for example, "Excuses," p. 131), sometimes to general and apparently congenital weaknesses of philosophy itself: "over-simplification, schematization, and constant obsessive repetition of the same small range of jejune 'examples' are . . . far too common to be dismissed as an occasional weakness of philosophers." And this characteristic weakness—something he refers to as "scholastic," following the call of the major line of British Empiricists—he attributes "first, to an obsession with a few particular words, the uses of which are over-simplified, not really understood or care-fully studied or correctly described; and second, to an obsession with a few (and nearly always the same) half-studied 'facts' " (*Sense and Sensibilia*, p. 3). So far the criticisms proceed on familiar Baconian or Cartesian ground; the philosopher of good will and the man of common sense will work together to see through philosophy and prejudice to the world as it is.

At some point Austin strikes into criticisms which go beyond the impatience and doubt which begin modern philosophy, new ones necessary perhaps just because philosophy seems to have survived that impatience and doubt (or emasculated them, in turn, into academic subjects). I find three main lines here. (1) Most notably in *Sense and Sensibilia*, he enters charges against philosophers which make it seem not merely that their weakness is somehow natural to the enterprise, imposed on men of ordinary decency by an ill-governed subject, but that their work is still more deeply corrupt: we hear of philosophers having "glibly trotted out" new uses of phrases (p. 19); of subtle "insinuation" which is "well calculated" to get us "where the sense-datum theorist wants to have us" (p. 25); of bogus dichotomies, gro-tesque exaggeration, gratuitous ideas (p. 54)—phrases which, at this point, carry the suggestion that they are deliberate or willful exag-gerations and the like, and pursued with an absence of obvious moti-vation matched only by an Iago. (2) On more than one occasion he suggests that philosophical delinquency arises from a tendency to Dionysian abandon: we are warned of the blindness created in the "*ivresse des grandes profondeurs*" (p. 127) and instructed in the size of problems philosophers should aim at—"*In vino*, possibly, '*veritas*,' but in a sober symposium '*verum*' " ("Truth," p. 85). (3) Finally, and quite generally, he conveys the impression that the philosophers he is attacking are not really serious, that, one may say, they have written inauthentically (cf. *Sense and Sensibilia*, p. 29).

I cannot attempt here to complete the list of Austin's terms of criticism, any more than I can now attempt to trace the particular target each of them has; and I have left open all assessment of their relative seriousness and all delineation of the particular points of view from which they are launched. I hope, however, that the bare suggestion that Austin's work raises, and helps to settle, such topics will have served my purposes here, which, in summary, are these: (1) To argue that, without such tracing and assessment and delineation, we cannot know the extent to which these criticisms are valid and the extent to which they project Austin's own temper. (2) To point out that Austin often gives no reasons whatever for thinking one or other of them true, never making out the application to a philosopher of a term like "mistaken" or "imprecise" or "bogus" or the like according to anything like the standards he imposes in his own constructions. This discrepancy is not, I believe, peculiar to Austin, however clearer in him than in other philosophers; my feeling is that if it could be understood here, one would understand something about the real limitations, or liabilities, of the exercise of philosophy. (3) To register the fact that his characteristic terms of criticism are new terms, new for our time at least, though not in all cases his alone; and that these new modes of criticism are deeply characteristic of modern philosophy. (4) To suggest that if such terms do not seem formidable directions of criticism, and perhaps not philosophical at all (as compared, say, with terms such as "meaningless," "contradiction," "circular," and so forth), that may be because philosophy is only just learning, for all its history of self-criticism and self-consciousness, to become conscious of itself in a new way, at further ranges of its activity. One could say that attention is being shifted from the character of a philosopher's argument to the character of the philosopher arguing. Such a shift can, and perhaps in the Anglo-American tradition of philosophy it generally does, serve the purest political or personal motive: such criticism would therefore rightly seem philosophically irrelevant, if sometimes academically charming or wicked. The shift could also, one feels, open a new literary-philosophical criticism, in a tradition which knows how to claim, for example, the best of Kierkegaard and Nietzsche. Whatever the outcome, however, what I am confident of is that the relevance of the shift should itself become a philosophical problem. (5) To urge, therefore, a certain caution or discrimination in following Austin's procedures, using his attempts to define in new and freer and more accurate terms the various failings —and hence the various powers—of philosophy, without imitating his complacency, and even prejudice, in attaching them where he sees (but has not proven) fit. It suggests itself that a sound procedure would be this: to enter all criticisms which seem right, but to treat them phenomenologically, as temptations or feelings; in a word, as data, not as answers.

These purposes are meant to leave us, or put us, quite in the

dark about the sources of philosophical failure, and about the relation between the tradition of philosophy and the new critics of that
tradition, and indeed about the relation between any conflicting philosophies. For quite in the dark is where we ought to know we are. If,
for example, that failure of Moore's which we discussed earlier is
not to be understood as a mistake, then what is it? No doubt it would
be pleasanter were we able not to ask such a question—except that
philosophy seems unable to proceed far without criticizing its past,
any more than art can proceed without imitating it, or science without summarizing it. And anything would be pleasanter than the
continuing rehearsals—performable on cue by any graduate student
in good standing—of how Descartes was mistaken about dreams, or
Locke about truth, or Berkeley about God, or Kant about things-in-
themselves or about moral worth, or Hegel about "logic," or Mill
about "desirable," and so forth; or about how Berkeley mistook
Locke, or Kant Hume, or Mill Kant, or everybody Mill, and so forth.
Such "explanations" are no doubt essential, and they may account for
everything we need to know, except why any man of intelligence and
vision has ever been attracted to the subject of philosophy. Austin's
criticisms, where they stand, are perhaps as external and snap as any
others, but he has done more than any philosopher (excepting Wittgenstein) in the Anglo-American tradition to make clear that there is
a coherent tradition to be dealt with. If he has held it at arm's length,
and falsely assessed it, that is just a fault which must bear its own
assessment; it remains true that he has given us hands for assessing it
in subtler ways than we had known. The first step would be to grant
to philosophers the ordinary rights of language and vision Austin
grants all other men: to ask of them, in his spirit, why they should
say what they say where and when they say it, and to give the *full story*
before claiming satisfaction. That Austin pretends to know the story,
to have heard it all before, is no better than his usual antagonist's
assumption that there is no story necessary to tell, that everything is
fine and unproblematic in the tradition, that philosophers may use
words as they please, possessing the right or power—denied to other
mortals—of knowing, without investigating, the full source and significance of their words and deeds.

It is characteristic of work like Austin's—and this perhaps carries a certain justice—that criticism of it will often take the form of
repudiating it as philosophy altogether. Let me conclude by attempt-

ing to make one such line of criticism less attractive than it has seemed to some philosophers to be.

A serviceable instance is provided by a sensational book published a few years ago by Mr. Ernest Gellner (*Words and Things*, London: 1959; Boston: The Beacon Press, 1960) in which this author congratulates himself for daring to unmask the sterility and mystique of contemporary English philosophy by exposing it to sociology. First of all, unmasking is a well-turned modern art, perhaps *the* modern intellectual art, and its practitioners must learn not to be misled themselves by masks, and to see their own. I mean both that unmasking is itself a phenomenon whose sociology needs drawing, and also that the philosophy Gellner "criticizes" is itself devoted to unmasking. If, as one supposes, this modern art develops with the weakening or growing irrelevance of given conventions and institutions, then the position of the unmasker is by its nature socially unhinged, and his responsibility for his position becomes progressively rooted in his single existence. This is the occasion for finding a mask or pose of one's own (sage, prophet, saint, and so forth). Austin was an Englishman, an English professor. If I say he *used* this as a mask, I mean to register my feeling that he must, somewhere, have known his criticisms to be as unjustified as they were radical, but felt them to be necessary in order that his work get free, and heard. It would have served him perfectly, because its Englishness made it unnoticeable as a pose, because what he wanted from his audience required patience and co-operation, not depth and upheaval, and because it served as a counterpoise to Wittgenstein's strategies of the sage and the ascetic (which Nietzsche isolated as the traditional mask of the Knower; that is, as the only form in which he could carry authority).

Far from a condemnation, this is said from a sense that in a modern age to speak the truth may require the protection of a pose, and even that the necessity to posture may be an authentic mark of the possession of truth. It may not, too; that goes without saying. And it always is dangerous, and perhaps self-destructive. But to the extent it is necessary, it is not the adoption of pose which is to be condemned, but the age which makes it necessary. (Kierkegaard and Nietzsche, with terrible consciousness, condemned both themselves and the age for their necessities; and both maintained, at great cost, the doubt that their poses were really necessary—which is what it must feel like to know your pose.)

The relation of unmasking to evaluation is always delicate to trace. Gellner vulgarly imagines that his sociological reduction in itself proves the intellectual inconsequence and social irrelevance or political conservatism of English philosophy. (His feeling is common enough; why such psychological or sociological analyses appear to their performers—and to some of their audience—as reductive in this way is itself a promising subject of psychological and sociological investigation.) Grant for the argument that his analysis of this philosophy as a function of the Oxford and Cambridge tutorial system, the conventions of Oxford conversation, the distrust of ideology, the training in classics and its companion ignorance of science, and so forth, is accurate and relevant enough. Such an analysis would at most show the conditions or outline the limitations—one could say it makes explicit the conventions—within which this work was produced or initiated. To touch the question of its value, the value of those conventions themselves, as they enter the texture of the work, would have to be established. This is something that Marx and Nietzsche and Freud, our teachers of unmasking, knew better than their progeny.

Still, it can seem surprising that radical and permanent philosophy can be cast in a mode which merges comfortably in the proprieties of the common room—in the way it can seem surprising that an old man, sick and out of fortune, constructing sayings (in consort with others) polite enough for the game in a lady's drawing room, and entertaining enough to get him invited back, should have been saying the maxims of La Rochefoucauld.

Seven published papers are not many, and those who care about Austin's work will have felt an unfairness in his early death, a sense that he should have had more time. But I think it would be wrong to say that his work remains incomplete. He once said to me, and doubtless to others: "I had to decide early on whether I was going to write books or to teach people how to do philosophy usefully." Why he found this choice necessary may not be clear. But it is as clear as a clear Berkeley day that he was above all a teacher, as is shown not merely in any such choice, but in everything he wrote and (in my hearing) spoke, with its didactic directions for profitable study, its lists of exercises, its liking for sound preparation and its disapproval of sloppy work and lazy efforts. In example and precept, his work is complete, in a measure hard to imagine matched. I do not see that it is anywhere being followed with the completeness it describes and exemplifies. There must be, if this is so, various reasons for it. And it would be something of an irony if it turned out that Wittgenstein's manner were easier to imitate than Austin's; in its way, something of a triumph for the implacable professor.

# V

# Ending the Waiting Game
## A READING OF BECKETT'S *ENDGAME*

Various keys to its interpretation are in place: "Endgame" is a term of chess; the name Hamm is shared by Noah's cursed son, it titles a kind of actor, it starts recalling Hamlet. But no interpretation I have seen details the textual evidence for these relations nor shows how the play's meaning opens with them. Without this, we will have a general impression of the play, one something like this: Beckett's perception is of a "meaningless universe" and language in his plays "serves to express the breakdown, the disintegration of language"—by, one gathers, itself undergoing disintegration. Such descriptions are usual in the discussions of Beckett I am aware of, but are they anything more than impositions from an impression of fashionable philosophy? [1]

---

[1] When the ideas which prompted this essay started occurring to me, I read Martin Esslin's *The Theatre of the Absurd,* Anchor Book, 1961; Hugh Kenner's *Samuel Beckett,* Grove Press, 1961; David Grossvogel's *Four Playwrights,* Cornell University Press, 1962; and, I'm afraid, little else, and incompletely in Beckett's other works. But I felt compelled to have my say about this play once the methodological route to it opened for me and when the detailed closeness to Noah, Hamlet, Lear, and the Sermon on the Mount made themselves felt; and I did not want to get talked out of it by arguing with others. This may mean that what I have said, so far as it is valid, is known. Three of the four "keys" listed in the opening sentence are mentioned by Kenner, two of them, the allusion to acting and to chess, forming the basis for much of what he says about it. The fourth, Noah's son, is noted by Grossvogel, but nothing further, as I recall, is made of it. Any further resemblances between what I have said and those writings should therefore be credited as due to them. All page references to *Endgame* are to the Grove Press edition, 1958, and selections are used by permission of the Grove Press.

Martin Esslin, from whom I was just quoting, applauds Beckett for his veridical registering of the modern world. Georg Lukacs deplores Beckett as an instance of the modernist writer who, while accurately registering something about our world, fails to see that his response to that world (in subjectivity, *angst*, formalism, psychopathology) is chosen, and partial—in particular, a choice against a socialist perspective from which alone possibilities for the future of human society can be spoken for by artists.[2] One recognizes the sorts of production which fit Lukacs' descriptions, the amusements which sell the world its own weirdness. Both Esslin and Lukacs take Beckett's work much as any corrupted audience takes it, except that Lukacs maintains the classical demand of art, that the artist achieve perspective which grants independence from the world within which he is centered; that he not allow himself merely to pander to the world, becoming one of its typical phenomena, but that he witness it, helping the world to see its phenomena by providing his perspective. Esslin speaks with those who have forgotten that such a perspective is necessary, or who assume that it is no longer possible. Lukacs proposes to bring society and art back together by demanding that the artist's perspective be provided by a particular social attitude or choice. Both views are blind to the fact that in modernist arts the achievement of the autonomy of the object is a *problem*—the artistic problem. Autonomy is no longer provided by the conventions of an art, for the modernist artist has continuously to question the conventions upon which his art has depended; nor is it furthered by any position the artist can adopt, towards anything but his art. (Contrariwise, the success of socialism is not to be measured by its providing artists with perspective, but by its providing conditions under which artists are free to find their own, without punishing eccentricity or isolation, and in which the members of his community are each in a position to expose themselves to those discoveries, or not to.)

Neither Esslin's praise nor Lukacs' blame ought to guide or to depress us, for the former does not see the problem and the latter does not see Beckett's solution to the problem. The first critical problem is to discover how Beckett's objects mean at all, the original source of their conviction for us, if they have conviction. My argument will be that Beckett, in *Endgame*, is not marketing subjectivity,

[2] See, for example, Georg Lukacs, *Realism in Our Time* (New York: Harper & Row, 1964).

popularizing *angst,* amusing and thereby excusing us with pictures of our psychopathology; he is outlining the facts—of mind, of community—which show why these have become our pastimes. The discovery of *Endgame,* both in topic and technique, is not the failure of meaning (if that means the lack of meaning) but its total, even totalitarian, success—our inability *not* to mean what we are given to mean.

## I

Who are these people? Where are they, and how did they get there? What can illuminate their mood of bewilderment as well as their mood of appalling comprehension? What is the source of their ugly power over one another, and of their impotence? What gives to their conversation its sound, at once of madness and of plainness?

I begin with two convictions. The first is that the ground of the play's quality is the *ordinariness* of its events. It is true that what we are given to see are two old people sticking half up out of trash cans, and an extraordinarily garbed blind paraplegic who imposes bizarre demands on the only person who can carry them out, the only inhabitant of that world who has remaining to him the power of motion. But take a step back from the bizarrerie and they are simply a family. Not just any family perhaps, but then every unhappy family is unhappy in its own way—gets in its own way in its own way. The old father and mother with no useful functions any more are among the waste of society, dependent upon the generation they have bred, which in turn resents them for their uselessness and dependency. They do what they can best do: they bicker and reminisce about happier days. And they comfort one another as best they can, not necessarily out of love, nor even habit (this love and this habit may never have been formed) but out of the knowledge that they were both there, they have been through it together, like comrades in arms, or passengers on the same wrecked ship; and a life, like a disaster, seems to need going over and over in reminiscence, even if that is what makes it disastrous. One of their fondest memories seems to be the time their tandem bicycle crashed and they lost their legs: their past, their pain, has become their entertainment, their pastime. Comfort may seem too strong a term. One of them can, or could, scratch the other where the itch is out of reach, and Nagg will tolerate Nell's girlish re-rhapsodizing the beauties of Lake Como if she will bear his telling again his favorite funny story. None of this is very *much* comfort perhaps, but then there never is very *much* comfort.

The old are also good at heaping curses on their young and at controlling them through guilt, the traditional weapons of the weak and dependent. Nagg uses the most ancient of all parental devices, claiming that something is due him from his son for the mere fact of having begot him. Why that should ever have seemed, and still seem, something in itself to be grateful for is a question of world-consuming mystery—but Hamm ought to be the least likely candidate for its effect, wanting nothing more than to wrap up and send back the gift of life. (His problem, as with any child, is to find out where it came from.) Yet he keeps his father in his house, and lays on his adopted son Clov the same claim to gratitude ("It was I was a Father to you"). Like his father, powerless to walk, needing to tell stories, he masks his dependence with bullying—the most versatile of techniques, masking also the requirements of loyalty, charity, magnanimity. All the characters are bound in the circle of tyranny, the most familiar of family circles.

Take another step back and the relationship between Hamm and his son-servant-lover Clov shows its dominance. It is, again, an ordinary neurotic relationship, in which both partners wish nothing more than to end it, but in which each is incapable of taking final steps because its end presents itself to them as the end of the world. So they remain together, each helpless in everything save to punish the other for his own helplessness, and play the consuming game of manipulation, the object of which is to convince the other that you yourself do not need to play. But any relationship of absorbing importance will form a world, as the personality does. And a critical change in either will change the world. The world of the happy man is different from the world of the unhappy man, says Wittgenstein in the *Tractatus*. And the world of the child is different from the world of the grown-up, and that of the sick from that of the well, and the mad from the un-mad. This is why a profound change of consciousness presents itself as a revelation, why it is so difficult, why its anticipation will seem the destruction of the world: even where it is a happy change, a world is always lost. I do not insist upon its appearing a homosexual relationship, although the title of the play just possibly suggests a practice typical of male homosexuality, and although homosexuality figures in the play's obsessive goal of sterility—the non-consummation devoutly to be wished.

The language sounds as extraordinary as its people look, but it imitates, as Chekhov's does, the qualities of ordinary conversation among people whose world is shared—catching its abrupt shifts and sudden continuities; its shades of memory, regret, intimidation; its opacity to the outsider. It is an abstract imitation, where Chekhov's is objective. (I do not say "realistic," for that might describe Ibsen, or Hollywoodese, and in any case, as it is likely to be heard, would not emphasize the fact that art had gone into it.) But it is an achievement for the theater, to my mind, of the same magnitude. Not, of course, that the imitation of the ordinary is the only, or best, option for writing dialogue. Not every dramatist wants this quality; a writer like Shakespeare can get it whenever he wants it. But to insist upon the ordinary, keep its surface and its rhythm, sets a powerful device. An early movie director, René Clair I believe, remarked that if a person were shown a film of an ordinary whole day in his life, he would go mad. One thinks, perhaps, of Antonioni. At least he and Beckett have discovered new artistic resource in the fact of boredom; not as a topic merely, but as a dramatic technique. To miss the ordinariness of the lives in *Endgame* is to avoid the extraordinariness (and ordinariness) of our own.

## II

I said there are two specific convictions from which my interpretation proceeds. The second also concerns, but more narrowly, the language Beckett has discovered or invented; not now its use in dialogue, but its grammar, its particular way of making sense, especially the quality it has of what I will call *hidden literality*. The words strew obscurities across our path and seem willfully to thwart comprehension; and then time after time we discover that their meaning has been missed only because it was so utterly bare—totally, therefore unnoticeably, in view. Such a discovery has the effect of showing us that it is *we* who had been willfully uncomprehending, misleading ourselves in demanding further, or other, meaning where the meaning was nearest. Many instances will come to light as we proceed, but an example or two may help at the outset.

At several points through the play the names God and Christ appear, typically in a form of words which conventionally expresses a curse. They are never, however, used (by the character saying them, of course) to curse, but rather in perfect literalness. Here are two instances: "What in God's name could there be on the horizon?" (p. 31); "Catch him [a flea] for the love of God" (p. 33). In context, the first instance shows Hamm really asking whether anything on the horizon is appearing in God's name, as his sign or at his bidding; and the second instance really means that if you love God, have compassion for him, you will catch and kill the flea. Whether one will be convinced by such readings will depend upon whether one is convinced by the interpretation to be offered of the play as a whole, but they immediately suggest one motive in Beckett's uncovering of the literal: it removes curses, the curses under which the world is held. One of our special curses is that we can use the name of God naturally only to curse, take it only in vain. Beckett removes this curse by converting the rhetoric of cursing; not, as traditionally, by using the name in prayer (*that* alternative, as is shown explicitly elsewhere in the play, is obviously no longer open to us) but by turning its formulas into declarative utterances, ones of pure denotation —using the sentences "cognitively," as the logical positivists used to put it. Beckett (along with other philosophers recognizable as existentialist) shares with positivism its wish to escape connotation, rhetoric, the noncognitive, the irrationality and awkward memories of ordinary language, in favor of the directly verifiable, the isolated and perfected present. Only Beckett sees how infinitely difficult this escape will be. Positivism said that statements about God are meaningless; Beckett shows that they mean too damned much.

To undo curses is just one service of literalization; another is to unfix clichés and idioms:

HAMM. Did you ever think of one thing?
CLOV. Never.

(p. 39)

The expected response to Hamm's question would be, "What?"; but that answer would accept the question as the cliché conversational gambit it appears to be. Clov declines the move and brings the gesture to life by taking it literally. His answer means that he has always thought only of *many* things, and in this I hear a confession of failure in following Christ's injunction to take no thought for your life, what ye shall eat, or what ye shall drink; nor yet for your body, nor for tomorrow—the moral of which is that "thine eye be single." Perhaps I hallucinate. Yet the Sermon on the Mount makes explicit appearance in the course of the play, as will emerge. Our concerns with God have now become the greatest clichés of all, and here is another curse to be undone.

> CLOV. Do you believe in the life to come?
> HAMM. Mine was always that.
>
> (p. 49)

Hamm knows he's made a joke and, I suppose, knows that the joke is on us; but at least the joke momentarily disperses the "belief" in the cliché "life to come," promised on any Sunday radio. And it is a terribly sad joke—that the life we are living is not our life, or not alive. Or perhaps it's merely that the joke is old, itself a cliché. Christ told it to us, that this life is nothing. The punch line, the knock-out punch line, is that there is no other but this to come, that the life of waiting for life to come is all the life ever to come. We don't laugh; but if we could, or if we could stop finding it funny, then perhaps life would come to life, or anyway the life of life to come would end. (Clov, at one point, asks Hamm: "Don't we laugh?", not because he feels like it, but out of curiosity. In her longest speech (p. 19), Nell says: "Nothing is funnier than unhappiness . . . It's like the funny story we have heard too often, we still find it funny, but we don't laugh any more.") As it is, we've heard it all, seen it all too often, heard the promises, seen the suffering repeated in the same words and postures, and they are like any words which have been gone over so much that they are worn strange. We don't laugh, we don't cry; and we don't laugh that we don't cry, and we obviously can't cry about it. That's funny.

So far all that these examples have been meant to suggest is the sort of method I try to use consistently in reading the play, one in which I am always asking of a line either: What are the most ordinary circumstances under which such a line would be uttered? Or: What do the words literally say? I do not suggest that every line will yield to these questions, and I am sharply aware that I cannot provide answers to many cases for which I am convinced they are relevant. My exercise rests on the assumption that different artistic inventions demand different routes of critical discovery; and the justification for my particular procedures rests partly on an induction from the lines I feel I have understood, and partly on their faithfulness to the general direction I have found my understanding of the play as a whole to have taken. I have spoken of the effect of literalizing curses and clichés as one of "undoing" them, and this fits my sense, which I will specify as completely as I can, that the play itself is about an effort to undo, to end something by undoing it, and in particular to end a curse, and moreover the commonest, most ordinary curse of man—not so much that he was ever born and must die, but that he has to figure out the one and shape up to the other and justify what comes between, and that he is not a beast and not a god: in a word, that he is a man, and alone. All those, however, are the facts of life; the curse comes in the ways we try to deny them.

I should mention two further functions of the literal which seem to me operative in the play. It is, first, a mode which some forms of madness assume. A schizophrenic can suffer from ideas that he is literally empty or hollow or transparent or fragile or coming apart at the seams.[3] It is also a mode in which prophecies and wishes are

---

[3] On this topic see Stanley R. Palombo and Hilde Bruch, "Falling Apart: The Verbalization of Ego Failure," *Psychiatry*, Vol. 27, No. 3, August, 1964. But the issue is philosophically complex. Drs. Palombo and Bruch emphasize the *spatial* and *physical* basis of such terms, whereas I was led to speak of it as the *literal*. I do not, however, wish to pre-judge the possible identity of spatiality (or physicality) with literality, and in particular I do not mean to suggest that when one is not meaning one's words with purely spatial or physical reference one is then using them metaphorically. For two sorts of reasons: The metaphorical statement "Juliet is the sun" refers to two physical objects, grammatically equating them, and it would not work as a metaphor unless one knew what those two objects were. Contrariwise, a statement like "It will take a long time" is not metaphorical even though time does not come in (spatial) lengths. There are two grounds for denying that it is metaphorical: (1) There are good reasons (one could say, there are facts which explain) why the concept of length is applied to the measurement of time; in particular the facts of our world which make it normal for longer distances to take longer to traverse than shorter distances. There are not comparable facts which explain why Juliet is equated with the sun, though the metaphor depends upon one's knowing facts about the sun (e.g., that the day begins with it, that it is the source of life) and it summarizes many things Romeo takes to be facts about Juliet. (2) What Empson calls the "pregnancy" of metaphor—the fact that its paraphrase is indefinitely long and elaborate—is essential to it. Whereas in statements about the length of time it is not up to each of us to determine how much of the concept of length, or which facts about measuring lengths, apply to the measurement of time. This is related to the fact that no one could have *invented* the normal application of length to time. But the topic is enormous, and needs investigation.

fulfilled, surprising all measures to avoid them. Birnam Forest coming to Dunsinane and the overthrow by a man of no woman born are textbook cases. In the *Inferno*, Lucifer is granted his wish to become the triune deity by being fixed in the center of a kingdom and outfitted with three heads. *Endgame* is a play whose mood is characteristically one of madness and in which the characters are fixed by a prophecy, one which their actions can be understood as attempting both to fulfill and to reverse.

A central controversy in contemporary analytic philosophy relates immediately to this effort at literalizing. Positivism had hoped for the construction of an ideal language (culminating the hope, since Newton and Leibniz at the birth of modern science, for a *Characteristica Universalis*) in which everything which could be said at all would be said clearly, its relations to other statements formed purely logically, its notation perspicuous—the form of the statement *looking* like what it means. (For example, in their new transcription, the statements which mean "Daddy makes money" and "Mommy makes bread" and "Mommy makes friends" and "Daddy makes jokes" will no longer look alike; interpretation will no longer be required; thought will be as reliable as calculation, and agreement will be as surely achieved.) Post-positivists (the later Wittgenstein; "ordinary language philosophy") rallied to the insistence that ordinary language—being *speech*, and speech being more than the making of statements—contains implications necessary to communication, perfectly comprehensible to anyone who can speak, but not recordable in logical systems. If, for example, in ordinary circumstances I ask "Would you like to use my scooter?", I must not simply be *inquiring* into your state of mind; I must be *implying* my willingness that you use it, offering it to you. —I *must*? Must not? But no one has been able to explain the force of this *must*. Why mustn't I just be inquiring? A positivist is likely to answer: because it would be bad manners; or, it's a joke; in any case most people wouldn't. A post-positivist is likely to feel: That isn't what I meant. Of course it *may* be bad manners (even unforgivable manners), but it *may* not even be odd (e.g., in a context in which you have asked me to guess which of my possessions you would like to use). But suppose it isn't such contexts, but one in which, normally, people *would* be offering, and suppose I keep insisting, puzzled that others are upset, that I simply want to know what's on your mind. Then aren't you going to have to say something like: You don't know what you're saying, what those words mean—a feeling that I have tuned out, become incomprehensible. Anyway, why is the result a *joke* when the normal implications of language are defeated; what kind of joke?

Hamm and Clov's conversations sometimes work by defeating the implications of ordinary language in this way.

> HAMM. I've made you suffer too much.
> (*Pause.*)
> Haven't I?
> CLOV. It's not that.
> HAMM (*shocked*). I haven't made you suffer too much?
> CLOV. Yes!
> HAMM (*relieved*). Ah you gave me a fright!
> (*Pause. Coldly.*)
> Forgive me.
> (*Pause. Louder.*)
> I said, Forgive me.
> CLOV. I heard you.
>
> (pp. 6–7)

Hamm's first line looks like a confession, an acknowledgment; but it is just a statement. This is shown by the question in his next speech, which is to determine whether what he said was true. His third speech looks like an appeal for forgiveness, but it turns out to be a command—a peculiar command, for it is, apparently, obeyed simply by someone's admitting that he heard it. How could a *command for forgiveness* be anything but peculiar, even preposterous? (Possibly in the way the Sermon on the Mount is preposterous.) An ordinary circumstance for its use would be one in which someone needs forgiveness but cannot *ask* for it. Preposterous, but hardly uncommon. (One of Hamm's lines is: "It appears the case is . . . was not so . . . so unusual" (p. 44); he is pretty clearly thinking of himself. He is *homme*. And "Ha-am" in Hebrew means "the people." Probably that is an accident, but I wouldn't put anything past the attentive friend and disciple of James Joyce.[4]) In Hamm's case, moreover, it

---

[4] Though it is hard to be reasonable. I am thinking of the syllable "Om," holy in Eastern mysticism. Rudolf Otto, in *The Idea of the Holy* (New York: Oxford University Press, 1958; first published in 1923) says this about it: ". . . no word, nor even a complete syllable, for the *m* in which it ends is not an ordinary 'm,' but simply the

would have been trivially preposterous, and less honest, had he really been *asking* for forgiveness "for having made you suffer too much": How much is just enough? We have the need, but no way of satisfying it; as we have words, but nothing to do with them; as we have hopes, but nothing to pin them on.

Sometimes the effect of defeating ordinary language is achieved not by thwarting its "implications" but by drawing purely logical ones.

> HAMM. I'll give you nothing more to eat.
> CLOV. Then we'll die.
> HAMM. I'll give you just enough to keep you from dying.
> You'll be hungry all the time.
> CLOV. Then we won't die.
>
> (pp. 5–6)

Clov can hardly be meaning what his words, taken together and commonly, would suggest, namely "It makes no difference whether we live or die; I couldn't care less." First, in one sense that is *so trivial* a sentiment, at their stage, that it would get a laugh—at least from clear-headed Hamm. Second, it is not true. How could it make no difference when the point of the enterprise is to die to that world? (Though of course *that* kind of living and dying, the kind that depends on literal food, may make no difference.) And he *could* care less, because he's *trying* to leave (as he says, p. 7). If he were really empty of care, then maybe he could stop trying, and then maybe he could do it. The conventional reading takes Hamm's opening remark

---

long-protracted nasal continuation of the deep 'o' sound. It is really simply a sort of growl or groan, sounding up from within as the quasi-reflex expression of profound emotion in circumstances of a numinous-magical nature, and serving to relieve consciousness of a felt burden, almost physical in its constraining force" (p. 193). A conjunction of three intimations lead me to look up, and constrain me to quote, that passage: (1) Wondering, and skeptical, about the Hebrew word, I noted that the "a" is not doubled in Hamm's name, but that the "m" is, and I looked for significance in that. (2) Hamm is not called by name by any of the other characters, though each of the others is. He does say his own name once, however (in a line in which it is followed by a word clearly echoing it): "But for me, no father. But for Hamm, no home" (p. 38). (". . . but the Son of man hath not where to lay his head.") (3) A critical moment at the end of the play concerns the sudden appearance of a young boy outside the shelter: in a passage omitted from the English version, he is said to be looking at his navel. The whole passage is given in Esslin, pp. 35–36.

The succeeding paragraph in Otto further encourages, or discourages, speculation: "This *Om* is exactly parallel to the similar sound in Sanskrit, *Hum* . . .". Hm.

as a *threat*; but there are no more threats. It is a plain statement and Clov makes the inference; then Hamm negates the statement and Clov negates the conclusion. It is an exercise in pure logic; a spiritual exercise.

The logician's wish to translate out those messy, non-formal features of ordinary language is fully granted by Beckett, not by supposing that there is a way out of our language, but by fully accepting the fact that there is nowhere else to go. Only he is not going to call that rationality. Or perhaps he will: this is what rationality has brought us to. The strategy of literalization is: you say *only* what your words say. That's the game, and a way of winning out.

I refer to contemporary analytical philosophy, but Hamm presents a new image of what the mind, in one characteristic philosophical mood, has always felt like—crazed and paralyzed; this is part of the play's sensibility. One thinks of Socrates' interlocutors, complaining that his questions have numbed them; of Augustine faced with his question "What is Time?" (If you do not ask me, I know; if you ask me, I do not know). Every profound philosophical vision can have the shape of madness: The world is illusion; I can doubt everything, that I am awake, that there is an external world; the mind takes isolated bits of experience and associates them into a world; each thing and each person is a metaphysical enclosure, and no two ever communicate directly, or so much as perceive one another; time, space, relations between things, are unreal. . . . It sometimes looks as if philosophy had designs on us; or as if it alone is crazy, and wants company. Then why can't it simply be ignored? But it *is* ignored; perhaps not simply, but largely so. The question remains: What makes philosophy possible? Why can't men *always* escape it? Because, evidently, men have minds, and they think. (One mad philosophical question has long been, Does the mind *always* think? Even in sleep? It is a frightening thought.) And philosophy is what thought does to itself. Kant summarized it in the opening words of the *Critique of Pure Reason*: "Human reason has this peculiar fate that in one species of its knowledge it is burdened by questions which . . . it is not able to ignore, but which . . . it is also not able to answer." And Wittgenstein, saying in his *Investigations* that his later methods (he compared them to therapies) were to bring philosophy peace at last, seemed to find opportunity, and point, within such disaster: "The philosopher is the man who has to cure himself of many sicknesses of the understanding before he can arrive at the notions of the sound human understanding" (*Remarks on the Foundations of Mathematics*, p. 157)—as though there were no other philosophical path to sanity, save through madness. One will not have understood the opportunity if one is *eager* to seize it. Genuine philosophy may begin in wonder, but it continues in reluctance.

## III

The medium of Beckett's dialogue is repartée, adjoining the genres of Restoration comedy, Shakespearean clowning, and the vaudeville gag, but also containing the sound of some philosophical argument and of minute theological debate. It is the sound in which victory or salvation consists (not exactly in proving a point or defending a position but) in coming up with the right answer—or rather, with the *next* answer, one which continues the dialogue, but whose point is to win a contest of wits by capping a gag or getting the last word. And within stringent conventions: for example, your entry must include an earlier bit of the dialogue, which it furthers or overturns, and it must be at least as witty as the entry it follows. The game is won by the one who gets off the last word, and no reply is a priori the last, hence best; no direction of reply the most likely; you never know, on hearing it, that a given reply will be the end; it is solely a matter of personal invention and resourcefulness. This is perhaps why defeat here can have its special pang of humiliation and why the knack of answering is so powerful a weapon. With it one can control not only cocktail parties and revolutionary movements, but relationships whose medium is an interminable, if frequently interrupted, discussion; and usually a discussion whose principal theme is the sickness of the relationship itself. What counts as insight or perceptiveness in such dialectic is the wit to come up with an answer, resulting in that special state of impotence in which the other knows he is not convinced but feels he hasn't the right not to be convinced. (A conclusion endemic in philosophical and theological exchange.) He may think of the right, and the right answer, in thirty minutes, or thirty years. And wittiness need not make you laugh. The device of aphorism depends upon the sound of wit, and its effect is of hilarity, but with all passion spent.

A necessary task of critical description in grasping Beckett would be to capture his particular force of wit, distinguishing it from its neighbors. One element in this description must be that literalizing of words I have taken as characteristic of his writing. One effect Beckett achieves with his dexterity of the curt, stunted line is that of the riddle posed, a situation in which you know that the correctness of the answer logically depends upon its being witty. (This effect, if it occurs, would express Hamm and Clov's constant air of strained puzzlement.) Not so much the sort of riddle which depends upon a play of words ("What snake is a mathematician?" "An adder"), nor on distracting clues ("What coat has no buttons and is put on wet?" "A coat of paint"), nor upon finding a verbal twist ("What is the difference between a schoolteacher and a railroad conductor?" "One trains the mind, the other minds the train"), but one whose difficulty lies in avoiding a conventional reading, seeing the syntax a new way, whose answer, therefore, is not recognized to be right immediately on being told it (you have first to go over and refigure the syntax), but which is suddenly seen to make perfect sense ("What can go up a chimney when it's down, but can't go down when it's up?" "An umbrella").

Another technique is harder for me to characterize, partly because I know of no literary form or figure with which to compare it. It is a phenomenon I have often encountered in conversation and in the experience of psychotherapy—the way an utterance which has entered naturally into the dialogue and continues it with obvious sense suddenly sends out an intense meaning, and one which seems to summarize or reveal the entire drift of mood or state of mind until then unnoticed or unexpressed. I am remembering a conversation in which a beautiful and somewhat cold young lady had entered a long monologue about her brother, describing what it was like to live for the summer with him alone in their step-mother's New York apartment, telling of her fears that he was becoming more and more unhappy, more than once mentioning suicide; a beautiful young man like that. And then she said: "When I was in the shower, I was afraid of what my brother might do." The line came at us; I seemed to know that she had not been talking about her fears for her brother, but her fears of him. "What might your brother do?" But she had become perplexed, we were both rather anxious, the subject got lost; the line, however, stayed said. It would not be quite right to say that something was revealed; but there was as it were an air of revelation among us.

There are several examples of this effect in *Endgame*; two or three achieve the spiritual climaxes of the play, letting its meaning swell out suddenly, like a child playing with the volume control of a radio. Twice (p. 53, p. 68) Hamm comes out with: "Use your head can't you, use your head, you're on earth, there's no cure for that!". The natural, or conventional, reading will emphasize the word *that*, and this way makes a stunning enough effect. But another reading becomes possible, emphasizing the word *cure*; and with that I have the feeling of revelation stirring. No *cure* for that, but perhaps there is something else for it—if we could give up our emphasis upon cure. There is faith, for example.

Other instances must wait for more context, but after convincing myself of several of them, I am able, perhaps too willing, to hear it happening in Hamm's early, very innocuous line: "Quiet, quiet, you're keeping me awake" (p. 18)—said to his parents shortly after they have popped up. What is keeping him awake? His parents talking, obviously; but they are not talking loudly. It seems Hamm is curious, cannot not listen. What are they talking about, what does Hamm hear? Some moments earlier Hamm had said, "It's the end of the day like any other day," and dismissed Clov. A few lines earlier still his father Nagg had lifted the lid of his bin and stared listening to Hamm and Clov. When Clov leaves and Hamm quiets down, Nagg knocks on the lid of Nell his wife. She comes up with:

> What is it my pet?
> (*Pause.*)
> Time for love?
> NAGG. Were you asleep?
> NELL. Oh no!
> NAGG. Kiss me.

(p. 14)

The husband of an old married couple nudges his dozing wife and she turns to him with encouragement. That is what Hamm may be hearing to keep him awake. This idea would naturally explain Hamm's silence, save for his complaint at being kept awake and for one later brief speculation, throughout the long intercourse which now ensues between his parents. They have meant not to disturb him, but he is disturbed, and powerless to intervene. If this is accepted, something definite follows about the way the scene is to be played. Hamm will not then say "Quiet, quiet . . ." *to* his parents, as a straight request; rather he will say it to them as if in reverie, remembering something, not seeing them here and now but as characters of his imagination. An imagination stuffed with jealousy, competition, disgust, murderousness, guilt—states in which little boys begin their lives. Some are paralyzed in them, never stand on their own feet. His parents certainly do not think he has spoken to them. Nagg says—and the stage direction is (*Soft*)—"Do you hear him?". They are over-hearing him, as he is over-hearing them, and soon they go back to over-looking him. They will play most of the scene in bed-whispers.

The sudden turning of an obvious line into a cry of anxiety is something one expects of Chekhov, who is, I suppose, the closest classical equivalent to Beckett's glazing of calm onto terror. But in Chekhov the lines implode a different way: first, they characterize their speakers; second, their effect, like the effect of gestures, depends upon when and to whom they are made; third, they shape the silence which surrounds them so that what is unsaid leads a life of its own, sapping the life of the speakers and cursing what is left. His characters speak in order that they not have to hear themselves: that is the drama of his plays. Beckett has no such resources. Chekhov, in a word, is the greater dramatist, but Beckett is the superior showman, or raconteur; and like any strong performer he exploits his limitations. His lines do not individuate his characters nor further the action of the play; their interest is intrinsic. Words, we feel as we hear them, *can* mean in these combinations, and we want them to, they speak something in us. But what do they mean, and what in us, who in us, do they speak for? Nothing is left unsaid, but the speakers are anonymous, the words lead a life of their own. To own them, to find out who says them, who can mean them when, is the drama of the play.

Our relationship to the characters, accordingly, is different. About Vershinin we can say: He cannot bear not to dream; the future which he can be no part of is more precious to him than any present, *is* his present. About Irina we can say: She says she wants to go to Moscow, but there is no Moscow, and she cannot survive that knowledge. It is not that our relationship to Beckett's characters is more intimate, but that there is no distance at all or no recognizable distance between them and us. After Chekhov we know that each of us has his Moscow and that each has his way of foregoing reality. From Beckett no such statements emerge, or not this way. We cannot see ourselves *in* his characters, because they are no more characters than cubist portraits are particular people. They have the abstraction, and the intimacy, of figures and words and objects in a dream. Not that what we see is supposed to be our dream, or any dream. It is not surrealism, and its conventions are not those of fantasy. If this were a movie its director would not be Cocteau but Hitchcock.

There is no world just the other side of this one, opened onto through mirrors; escapes, if they come, will be narrower than this. There is only this world, unenchanted, unsponsored, but more fantastic than we can tell. The unbelievable, the plain truth which you cannot tell, that others will think you mad when you try to tell, is one of Hitchcock's patented themes. Take two people as pointedly ordinary as Robert Cummings and Priscilla Lane, have them discover, during the war, a plot to blow up a ship in the Brooklyn Navy Yard, have them momentarily elude the plotters only to find themselves in the midst of a private charity ball, the house owned by a colleague of the enemies, the immaculately proper servants guarding each exit, their only hope of escape lying in convincing the unknowing among the well-dressed mob of dancers and patrons under the crystal chandeliers and the spell of society dance music that their socially prominent and conscientious hostess is a Nazi sympathizer sheltering a gang of saboteurs—why anyone present would have to be mad to believe such a tale.

Beckett's characters have such a tale to tell, but their problem is not to distinguish friends from foes under the tuxedos, for there are neither friends nor foes any more; nor to prevent a disaster from happening or a culprit from escaping justice, for no one in particular is the culprit and all disasters have taken place. Their problem is not to become believable, but to turn off the power of belief altogether since it has become, because useless, the source of unappeasable, unbelievable pain. Suspense is for Hitchcock what faith is for the Christian, an ultimate metaphysical category, directing life's journey and making the universe come clear, and clean at the end. The overwhelming question for both is: How will the truth come out at last?

Beckett's couples have discovered the final plot: that there is no plot, that the truth has come out, that *this* is the end. But they would be mad to believe it and they cannot, being human, fully give up suspense. So they wait. Not *for* something, for they know there is nothing to wait for. So they try not to wait, but they do not know how to end.

But why should ending it be a problem, and why should the problem be an intellectual one, going beyond assembling the stamina for suicide? Because, evidently, suicide is not the end. I do not mean what Hamlet seems to mean (and perhaps he didn't either) that such an end has consequences, and hence is not the end. I mean it is not the *right* end, not the right solution to some particular problem. This has two implications: (1) Man is the animal for whom to be or not to be is a *question*: its resolution therefore must have the form of an *answer*. (2) It must form the answer to a *particular* reason for ending. Hamlet shuns suicide not because of the divine canon against self-slaughter; there is ample canon against other-slaughter as well, which he does not often hesitate to break. His real hesitations are over the right of vengeance and the belief in ghosts,[5] hesitations which have survived the God-slaughter of the succeeding centuries. He shuns suicide just because it makes no sense for his unhappiness. His problem is not one of radical failure or dishonor or abandonment. (I take it that suicide can solve these unhappinesses: in the first case because it serves as punishment, in the second because it serves as sacrifice, in the third because it vengefully turns the tables, turning the abandoner into the abandoned. All convert suffering into action; in all, impotence has become unbearable; in all, the act is toward silence, toward a shelter from a torment of accusation.) Hamlet's problem, on the contrary, is that he alone has the success of knowledge, the honor of succession, and the presence of motive to doctor the time. It makes no sense to run from that conjunction through use of suicide, though the thought of running from it may move him closer to suicide.

Why do men stay alive in the face of the preponderance of pain over pleasure, of meaninglessness over sense? Camus' answer is, in effect, that suicide, as a response to the general condition of human life, is a contradiction, because the condition to which it would be a response is life's absurdity, and suicide does not *respond* to this

---

[5] In *The Question of Hamlet* (New York: Oxford University Press, 1959), Harry Levin points to these as Hamlet's "double dilemma" (p. 24).

absurdity, but removes it. That seems a very academic way of putting the problem. Camus is right that this is *the* philosophical problem, because until it is answered one's chance for moral existence has not begun—or ended; one has not taken one's life into one's own hands. And after it is answered the supposed need for a philosophical "foundation" for morality vanishes, which is the reason all such foundations—metaphysical, epistemological, political or religious—strike one as conceived in bad faith.

It is true that Hamm wants death, at least there is no life he wants, and one can say that his entire project is to achieve his death. Why will suicide not answer? Because he cannot imagine his death apart from imagining the death of the world. *That* is what he wants, and his death is wanted as a necessary, and welcome, entailment of that. If the imagination of death requires the imagination of *leaving*, of farewells, then Hamm is not imagining his death. (Perhaps this means he cannot imagine his life either. In the eighth *Duino Elegy*: ". . . so leben wir und nehmen immer Abschied.") He wants to end, but without taking leave. But where does the motive come from to destroy the whole world?

It is as if personal escape, individual non-existence, private relief, are insufficient to neutralize the pain which would motivate suicide; as long as *anyone* can remember, the memory which is to die has not died; as long as anything breathes, I am not at rest. But how can anyone take in, or even conceive, an ambition or obligation large enough to encompass the death of the world? Perhaps, however, largeness is not at issue. If we are to speak of ambition or obligation, the question is: How does this *specific* obligation come to be shouldered?

Merely the connection between the death of personal existence and the death of the world is not new. Hamlet and Lear both crave death, and knowing they must be the *last* to die, crave the death of their worlds. Certainly Hamm, for all his efforts, cannot surpass them in their *disgust* with the world, especially with its fruitfulness. But their worlds were limited to the coherent state; the universe outside that was not their responsibility. Christ had wished the death of all, but in order for the re-birth of all. What is new is to wish for unlimited surcease, and without the plan of redemption.

It must be some widening knowledge of such a wish—heard by Nietzsche before this century turned on us the news now reaching our ears—which functions in our awareness of the Bomb. I would scarcely deny its objective threat, but one senses reactions to it that are not reactions to an objective threat. Sometimes they are hysterically fearful ("Better Red than dead," as though the *others* are willing to send them over at any moment), sometimes hysterically repressive and rational (the mode of all official rhetoric employing concepts of deterrence, over-kill, etc.—language breaking down in front of our ears, denoting nothing we know or imagine). I do not suggest that there is some *right* reaction waiting to be had. The situation *is* in fact mad. We know, sort of, that the world may end in twenty minutes (and to qualify this by calculating whether 30,000,000 or 50,000,000 persons will survive, or to speculate whether plant life will continue, is merely tragic relief). And we know there is nothing we can do to stop it which is not absurdly disproportionate to the event. So we treat it, or improvise around it, using the reactions we know: forgetfulness, habit, hope against hope, humor, hysteria, fantasy. The Three Sisters are no more out of touch with their world than we are with ours. We are a billion times three sisters.

One thinks of *Dr. Strangelove*. The film has been criticized because it presents superficial explanations of our final difficulties (it's all due to mad Generals, boy scout Generals, German rocket designers, bullies and dupes in high places) and childish solutions to them (get the bastards out, we want anarchy). Perhaps these are motives of the film, and doubtless some of its ardent fans have been fans of those explanations and solutions. But the issue is a false one. The clearest fact about the film is its continuous brilliance, and any understanding of it must understand that. It is not, for example, the result of brilliant movie-making, at which it is quite routine; nor the result of brilliant ideas, for it has no ideas (which is perhaps sufficient reason not to defend it, as has been tried, as satire). Its brilliance is that of farce, with its stringent rhythm of entrances and concealments; and of silent comedy, with its sight gags. Only it is abstract. The figure displaced under the bed or into the closet is not a person but a turn of mind; the object that drops on the head is not a loose chandelier but a tight loyalty; the inappropriate get-up is not a feather boa or a spittoon on the foot from which you cannot extricate yourself, but a habit of response. It is a collage whose bits are as common as sand: Who has never endowed a pop tune with Proustian power of recall and summary; or straightened out an awkward moment with a piece of pop seriousness ("Of course it's not just physical; I respect you as a person"); or thrilled when, at Saturday matinees, the tight-faced soldier nudges the door open with one hand and in the other holds a sub-machine gun upright in world-preserving coolness? If these fantasies are worthless, we are worthless. And nothing in all of Beckett's sadness is sadder than the scene in which Slim Pickens encourages his crew of doom by reminding them that the folks back home are counting on them. Inappropriate no doubt now; but the Second World War—and it is from movies about that War that this scene is taken—depended upon scenes like that, and it is not clear that without such scenes the outcome of the War would have been the same. What is so sad is that it is something good in us that has turned out to be so inappropriate. What is the solution? To see to it that our minds are no longer composed of trivial tunes, adolescent longings and movie clips? No doubt. Exactly what would one have in mind?

*Dr. Strangelove*'s strategies of sacrifice are singly clear to laugh at; but they amount to that mood of hilarity which does not produce laughter. It also suggests, what I take *Endgame* to be about, that we think it is right that the world end. Not perhaps morally right, but inevitable; tragically right. In a world of unrelieved helplessness, where Fate is not a notable Goddess but an inconspicuous chain of command, it would be a relief to stop worrying and start loving the Bomb (the extent to which these are accepted as our fixed alternatives is a measure of our madness.) A love too precious for this world, no doubt; but God will witness how powerful and true to itself. (I can hear the lyrics for the new *Liebestod*. They begin: "Extremism in the defense of liberty is no vice. I regret that I have but three billion lives to give for my country.") The official rhetoric is rational, but it bears to ordinary consciousness the same relation as advanced theology to the words and the audience of a revivalist. What *does* an ordinary Christian think when he says, or hears, that Christ died to save sinners? What does an ordinary citizen think when he says, or hears, that our defense systems provide such and such a margin of warning, or sees a sign saying "Fallout Shelter"? We speak about the dangers of "accidental war," but what does this mean? Not that the *whole* war will be an accident, but that it will *start* accidentally. From then on it will be planned. We are imagining that, if ordered to, men will "push buttons" which they *know* will mean the destruction of their world. Why do we imagine they will do this? Because they are soldiers and will be following orders and thereby doing a soldier's duty? That seems no more satisfactory an explanation here than its use to explain the behavior of extermination squads. In both cases, what is suppressed is the fact that the content of an act is essentially related to that action's counting as a duty. (Kant, I believe, is still thought to have denied this, and thus, I suppose, to have contributed to the moral destruction of Germany. What Kant denies, however, is only that anything *other* than the content of an act—in particular, its being performed from a particular motive (other than duty itself) or its having certain consequences—can make the act morally right.) For an action even to seem to be a duty it must be taken as on the whole good, or to lead to good; or at the least a regrettable necessity —and necessary on grounds other than the mere fact that it has been commanded: it is necessary in order that a greater good may supervene.

Someday, if there is someday, we will have to learn that evil thinks of itself as good, that it could not have made such progress in the world unless people planned and performed it in all conscience. Nietzsche was not crazy when he blamed morality for the worst evils, though he may have become too crazy about the idea. This is also why goodness, in trying to get born, will sometimes look like the destruction of morality. I am scarcely to be taken as presenting a theory of Nazism, any more than of the acquiescence to world destruction, so it would be irrelevant to point to other considerations which help explain human involvement in events of such catastrophe, for example to ways in which one denies to oneself the name and meaning and consequence of one's actions, to ways in which one merely hopes, out of a helplessness to see or to take any alternative, that one will be justified, and so on. What I am suggesting is that one dimension of our plight can only be discovered in a phenomenology of the Bomb.[6] For it has invaded our dreams and given the brain, already

---

[6] An instance of what I have in mind is Resnais' film *Hiroshima Mon Amour*. It has been called an anti-war film, on the ground, I suppose, of its display of the evil of the Bomb. But while it doubtless contains such an awareness (that evil is, after all, pretty obvious) its real subject is the evil of using the Bomb as an excuse—or, which is perhaps the same, a symbol—for inner horror, and thence about the oblique and ironic relations between inner and outer worlds generally. This suggests both a political and aesthetic problem. (1) While one does not expect, and does not want, politicians to become phenomenologists, nor to give up the most practical worries they can find, one of their biggest worries, and perhaps a new one, is this new importance, and power, of phenomenological awareness, making realistic appraisal and accommodation difficult in a new way. (2) The aesthetic problem concerns what limits there may be to subjects of art. Is, for example, the Bomb too practically engulfing to fit requirements of artistic treatment?

wrinkled with worry, a new cut. And it has finally provided our dreams of vengeance, our despair of happiness, our hatreds of self and world, with an instrument adequate to convey their destructiveness, and satisfaction.

I raise the image of the Bomb because Beckett's play has seemed to raise it for some of its audience, and this is as good a place as any to begin pursuing systematically the textual evidence for the pile of claims which has been so long accumulating.

## IV

Does the play take place, as is frequently suggested, after an atomic war? Are these its last survivors? Well, Beckett suggests they are, so far as they or we know, the last life. And he says twice that they are in "the shelter" (p. 3; p. 69). Is it a bomb shelter? These considerations are doubtless resonant in the play's situation; it tells its time. But the notion leaves opaque the specific goings on in the shelter. Do these people want to survive or not? They seem as afraid of the one as of the other. Why do they wish to *insure* that nothing is surviving? Why are they *incapable* of leaving? That Hamm and Clov want (so to speak) the world to end is obvious enough, but an understanding of the way they imagine its end, the reason it must end, the terms in which it can be brought to an end, are given by placing these characters this way: The shelter they are in is the ark, the family is Noah's, and the time is sometime after the Flood.

Many surface details find a place within this picture. Most immediately there is the name of Hamm. He is, in particular, the son of Noah who saw his father naked, and like Oedipus, another son out of fortune, he is blinded by what he has seen. Because of his transgression he is cursed by his father, the particular curse being that his sons are to be the servants of men. Clov, to whom Hamm has been a father, is his servant, the general servant of all the other characters. We are told (Genesis 9:23) that Shem and Japheth, the good brothers, cover their father while carefully contriving not to look at him. I hear a reference to their action when Hamm directs Clov (p. 10) to "bottle him" (i.e., clamp the lid down on his father)—one of the most brutal lines in the play, as if Hamm is commenting on what has passed for honorable conduct; he is now the good son, with a vengeance. At two points Hamm directs Clov to look out of the windows, which need to be reached by a ladder (they are situated, as it were, above the water line) and he looks out through a telescope, a very nautical instrument. (Another significant property in the shelter is a gaff.) One window looks out at the earth, the other at the ocean, which means, presumably, that they are at the edge of water, run aground perhaps. Earlier he has asked about the weather, and there was a little exchange about whether it will rain and what good that would do. Now he asks Clov to look at the earth and is told, what both knew, that all is "corpsed": Man and beast and every living thing have been destroyed from the face of the earth. Then Hamm directs Clov to look at the sea, in particular he asks whether there are gulls. Clov looks and answers, "Gulls!", perhaps with impatience (how could there be?), perhaps with longing (if only there were!), perhaps both. Hamm ought to *know* there aren't any, having looked for them until he is blind, and being told there are none day after day. And Hamm ought to ask what he really wants to know but is afraid to know, namely, whether there is a raven or a dove.

Let this suffice to establish a serious attention to the tale of Noah. Its importance starts to emerge when we notice that the entire action of the play is determined by the action of that tale. After the flood, God does two things: he establishes a covenant with Noah that the earth and men shall no more be taken from one another; and presses a characteristic commandment, to be fruitful and multiply and replenish the earth. Hamm's behavior is guided by attempts to undo or deny these specific acts of God.

Something has happened in the ark during those days and nights of world-destroying rain and the months of floating and waiting for the end, for rescue. Hamm has seen something in the ark of the covenant. I imagine it this way.

He has seen God naked. For it is, after all, the most fantastic tale. God repented, it says, that he created man. How does a God repent? How does anyone? Suppose he has a change of heart about something he has done. If this is not mere regret, then the change of heart must lead to mending one's ways or making amends. How does a God mend his ways; can he, and remain God? A further question is more pressing: How does God justify the destruction of his creation? A possible response would be: Man is sinful. But that response indicates at most that God had to do *something* about his creatures, not that he had to separate them from earth. He might have found it in himself to forgive them or to abandon them—alternatives he seems to have used, in sequence, in future millennia. Why destruction? Suppose it is said: God needs no justification. But it is not clear that God would agree; besides, all this really means is that men are God's creatures and he may do with them as he pleases. Then what did he in fact do? He did not, as he said, cause the end of flesh to come before him, for he preserved, with each species, Noah's family; enough for a new beginning. He hedged his bet. Why? And why Noah picked from all men? Those are the questions I imagine Hamm to have asked himself, and his solution is, following God, to see the end of flesh come before him. As before he imitates his good brothers, so now he imitates his God—a classical effort. Why is this his solution?

God saves enough for a new beginning because he cannot part with mankind; in the end, he cannot really end it. Perhaps this means he cannot bear not to be God. (Nietzsche said that this was true of himself, and suggested that it was true of all men. It seems true enough of Hamm. We need only add that in this matter men are being faithful to, i.e., imitating, God.) Not ending it, but with the end come before him, he cannot avoid cruelty, arbitrariness, guilt, repentance, disappointment, then back through cruelty . . . Hamm and Clov model the relationship between God and his servants.

And if the bet must be hedged, why with Noah? The tale says, "Noah walked with God." That's all. Well, it also says that he was a just man and perfect in his generations, and that he found grace in the eyes of the Lord. Is that enough to justify marking him from all men for salvation? It is incredible. Perhaps God has his reasons, or perhaps Noah does not deserve saving, and perhaps that doesn't matter. Doesn't matter for God's purposes, that is. But how can it *not* matter to those who find themselves saved? The tale is madly silent about what Hamm saw when he saw his father naked, and why it was a transgression deserving an eternal curse. Perhaps all he saw was that his father was ordinary, undeserving of unique salvation. But he saw also that his father was untroubled by this appalling fact. Nell, at one point in her reminiscence of Lake Como, says to Nagg: "By rights we should have been drowned" (p. 21)—a line which both undoes a cliché ("by rights" here literally means: it would have been right if we had, and hence it is wrong that we weren't) and has the thrill of revelation I spoke of earlier (it is not Lake Como she is thinking of). But Nagg misses the boat. So blind Hamm sees both that he exists only as a product of his father ("Accursed fornicator!" p. 10), and that if either of their existences is to be provided with justification, he must be the provider; which presents itself to him as taking his father's place—the act that blinds Oedipus.

And how is one to undertake justifying his own—let alone another's—existence? One serious enough solution is to leave this business of justification to God; that is what he is for. But God has reneged this responsibility, and doubly. In meaning to destroy all flesh, he has confessed that existence cannot be justified by him. And in saving one family and commanding them to replenish the earth, there is the high hint that man is being asked to do a god's work, that he is not only abandoned to his own justification, but that he must undertake to justify God himself, to redeem God's curse and destruction. God cursed the world, and he is cursed. This seems to me to set the real problem of Theodicy, to justify God's ways to God. Its traditional question—Why did God create man and then allow him to suffer?—has a clear answer: Because it is man that God created; all men are mortal, and they suffer.

The Covenant, therefore, is a bad bargain, and the notion of replenishing the earth is a losing proposition. Promising not to destroy man *again* is hardly the point, and is not so much a promise as an apology. (As the rainbow is more a threat than a promise.) The point is to understand why it was done the first time, and what man is that he can accept such an apology. As for replenishing the earth, what will that do but create more fathers and sons, and multiply the need for justification? God was right the first time: the end of flesh is come, God's destruction is to be completed. Or rather, what must end is the mutual dependence of God and the world: *this* world, and its god, must be brought to a conclusion. Hamm's strategy is to undo all covenants and to secure fruitlessness. In a word, to disobey God perfectly, to perform man's last disobedience. No doubt Hamm acts out of compassion. ("Kill him, for the love of God.") The creation and destruction of a world of men is too great a burden of responsibility even for God. To remove that responsibility the world does not so much need to vanish as to become *un-created*. But to accomplish that it seems that we will have to become gods. For mere men will go on hoping, go on waiting for redemption, for justification, for meaning. And these claims ineluctably retain God in creation—to his, and to our, damnation. And yet, where there is life there is hope. That is Hamm's dilemma.

(At some such point another feature of our time is apt to enter the resonance of these lines, another mine of response running under the original meaning of Hamm's name: the new sense of blackness. The demand for the end of the world in which blacks and whites are dependent upon one another for their own view of themselves, for their own sense of worth—this demand is now irreversible. And the reversal of the curses and covenants which have created this world will feel like the loss of the world. Whether it also feels to a given man like the hope of the world depends upon whether that man relocates his sense of worth inside his single skin. That this preposterously simple demand should be so preposterously complex to fulfill is itself maddening. It is simply crazy that there should ever have come into being a world with such a sin in it, in which a man is set apart because of his color—*the* superficial fact about a human being. Who could *want* such a world? For an American, fighting for his love of country, that the last hope of earth should from its beginning have swallowed slavery, is an irony so withering, a justice so intimate in its rebuke of pride, as to measure only with God. The question is whether enough men can afford the knowledge that the way the world is comes down in the end to what each son is doing now, sitting within his ordinary walls, making his everyday demands. And whether enough men can divine the difference, and choose, between wanting this world to stop itself, and wanting all world to end.)

Hamm's problem, like Job's, is that of being singled out. Job is singled out for suffering, Hamm for rescue, and it is something of an insight to have grasped the problem still there. Job, presumably, has his answer in recognizing that there *is* no humanly recognizable reason for being singled out to suffer. That is, none having to do with *him*. Life becomes bearable when he gives up looking for such a reason. Couldn't we give up looking for a reason for being singled out for rescue? For certain spirits that is harder, for the good Christian reason that others are there, unrescued.

It is in some such way that I imagine Hamm's thoughts to have grown. It is from a mind in such straits that I can make sense (1) of his attempt to reverse creation, to empty the world of salvation, justification, meaning, testaments; and (2) of the story he tells, the composing of which is the dominant activity of his days.

He calls his story a "chronicle," suggesting that it is a record of fact. It concerns a man who had come to him for help, begging him at least to "take his child in" (p. 53). And we learn that this is not an isolated case, for Hamm refers to

> All those I might have helped.
> (*Pause.*)
> Helped!
> (*Pause.*)
> Saved.
> (*Pause.*)
> Saved!
> (*Pause.*)
> The place was crawling with them!

"Might have." With those words every man takes his life. Hamm is remembering something that actually happened. I imagine him to be remembering the ark being built. It would have taken a while—all those cubits to arrange, and all that food and all the paired beasts to collect. People would have got wind of it, perhaps some were hired to help in the preparations. God, the tale says, went away while it was being done, perhaps to let the family get used to the idea of their special fortune, and to get a full appreciation of God's love. Then he returned to order them into the ark, and when the family and each kind had gone in unto Noah into the ark, "the Lord shut him in" (Genesis 7:7), preserved him, bottled him. At first people would have been skeptical at Noah's folly rising there in the middle of land, but some would eventually have believed, and even if these were the gullible and lunatic who believe every announcement of doom, Noah would have known that this time they were right; but he would have had to refuse their crazed petitions to be let in. Finished, the ark stood there closed for seven days, then the rain began, and some days would have passed before it lifted off its scaffolding to be held up in the palm of God's sea. Suppose it had been built just by the family, in secret. But now the water is deep, raising the general horizon, and the ark is visible for as far as the eye can see, to anyone who is still afloat. Perhaps no one is, but Noah's family doesn't know that. Perhaps the sounds of pounding are not survivors screaming for rescue, only dead wreckage in the water. They don't know that either, but it wouldn't require much imagination to wonder whether it was. They must not imagine, or they must be mad. Imagination has to be bottled. But in Hamm it has started to leak out. He complains twice that "There's something dripping in my head"; both times his father has to suppress a laugh—how comical the young are, so serious, so pure; they'll learn. The first time is his over-hearing his parents together; he tells himself it's a heart, "A heart in my head" (p. 18). Something is pounding. Children will give themselves *some* explanation. The second time he thinks of it as splashing, "Splash, splash, always on the same spot" (p. 50). Now he tries pressing his earlier thought that it is a little vein, and now adds the idea that it is a little artery; but he gives it up and begins working on his chronicle, his story, his art-work. (His art-ery? That could mean, following Eric Partridge on the origin of the suffix "-ery", either the action (cp. "drudgery"), the condition (cp. "slavery"), the occupation (cp. "casuistry"), the place of actions (cp. "nursery"), the product of the action (cp. "poetry"), or the collectivity (cp. "citizenry") of art. Each of these would fit this character and this play.) Art begins where explanations leave off, or before they start. Not everything has an explanation, and people will give themselves *some* consolation. The imagination must have something to contain it—to drip into, as it were—or we must be mad. Hamm is in both positions.

## V

Whatever God's idea in destroying men, to have saved one family for himself puts them in the position of denying life to all other men. To be chosen, to be special, singled out, for suffering *or* for salvation, is an inescapable curse. Perhaps this was something Christ tried to show, that even to be God is to be completely unspecial, powerless to claim exemption. To deny this is to be less than a man: we are all in the same boat. But can any man, not more than a man, affirm it?

It seems possible to me that this is what *Endgame* is about, that what it envisions is the cursed world of the Old Testament ("Ah, the old questions, the old answers, there's nothing like them," p. 38) and that what is to be ended is that world, followed by the new message, glad tidings brought by a new dove of redemption, when we are ready to receive it. Without it we are paralyzed.

But I do not think this is what is seen, though it may be a permanent segment. For the new message is also present in the play, and it too is helpless. Immediately after Hamm's first full telling of the story, his telling of it to date, he wonders how he is to continue (as anyone does, artist or man, in final difficulties) and says: "Let us pray to God" (p. 54). There are references to food (not to loaves, but to the bribe of a sugar-plum, and to calling Clov from the kitchen), and he finally persuades Clov and Nagg to join him. Nagg wants his sugar-plum before he prays, but Hamm insists "God first!"—thus summarizing the First Commandment, according to Christ the first and greatest commandment. Whereupon Nagg begins to recite the Lord's Prayer, taught during the Sermon on the Mount. That occasion is alluded to further in the way Hamm immediately interrupts his father's prayer: "Silence! In silence! Where are your manners?" (p. 55). Christ cautions that prayer be offered "in secret" immediately before he delivers *his* Father's Prayer. If here Hamm's teaching parodies Christ's he will later imitate him more directly, as in his chronicle he presents himself as in God's position, distributing life and death to supplicants. That's the position God has put him in.

The next time he tries to finish his story, instead of praying to God he ends by calling his father. "Father, Father" he says (p. 66), echoing the repeated among the seven last words, and addressed to the same old party. ("Father, Father" he says again near the end of his, and the play's, last speech.) And now it looks as if he is not only the son of the only spared man, hence has the same ancestor as all men; but the one and only son, with the father to end all fathers. No wonder he is confused about whether he is father or son.

He goes back to his chronicle, to try to end it, or make some continuation, a third time; again he gets to the point at which he is begged for salvation and again this is the stumbling block (pp. 68–69). Now he quotes the Sermon on the Mount more openly: "Get out of here and love one another! Lick your neighbor as yourself!" And now he becomes petulant: "When it wasn't bread they wanted it was crumpets." And wrathful: "Out of my sight and back to your petting parties." He can find no conclusion to the story of suffering and sin, and no answer to the prayer for salvation, no answer old or new. He has just told them again everything eternity knows: "Use your head can't you, use your head, you're on earth, there's no cure for that!". But they can't use their heads; men are enough to try the patience of a God. "How is it that ye do not understand that I spake it not to you concerning bread, that ye should beware of the leaven of the Pharisees and of the Sadducees? Then understood they how that he bade them not beware of the leaven of bread, but of the doctrine of the Pharisees and Sadduccees" (Matthew 16:11–12). Use your head, can't you? It was a parable! Get it? But he's said that before and he'll say it again, and nobody gets it. They want signs, miracles, some cure for being on earth, some way of getting over being human. Maybe that's just human; and there's no cure for that.

So Hamm renounces parable in favor of the perfectly literal. (People, he might say, have no head for figures.) Only it is just as hard to write his anti-testament that way. Maybe to receive either word one would have to have a heart in one's head. No doubt it is not very clear how that could be, but then Christ sees his disciples' lack of understanding as a lack of faith, and it has never seemed unusually clear what that would be either. ("Believe," said Augustine, "and you have eaten"; Luther thought he understood what that meant.) However it is to come, nothing less powerful than faith will be needed to remove God and his curse, the power to un-create God. Hamm, however, may believe, or half-believe—believe the way little children believe—that he really has got a blood-pumping organ upstairs. We have known for a long time that the heart has its reasons which reason knows not of. But we have come to think that reason *can* know them, that the knowing of them takes over the work of the heart, that what we require for salvation is more knowledge, knowledge of the sort we already know, that will fit the shape of our heads as they are. Hamm is half-crazy with his efforts at un-doing knowledge, at not knowing. But no half-crazier than we are at our frenzy for knowledge, at knowing where we should love, meaning our lives up.

Finally, he tries to imagine that it can end without ending his story. "If I can hold my peace and sit quiet, it will be all over with sound, and motion, all over and done with" (p. 69). But it seems to be just the same old story. "I'll have called my father and I'll have called my . . . [he hesitates] . . . my son." He hesitates, as if not knowing whether he is the new god or the old, son or father. But at least he is putting himself into the picture; no attitude is struck now towards father or son; the son is now not another's—as if to acknowledge that all sons are his. "I'll have called . . . I'll say to myself, He'll come back. [Pause] And then? [Pause] . . . He couldn't, he has

gone too far. [Pause] And then?" And then a description of confusion: "Babble, babble . . ." (Babel? If so, what does it mean? What
caused Babel and its aftermath? Our presumption, in desiring God's
eminence? Or our foolishness, in imagining that a tower is the way
to reach heaven? In either case the confusion of tongues is God's
punishment, hence proof of his existence. Or is the din rather the
sound of our success, that we reached heaven and found it empty?
Better to bite the tongue than admit that. Better to take over and
punish ourselves than to forgo that proof.)

Here is at least one possible endgame other than the act of
ending the story: I call; there is no answer. But this ending is unclear.
The problem seems to be that there is no way of *knowing* there is no
answer, no way of knowing the call was heard, and therefore *unanswered*. (An unconnected telephone cannot be left unanswered.)

One source of confusion seems clear enough. *Who* has gone too
far to come back? The father or the son? Is it God who has gone too
far, in inflicting suffering he cannot redeem? Or Christ, in really
dying of suffering we cannot redeem? What does it matter? The one
threatened, the other promised, the end of the world; and neither
carried through. We are left holding it.

There are three other allusions to Christ which need mentioning, one at the beginning, one near the middle, and one at the end
of the play. The first may seem doubtful: "Can there be misery loftier
than mine?" (p. 3). If confirmation is wanted beyond the fact that the
tone of this remark perfectly registers Hamm's aspiration (perhaps
the usual tone in which Christ is imitated) there is the refrain of
George Herbert's "The Sacrifice": "Was ever grief like mine?", in
which the speaker is Christ. The middle allusion is the only explicit
one, and it occurs with characteristic literality. After Hamm's instruction in the etiquette of prayer, the three men have a try at it, whereupon each confesses in turn that he has got nowhere. King Claudius,
in a similar predicament, gives the usual honest explanation for this
failure: "My words fly up, my thoughts remain below: words without
thoughts never to heaven go." Hamm has a different, perhaps more
honest, certainly no less responsible, explanation: "The bastard! He
doesn't exist." To which Clov's response, in full, is: "Not yet", and
the subject is dropped (p. 55). Removing the curse, what Hamm has
just said is that the bastard does not exist. That Christ was literally

a bastard was among the first of the few things I was ever told about him, and I suppose other Jewish children are given comparable help to their questions. I take it this exciting gossip makes its way in other circles as an advanced joke. So it is Christ whom Clov says does not exist yet. This may mean either that we are still, in the play, in the pre-christian age, with rumors, prophecies, hopes stirring; or that since we know there is a bastard, he has come, but not returned. (The French version notates the ambiguity: "Pas encore" is "Not yet." But also, I take it, "Not again.") Either way, "Not yet" is the most definite expression of hope—or, for that matter, of despair—in the play, the only expression of future which is left unchallenged, by contradiction, irony or giggles.

What weight is to be attached to this? Do those two words give *the* Endgame to this play of suffering, that with Christ's coming this will all have meaning? It seems unimaginable in this total context of run-down and the fallout of sense. Yet there is a coming at the end of the play, one which Hamm apparently takes to signal the awaited end, and upon which he dismisses Clov. Clov spies a small boy through the glass; it is a moment which is considerably longer in the French, but for some reason cut down in Beckett's English version. In the French, the boy is said to be leaning against a stone, and this seems a clear enough suggestion of the sepulchre. But even without this description, the character is sufficiently established by Hamm's response, which is to speculate about whether what Clov sees exists. (This is the only use of "exists" in the play outside the bastard remark.) The important fact for us is that after that earlier exchange between Hamm and Clov, it is Clov whose immediate response is to prepare to kill the newcomer, whereas Hamm, for the first time, prevents the destruction of a "potential procreator" (p. 78), saying in effect that he cannot survive anyway, that he will make no difference, present no problem. Earlier, Clov had expressed the straightest hopes for this coming, but he misses it when it comes; Hamm is now ready to admit that perhaps it has come but he sees that it is too late, that it was always too late for redemption; too late from the moment redemption became necessary. We are Christ or we are nothing—that is the position Christ has put us in.

## VI

Suppose this is what Hamm sees now that the boy has finally appeared. Does this mean the game ends, that Hamm now knows what he needs to know to end; that knowing there is no salvation from salvation or damnation, he can give up hope and fear, and end?

He knows nothing. His final soliloquy, like every other moment in the play, was planned, rehearsed. His first words are "Me to play"; it's his move, it's up to him. Over and over we are shown that everything that is happening has happened before. Just before his last speech Hamm the ham makes what he calls an aside and says he's "warming up for my last soliloquy" (p. 78). True, this is said immediately before the boy appears, so that what is in fact his last soliloquy may not be the one he had planned. However, the last soliloquy contains the same reference to conscious composition as the former ones do ("Nicely put, that," p. 83), and its content is about the same. Still, Clov is "dressed for the road," standing at the exit, and Hamm, a stage direction informs us, "gives up" (p. 82). Does Clov really leave? There is evidence for believing he does and evidence the other way. We don't know, they don't know. And if he does leave, is *that* the end?

This can't, I think, be the right track. The end Hamm seeks must be shown in the efforts made throughout the play. What are these efforts? Take these:

1. To play out a game, or drama, to a conclusion.
2. To finish a story.
3. To secure fruitlessness, and in particular:
4. To defeat meaning, of word and deed.

This ought to seem a set of goals split against itself: as though the end of the game will be to show that the game has no winner, the moral of the story to show there is no moral anyone can draw, its art directed to prove that art—the grouping of details to an overwhelming expression—does not exist; that games, plays, stories, morals, art —all the farcing of coherent civilizations—come to nothing, are nothing. To accomplish this will seem—will be—the end of the world, of *our* world. The motive, however, is not death, but life, or anyway human existence at last. Because what has happened since the Gods of the world went too far is that what used to seem life's leaven, the sources of meaning and coherence, the shelters from chaos and destruction, have now grown to shut out existence; morality, art, religion and the rest, lead lives of their own, grown out of hand, that shear man's existence from him. God shut us in. The result is that the earth is blotted out for man, sealed away by a universal flood of meaning and hope. The price of soaking it up will be no less high, for there is nothing to soak it up with except ourselves. A hope precipitated and concentrated through millennia will not swiftly recede, it comes back in waves. Splash, splash, always on the same spot.

Suppose what Hamm sees is that salvation lies in the ending of endgames, the final renunciation of all final solutions. The greatest endgame is Eschatology, the idea that the last things of earth will have an order and a justification, a sense. That is what we hoped for, against hope, that was what salvation would look like. Now we are to know that salvation lies in reversing the story, in ending the story of the end, dismantling Eschatology, ending this world of order in order to reverse the curse of the world laid on it in its Judeo-Christian end. Only a life without hope, meaning, justification, waiting, solution—as we have been shaped for these things—is free from the curse of God.

But Hamm can't do it. At one point, though he and Clov seem, as he puts it, to be "getting on," getting on together by getting on with the game of un-doing, still he doubts: "We're not beginning to . . . to . . . mean something?" Clov apparently laughs at the idea, but Hamm's doubt remains a moment, and he comes out with, "To think perhaps it won't all have been for nothing!", a climactic exclamation whose force, for me, indicates another of the revelatory utterances I have tried to describe. The exclamation remains perfectly ambiguous in attitude, poised between hope and despair. The obvious rhetoric is that of hope: Only think! The super-human effort won't have been for nothing, won't have been wasted; against divine odds we shall have come through. But in context it is a cry of despair (the stage direction leading to the question cites Hamm as "anguished"): Only think! The effort won't have been for nothing; therefore it will have been for something; but since divine odds insure that we can only mean the old things—namely the very things that have brought us into the sealing shelter—we cannot come through.

I think here of the quotation from St. Augustine which Beckett is reported to have offered as a help to *Godot*. Somewhere Augustine cautions: "Do not despair, for one of the thieves was saved. Do not presume, for one of the thieves was damned." The implication is that the correct attitude is hung between; between the despair and the presumption of salvation, absorbing both. That is the poise I hear in Hamm's exclamation, and perhaps as difficult to sustain.

The allusion in *Godot* is perfectly clear. Near its opening there is a discussion which begins: "One of the thieves was saved. A reasonable percentage." Reasonable indeed. Just the percentage you'd expect on the basis of chance alone, if there were no third. And an appropriate speculation beneath an empty tree, one on which there is no hanging man, no third. *Godot* is about waiting, about the inescapable fact that human beings are suspended, between future and past, hope and despair, beast and angel, mother and father, parent and child, birth and death, good and evil, heaven and earth. They wait; therefore they wait *for* something; and because they cannot not wait, what is waited for cannot, logically cannot, come; otherwise waiting would stop. "Man," says Nietzsche at the close of *The Genealogy of Morals*, a book which wants the end of morality, and of art, of knowledge, of hope, of man—"Man would rather take the void for his purpose than to be void of purpose." Hamm may not be much in the way of a Superman (but who is?), yet he faces the hard Nietzschean alternatives: either nihilism or else the task of purposely undoing, re-evaluating all the purposes we have known, re-locating the gravity of purpose itself. Perhaps it's not clear, perhaps he doesn't know, which alternative he has chosen. But who, having faced them, does know? They look so much alike.

What Hamm sees is that waiting is the final losing game, that waiting itself is damnation: for one waits either for damnation or salvation, and both are impossible. To destroy all flesh *save mine* is not a reasonable percentage. Sense cannot come of it, or rather sense *must* not come of it for it is damnation to think it can—but what else can we think as long as we wait and hope? The endgame Hamm centers is meant to end the waiting. Why does this require a game of strategy and skill? Because a man cannot simply *stop* waiting anymore than he can overcome a lack of air by stopping breathing. One solution is to wait for nothing, for zero, to make every goal empty, to accompany each wish by a wish for the opposite. (To wish that it will rain and that it will not rain is to wish for nothing; the same goes for the wish simultaneously to get out of and to stay in a relationship, or any shelter.) The result may be paralyzing, but at least it is not waiting, and therefore contains a seed of truth, that there is nothing to wait for. Another strategy would be to wait better, more effectively; to wear out waiting like a shirt.

This is also tried by Hamm and Clov. The canonical forms of waiting are Jewish messianism and Christian suffering. We've said something about the former, but the latter is coiled together with it in the play, in the play of our Jewish-Christian minds. Clov opens the play with a speech which declares, "I can't be punished any more." His meaning here is amplified in his last soliloquy, just before Hamm's last: "I say to myself—sometimes, Clov, you must learn to suffer better than that if you want them to weary of punishing you— one day . . . You must be there better than that if you want them to let you go . . ." And we heard Hamm at the start of his opening speech ask: "Can there be misery [he yawns] loftier than mine?" These beginning utterances suggest the uses to which suffering (or waiting), since we were taught to suffer, has been put, in order to end itself. Either it can make us good, worthy of pardon, or it can make us powerful, ascendant, worthy of praise. These are the endgames of suffering with which we begin: I win, my suffering ends, either when I learn perfectly that suffering is punishment, that is to say, that I deserve it, that I am perfectly sinful; or when I win the competition of suffering itself. These exhaust the strategies of suffering used in the shelter. To get out, these ways of winning have to be brought to an end; suffering has to stop being *used,* has to stop *meaning* anything, and become the simple fact of life. Where it is a game, it is a losing game; where existence is interpreted, sheltered, it is lost. Hamm and Clov both know this, and the play is about their efforts to forgo the losing win of suffering. This is why they try to give each other up, because apart from one another the strategies are pointless. Each requires his audience: Clov, because his worthiness must be seen; Hamm, because his loftiness must be appreciated. And the giving up of audience must present itself, both to the theologian and to the artist, as death.

Hamm, the artist, still hopes for salvation through his art; hopes to move his audience to gratitude, win their love through telling his story. It is the usual story of private guilt, complete with self-justifications and vengeance on his characters, and he's been telling himself that, told well enough, the burden of his guilty secret will be shared. His end of endgame will come when he is able to "speak no more about it" (p. 84), stop telling himself the old stories of justification, or the new story that salvation can be found in art, or indeed that art, as we have conceived and practiced it, has any relevance at all to our current necessities. I imagine all this is meant when Clov refers to Hamm's composition as "The story you've been telling yourself all your days" (p. 58). Perhaps he also means, most directly, that the biggest fiction is that one's days form a story, that you can capture them by telling them. (This is Sartre's best subject—purest in *Nausea*—and if he is relevant anywhere to the play, he is here.) Nowadays, if you pour the wine of new meaning into old bottles, it is the wine which breaks. And all bottles are old.

I am reminded here of another of the precious few properties called for in the description of the set: a picture, "its face to the wall." Someone is in disgrace, has disgraced those left behind. The suggestion is too salient for Beckett not to have meant us to make something of it. But who is out of grace? All of us, none of us? What pictures, turned to the wall, would mean either of these? It is possible we are to be left guessing, like his characters. I have imagined it variously: as an illustration of a biblical scene (perhaps of the Creation); as an icon portrait of Christ; as a family portrait of the four characters. It now seems to me that the picture may be turned not because anyone special is in disgrace, nor everyone special, but just because it is a picture. It is art itself which is disgraced, cursed because it makes the artist special, bullies his audience into suffering for him, contains his meaning, tells stories, loves floods.

As the play starts toward its close, Clov takes down the picture, keeping its face to the wall, and in its place hangs up an alarm clock. Hamm asks what he's doing and he replies, "Winding up" (p. 72). That is, ending; but literally—since the subject is a clock—starting. Apparently important business has focussed around that clock before, but only with reference to its alarm, not as something which tells time. What time it is has significance only when it may be time for something. Recurrently, Hamm asks whether it is time (for his pain-killer, or his story—which perhaps are the same) and says that it is time; but it is time no clock can tell. What is alarming is just time itself—that it is always time, that it is never time.

Once Clov suggests setting the alarm to signal Hamm that he has departed, not just died, and this is what happens as they try the alarm to see if it works, listening to its ringing to the end:

CLOV. Fit to wake the dead! . . .
    The end is terrific!
HAMM. I prefer the middle.

(Clov is the eschatologist to the end; Hamm, as usual, is caught in the middle.) They use it as a toy, or a musical instrument; they have their resources. Gabriel's is the other musical alarm to wake the dead (and is alluded to when Clov, as he and Hamm are winding up, removes the clock from the wall and puts it on the lid of Nagg's bin). But that cannot be what the alarm clock, run out, is supposed to mean —the significant, terrific end of time. They need to test the alarm because:

HAMM. The alarm, is it working?
CLOV. Why wouldn't it be working?
HAMM. Because it's worked too much.
CLOV. But it's hardly worked at all.
HAMM (angrily). Then because it's worked too little.

(p. 47)

Worked too little, because it's worked too much: we have been alarmed too often. What in God's name could there be, finally, to be alarmed about? Hang it on the wall, bury it on the tomb, as a monument, or memento, to time and to eternity. Hang the run-out object where art used to hang, for if only art is worth looking at, nothing is. Hang it up because it is a real thing, empty of function and alarm; and in the place of art, which is not able to recover for us the things of this world or of the next.

Clov had not, so far as we know, rewound the alarm, so we are not to assume that he has set the signal of his departure. Not that it matters, because if Clov's leaving Hamm is to secure their mutual lack of audience, this too is no end. An audience remains, in two locales: in each self and in heaven.

Self-consciousness is many kinds of curse, but specifically here in providing a witness for actions whose entire point is that they have no point. But a witness will, ineluctably, give them a point. That is the danger of strangers, that they will misunderstand, or that they will understand. It is the thought of this invasion of the self that produces Hamm's outcry, "Perhaps it won't all have been for nothing!". But even if the last man goes, how can I keep the point from myself, how not let the left man know what the left man is doing? If I could do that I would know prayer and charity; but that is back to the endgames we know about, and have tried and have lost.

The danger remains in heaven. The audience of the play is God, and its object is the reverse of prayer. I do not mean that its object is to achieve damnation; that is not the reverse of prayer but a parody of it, or a prayer to the Devil (which perhaps comes to the same). Its object is to show God not that he must intervene, bear witness to our efforts and aid and mitigate them, but that he owes it to us, to our suffering and our perfect faithfulness, to depart forever, to witness nothing more. Not to fulfill, but to dismantle all promises for which we must await fulfillment. "Lord, I believe; help thou my unbelief" now means: Help me not to believe.

Hamm's kinship to Hamlet has been mentioned. Abandoned sons, each is forced to redeem his father's soul, knowing that the task is a curse which requires taking his father's place; each uses the antics of methodical madness as his characteristic tactic; both are in a shelter which is thought of as a prison; the situations of both are paralyzing. (Nietzsche gave the answer to suggestions that Hamlet "cannot make up his mind." What Hamlet sees is the *cost* of action, the hardest of all truths, that redemption is impossible, that nothing makes up for anything. "All is absolute" says Hamm at the beginning of his play, and *Hamlet* is the Revenge Play to end revenge, which sees that revenge, getting even, is only the hardest of lies, in denying the hardest truth: we are never even and we are always even; the uniqueness of the human soul, held to be its greatest value, is its greatest curse. We are alone, separate. Who has made up his mind to that?) Finally, they are alike in helping to compose a play within the play, only Hamm's is the entire play. The surrounding play is the mind to date, with its cursing self-performances, its inheritance of testaments, its ghosts and their tasks. The play within the play is to show us how to acquit ourselves. And it is still to perform its work by catching the conscience of the King.

There are two Kings of the world of *Endgame,* Hamm and the old King, the King of Kings. That Hamm is a King, or takes a King's place, is shown in many ways. His identification with the Gods has been mentioned; and it is the clearest implication of the chess title. Further, he picks up direct lines from two of Shakespeare's rulers: from the most isolated, Richard the Third ("My kingdom for a night-man"(on drayhorse), p. 23) and from the most powerful, Prospero ("Our revels now are ended," p. 56). Above all he resembles Lear, and his world Lear's: there is the sexual disgust related, as also in *Hamlet,* to unassimilable revelations about a parent or child; there is, further, the catastrophic reversal of roles (Lear with the Fool; father with children; sanity with madness); it is a world pervaded by madness and the fear of madness—a fear not of chaos but of naked meaning; there is the attempt, and the inability, at renunciation; there is the obsession with Gods; there is the emphasis upon *nothing,* a thematic word in the play; it is the great secular play about suffering —showing that it has no known limits, and is absolute, unredeemable; and finally it is about life outside the shelter (of authority, family, place, sanity).

The ambition of Hamm's play, knowing all bounds, is to catch the conscience of both Kings. It is to catch Hamm's own, as has been suggested, by embodying it, turning it into art. It is to catch God's by showing him to himself naked. In it he will see a King, made in his own image, cursing his Kingdom, betraying his subjects and being betrayed by them, and having the poison of covenants and salvation poured into his ears. Claudius, at this point in his performance, calls for light. If God picks up his cue, he will remove the light he called forth to begin this entire business, and let earth find its own; or not find it. In the beginning God created the heaven *and* the earth; in the end the conjunction must be denied. That is the only effective Theodicy. God, accordingly, must repent once more—not indeed by destroying, nor again by sending salvation, but by doing nothing more: by repenting precisely all repentance. Above all, by stopping waiting. We waited for him and we were left waiting; now he waits for us and we keep him waiting. But that is vengeance, the game nobody can win, because nobody can end. If God would stop waiting, maybe then we could imitate him, finally, in that.

156 ✳ MUST WE MEAN WHAT WE SAY?

## VII

Solitude, emptiness, nothingness, meaninglessness, silence—
these are not the *givens* of Beckett's characters but their goal, their
new heroic undertaking. To say that Beckett's message is that the
world *is* meaningless, etc. is as ironically and dead wrong as to say it
of Kierkegaard or Nietzsche or Rilke, for whom emptiness or perfect
singleness are not states—not here and now—but infinite tasks.
Achieving them will require passing the edge of madness, maybe
passing over, and certainly passing through horror, bearing the
nausea Zarathustra knows or the vision of oneself as a puppet ("the
husk, the wire, even the face that's all outside") as in Rilke's fourth
*Duino Elegy*—not protesting one's emptiness, but *seeing* what one is
filled with. Then the angel may appear, then nature, then things,
then others, then, if ever, the fullness of time; then, if ever, the
achievement of the ordinary, the faith to be plain, or not to be.

If this is right, how can it be acted? How spoken? I am now not
thinking of the lines as directed between the actors, where there will
be many particular choices whether to read according to the literalization or to leave it latent. For example, the phrase "for the love of
God" *sounds* different as a cliché curse and as a literal appeal. Again,
it is possible that a given actor will be led to try the Hamm/home
utterance as the "growl or groan, sounding up from within" which
Rudolf Otto speaks about (cf. note 4). The problem arises in the
relation between an analysis of a piece of music and a performance of
it. The *Hammerklavier* Sonata can be analyzed as sequences of falling
and rising thirds, but it would be mad to perform the piece accenting
all intervals of a third. How much, or what points, of an analysis, do
you *play*? (Not, of course, that every performance must allow the
same resolution.) I raise the question just to suggest that it is not
unique to Beckett, or to modern theater, or to theater, but is one of
performance (or reading) generally. The first aesthetic fact about
performances is that they have audiences. And my question now is:
How are we to conceive of the audience of Beckett's (not Hamm's)
play? If we say, not that there *is* no audience, but that the goal of the
play is that there be no audience, then what are we to make of all
those people sitting out there in the dark, watching and listening?

These questions have seemed to me crucial and unanswerable, but now I think that I was looking for the wrong kind of answers, ones too new or too special. Partially the problem is one as old as Aristotle's about tragedy: How can such events give pleasure? The aesthetic problem about Beckett's dramaturgy is no more difficult, and perhaps no different: it still concerns how the people comprising the audience are different from those same people when they are not an audience. Partially the answer has to do with the conventions of the theater: getting rid of the audience is not necessarily a matter of emptying the theater, but of removing the concept and the status of *audience*.

What is an audience? A theoretical answer to this is not in question now, except to take encouragement from remembering that the audience, as we conceive it, is a fairly recent invention in the history of theater; so its disappearance or transcendence is not unthinkable. One recalls *The Birth of Tragedy*: "An audience of spectators, such as we know it, was unknown to the Greeks" (Anchor Book edition, p. 54). Nietzsche's is the profoundest discussion, to my knowledge, of the problem of audience—and hence, I suppose, of the aesthetics of theater generally. And his profoundest wish was to remove the audience from art, something that must present itself as an attempt to remove art altogether, an experience hardly foreign to us today, however little understood. Whatever philosophical difficulties must be faced, practical solutions are not hard to see. Practically, or conventionally, "audience"—for theater in the period after Shakespeare through, say, the 19th century—means "those present whom the actors ignore," those beyond the fourth wall. Deny that wall—that is, recognize those in attendance—and the *audience* vanishes. It seems a reasonable hypothesis that if anything is sensibly to be grasped as "modern theater" one of its descriptions would be the various ways in which modern dramatists have denied the wall.

Beckett's way is two-fold. First, while he does not speak *to* those out there (a possible form of denial) he never lets them forget that those on the stage are acting, and know they are acting. He makes the fact that they are acting one of their constant topics and problems. This is scarcely original. Second, he has his own way of putting the audience in the position of the actors; I mean in the position of the characters. In other theater the audience knows more than any character (for example, they know what happens when he is off stage); or some character knows more than the audience (for example, what is happening to him off stage). Not that it is a matter merely of entrances and exits—though to have called attention to these *as* conventions may itself be something of a dramaturgical discovery. It is a matter of our feeling that no one in the place, on the stage or in the house, knows better than anyone else what is happening, no one has a better right to speak than anyone else. Something is happening, something is happening to the actors (I mean the characters). In *Waiting for Godot*: "Nothing happens, nobody comes, nobody goes, it's awful." But in *Endgame* there is something more awful, namely the experience of something happening. Near the beginning (p. 13) Hamm asks (and the direction is, "anguished") "What's happening, what's happening?", and later (p. 32, and again "anguished") he reiterates the question. It's a normal question for a blind man, but both times Clov answers: "Something is taking its course." Near the end (pp. 74–5) Hamm says: "It all happened without me. I don't know what's happened." Then he asks if Clov knows what's happened, and in his next three small speeches he asks three more times. The concept is thematic, but at this point we can hardly enter a new theme. The suggestion is, partly, that for *anything* to happen is anguishing because that means the end has not come. But it also suggests that so far as something is *happening* to us, we are not *acting,* and if we are not acting, we are not in control; we have moved from the waiting of patience to the waiting of passion. And then anything can happen, in particular the most anguishing thing of all, that we may *change.* Any misery is better than that, I can always find some attitude toward my misery which exploits it, for the entertainment or enchantment of others, and to my fuller love of myself. But if I change, *I* am no longer intact; I die to my world. I would rather die.

To the extent the figures up there are not *acting,* but undergoing something which is taking its course, they are not *characters.* And we could also say: the words are not spoken by them, to one another; they are occurring to them. It is a play performed not by actors, but by sufferers. Clowns. Beckett has discovered how clowns would talk if they were given the power of speech, and if they couldn't be slapped any more (nobody has the strength), or trip (they can't walk), or do prat-falls (they can't sit). Their words take the falls for them, since they have to fall.

That what is now happening to them is not now happening to

us is our only difference from them—the deepest, the only unbreachable difference there is between two people: that they are two. The only difference, in the end, that counts.

Perhaps the sense of *happening* (vs. *acting*) is an effect of theater generally; and perhaps the point of Method acting is to demonstrate our new appreciation of this effect. I am far from clear about it, and I do not imagine that I have conveyed my experience of it, if it is there, in these poor descriptions. A good test case here is Paul Scofield's performance of Lear in the Peter Brook production. It shares with other great performances the immediacy, conviction, absorption of actor into character, of technique into expression, that we know how to expect, if rarely expect. But in Scofield the process occurs at a further stage, a place in which technique is not merely absorbed, but in which it seems altogether irrelevant; one does not see how the part can be entered gradually, and improved. One wants to say not that the character we know is embodied for us, but that the performance is about embodiment; it displays not merely the end-points of thought and impulse, but the drama by which impulse and thought find (and lose) their way through the body. Or: it is not merely that the words are so perfectly motivated that they appear to be occurring to the character, but that the style or delivery is itself one of *occurring*: the words do not so much express thought as they represent after-thought, or pre-thought. They are not so much what the character wishes to say as they are what he cannot help saying, the result not of expression but of failed suppression. Whether such a style can function as well in plays which are not themselves about madness and radical dissolution, is a further question. One would not expect Congreve and Shaw to yield to it; Chekhov certainly, and I have seen a performance of Alceste in Molière's *Misanthrope* which could be described this way.[7]

---

[7] The Brook production is relevant to what I have written in another way. It is said to have been inspired by the writing of Jan Kott in *Shakespeare Our Contemporary* (New York: Doubleday, 1964), one of whose chapters is titled "King Lear or Endgame." I have now read that essay (in the *Evergreen Review*, August–September 1964) and it may be worth mentioning briefly some reactions to work which may appear similar, which is, in some ways, obviously similar, and yet opposed in spirit to what I have wished to suggest. (1) Its momentum is provided by a *theory* which contrasts the tragic with the grotesque. Not that anything is wrong with theory as such, and even obscure theory can be enlightening. But in Kott's essay the theory seems too often not merely irrelevant to the lines of the play quoted as evidence, but to violate them, not by over-interpreting them but by muffling them. Whatever the limitations of the New Criticism

Beckett's peculiar value is most evident, to my mind, in his radical sense of the problem developing in our relation to our own words. (Wittgenstein indicates the level of this problem when he expresses dissatisfaction with the idea that we *hear* our own words (cf. *Investigations*, p. 199ff.). This suggests an exercise for the actor: not merely that he not listen to the words he always knew he would be saying, but that he not anticipate, in forward memory as it were, what he is about to say. Improvisation becomes an effort to regain a lost knack of spontaneity; and improvisation can itself become mechanical.) This is a discovery for the theater which goes beyond any obvious solution in given theatrical terms. Brecht calls for new relations between an actor and his role, and between the actor and his audience: theater is to defeat theater. But in Beckett there *is* no role towards which the actor can maintain intelligence, and he has nothing more to *tell* his audience than his characters' words convey. Theater becomes the brute metaphysical fact of separateness; damnation lies not in a particular form of theater, but in theatricality as such. If, against that awareness, theater were to defeat theater, then while theater loses, it thereby wins; we have not found our way outside, we have merely extended the walls.  —This is what makes one want to say to Beckett: Other writers claim that words are meaningless, that communication is impossible, etc.; but *you* really *mean* it, so why do you write? Other playwrights claim that there is no audience, but you really mean it, so why do you write plays? Esslin reports

(and one of the most serious is its lack, or casualness, of theory), its permanent contribution to the activity of literary criticism has been its renewed concentration on the autonomy of the given text. (2) The suggestion that Shakespeare can only be made "our contemporary" by virtue of a particular theory of his work seems to me philosophically disastrous (turning aesthetic theory into political ideology) and to falsify and cheapen what it is which makes certain literature "classic"—the fact that it is *always* our contemporary, though in any age it will turn a different side, and sometimes one very thin, to our immediate gaze. (3) The fact that a period's productions (or readings) of classics will be formed from within the art and sensibility contemporary with that period, is just that—a fact. To argue that it *must* be so is to miss the significance of the fact. It substitutes an ideology of modernity for the ineluctable shifts of consciousness which naturally yield what we will understand as relevantly modern. It seems to me to imply a distrust both of the contemporary and of the classic, to wish to *insure* their relation a priori rather than to determine what, in a given moment of history, the relation, in its complexity, is. Of course *productions* are events at which various histories of conventions—artistic, economic, political and social—meet; so that productions of operas and symphony concerts and commercial films as well as productions within professional theater, are dragged from contemporary relevance by their forced responsiveness to perceptions and conventions which are themselves unresponsive to live art. What therefore needs to be argued, and fought for, is not that productions become contemporary but that they be freed from the holds which prevent them from being contemporary.

this incident: "When Gessner asked him about the contradiction between his writing and his obvious conviction that language could not convey meaning, Beckett replied, "Que voulez-vous, Monsieur? C'est les mots; on n'a rien d'autre." Esslin's reaction to this continues: "But in fact his use of the dramatic medium shows that he has tried to find means of expression beyond language"—which strikes me as about as useful to say of Beckett as of Tennessee Williams or Mallarmé; and less true of these than of Al Capone, or Werther. I do not know what Gessner thought, but one hopes he knew it was Beckett speaking and knew he hadn't given an answer—or that he had made room for the next question: Why, if there are only words, do you use *any*? Which means: Why talk? To which Beckett's answer might have been: That's what I'd like to know.

Is there a *contradiction* between Beckett's "obvious conviction" about words and his going on using them? One could say: He doesn't use them just *any* way; and even: He doesn't *use* them at all (for example, to promise, to threaten, to pray, to apologize—the things words are used for) or sees how far he can go in not, in not saying more than the words. And one should add that "contradiction" is a good word, useful for describing a particular relation between two statements. Does it name accurately the relation between a conviction and an action which apparently proceeds as if the conviction weren't there? If it did, Beckett's problem, and ours, would be less serious than it is. (Mutually contradictory statements cannot both be true; but a conviction and an action which counters it can both be present.) We *have* to talk, whether we have something to say or not; and the less we want to say and want to hear the more willfully we talk and are subjected to talk. How did Pascal put it? "All the evil in the world comes from our inability to sit quietly in a room." To keep still.

More than once I have had to suppress an impulse to bring in *Ash Wednesday*, and in the end it had better at least be mentioned. The clearest connections, to my reading, are these: "Teach us to sit still"; "Teach us to care and not to care"; "Redeem the time"; "the Word unheard, the Word without a word"; and the Christian ambiguities in the ideas of birth and death, of the exhaustion of spirit and the inability to "turn." The claims are undeniable; but just because the confrontation with Christian writing would perhaps be the final test of the power of Beckett's sensibility (as the confrontation with a Marxian criticism was the initial test of his seriousness), it is too webbed and delicate to be handled quickly. I should hope, however, that the work I have wished to show in what I have written would seem a necessary preliminary to its description. In particular, the problem I see is this: Both Beckett and Eliot begin with a decisive experience of the truth of *Ecclesiastes*: e.g., the profitlessness of labor, the absoluteness of time. Section I of Eliot's poem is a virtual transcription of this position, including the injunction to "rejoice." But from here Eliot manages, as the poem progresses, to move from the joy of surcease to the joy of surrender; the direction is up. But can it really be *taken,* or does Eliot's assurance rely only on knowing his religion like a book? Eliot's Christianity ought to raise raw the fundamental aesthetic question of the relation of belief to art, since it contains the highest versions of both—where his belief is organizing his art and his art is testing his belief. If the direction Eliot descries can really be described, then Beckett's vision can be encompassed within Christianity. Within it, we could explain why we lack words, and have too many. We could re-understand the sense in which redemption is impossible, and possible: impossible only so long as we live solely in history, in time, so long as we think that an event near 2,000 years ago relieves us of responsibility rather than nails us to it —so long, that is, as we live in magic instead of faith. And we can re-interpret suffering yet again: I had occasion to complain that we take suffering as proof of connection with God; but a sounder theology will take *that* suffering to prove exactly that the connection has not been made, but resisted; for, as Luther's confessor had to remind him, God appears only in love. —But can we really believe all this, or *must* these explanations be given in bad faith, blinding us to what we *do* believe? Beckett tests this because he is the contemporary writer complex and single enough to match with Eliot. I do not mean that Rilke or Stevens or Frost are not large enough; but their worlds do not measure together, or they scrape, where Eliot's and Beckett's eclipse one another. It is not everyone's problem; but it may be anyone's.

Shall we blame Beckett because he cannot keep still? Then blame Hamlet because he cannot keep going? Why won't somebody stop us, or start us? Perhaps we've got something to complain about, and maybe it has to do with our efforts first to create and then to destroy our Gods. Nietzsche said we will have to become Gods ourselves to withstand the consequences of such deeds. Camus said we will never be men until we give up trying to be God. Que voulez-vous, Monsieur? Which do you pick? —We hang between.

# VI

# Kierkegaard's

## ON AUTHORITY AND REVELATION

"I myself perceive only too well," Kierkegaard says in beginning a second Preface to his Cycle of Ethico-Religious Essays, "how obvious is the objection and how much there is in it, against writing such a big book dealing in a certain sense with Magister Adler." His first answer to this objection is just that the book is "about" Adler only in a certain sense, the sense, namely, in which he is a Phenomenon, a transparence through which the age is caught. But that is scarcely a serious answer, because what the objection must mean is: Why use the man Adler in this way? And Kierkegaard has an answer to this as well: it enabled him to accomplish something which "perhaps it was important for our age that [I] should accomplish and which could be accomplished in no other way." This is not a moral defense for his treatment; it does not, for example, undertake to show that an action which on the surface, or viewed one way, appears callous or wanton, is nevertheless justified or anyway excusable. Kierkegaard goes on to offer what looks like an aesthetic defense of his treatment of Adler— "without him [I] could not have given my presentation the liveliness and the ironical tension it now has." This moral shock is succeeded by another as we realize that the presentation in question is not offered for its literary merit, but for its value as a case study; it is the justifi-

This book, *On Authority and Revelation: The Book on Adler, or a Cycle of Ethico-Religious Essays,* was translated, with an Introduction and Notes, by Walter Lowrie (Princeton: Princeton University Press, 1955). All references are to this edition.

cation of a surgeon, whose right to cut into people is based on his skill
and credentials and whose right to present his cases to others is based
on his office and on the obligation to transmit his knowledge to his
peers.

Why, on this ground, is the Adler case of profit? Of what is he a
typical, and until now undiagnosed, case? He is a case of a particular
and prevalent and virulent confusion, and an initial diagnosis is
broached: "Disobedience is the secret of the religious confusion of
our age" (xviii). But what is the secret? Isn't this just what the case
was widely known to be all about? Adler's claim to have had a revelation was certainly a case for the Church, and in particular a case of
confusion; he was suspended on the ground that his mind was deranged (Lowrie's Preface, p. ix) and finally deposed after replying
evasively to the ecclesiastical interrogatories. This seems patently a
case of trying unsuccessfully to evade the Church's authority. But it
seems Kierkegaard's view of the case is different: ". . . the whole
book is essentially . . . about the confusion from which the concept
of revelation suffers in our confused age. Or . . . about the confusion
involved in the fact that the concept of authority has been entirely
forgotten in our confused age" (p. xvi). The concept is *entirely forgotten*. This suggests not merely that Adler, for instance, was disobedient in this particular case; it suggests that Adler would not have
known what obedience consisted in. And it implies that no one else
would have known either, in particular not the Church. The concept
of revelation, on the other hand, is not forgotten; it is confused.
Adler suffers from this, but so do all men in our age, in particular
men of the Church. When Bishop Mynster appealed to Adler's mental derangement as the ground for suspending him, he was evading
the same thing Adler would come to evade, the claim to a revelation;
and in this evasion the Church is disobedient to its divine command
to preach and clarify, to hold open, the word of God.

So the case deepens. For it is not merely that the situations of the
extraordinary preacher and the ecclesiastical authority are morally
analogous, each suffering his own confusion and each falling into his
own disobedience. The third Preface Kierkegaard composed seems to
me to go farther, almost saying that they suffer identical consequences, the same confusion of mind, that they are both, as the age
is, spiritually deranged. The political events of 1848, which called out
this final Preface, are interpreted by Kierkegaard as an attempt to

solve a religious problem in political terms, an attempt which will go on, and with increasing confusion and fury, until men turn back to themselves:

> Though all travel in Europe must stop because one must wade in blood, and though all ministers were to remain sleepless for ruminating [about constitutional amendments, votes, equality, etc.] and though every day ten ministers were to lose their reason, and every next day ten new ministers were to begin where the others left off, only to lose their reason in turn—with all this not one step forward is made, an obstacle to it is sternly fixed, and the bounds set by eternity deride all human efforts. . . . Ah, but to get the conflagration quenched, the spontaneous combustion brought about by the friction of worldliness, i.e., to get eternity again—bloodshed may be needed and bombardments, *item* that many ministers shall lose their reason (p. xxi).

The book on Adler is about a minister who has lost his reason, and the flat ambiguity of Kierkegaard's "many ministers" registers exactly the ambiguity of concepts, the confusion of realms, which he finds the cause, and the content, of our sickness. Both political and religious ministers madly try to solve religious problems with political means, the one by "levelling" worldly differences into a horrible parody of what is, Christianly, already a fact; the other by trying to approach by reason what is always grasped by faith, or by trying to make a shift of emotion do what only a change of heart can do. This points to a second ambiguity in Kierkegaard's prediction, recorded in the phrase "shall lose their reason." To lose their reason, religiously understood as "[letting] the understanding go" (p. xxii) is precisely what the ministers, what we all, should do; it is precisely because we are incapable of that "leap into the religious" (but equally incapable of letting go of religious categories, of "Christianity of a sort") that we are confused. This is one way Adler is seen by Kierkegaard as a Satire upon the Present Age, and one prompting, throughout the book, for Kierkegaard's recourse to his categories of the comic and ironic. Adler performed the one saving act, he lost his reason; only he did it the way he does everything else, the way things normally are done in our reflective age: he did it literally, not religiously. He went crazy. But just in this lies the real defense of Adler, the *moral* answer to the question "Why expose Adler?" The derangement of this minister is shared by all ministers. Of course in his case the derangement may have got out of hand, he went too far; but this, as Kierkegaard says in the concluding sections of his book, is to his "advantage" as a Christian, because it came from a real spiritual movement toward inner self-concern. Religiously considered, other ministers are in the same, or in a worse, state; so it is unjust that Adler should be singled out for deposition on the ground of derangement. And the Bishop should have considered it religiously. For the Church, Adler is not a transparent medium, but an opaque glass, a mirror. Perhaps this is a way of seeing why, while Kierkegaard calls Adler a satire on the present *age*, he calls him an epigram on the Christendom of our age —a terse and ingenious expression of it.

Of course this does not mean that there are no valid religious grounds on which to question and perhaps depose Adler. What it means is that providing these religious grounds, in our age, for our age, will require *overcoming the specific confusion* which has deprived us of religious ground altogether; hence the form of activity will be one of *regaining clarity*. (In this book, Kierkegaard characterizes our age in a few, very specific, and often repeated, ways; his task is to provide correctives specific to them. For example, he finds that we are absent-minded, so his task is to provide presence of mind; he finds us lightminded (lightheaded?), so his task is to inject seriousness and balance; he finds us *distrait,* so his task is to attract our attention.) In his first Preface Kierkegaard says he uses the Adler case "to defend dogmatic concepts," and in the second Preface he claims that from the book one will "get a clarity about certain dogmatic concepts and an ability to use them" (p. xv). By "defend dogmatic concepts" he does not mean "provide a dogmatic backing for them," but rather something like "defend them as themselves dogmatic"; as, so to speak, carrying their own specific religious weight—something, it is implied, theology now fails to do—and this is a matter of coming to see clearly what they mean. So his task is one of providing, or re-providing, their meaning; in a certain sense, giving each its definition. This definition is not to provide some new sense to be attached to a word, with the purpose of better classifying information or outfitting a new theory; it is to clarify what the word does mean, as we use it in our lives— what it means, that is, to anyone with the ability to use it. Now an activity which has the form of taking us from confusion to clarity by means of defining concepts in such a way has, from Socrates to Wittgenstein, signalled philosophical activity.

As I do not insist that philosophy is exhausted in this activity, so I do not insist that Kierkegaard is, in this book, exclusively philosophical. The question I want to turn to is, rather: How far is the book on Adler to be considered a book of philosophy? There are several reasons for pressing this question:

1. It recognizes that the *kind* of writing before us is problematic, and so keeps faith with Kierkegaard's own efforts, as an author and as a Christian, to write distinct kinds of works.

2. This book is itself about writing, about the differences between real and fake authors: our amnesia of the concept of authority is expressed by an amnesia of genuine writing and reading: speech, never easy, has now fully become talk. Adler's confused disobedience to religious authority is not merely analogous to, but is instanced by his disobedience, as an author, to the requirements of art. Adler's books are not only fake religion, they are fake books—and the one because of the other.

3. The emphasis on philosophy distinguishes Kierkegaard's effort here from other efforts with which it may be confused:

*a)* If one says he writes to defend Christianity and to reform Christendom, then one must know his differences from (say) Luther. "[Luther's] . . . day is over," Kierkegaard said in a work composed during the period in which he was reading and writing about Adler; "No longer can the individual . . . turn to the great for help when he grows confused." [1] Luther saw the Church in bondage, Kierkegaard sees it in a position of false mastery and false freedom; Luther's problem was to combat a foreign institution motivated politically and economically, but Kierkegaard's problem is that the mind itself has become political and economic; Luther's success was to break the hold of an external authority and put it back into the individual soul, but what happens when *that* authority is broken? Luther's problem was to combat false definitions of religious categories, but Kierkegaard has to provide definition for them from the beginning; Luther could say, "The mass is not a sacrifice, but a promise," and now Kierkegaard's problem is that no one remembers what a promise is, nor has the authority to accept one.

*b)* The emphasis on philosophy serves as a corrective to calling it psychology. Kierkegaard is often praised in our age as a "profound

[1] Søren Kierkegaard, *The Present Age* (New York: Harper & Row, 1962, Torchbook), pp. 58, 81.

psychologist," and while I do not wish to deny him that, it seems to me attractively misleading praise, especially about such efforts as the present book; because what is profound psychology in Kierkegaard's work is Christianity itself, or the way in which Kierkegaard is able to activate its concepts; and because the way he activates them, wherever else it is, is through philosophy, through attention to the distinct applicability of concepts—perhaps one could say, attention to the a priori possibility of applying the concepts in general: it is what Kant called Transcendental Logic, what Hegel called Logic, why Oxford philosophers are moved to speak of their attention to words as a question of logic; Wittgenstein called it "grammar." Take the originating concern of the book on Adler: "How far a man in our age may be justified in asserting that he had a revelation" (p. 91). This is the question the Church ought to have confronted—in order to confront itself, as it stands, with the fact that it cannot answer it. Because this question of being "justified in asserting" is not a matter of determining how likely it is, given a certain man's psychological make-up and given a particular historical condition, that he had or will have a revelation (it is always unlikely); nor a matter of determining whether one is religiously prepared to receive a revelation (for, religiously speaking, there is no human preparation possible); nor a matter of determining psychological variation and nuance in different instances of the experience of a revelation and tracing its antecedents and consequences in a particular man's worldly existence. The question is whether, no matter *what* occurs in a man's life, we are conceptually prepared to call it a revelation, whether we have the power any longer to recognize an occurrence as a revelation, whether anything any longer could conceivably count for us as a revelation— could, so to speak, *force us to assert* that what has taken place is a revelation. Of course, anyone can, and occasionally will, *use the word* "revelation," to refer perhaps to a striking or unexpected experience —this, as emerged in the interrogation of Adler, is what happened in his case. And quite generally: ". . . every Christian term, which remaining in its own sphere is a qualitative category, now, in reduced circumstances, can do service as a clever expression which may signify pretty much everything" (p. 103). The serious issue, which is simultaneously the logico-philosophical and the Christian issue, remains: for a Christian church to be in a position in which it has to say that God is hidden or distant or silent, is one thing; for it to be in a position in which it would not find it conceivable that God should speak to us, is something else. In the latter case, the implication is, one should stop referring to such a thing as Christianity altogether.

Let me, then, call attention to two procedures characteristic of Kierkegaard's writing which I think of as philosophical, and philosophically correct:

1. He frequently wishes to show that a question which appears to need settling by empirical means or through presenting a formal argument is really a conceptual question, a question of grammar. (This is one way of putting the whole effort of the book on Adler.) Take the question John Stuart Mill raises in his essay on Revelation (Part IV of *Theism*): "Can any evidence suffice to prove a divine revelation?" Mill's answer, after careful consideration and reasoning is that "miracles have no claim whatever to the character of historical facts and are wholly invalid as evidences of any revelation"; but he adds to this the concession that if a certain sort of man ". . . openly proclaimed that [a precious gift we have from him] did not come from him but from God through him, then we are entitled to say that there is nothing so inherently impossible or absolutely incredible in this supposition as to preclude anyone from hoping that it may perhaps be true. I say from hoping; I go no further. . . ." From a Kierkegaardian perspective, Mill has gone nowhere at all, and indeed there is nowhere to go along those lines. For the answer to his question is just, No. The statement "A revelation cannot be proven by evidence" is not an empirical discovery, nor a sensible topic for an argument; it is a grammatical remark. (Religiously speaking, such a thing *is* "absolutely incredible.") One factor of Mill's hope is that there is a God through whom the gift can have come; and he regards someone as "entitled" to this hope because there is some evidence for his existence. For Kierkegaard, to hope for such a thing on such a ground is not an act of piety and intellectual caution; it is a hope for nothing: *hoping it* is as incoherent as *believing it firmly*. Other grammatical remarks in, or to be elicited from, the book on Adler are, for example, "Religion only conquers without force"; "One must *become* a Christian"; "Christianity is not plausible."

2. The other philosophical procedure to be mentioned is what Kierkegaard calls "qualitative dialectic." Very generally, a dialectical examination of a concept will show how the meaning of that concept changes, and how the subject of which it is the concept changes, as

the context in which it is used changes: the dialectical meaning is the history or confrontation of these differences. For example, an examination of the concept of *silence* will show that the word means different things—that silence is different things—depending on whether the context is the silence of nature, the silence of shyness, the silence of the liar or hypocrite, the short silence of the man who cannot hold his tongue, the long silence of the hero or the apostle, or the eternal silence of the Knight of Faith. And the specific meaning of the word in each of those contexts is determined by tracing its specific contrasts with the others—the way its use in one context "negates" its use in another, so to speak.

There is one dialectical shift which is of critical importance for Kierkegaard, that which moves from "immanent" to "transcendent" contexts. It is, I believe, when he is speaking of this shift that he characteristically speaks of a *qualitative* (sometimes he adds, decisive) difference in meaning. (This is the point at which his insistence on God as "wholly other" finds its methodological expression.) The procedure is this: he will begin with an immanent context, appealing to ordinary contexts in which a concept is used, for example, ordinary cases of silence, or of authority, or of coming to oneself, or of being shaken, or of living in the present, or of offense . . . ; and then abruptly and sternly he will say that these concepts are decisively or qualitatively different when used in a transcendental sense, when used, that is, to characterize our relationship to God. ("The situation is quite otherwise . . ."; "It is quite another matter with . . .") Sometimes he is *merely* abrupt and stern, and offers us no further help in understanding; as if to say, You know perfectly well what I mean; as if to rebuke us for having forgotten, or for refusing to acknowledge, something of the clearest importance. Sometimes, of course, he does go further; then he will describe what the life of a man will look like which calls for description, which can only be understood in terms of—which (he sometimes puts it) *is lived in*— Christian categories. A man's life; not a striking experience here and there, or a pervasive mood or a particular feeling or set of feelings. As if to say: in that life, and for that life, the Christian categories have their full, mutually implicating meaning, and apart from it they may have any or none (pp. 103, 104, 115, 165). And contrariwise, a life which does not invite, require description in terms of (is not lived within) the mutual implications of these categories—no matter how religious it is in some sense, and however full it may be of sublime and intricate emotion—is not a Christian life.

When I said that I thought this procedure was philosophically correct, I did not mean to suggest that I found it philosophically clear. As an *account* of "qualitative differences of meaning" (in terms of "immanence," "transcendence," "qualitative," etc.), I find it all but useless. But it begins and ends in the right place, with the description of a human existence; and each difference in each existence makes what seems intuitively the right kind of difference. And it seems to me right that Kierkegaard should suggest that we *do* or could know, without explanation, what it means to say that a man "stands before God" or that "This night shall thy soul be required of thee"; know what they mean not just in *some* sense, but know what they mean in a sense which we may wish to call *heightened*. That we may not know this all the time is no proof against our knowing; this may only indicate what kind of knowledge it is—the kind of knowledge which can go dead, or become inaccessible. Nor would the fact that we cannot *explain* the (heightened) meaning of such utterances prove that we do not understand them, both because it is not clear what an explanation would consist in, and because knowing where and when to use an utterance seems proof that one knows what it means, and knowing where and when to use it is not the same as being able to give an explanation of it. It is true that in the religious case an explanation seems *called for*; but this may only mean, one might say, that we are perplexed about *how* we know its meaning, not whether we do; and even that not all the time. And, again, this particular situation may be characteristic of a particular kind of meaning rather than a situation in which meaning is absent. There might even be an explanation for the sense, as I wish to put it, that we are balancing on the edge of a meaning. And Kierkegaard's explanations, however obscure, are not obviously wrong. He does not, for example, say that religious utterances are metaphorical.

While Kierkegaard's account sometimes refuses explanations of meaning, sometimes seems to rebuke us for being confused about a meaning which should be clear with a qualitatively decisive clarity, sometimes seems to suggest a mode of explanation for that sense of "balancing on the edge of a meaning," he would nevertheless not be surprised at Positivism's claim, or perception, that religious utterances have *no* cognitive meaning. Indeed, he might welcome this fact. It indicates that the crisis of our age has deepened, that we are no longer *confused,* and that we have a chance, at last, to learn what our lives really depend upon. Utterances we have shared about our infinite interests no longer carry any cognitive meaning. Well and good; we have now completely forgotten it. Then it is up to each man to find his own.

"To imagine a language," says Wittgenstein in one of his best mottoes, "is to imagine a form of life." When a form of life can no longer be imagined, its language can no longer be understood. "Speaking metaphorically" is a matter of speaking in certain ways using a definite form of language for some purpose; "speaking religiously" is not accomplished by using a given form, or set of forms, of words, and is not done for any further purpose: it is to speak from a particular perspective, as it were to mean anything you say in a special way. To understand a metaphor you must be able to interpret it; to understand an utterance religiously you have to be able to share its perspective. (In these ways, speaking religiously is like telling a dream.) The religious is a Kierkegaardian Stage of life; and I suggest it should be thought of as a Wittgensteinian form of life. There seems no reason not to believe that, as a given person may never occupy this stage, so a given age, and all future ages, may as a whole not occupy it—that the form will be lost from men's lives altogether. (It would be a phenomenon like everyone stopping having dreams.)

It is Kierkegaard's view that this has happened to the lives of the present age. Wittgenstein, late in the *Investigations,* remarks that "One human being can be a complete enigma to another. We learn this when we come into a strange country with entirely strange traditions; and, what is more, even given a mastery of the country's language. We do not *understand* the people. (And not because of not knowing what they are saying to themselves.) We cannot find our feet with them." Toward the end of the book on Adler, Kierkegaard has this:

> Most men live in relation to their own self as if they were constantly out, never at home. . . . The admirable quality in Magister A. consists in the fact that in a serious and strict sense one may say that he was fetched home by a higher power; for before that he was certainly in a great sense "out" or in a foreign land . . . spiritually

and religiously understood, perdition consists in journeying into a foreign land, in being "out" . . . (pp. 154–55).

One may want to say: A human being can be a complete enigma to himself; he cannot find his feet with himself. Not because a particular thing he does puzzles him—his problem may be that many of the puzzling things he does do *not* puzzle him—but because he does not know why he lives as he does, what the point of his activity is; he understands his words, but he is foreign to his life.

Other major writers of the 19th century share the sense of foreignness, of alienation, Kierkegaard describes; and not merely their own alienation from their societies, but of self-alienation as characteristic of the lives common to their time; which is perhaps the same as seeing their time as alienated from its past. They can be understood as posing the underlying concern of Kierkegaard's book: ". . . how it comes about that a new point of departure is created in relation to the established order" (p. 192; cf. p. xxi). Kierkegaard's answer is that it comes "from ABOVE, from God," but the test of this answer depends on confronting it with the major answers given it by (say) Marx, and Freud, and Nietzsche (both the Nietzsche of the *Birth of Tragedy* and the Nietzsche of *Zarathustra*). This should forcibly remind one how little of the complexity of Kierkegaard's book I have brought out; for politics, psychology, art, and the final break with God are all themes of the dialectical situation within which *The Book on Adler*, like Adler himself, is produced. I began by indicating some lines through which the religious plane intersects the psychological; let me end with a word or two about its intersection in this book with the political and with the aesthetic.

The Introduction, written one year before the *Communist Manifesto*, starts the imagery of the newspaper which recurs throughout the book—the image of its gossip, of its volatilization of concepts, the universal (no-man's) intelligence it wishes to be, the fourth estate which undermines the idea of *estates* altogether with their recognized authority and responsibilities, pulverizes them into a gritty mixture called the public, from whom nothing but violence and distraction can be expected. Four years earlier Marx had written some articles for his newspaper[2] against a rival editor who had raised the

---

[2] These pieces are collected under the title "The Leading Article of No. 179 of *Kölnische Zeitung*," in a volume of selected writings of Marx and Engels entitled *On Religion* (Moscow: Foreign Languages Publishing House, n.d.).

question: "Should philosophy discuss religious matters in newspaper articles?" Marx despises the mind which could frame this question as passionately as Kierkegaard would, and Marx responds to it by criticizing it, as Kierkegaard would; that is to say, he responds dialectically. The point of application of his criticism is evidently different, not to say opposite from Kierkegaard's, but it clarifies for me a particular lack in Kierkegaard's "ethico-religious investigation" of his age and of the way that determines its possibilities for a new departure. He was deeply responsive with the "criticism of religion" which Marx said is now (in 1844) complete in Germany (*Critique of Hegel's Philosophy of Right*). Kierkegaard can be seen as attempting to carry its completion to the North, while at the same time one of his dominating motives would be to criticize religion's criticizers. Nothing an outsider can say about religion has the rooted violence of things the religious have themselves had it at heart to say: no brilliant attack by an outsider against (say) obscurantism will seem to go far enough to a brilliant insider faced with the real obscurity of God; and attacks against religious institutions in the name of reason will not go far enough in a man who is attacking them in the name of faith. The criticism of religion, like the criticism of politics which Marx invented, is inescapably dialectical (which is, I take it, a reason Marx said it provided the origin for his criticism), because everything said on both sides is conditioned by the position (e.g., inside or outside) from which it is said. (This emerges in so differently conceived a work as Hume's *Dialogues,* in its outbreaks of irony.) Kierkegaard is fully dialectical where religious questions are concerned, as is displayed not merely in his long attention to different Stages of life, but in the many particular examples in which the same sentence is imagined to be said by men in different positions and thereby to mean differently. (On the recognition that they mean differently depends salvation, for the Gospel saves not because of what it says but because of who it is who has said it.) But his dialectical grasp is loosened when he comes to politics, where his violence does not see its own position and where the object he attacks is left uncriticized. He attacks newspapers and gossip and the public, as no doubt they deserve (on religious and on every other ground); but he does not consider, as it is Marx's business to consider, that what is wrong with them is itself a function of the age (not the other way around), and that a press which really belonged to the public (a public which belonged to itself) would reflect its audience otherwise than in gossip, and that its information would become, thereby, personal—existential in the relevant sense. We now know that this has not happened, but we should not therefore know that it is inevitable that it has not happened. I do not suggest that if it did happen Kierkegaard's problems would become solved, or irrelevant. But to the extent such a question is neglected, Kierkegaard's damning of society to perdition and his recourse to the individual, is suspect—it may be that a fear of the public is only the other side of a fearful privacy, which on his own ground would create the wrong silence and the wrong communication and provide no point for a new departure.

✳ ✳

In our age, as yet an unknown distance from that of Kierkegaard, we are likely to read his books as aesthetic works, thus apparently denying his fervent claims that they are religious (even, with the present book, ignoring his claim that it can be understood essentially only by theologians—a remark I choose to interpret ironically or aesthetically, as a rebuke to theologians for not attending to their job of defending the faith, in the categories of the faith, but instead help deliver it bound and gagged into the hands of philosophy). We read him running the risk, and feeling the pinch, of his damning outbursts against the merely curious, who translate the real terrors of the religious life into sublime spectacles of suffering with which to beguile their hours of spiritual leisure (cf. pp. 158–59). I take heart from the realization that both his and our concepts of aesthetics are historically conditioned; that the concepts of beauty and sublimity which he had in mind (in deploring the confusion between art and religion) are ones which our art either repudiates or is determined to win in new ways; that, in particular, our serious art is produced under conditions which Kierkegaard announces as those of apostleship, not those of genius. I do not insist that for us art has become religion (which may or may not describe the situation, and which as it stands describes phenomena other than those I have in mind) but that the activity of modern art, both in production and reception, is to be understood in categories which are, or were, religious.

The remarkable Introduction is, in effect, an essay in aesthetics

—or is something I wish aesthetics would become. Its distinction between "premise-authors" and "genuine authors" is drawn in a vital place—the place at which one must criticize a given work, perhaps the work of a given period, not as deficient in this or that respect, but dismiss it as art altogether. This kind of occasion is characteristic of the modern in the field of art. It does not arise as a problem until some point in the 19th century. I might call the problem "the threat of fraudulence," something I take to be endemic to modern art. One cannot imagine an audience of new music before Beethoven, or viewers of the paintings or spectators of the theater of that period, as wondering, or having the occasion to wonder, whether the thing in front of them was a piece of genuine art or not. But sometime thereafter audiences did begin to wonder, until by now we grow up learning and cherishing stories of the outrage and rioting which accompanied the appearance of new works, works *we* know to be masterpieces. At the same time, the advanced critics of the period in which this is becoming manifest (e.g., Matthew Arnold, Tolstoy, Nietzsche) were finding that it was precisely the work acceptable to the public which was the real source of fraudulence. It is characteristic of our artistic confusion today that we no longer know, and cannot find or trust ourselves to find occasion to know, which is which, whether it is the art or its audience which is on trial. Kierkegaard, who knew one when he saw one, defines the genuine author in terms of his moral relation to his work and to his audience: having a position of his own, the real author can give to the age what the age needs, not what it demands, whereas the fraudulent artist will "make use of the sickness of our age" (p. 5) by satisfying its demands; the genuine author "needs to communicate himself" (p. 8) whereas the false author is simply in need (of praise, of being in demand, of being told whether he means anything or not); the genuine is a physician who provides remedies, the false is a sick man, and contagious (p. 11). Kierkegaard has other ways of capturing the experience of this difference (which he calls a qualitative difference), and when we find him saying that

> . . . it is a suspicious circumstance when a man, instead of getting out of a tension by resolution and action, becomes literarily productive about his situation in the tension. Then no work is done to get out of the situation, but the reflection fixes the situation before the eyes of reflection, and thereby fixes (in a different sense of the word) the man . . . (p. 173)

we recognize that writers in our time, such as Georg Lukacs and Sartre, have not deepened this definition of the problem of modernism. Adler is, of course, a premise-author, and Kierkegaard goes on in the body of his book to use the out-throw of imagery and contrasts which emerge in this Introduction to mark the features by which one knows that Adler is no better an apostle than he is an author; in both fields he lacks, in a word, the authority. I do not suppose Kierkegaard meant to suggest that a genuine author has to have, or claim, God's authority for his work, but his description of the apostle's position characterizes in detail the position I take the genuine modern artist to find himself in: he is pulled out of the ranks by a message which he must, on pain of loss of self, communicate; he is silent for a long period, until he finds his way to saying what it is he has to say (artistically speaking, this could be expressed by saying that while he may, as artists in former times have, begin and for a long time continue imitating the work of others, he knows that this is merely time-marking—if it is preparation, it is not artistic preparation—for he knows that there are no techniques at anyone's disposal for saying what he has to say); he has no proof of his authority, or genuineness, other than his own work (cf. p. 117) (artistically speaking, this is expressed by the absence of conventions within which to compose); he makes his work repulsive, not, as in the case of the apostle, because of the danger he is to others (p. 46) but because mere attraction is not what he wants (artistically, this has to do with the various ways in which art has today withdrawn from, or is required to defeat, its audience); he must deny his personal or worldly authority in accomplishing what he has to do (artistically, this means that he cannot rely on his past achievements as securing the relevance of his new impulse; each work requires, spiritually speaking, a new step); art is no longer a profession to which, for example, a man can become apprenticed (religiously speaking, it is a "call," but there is no recognized calling in which it can be exercised); finally, the burden of being called to produce it is matched by the risk of accepting it (religiously speaking, in accepting or rejecting it, the heart is revealed). Art produced under such spiritual conditions will be expected to have a strange, unheard of *appearance*. Kierkegaard puts it this way:

> That a man in our age might receive a revelation cannot be absolutely denied [i.e., I take it, denying it would suffer the same con-

fusion as affirming it], but the whole phenomenal demeanor of such an elect individual will be essentially different from that of all earlier examples . . . (p. 46).

All this does not mean (it is not summarized by saying) that the artist *is* an apostle; because the concept of an apostle is, as (because) the concept of revelation is, forgotten, inapplicable. So, almost, is the concept of art.

To the extent that one finds such considerations an accurate expression of one's convictions about the modern enjambment of the impulse to art and to religion, one will want to re-examine the whole question of Kierkegaard's own authorship—a task which could take a form related to Kierkegaard's book on Adler: for Kierkegaard is a "case" with the same dimensions, and no less a phenomenon than Adler, if harder to see through. In particular, in the light of our un-aestheticizing of aesthetics, what shall we make of Kierkegaard's famous claim for himself that he was, from the beginning, a *religious* author, that the Pseudonymous works were part of a larger design which, at the appropriate moment, emerged in directness? [3] Since, presumably, he denied being an apostle, his claim says nothing about any special spiritual position he occupies as a Christian; he, like many others—like Adler—is a writer about religious matters. What the claim means, to our position, is that he is a *genuine* author, that he shares *that* fate. One fate of the genuine modern author is exactly his indirectness; his inability, somehow just because of his genuineness, to *confront* his audience directly with what he must say. Kierkegaard's claim to religious authorship sounds too much as though the Pseudonymous works were a strategy he employed for the benefit of others; whereas those works ought to be seen as a function of his inner strategy, as a genuine writer, to find ways of saying what he has it at heart to say. For it is very peculiar to us—in an age of Rilke, Kafka, Joyce, Mann, Beckett, non-objective painting, twelve-tone music—to hear an artist *praising* the strategy of indirectness, thinking to encompass its significance by acknowledging its usefulness as a medium of communication. What else have we had, in major art of the past hundred years, but indirectness: irony, theatricality, yearning, broken forms, denials of art, anti-heroes, withdrawals from

[3] See Søren Kierkegaard, *The Point of View for My Work as an Author* (New York: Harper & Row, 1962, Torchbook).

nature, from men, from the future, from the past. . . . What is admirable in a work like *Fear and Trembling* is not its indirectness (which, so far as this is secured by the Pseudonym, is a more or less external device) nor its rather pat theory about why Abraham must be silent. What is admirable, exemplary, is its continuous awareness of the pain, and the danger, of that silence—of the fear of the false word, and the deep wish that the right word be found for doing what one must: what, to my mind, Kierkegaard's portrait of Abraham shows is not the inevitability of his silence, but the completeness of his wish for directness, his refusal of anything less. Exemplary, because while we are stripped of Abraham's faith and of his clarity, it is still his position we find ourselves in. For certainly we cannot see ourselves in Kierkegaard's alternative, we are not Tragic Heroes: our sacrifices will not save the State. Yet we are sacrificed, and we sacrifice. Exemplary, because in our age, which not only does not know what it needs, but which no longer even demands anything, but takes what it gets, and so perhaps deserves it; where every indirectness is dime-a-dozen, and any weirdness can be assembled and imitated on demand —the thing we must look for, in each case, is the man who, contrary to appearance, and in spite of all, speaks.

# VII

# Music Discomposed

## I

It is a widespread opinion that aesthetics, as we think of it, became a subject, and acquired its name, just over two hundred years ago; which would make it the youngest of the principal branches of philosophy. Nothing further seems to be agreed about it, not even whether it is one subject, nor if so, what it should include, nor whether it has the right name, nor what the name should be taken to mean, nor whether given its problems, philosophers are particularly suited to venture them. Various reasons for these doubts suggest themselves: (1) The problems of composers, painters, poets, novelists, sculptors, architects . . . are internal to the procedures of each, and nothing general enough to apply to all could be of interest to any. One cannot, I think, or ought not, miss the truth of that claim, even while one feels that its truth needs correct placement. There *are* people recognizable as artists, and all produce works which we acknowledge, in some sense, to call for and warrant certain kinds of experience. (2) There is an established activity and a recognizable class of persons whose established task it is to discuss the arts, namely the criticism and the critics of literature, painting, music. . . . This fact faces two ways: One way, it suggests that there *is* something importantly common to the arts, namely, that they all require, or tolerate, such an activity; and that itself may incite philosophical reflection. Another way, it suggests that only someone competent as a critic of art is competent to speak of art at all, at least from the point of view of the experience which goes into it or which is to be found in it, so that an aesthetician incapable of producing criticism is simply incapable of recognizing and relevantly describing the objects of his discourse. (3) It is not clear what the data of the subject shall be. The enterprise of epistemologists, however paradoxical its conclusions have been, begins and continues with examples and procedures common to all men; and moral philosophers of every taste agree in appealing to the experience, the concepts, and the conflicts all men share. But upon what, or whom, does the aesthetician focus? On the artist? On the work he produces? On what the artist says about his work? On what critics say about it? On the audience it acquires?

One familiar resolution of these questions has been to commend the artist's remarks, and his audience's responses, to the attention of psychologists or sociologists, confining philosophy's attention to "the object itself." The plausibility of this resolution has strong sources. There is the distinction established in the philosophy of science according to which the philosopher's concern is confined to the "context of justification" of a theory, its "context of discovery" yielding, at best, to history and psychology. There is the decisive accomplishment, in literary criticism, of the New Critics, whose formalist program called for, and depended upon, minute attention concentrated on the poem itself. There is, finally, the realization on the part of anyone who knows what art is that many of the responses directed to works of art are irrelevant to them as art and that the artist's intention is *always* irrelevant—it no more counts toward the success or failure of a work of art that the artist intended something other than is *there,* than it counts, when the referee is counting over a boxer, that the boxer had intended to duck.

I cannot accept such a resolution, for three main sorts of reasons: (1) The fact that the criticism of art may, and even must, be formal (in the sense suggested) implies nothing whatever about what the content of aesthetics may or must be. Kant's aesthetics is, I take it, supposed to be formal, but that does not deter Kant from introducing intention (anyway, "purposiveness") and a certain kind of response ("disinterested pleasure") in determining the grounds on which anything is to count as art. And such books as *The Birth of Tragedy* and *What Is Art?* rely fundamentally on characterizing the experience of the artist and of his audience, and I am more sure that Nietzsche (for all his reputedly unsound philology) and Tolstoy (for all his late craziness) know what art is than I know what philosophy or psychology are, or ought to be. (2) The denial of the relevance of the artist's intention is likely not to record the simple, fundamental fact that what an artist meant cannot alter what he has or has not accomplished, but to imply a philosophical *theory* according to which the artist's intention is something in his mind while the work of art is something out of his mind, and so the closest connection there could be between them is one of causation, about which, to be sure, only a psychologist or biographer could care. But I am far less sure that any such philosophical theory is correct than I am that when I experience a work of art I feel that I am *meant* to notice one thing and not another, that the placement of a note or rhyme or line has a *purpose*, and that certain works are perfectly realized, or contrived, or meretricious. . . . (3) Nothing could be commoner among critics of art than to ask *why* the thing is as it is, and characteristically to put this question, for example, in the form "Why does Shakespeare follow the murder of Duncan with a scene which begins with the sound of knocking?", or "Why does Beethoven put in a bar of rest in the last line of the fourth Bagatelle (Op. 126)?" The best critic is the one who knows best where to ask this question, and how to get an answer; but surely he doesn't feel it necessary, or desirable even were it possible, to get in touch with the artist to find out the answer. The philosopher may, because of his theory, explain that such questions are misleadingly phrased, and that they really refer to the object itself, not to Shakespeare or Beethoven. But who is misled, and about what? An alternative procedure, and I think sounder, would be to accept the critic's question as perfectly appropriate—as, so to speak, a philosophical datum—and then to look for a philosophical explanation which can accommodate that fact. Of course, not just *any* critic's response can be so taken. And this suggests a further methodological principle in philosophizing about art. It seems obvious enough that in setting out to speak about the arts one begins with a rough canon of the objects to be spoken about. It seems to me equally necessary, in appealing to the criticism of art for philosophical data, that one begin with a rough canon of criticism which is not then repudiated in the philosophy to follow.

Confusion prescribes caution, even if the confusion is private and of one's own making. Accordingly, I restrict my discussion here primarily to one art, music; and within that art primarily to one period, since the second World War; and within that period to some characteristic remarks made by theorists of music about the *avant garde* composers who regard themselves as the natural successors to the work of Schoenberg's greatest pupil, Anton Webern. Though narrow in resource, however, my motives will seem extremely pretentious, because I am going to raise a number of large questions about art and philosophy and ways they bear on one another. Let me therefore say plainly that I do not suppose myself to have *shown* anything at all; that what I set down I mean merely as suggestions; and that I am often not sure that they are philosophically relevant. They are the result, at best, of a clash between what I felt missing in the philosophical procedures I have some confidence in, and what I feel present and significant in some recent art.

## II

I believe it is true to say that modernist art—roughly, the art of one's own generation—has not become a problem for the philosophy contemporary with it (in England and America anyway); and perhaps that is typical of the aesthetics of any period. I do not wish to insist upon a particular significance in that fact, but I am inclined to believe that there is decisive significance in it. For example, it mars the picture according to which aesthetics stands to art or to criticism as the philosophy of, say, physics stands to physics; for no one, I take it, could claim competence at the philosophy of physics who was not immediately concerned with the physics current in his time. One may reply that this is merely a function of the differences between science and art—the one progressing, outmoding, or summarizing its past, the other not. I would not find that reply very satisfactory, for two related reasons: (1) It obscures more than it reveals. It is not clear what it is about science which allows it to "progress" or, put another way, what it is which is called "progress" in science (for example, it does not progress evenly);[1] moreover, the succession of styles of art, though doubtless it will not simply constitute progress, nevertheless seems not to be mere succession either. Art critics and historians (not to mention artists) will often say that the art of one generation has

[1] See Thomas S. Kuhn, *The Structure of Scientific Revolutions* (Chicago: University of Chicago Press, 1962).

"solved a problem" inherited from its parent generation; and it seems right to say that there is progress during *certain* stretches of art and with respect to certain developments within them (say the developments leading up to the establishment of sonata form, or to the control of perspective, or to the novel of the nineteenth century). Moreover, the succession of art styles is *irreversible,* which may be as important a component of the concept of progress as the component of superiority. And a new style not merely replaces an older one, it may change the significance of any earlier style; I do not think this is merely a matter of changing taste but a matter also of changing the *look,* as it were, of past art, changing the ways it can be described, outmoding some, bringing some to new light—one may even want to say, it can change what the past *is,* however against the grain that sounds. A generation or so ago, "Debussy" referred to music of a certain ethereal mood, satisfying a taste for refined sweetness or poignance; today it refers to solutions for avoiding tonality: I find I waver between thinking of that as a word altering its meaning and thinking of it as referring to an altered object. (2) Critics, on whom the philosopher may rely for his data, *are* typically concerned with the art of their time, and what they find it relevant to say about the art of any period will be molded by that concern. If I do not share those concerns, do I understand what the critic means? Virtually every writer I have read on the subject of non-tonal music will at some point, whether he likes it or not, compare this music explicitly with tonal music; a critic like Georg Lukacs will begin a book by comparing (unfavorably) Bourgeois Modernism with the Bourgeois Realism of the nineteenth century; Clement Greenberg will write, "From Giotto to Courbet, the painter's first task had been to hollow out an illusion of three-dimensional space on a flat surface. . . . This spatial illusion or rather the sense of it, is what we may miss [in Modernism] even more than we do the images that used to fill it." Now, do I understand these comparisons if I do not share their experience of the modern? I do not mean merely that I shall not then understand what they say about modern art; I mean that I shall not then understand what they see in traditional art: I feel I am *missing* something about art altogether, something, moreover, which an earlier critic could not give me.

## III

The writing I have begun studying, and upon which I base my observations, occurs largely in two sets of professional periodicals: *Die Reihe*, whose first issue appeared in 1955; and *Perspectives of New Music*, starting in 1962.[2] Both were created in direct response to "the general problems relating to the composition of music in our time," as the prefatory note to *Die Reihe*'s first number puts it. Opening these periodicals, and allowing time to adapt to the cross-glare of new terms, symbols invented for the occasion, graphs, charts, some equations . . . several general characteristics begin to emerge as fairly common to their contents. There is, first, an obsession with *new-ness* itself, every other article taking some position about whether the novelty of the new music is radical, or less than it seems, whether it is aberrant or irreversible, whether it is the end of music as an art, or a reconception which will bring it new life. None, that I recall, raises the issue as a problem to be investigated, but as the cause of hope or despair or fury or elation. It is characteristic to find, in one and the same article, analyses of the most intimidating technicality and arcane apparatus, combined or ended with a mild or protracted cough of philosophy (e.g., "The new music aspires to Being, not to Becoming"). If criticism has as its impulse and excuse the opening of access between the artist and his audience, giving voice to the legitimate claims of both, then there is small criticism in these pages— although there is a continuous reference to the *fact* that artist and audience are out of touch, and a frequent willingness to assign blame to one or the other of them. One is reminded that while the history of literary criticism is a part of the history of literature, and while the history of visual art is written by theorists and connoisseurs of art for whom an effort at accurate phenomenology can be as natural as the deciphering of iconography, histories of music contain virtually no criticism or assessment of their objects, but concentrate on details of its notation or its instruments or the occasions of its performance. The serious attempt to articulate a *response* to a piece of music, where more than reverie, has characteristically stimulated mathe-

---

[2] *Die Reihe*, Theodore Presser Co., Bryn Mawr, Pennsylvania, in association with Universal Edition. *Perspectives of New Music*, Princeton University Press.

matics or metaphysics—as though music has never quite become one of the facts of life, but shunts between an overwhelming directness and an overweening mystery. Is this because music, as we know it, is the newest of the great arts and just has not had the time to learn how to criticize itself; or because it inherently resists verbal transcriptions? (Both have been said, as both are said in accounting for the lack of a canon of criticism about the cinema.) Whatever the cause, the absence of humane music criticism (of course there are isolated instances) seems particularly striking against the fact that music has, among the arts, the most, perhaps the only, systematic and precise vocabulary for the description and analysis of its objects. Somehow that possession must itself be a liability; as though one now undertook to criticize a poem or novel armed with complete control of medieval rhetoric but ignorant of the modes of criticism developed in the past two centuries.

A final general fact about the writing in these periodicals is its concentration on the composer and his problems; a great many of the articles are produced by composers themselves, sometimes directly about, sometimes indirectly, their own music. Professor Paul Oskar Kristeller, in his review of the writing about the arts produced from Plato to Kant, notices in his final reflections that such writing has typically proceeded, and its categories and style thereby formed, from the spectator's or amateur's point of view.[3] Does the presence of these new journals of music indicate that the artist is, some place, finally getting the attention he deserves? But one can scarcely imagine a serious journal contributed to by major poets, novelists, or painters devoted to the problems of the making of poems and novels and paintings, nor that any such artist would find it useful if somehow it appeared. It might even be regarded by them as unseemly to wash these problems in public, and at best it distracts from the job of getting on with real work. Magazines are for interviews or for publishing one's work and having others write about it. Why is it not regarded as unseemly or distracting by composers? Perhaps it is. Then what necessity overrides a more usual artistic reticence? Perhaps it is an awareness that the problems composers face now are no longer merely private but are the problems of their art in general, "the general problems relating to the composition of music in our time."

[3] "The Modern System of the Arts," reprinted in *Renaissance Thought II* (New York, 1965), p. 225.

(This is likely to seem at once unmentionably obvious to composers and unintelligible to spectators, which is itself perhaps a measure of the problems of composition in our time.) This further suggests, as in the case of ordinary learned journals, the emergence of a new universal style or mode of procedure, implying an unparalleled dispersal of those who must inescapably be affected by one another's work. Painting still grows, as it always has, in particular cities; apprenticeship and imitation are still parts of its daily life. Writers do not share the severe burden of modernism which serious musicians and painters and sculptors have recognized for generations: a writer can still work with the words we all share, more or less, and have to share; he still, therefore, has an audience with the chance of responding to the way *he* can share the words more than more or less. My impression is that serious composers have, and feel they have, all but lost their audience, and that the essential reason for this (apart, for example, from the economics and politics of getting performances) has to do with crises in the internal, and apparently irreversible, developments within their own artistic procedures. This is what I meant by "the burden of modernism": the procedures and problems it now seems necessary to composers to employ and confront to make a work of art at all *themselves* insure that their work will not be comprehensible to an audience.

This comes closer to registering the dissonant and unresolved emotion in the pages to which I refer. They are prompted by efforts to communicate with an audience lost, and to compose an artistic community in disarray—efforts which only the art itself can accomplish. So the very existence of such periodicals suggests that they cannot succeed.

But here a difference of animus in these two periodicals becomes essential. *Die Reihe* began first, with an issue on electronic music, and its general tone is one of self-congratulation and eagerness for the future, whether it contains art and composers and performers or not. *Perspectives* began publication seven years later (and lean years or fat, seven years in our period may contain an artistic generation); and for a variety of reasons its tone is different. It is committed to much of the same music, shares some of the same writers, but the American publication is quite old world in its frequent concern with tradition and the artist and the performer, and in its absence of belief that progress is assured by having *more* sounds and rhythms, etc., available for exploitation. Whatever the exact pattern of rancors and rites in these pages, the sense of conflict is unmistakable, and the air is of men fighting for their artistic lives. Perhaps, then, their theories and analyses are not addressed to an audience of spectators, but as has been suggested about their music itself, to one another. The communications often include artistic manifestos, with declarations of freedom and promises for the future. But unlike other manifestos, they are not meant to be personal; they do not take a position against an establishment, for they represent the establishment; a young composer, therefore, seems confronted not by one or another group of artists but by one or another official philosophy, and his artistic future may therefore seem to depend not on finding his own conviction but on choosing the right doctrine. Sometimes they sound like the dispassionate analyses and reports assembled in professional scientific and academic journals. But unlike those journals they are not organs of professional societies with fairly clear requirements for membership and universally shared criteria for establishing competence, even eminence, within them. One comes to realize that these professionals themselves do not quite know who is and who is not rightly included among their peers, whose work counts and whose does not. No wonder then, that we outsiders do not know. And one result clearly communicated by these periodicals is that there is no obvious way to find out.

What they suggest is that the possibility of fraudulence, and the experience of fraudulence, is endemic in the experience of contemporary music; that its full impact, even its immediate relevance, depends upon a willingness to trust the object, knowing that the time spent with its difficulties may be betrayed. I do not see how anyone who has experienced modern art can have avoided such experiences, and not just in the case of music. Is Pop Art art? Are canvases with a few stripes or chevrons on them art? Are the novels of Raymond Roussel or Alain Robbe-Grillet? Are art movies? A familiar answer is that time will tell. But my question is: *What* will time tell? That certain departures in art-like pursuits have become established (among certain audiences, in textbooks, on walls, in college courses); that *someone* is treating them with the respect due, we feel, to art; that one no longer has the right to question their status? But in waiting for time to tell that, we miss what the present tells—that the dangers of fraudulence, and of trust, are essential to the experience of art. If anything in this paper should count as a thesis, that is my thesis. And it is meant quite generally. Contemporary music is only the clearest case of something common to modernism as a whole, and modernism only makes explicit and bare what has always been true of art. (That is almost a definition of modernism, not to say its purpose.) Aesthetics has so far been the aesthetics of the classics, which is as if we investigated the problem of other minds by using as examples our experience of *great* men or *dead* men. In emphasizing the experiences of fraudulence and trust as essential to the experience of art, I am in effect claiming that the answer to the question "What is art?" will in part be an answer which explains why it is we treat certain objects, or how we *can* treat certain objects, in ways normally reserved for treating persons.

Both Tolstoy's *What Is Art?* and Nietzsche's *Birth of Tragedy* begin from an experience of the fraudulence of the art of their time. However obscure Nietzsche's invocation of Apollo and Dionysus and however simplistic Tolstoy's appeal to the artist's sincerity and the audience's "infection," their use of these concepts is to specify the genuine in art in opposition to specific modes of fraudulence, and their meaning is a function of that opposition. Moreover, they agree closely on what those modes of fraudulence are: in particular, a debased Naturalism's heaping up of random realistic detail, and a debased Romanticism's substitution of the stimulation and exacerbation of feeling in place of its artistic control and release; and in both, the constant search for "effects."

## IV

How can fraudulent art be exposed? Not, as in the case of a forgery or counterfeit, by comparing it with the genuine article, for there *is* no genuine article of the right kind. Perhaps it helps to say: If we call it a matter of comparing something with the genuine article, we have to add (1) that what counts as the genuine article, is not *given*, but itself requires critical determination; and (2) that what needs to be exposed is not that a work is a *copy*. (That of course *may* be an issue, and that *may* be an issue of forgery. Showing fraudulence is more like showing something is imitation—not: *an* imitation. The emphasis is not on copying a *particular* object, as in forgery and counterfeit, but on producing *the effect* of the genuine, or having some of its properties.) Again, unlike the cases of forgery and counterfeit, there is no one feature, or definite set of features, which may be described in technical handbooks, and no specific tests by which its fraudulence can be detected and exposed. Other frauds and imposters, like forgers and counterfeiters, admit *clear* outcomes, conclude in dramatic discoveries—the imposter is unmasked at the ball, you find the counterfeiters working over their press, the forger is caught signing another man's name, or he confesses. There are no such proofs possible for the assertion that the art accepted by a public is fraudulent; the artist himself may not know; and the critic may be shown up, not merely as incompetent, nor unjust in accusing the wrong man, but as taking others in (or out); that is, as an imposter.

The only exposure of false art lies in recognizing something about the object itself, but something whose recognition requires exactly the same capacity as recognizing the genuine article. It is a capacity not insured by understanding the language in which it is composed, and yet we may not understand what is said; nor insured by the healthy functioning of the senses, though we may be told we do not *see* or that we fail to *hear* something; nor insured by the aptness of our logical powers, though what we may have missed was the object's consistency or the way one thing followed from another. We may have missed its tone, or neglected an allusion or a cross current, or failed to see its point altogether; or the object may not have established its tone, or buried the allusion too far, or be confused in its point. You often do not know which is on trial, the object or the viewer: modern art did not invent this dilemma, it merely insists upon it. The critic will have to *get* us to see, or hear or realize or notice; help us to appreciate the tone; convey the current; point to a connection; show how to take the thing in. . . . What this getting, helping, conveying, and pointing consist in will be shown in the specific ways the critic accomplishes them, or fails to accomplish them. Sometimes you can say he is exposing an object to us (in its fraudulence, or genuineness); sometimes you can say he is exposing us to the object. (The latter is, one should add, not always a matter of noticing fine differences by exercising taste; sometimes it is a matter of admitting the lowest common emotion.) Accordingly, the critic's anger is sometimes directed at an object, sometimes at its audience, often at both. But sometimes, one supposes, it is produced by the frustrations inherent in his profession. He is part detective, part lawyer, part judge, in a country in which crimes and deeds of glory look alike, and in which the public not only, therefore, confuses one with the other, but does not know that one or the other has been committed; not because the news has not got out, but because what counts as the one or the other cannot be defined until it happens; and when it has happened there is no sure way he can get the news out; and no way at all without risking something like a glory or a crime of his own.

*One* line of investigation here would be to ask: Why does the assertion "You have to *hear* it!" mean what it does? Why is its sense conveyed with a word which emphasizes the function of a sense organ, and in the form of an imperative? The combination is itself striking. One cannot be commanded to hear a sound, though one can be commanded to listen to it, or for it. Perhaps the question is: How does it happen that the *achievement* or *result* of using a sense organ comes to be thought of as the *activity* of that organ—as though the aesthetic experience had the form not merely of a continuous effort (e.g., listening) but of a continuous achievement (e.g., hearing).

Why—on pain of what—must I hear it; what consequence befalls me if I don't? One answer might be: Well, then I wouldn't hear it—which at least says that there is no point to the hearing beyond itself; it is worth doing in itself. Another answer might be: Then I wouldn't *know* it (what it is about, what it is, what's happening, what is *there*). And what that seems to say is that works of art are objects of the sort that can only be *known in sensing*. It is not, as in the case of ordinary material objects, that I know *because* I see, or that seeing is *how* I know (as opposed, for example, to being told, or figuring it out). It is rather, one may wish to say, that *what* I know is what I see; or even: seeing *feels* like knowing. ("Seeing the point" conveys this sense, but in ordinary cases of seeing the point, once it's seen it's known, or understood; about works of art one may wish to say that they require a continuous seeing of the point.) Or one may even say: In such cases, knowing functions like an organ of sense. (The religious, or mystical, resonance of this phrase, while not deliberate, is welcome. For religious experience is subject to distrust on the same grounds as aesthetic experience is: by those to whom it is foreign, on the ground that its claims must be false; by those to whom it is familiar, on the ground that its quality must be tested.)

Another way one might try to capture the idea is by saying: Such objects are only *known by feeling,* or *in* feeling. This is not the same as saying that the object expresses feeling, or that the aesthetic response consists in a feeling of some sort. Those are, or may be, bits of a theory about the aesthetic experience and its object; whereas what I am trying to describe, or the descriptions I am trying to hit on, would at best serve as data for a theory. What the expression "known by feeling" suggests are facts (or experiences) such as these: (1) What I know, when I've *seen* or *heard* something is, one may wish to say, not a matter of *merely* knowing it. But what more is it? Well, as the words say, it is a matter of *seeing* it. But one could also say that it is not a matter of *merely* seeing it. But what more is it? Perhaps "merely knowing" should be compared with "not really knowing": "You don't really know what it's like to be a Negro"; "You don't really know how your remark made her feel"; "You don't really know what I mean when I say that Schnabel's slow movements give the impression not of slowness but of infinite length." You merely say the words. The issue in each case is: What would *express* this knowledge? It is not that my knowledge will be real, or more than *mere* knowledge, when I acquire a particular feeling, or come to see something. For the issue can also be said to be: What would express the acquisition of that feeling, or show that you have seen the thing? And the answer might be that I now *know* something I didn't know before. (2) "Knowing by feeling" is not like "knowing by touching"; that is, it is not a case of providing the *basis* for a claim to know. But one could say that feeling functions as a touchstone: the mark left on the stone is out of the sight of others, but the result is one of knowledge, or has the form of knowledge—it is directed to an object, the object has been tested, the result is one of conviction. This seems to me to suggest why one is anxious to communicate the experience of such objects. It is not merely that I want to tell you how it is with me, how I feel, in order to find sympathy or to be left alone, or for any other of the reasons for which one reveals one's feelings. It's rather that I want to tell you something I've seen, or heard, or realized, or come to understand, for the reasons for which *such* things are communicated (because it is news, about a world we share, or could). Only I find that I can't *tell* you; and that makes it all the more urgent to tell you. I want to tell you because the knowledge, unshared, is a burden—not, perhaps, the way having a secret can be a burden, or being misunderstood; a little more like the way, perhaps, not being believed is a burden, or not being trusted. It matters that others know what I see, in a way it does not matter whether they know my tastes. It matters, there is a burden, because unless I can tell what I know, there is a suggestion (and to myself as well) that I do *not* know. But I do—what I see is *that* (pointing to the object). But for that to communicate, you have to see it too. Describing one's experience of art is itself a form of art; the burden of describing it is like the burden of producing it. Art is often praised because it brings men together. But it also separates them.

The list of figures whose art Tolstoy dismisses as fraudulent or irrelevant or bad, is, of course, unacceptably crazy: most of Beethoven, all of Brahms and Wagner; Michelangelo, Renoir; the Greek dramatists, Dante, Shakespeare, Milton, Goethe, Ibsen, Tolstoy. . . . But the sanity of his procedure is this: it confronts the fact that we often do not find, and have never found, works we would include in a canon of works of art to be of importance or revelance to us. And the implication is that apart from this we cannot know that they are art, or what makes them art. One could say: objects so canonized do not exist for us. This strikes Tolstoy as crazy—as though we were to say we know that there are other minds because other people have told us there are.

V

But I was discussing some writing now current about the new music. Perhaps I can say more clearly why it leads, or has led me, to these various considerations by looking at three concepts which recur in it over and over—the concepts of composition, improvisation, and chance.

The reason for their currency can be put, roughly, this way. The innovations of Schoenberg (and Bartok and Stravinsky) were necessitated by a crisis of composition growing out of the increasing chromaticism of the nineteenth century which finally overwhelmed efforts to organize music within the established assumptions of tonality. Schoenberg's solution was the development of the twelve-tone system which, in effect, sought to overcome this destructiveness of chromaticism by accepting it totally, searching for ways to organize a rigidly recurring total chromatic in its own terms. History aside, what is essential is that no assumption is any longer to be made about how compositional centers or junctures could be established—e.g., by establishing the "dominant" of a key—and the problem was one of discovering what, in such a situation, could be heard as serving the structural functions tonality used to provide. Schoenberg's twelve-tone "rows" and the operations upon them which constitute his system, were orderings and operations upon pitches (or, more exactly, upon the familiar twelve classes of pitches). About 1950, composers were led to consider that variables of musical material other than its pitches could also be subjected to serial ordering and its Schoenbergian transformations—variables of rhythm, duration, density, timbre, dynamics, and so on. But now, given initial series of pitches, rhythms, timbres, dynamics, etc., together with a plot of the transformations each is to undergo, and a piece is written or, rather, determined; it is, so it is said, totally organized. What remains is simply to translate the rules into the notes and values they determine and see what we've got. Whether what such procedures produce is music or not, they certainly produced philosophy. And it is characteristic of this philosophy to appeal to the concepts of composition, chance, and improvisation.

The motives or necessities for these concepts are not always the same. In the writing of John Cage, chance is explicitly meant to *replace* traditional notions of art and composition; the radical ceding of the composer's control of his material is seen to provide a profounder freedom and perception than mere art, for all its searches, had found. In the defense of "total organization," on the contrary, chance and improvisation are meant to *preserve* the concepts of art and composition for music; to explain how, although the composer exercises choice only over the initial conditions of his work, the determinism to which he then yields his power itself creates the spontaneity and surprise associated with the experience of art; and either (a) because it produces combinations which are unforeseen, or (b) because it includes directions which leave the performer free to choose, i.e., to improvise. It is scarcely unusual for an awareness of determinism to stir philosophical speculation about the possibilities of freedom and choice and responsibility. But whereas the more usual motivation has been to preserve responsibility in the face of determinism, these new views wish to preserve choice by foregoing responsibility (for everything but the act of "choosing").

Let us listen to one such view, from Ernst Krenek, who was for years a faithful disciple of Schoenberg and who has emerged as an important spokesman for total organization.

> Generally and traditionally "inspiration" is held in great respect as the most distinguished source of the creative process in art. It should be remembered that inspiration by definition is closely related to chance, for it is the very thing that cannot be controlled, manufactured or premeditated in any way. It is what falls into the mind (according to the German term *Einfall*) unsolicited, unprepared, unrehearsed, coming from nowhere. This obviously answers the definition of chance as "the absence of any known reason why an event should turn out one way rather than another." Actually the composer has come to distrust his inspiration because it is not really as innocent as it was supposed to be, but rather conditioned by a tremendous body of recollection, tradition, training, and experience. In order to avoid the dictations of such ghosts, he prefers to set up an impersonal mechanism which will furnish, according to premeditated patterns, unpredictable situations . . . the creative act takes place in an area in which it has so far been entirely unsuspected, namely in setting up the serial statements. . . . What happens afterwards is predetermined by the selection of the mechanism, but not premeditated except as an unconscious result of the predetermined operations. The unexpected happens by necessity. The surprise is built in. ("Extents and Limits of Serial Techniques," *Musical Quarterly*, XLVI, 1960, pp. 228–229.)

This is not serious, but it is meant; and it is symptomatic—the way it is symptomatic that early in Krenek's paper he suggests that the twelve-tone technique "appears to be a special, or limiting, case of serial music, similar to an interpretation of Newtonian mechanics as a limiting expression of the Special Theory of Relativity, which in turn has been explained as a limiting expression of that General Theory." (Note the scientific caution of "appears to be.") The vision of our entire body of recollection, tradition, training, and experience as so many ghosts *could* be serious. It was serious, in their various ways, for Kierkegaard, Marx, Nietzsche, Emerson, Ibsen, Freud, and for most of the major poets and novelists of the past hundred years. It is not merely a modern problem; it is, one could say, the problem of modernism, the attempt in every work to do what has never been done, because what is known is known to be insufficient, or worse. It is an old theme of tragedy that we will be responsible for our actions beyond anything we bargain for, and it is the prudence of morality to have provided us with excuses and virtues against that time. Krenek turns this theme into the comedy of making choices whose consequences we accept as the very embodiment of our will and sensibility although we cannot, in principle, see our responsibility in them. He says that "the composer has come to distrust his inspiration," but he obviously does not mean what those words convey—that the composer (like, say, Luther or Lincoln) is gripped by an idea which is causing him an agony of doubt. What in fact Krenek has come to distrust is the composer's capacity to feel any idea as his own. In denying tradition, Krenek is a Romantic, but with no respect or hope for the individual's resources; and in the reliance on rules, he is a Classicist, but with no respect or hope for his culture's inventory of conventions.

It is less my wish here to detail the failings or to trace the symptoms in such philosophizing as Krenek's, than it is to note simply that theorizing of this kind is characteristic of the writing about new music—alternating, as was suggested, with purely technical accounts of the procedures used in producing the work. For this fact in itself suggests (1) that such works cannot be *criticized*, as traditional art is criticized, but must be defended, or rejected, as art altogether; and (2) that such work would not exist but for the philosophy. That, in turn, suggests that the activity going into the production, or consumption, of such products cannot be satisfied by the art it yields, but only in a philosophy which seems to give justification and importance to the activity of producing it. I am not suggesting that such activity is in fact unimportant, nor that it can in no way be justified, but only that such philosophizing as Krenek's does not justify it and must not be used to protect it against aesthetic assessment. (Cage's theorizing, which I find often quite charming, is exempt from such strictures, because he clearly believes that the work it produces is no more important than the theory is, and that it is not justified by the theory, but, as it were, illustrates the theory. That his work is performed as music—rather than a kind of paratheater or parareligious exercise—is only another sign of the confusions of the age. I do not speak of his music explicitly meant to accompany the dance.)

I have suggested that it is significant not only *that* philosophy should occur in these ways, but also that it should take the content it has. I want now to ask why it is that the concepts of chance and improvisation should occur at all in discussing composition; what might they be used to explain?

## VI

What is composition, what is it to compose? It seems all right to say, "It is to make something, an object of a particular sort." The question then is, "What sort?" One direction of reply would be, "An object of art." And what we need to know is just what an object of art is. Suppose we give a minimal answer: "It is an object in which human beings will or can take an interest, one which will or can absorb or involve them." But we can be absorbed by lots of things people make: toys, puzzles, riddles, scandals. . . . Still, something is said, because not *everything* people make is an object of this sort. It is a problem, an artistic problem—an experimental problem, one could say—to discover what will have the capacity to absorb us the way art does. Could someone be interested and become absorbed in a pin, or a crumpled handkerchief? Suppose someone did. Shall we say, "It's a matter of taste"? We might dismiss him as mad (or suppose he is pretending), or, alternatively, ask ourselves what he can possibly be *seeing in* it. That these *are* our alternatives is what I wish to emphasize. The situation demands an explanation, the way watching someone listening intently to Mozart, or working a puzzle, or, for that matter, watching a game of baseball, does not. The forced choice between the two responses—"He's mad" (or pretending, or on some drug, etc.) or else "What's in it?"—are the imperative choices we have when confronted with a new development in art. (A revolutionary development in science is different: not because the new move can initially be proved to be valid—perhaps it can't, in the way we suppose that happens—but because it is easier, for the professional community, to spot cranks and frauds in science than in art; and because if what the innovator does is valid, then it is *eo ipso* valid for the rest of the professional community, *in their own work*, and as it stands, as well.) But objects of art not merely interest and absorb, they move us; we are not merely involved with them, but concerned with them, and care about them; we treat them in special ways, invest them with a value which normal people otherwise reserve only for other people—*and* with the same kind of scorn and outrage. They *mean* something to us, not just the way statements do, but the way people do. People devote their lives, sometimes sacrifice them, to producing such objects just in order that they will have such consequences; and we do not think they are mad for doing so. We approach such objects not merely because they are interesting in themselves, but because they are felt as made by someone—and so we use such categories as intention, personal style, feeling, dishonesty, authority, inventiveness, profundity, meretriciousness, etc., in speaking of them. The category of intention is as inescapable (or escapable with the same consequences) in speaking of objects of art as in speaking of what human beings say and do: without it, we would not understand what they are. They are, in a word, not works of nature but of *art* (i.e., of act, talent, skill). Only the concept of intention does not function, as elsewhere, as a term of excuse or justification. We follow the progress of a piece the way we follow what someone is saying or doing. Not, however, to see how it will come out, nor to learn something specific, but to see what *it* says, to see what someone has been able to make out of these materials. A work of art does not express some particular intention (as statements do), nor achieve particular goals (the way technological skill and moral action do), but, one may say, celebrates the fact that men can intend their lives at all (if you like, that they are free to choose), and that their actions are coherent and effective at all in the scene of indifferent nature and determined society. This is what I understand Kant to have seen when he said of works of art that they embody "purposiveness without purpose."

Such remarks are what occur to me in speaking of compositions as objects *composed*. The concepts of chance and of improvision have natural roles in such a view: the capacities for improvising and for taking and seizing chances are virtues common to the activity leading to a composition. It suggests itself, in fact, that these are two of the virtues necessary to act coherently and successfully at all. I use "virtue" in what I take to be Plato's and Aristotle's sense: a capacity by virtue of which one is able to act successfully, to follow the distance from an impulse and intention through to its realization. Courage and temperance are virtues because human actions move precariously from desire and intention into the world, and one's course of action will meet dangers or distractions which, apart from courage and temperance, will thwart their realization. A world in which you could get what you want merely by wishing would not only contain no beggars, but no human activity. The success of an action is threatened in other familiar ways: by the lack of preparation or foresight; by the failure of the most convenient resources, natural or social, for implementing the action (a weapon, a bridge, a shelter, an extra pair of hands); and by a lack of knowledge about the best course to take, or way to proceed. To survive the former threats will require ingenuity and resourcefulness, the capacity for improvisation; to overcome the last will demand the willingness and capacity to take and to seize chances.

Within the world of art one makes one's own dangers, takes one's own chances—and one speaks of its objects at such moments in terms of tension, problem, imbalance, necessity, shock, surprise. . . . And within this world one takes and exploits these chances, finding, through danger, an unsuspected security—and so one speaks of fulfillment, calm, release, sublimity, vision. . . . Within it, also, the means of achieving one's purposes cannot lie at hand, ready-made. The means themselves have inevitably to be fashioned for *that* danger, and for *that* release—and so one speaks of inventiveness, resourcefulness, or else of imitativeness, obviousness, academicism. The *way* one escapes or succeeds is, in art, as important as the success itself; indeed, the way constitutes the success—and so the means that are fashioned are spoken of as masterful, elegant, subtle, profound. . . .

I said: in art, the chances you take are your own. But of course you are inviting others to take them with you. And since they are, nevertheless, your own, and your invitation is based not on power or authority, but on attraction and promise, your invitation incurs the most exacting of obligations: that *every* risk must be shown worthwhile, and every infliction of tension lead to a resolution, and every demand on attention and passion be satisfied—that risks those who trust you can't have known they would take, will be found to yield value they can't have known existed. The creation of art, being human conduct which affects others, has the commitments any conduct has. It escapes morality; not, however, in escaping commitment, but in being free to choose only those commitments it wishes to incur. In this way art plays with one of man's fates, the fate of being accountable for everything you do and are, intended or not. It frees us to sing and dance, gives us actions to perform whose consequences, commitments, and liabilities are discharged in the act itself. The price for freedom in this choice of commitment and accountability is that of an exactitude in meeting those commitments and discharging those accounts which no mere morality can impose. You cede the possibilities of excuse, explanation, or justification for your failures; and the cost of failure is not remorse and recompense, but the loss of coherence altogether.

The concept of improvisation, unlike the concept of chance, is one which has established and familiar uses in the practice of music theorists and historians. An ethnomusicologist will have recourse to the concept as a way of accounting for the creation-cum-performance of the music of cultures, or classes, which have no functionaries we would think of as composers, and no objects we would think of as embodying the intention to art; and within the realm of composed (written) music, improvisation is, until recent times, recognized as explicitly called for at certain sharply marked incidents of a performance—in the awarding of cadenzas, in the opportunities of ornamentation, in the realization of figured bass. In such uses, the concept has little explanatory power, but seems merely to name events which one knows, as matters of historical fact (that is, as facts independent of anything a critic would have to discover by an analysis or interpretation of the musical material as an aesthetic phenomenon), not to have been composed.

My use of the concept is far more general. I mean it to refer to certain qualities of music generally. Perhaps what I am getting at can be brought out this way. In listening to a great deal of music, particularly to the time of Beethoven, it would, I want to suggest, be possible to imagine that it was being improvised. Its mere complexity, or a certain kind of complexity, would be no obstacle. (Bach, we are told, was capable of improvising double fugues on any given subjects.) I do not suggest that a chorus or a symphony orchestra can be imagined to be improvising its music; on the contrary, a group improvisation itself has a particular *sound*. On the other hand I do not wish to restrict the sense of improvisation to the performance of one player either. It may help to say: One can hear, in the music in question, how the composition is *related* to, or could grow in familiar ways, from a process of improvisation; as though the parts meted out by the composer were re-enactments, or dramatizations, of successes his improvisations had discovered—given the finish and permanence the occasion deserves and the public demands, but containing essentially only such discoveries. If this could be granted, a further suggestion becomes possible. Somewhere in the development of Beethoven, this ceases to be imaginable. (I do not include *all* music after Beethoven. Chopin and Liszt clearly seem improvisatory, in the sense intended; so do Brahms Intermezzi, but not Brahms Symphonies; early Stravinsky, perhaps, but not recent Stravinsky.)

Why might such a phenomenon occur? It is, obviously enough, within contexts fully defined by shared formulas that the possibility of full, explicit improvisation traditionally exists—whether one thinks of the great epics of literature (whose "oral-formulaic" character is established), or of ancient Chinese painting, or of Eastern music, or of the theater of the Commedia dell'Arte, or jazz. If it seems a paradox that the reliance on formula should allow the fullest release of spontaneity, that must have less to do with the relation of these phenomena than with recent revolutions in our aesthetic requirements. The suggestion, however, is this. The context in which we can hear music as improvisatory is one in which the language it employs, its conventions, are familiar or obvious enough (whether because simple or because they permit of a total mastery or perspicuity) that at no point are we or the performer in doubt about our location or goal; there are solutions to every problem, permitting the exercise of familiar forms of resourcefulness; a mistake is clearly recognizable as such, and may even present a chance to be seized; and just as the general range of chances is circumscribed, so there is a preparation for every chance, and if not an inspired one, then a formula for one. But in the late experience of Beethoven, it is as if our freedom to act no longer depends on the possibility of spontaneity; improvising to fit a *given* lack or need is no longer enough. The entire enterprise of action and of communication has become problematic. The problem is no longer how to do what you want, but to know what would satisfy you. We could also say: Convention as a whole is now looked upon not as a firm inheritance from the past, but as a continuing improvisation in the face of problems we no longer understand. Nothing we now have to say, no *personal* utterance, has its meaning conveyed in the conventions and formulas we now share. In a time of slogans, sponsored messages, ideologies, psychological warfare, mass projects, where words have lost touch with their sources or objects, and in a phonographic culture where music is for dreaming, or for kissing, or for taking a shower, or for having your teeth drilled, our choices seem to be those of silence, or nihilism (the denial of the value of shared meaning altogether), or statements so personal as to form the possibility of communication without the support of convention—perhaps to become the source of new convention. And then, of course, they are most likely to fail even to seem to communicate. Such, at any rate, are the choices which the modern works of art I know seem to me to have made. I should say that the attempt to re-invent convention is the alternative I take Schoenberg and Stravinsky and Bartok to have taken; whereas in their total organization, Krenek and Stockhausen have chosen nihilism.

## VII

The sketches I have given of possible roles of improvisation and chance in describing composition obviously do not fit their use in the ideology of the new music; they may, however, help understand what that ideology is. When a contemporary theorist appeals to *chance,* he obviously is not appealing to its associations with taking and seizing chances, with risks and opportunities. The point of the appeal is not to call attention to the act of composition, but to deny that act; to deny that what he offers is composed. His concept is singular, with no existing plural; it functions not as an explanation for particular actions but as a metaphysical principle which supervises his life and work as a whole. The invocation of chance is like an earlier artist's invocation of the muse, and serves the same purpose: to indicate that his work comes not from *him,* but *through* him—its validity or authority is not a function of his own powers or intentions. Speaking for the muse, however, was to give voice to what all men share, or all would hear; speaking through chance forgoes a voice altogether—there is nothing to say. (That is, of course, by now a cliché of popular modernism.) This way of forgoing composition may perhaps usefully be compared with the way it is forgone in modernist painting. The contemporary English sculptor Anthony Caro is reported to have said: "I do not compose." Whatever he meant by that, it seems to have clear relevance to the painting of abstract expressionism and what comes after.[4] If you look at a Pollock drip painting or at a canvas consisting of eight parallel stripes of paint, and what you are looking for is *composition* (matters of balance, form, reference among the parts, etc.), the result is absurdly trivial: a child could do it; I could do it. The question, therefore, if it is art, must be: How is this to be seen? What is the painter doing? The problem, one could say, is not one of escaping inspiration, but of determining how a man could be inspired to do *this*, why he feels *this* necessary or satisfactory, how he can *mean* this. Suppose you conclude that he cannot. Then that will mean, I am suggesting, that you conclude that this is not art, and this man is not an artist; that in failing to mean what he's done, he is fraudulent. But how do you know?

In remarking the junctures at which composers have traditionally called for improvisation (cadenzas, figured bass, etc.), I might have put that by saying that the composer is at these junctures leaving something open to the performer. It is obvious that throughout the first decades of this century composers became more and more explicit in their notations and directions, leaving less and less open to the performer. One reason for allowing improvisation in the new music has been described as returning *some* area of freedom to the performer in the midst of specifications so complex and frequent (each note may have a different tempo, dynamic marking, and direction for attack, at extreme rates of speed) that it is arguable they have become unrealizable in practice. Does this use of "something left open" suggest that we have an idea of some notation which may be "complete," closing all alternatives save one to the performer? And is the best case of "leaving nothing open" one in which the composer codes his music directly into his "performer," thus obviating any need for an intermediary between him and his audience? What would be the significance of this displacement? A composer might be relieved that at least he would no longer have to suffer bad performances, and one might imagine a gain in having all performances uniform. But perhaps what would happen is that there would, for

[4] Reported by Michael Fried (who showed me its significance) in an article on Caro in *The Lugano Review*, 1965. See, in addition, his *Three American Painters*, the catalog essay for an exhibition of the work of Noland, Olitski, and Stella, at the Fogg Museum, in the spring of 1965; and his "Jules Olitski's New Paintings," *Artforum*, November 1965.

music made that way, no longer be anything we should call a "performance"; the concept would have no use there, anymore than it has for seeing movies. (One goes to see Garbo's performance as Camille, but not to see a performance of (the movie) *Camille*.) Perhaps, then, one would go to "soundings," "first plays," and "re-runs" of pieces of music. And then other musical institutions would radically change, e.g., those of apprenticeship, of conservatories, of what it is one studies and practices to become a composer. Would we then go on calling such people composers? But of course everything depends upon just what we are imagining his procedures to be. If, for example, he proceeds only so far as Krenek's "initial choices" and accepts whatever then results, I think we would not; but if, even if he begins that way, we believe that he has in some way tested the result on himself, with a view to satisfying himself—even if we do not know, or he does not know, what the source of satisfaction is—then perhaps we would. If we would not, would this suggest that the concept of a composition is essentially related to the concept of a performance? What it suggests is that it is not clear what is and is not essentially connected to the concept of music.

I do not, however, hesitate, having reminded myself of what the notion of improvisation suggests, to say that what is called for in a piece such as Stockhausen's *Pianostück Elf* (where nineteen fragments are to be selected from, in varying orders, depending upon certain decisions of the performer) is not improvisation. (The main reason, I think, for my withholding of the concept, is that nothing counts as the *goal* of a performance.) To call it improvisation is to substitute for the real satisfactions of improvisation a dream of spontaneity— to match the dream of organization it is meant to complement; as Krenek's fantasy of physics substitutes for the real satisfaction of knowledge. It also, since improvisation implies shared conventions, supposes that you can create a living community at a moment's notice. A similar point occurs when such a work is praised, as it has been, on the ground that it is graphically lovely. It is, I think, quite pretty to look at, but so is a Chopin or Bach or medieval manuscript graphically satisfying. To rest one's hope for organization on such an admittedly pleasant quality is to suppose that you can become a visual artist inadvertently. It expresses the same contempt for the artistic process as calling something musically organized (let alone totally organized) on grounds unrelated to any way in which it is, or is meant to be, heard.

## VIII

Why, instead of philosophy, didn't music made in these ways produce laughter and hostility? It did, of course, and does. But the response couldn't end there, because nobody could *prove* it wasn't music. Of course not, because it is not clear that the notion of "proving it is (or is not) music" is even intelligible, which means that it is not fully intelligible to say that nobody could do what it describes. (*What* can't anybody do here?) My suggestion is only that some composers would have had the remarkable feeling that their lives depended on performing this indescribable task. Why? Because those productions themselves seemed to prove something, namely, that music (or whatever it is) produced in those ways was indistinguishable from, or close enough to music produced in traditional ways—by composers, that is, artists, from their inspiration and technique, both painfully acquired, and out of genuine need—to be confused with it, and therewith certain to replace it. (It's just as good, and so much easier to make.) And it seemed to prove that the detractors of modernism were right all along: whatever artists and aestheticians may have said about the internal and coherent development of the art, it all turns out to have arrived at pure mechanism, it has no *musical* significance, a child could do it. This, or something like it, had been said about Beethoven, about Stravinsky, and doubtless about every *avant garde* in the history of the arts. Only no child ever *did* it before, and *some* people obviously did find it musically significant. Saint-Saëns stormed out of the first performance of *The Rite of Spring*. But Ravel and serious young composers stayed and were convinced. But now a child *has* done it, or might as well have, and a child could understand it as well as anyone else—you prove he couldn't. It is, I take it, significant about modernism and its "permanent revolution" that its audience recurrently tells itself the famous stories of riots and walkouts and outrages that have marked its history. It is as though the *impulse* to shout fraud and storm out is always present, but fear of the possible consequence overmasters the impulse. Remember Saint-Saëns: He said the Emperor had no clothes, and then history stripped him naked. The philistine audience cannot afford to admit the new; the *avant garde* audience cannot afford not to. This bankruptcy means that both are at the mercy of their tastes, or fears, and that no artist can test his work either by their rejection or by their acceptance.

These may or may not exhaust all the audiences there are, but they certainly do not include all the people there are. This suggests that genuine responses to art are to be sought in individuals alone, as the choice or affinity for a canon of art and a canon of criticism must be made by individuals alone; and that these individuals have no audience to belong in as sanctioning, and as sharing the responsibility for, the partiality they show for the work of individual artists and particular critics. (As the faithful auditor of God is perhaps no longer to be expected, and cannot receive sanction, through membership in a congregation.) This records one way of putting the modern predicament of audience: taste now appears as partialness.

This is the point at which Nietzsche's perception outdistances Tolstoy's. Tolstoy called for sincerity from the artist and infection from his audience; he despised taste just because it revealed, and concealed, the loss of our *appetite* for life and consequently for art that matters. But he would not face the possible cost of the artist's radical, unconventionalized sincerity—that his work may become uninfectious, and even (and even deliberately) unappetizing, forced to defeat the commonality which was to be art's high function, in order to remain art at all (art in exactly the sense Tolstoy meant, directed from and to genuine need). Nietzsche became the unbalanced ledger of that cost, whereas Tolstoy apparently let himself imagine that we could simply *stop* our reliance on taste once we were told that it was blocking us to satisfaction—and not merely in art. What modern artists realize, rather, is that taste must be *defeated*, and indeed that this can be accomplished by nothing less powerful than art itself. One may see in this the essential moral motive of modern art. Or put it this way: What looks like "breaking with tradition" in the successions of art is not really that; or is that only after the fact, looking historically or critically; or is that only as a result not as a motive: the unheard of appearance of the modern in art is an effort not to break, but to keep faith with tradition. It is perhaps fully true of Pop Art that its motive is to break with the tradition of painting and sculpture; and the result is not that the tradition is broken, but that these works are irrelevant to that tradition, i.e., they are not paintings, whatever their pleasures. (Where history has cunning, it is sometimes ironic, but sometimes just.)

## IX

I said earlier that the periodicals about music which we were discussing were trying to do what only the art of music itself could do. But maybe it just is a fact about modern art that coming to care about it demands coming to care about the problems in producing it. Whatever painting may be about, modernist painting is about *painting*, about what it means to use a limited two-dimensional surface in ways establishing the coherence and interest we demand of art. Whatever music can do, modern music is concerned with the making of music, with what is required to gain the movement and the stability on which its power depends. The problems of composition are no longer irrelevant to the audience of art when the solution to a compositional problem has become identical with the aesthetic result itself.

In this situation, criticism stands, or could, or should stand, in an altered relation to the art it serves. At any time it is subordinate to that art, and expendable once the experience of an art or period or departure is established. But in the modern situation it seems inevitable, even, one might say, internal, to the experience of art. One evidence of what I have in mind is the ease with which a new departure catches phrases which not merely free new response, but join in the creation of that response; moreover, the phrases do not cease to matter once the response is established, but seem required in order that the response be sustained. New theater is "absurd"; new painting is "action"; Pop Art exists "between life and art"; in serial music "chance occurs by necessity." Often one does not know whether interest is elicited and sustained primarily by the object or by what can be said about the object. My suggestion is not that this is bad, but that it is definitive of a modernist situation. Perhaps it would be nicer if composers could not think, and felt no need to open their mouths except to sing—if, so to say, art did not present problems. But it does, and they do, and the consequent danger is that the words, because inescapable, will usurp motivation altogether, no longer tested by the results they enable. I think this has already happened in the phrases I cited a moment ago, and this suggests that a central importance of criticism has become to protect its art against criticism. Not just from bad criticism, but from the critical impulse altogether, which no longer knows its place, perhaps because it no longer has *a* place. In a Classical Age, criticism is confident enough to prescribe to its art without moralism and its consequent bad conscience. In a Romantic Age, art is exuberant enough to escape criticism without the loss of conscience—appealing, as it were, to its public directly. In a Modern Age, both that confidence and that appeal are gone, and are to be re-established, if at all, together, and in confusion.

If we say it is a gain to criticism, and to art, when we know that criticism must not be prescriptive (e.g., tell artists what they ought to produce), then we should also recognize that this injunction is *clear* only when we already accept an object as genuine art and a man as an authentic artist. But the modernist situation forces an awareness of the *difficulty* in avoiding prescription, and indeed of the ways in which criticism, and art itself, are ineluctably prescriptive—art, because its successes garner imitations, not just because there are always those who want success at any price, but because of the very authority which has gone into the success; criticism, not because the critic cannot avoid prescriptive utterances, but because the terms in which he defines his response themselves define which objects are and which are not relevant to his response. When, therefore, artists are unmoored from tradition, from taste, from audience, from their own past achievement; when, that is, they are brought to rely most intimately on the critic, if only the critic in themselves; then the terms in which they have learned to accept criticism will come to dictate the terms in which they will look for success: apart from these, nothing will count as successful because nothing will be evaluable, nothing have a chance of validity. Here the artist's survival depends upon his constantly eluding, and constantly assembling, his critical powers.

A certain use of mathematical-logical descriptions of tone-row occurrences is only the clearest case of these difficulties, as it is also the case which most clearly shows the force of the aesthetically and intellectually irrelevant in establishing a reigning criticism—in this case, the force of a fearful scientism, an intellectual chic which is at once intimidating and derivative, and in general the substitution of precision for accuracy. This is hardly unusual, and it should go without saying that not *all* uses of such techniques are irrelevant, and that they represent an indispensable moment in coming to understand contemporary music. The issue is simply this: we know that criticism ought to come only after the fact of art, but we cannot *insure* that it will come only after the fact. What is to be hoped for is that criticism learn to criticize itself, as art does, distrusting its own success.

This is particularly urgent, or perhaps particularly clear, in the case of music, because, as suggested, the absence of a strong tradition of criticism leaves this art especially vulnerable to whatever criticism becomes established, and because the recent establishment of criticism is peculiarly invulnerable to control (because of its technicalities, its scientific chic . . . ). But if it is not technicality as such which is to be shunned, only, so to speak, its counterfeit, how do you tell? The moral is again, as it is in the case of the art itself: you cannot tell from outside; and the expense in getting inside is a matter for each man to go over. And again, this strict economy is not new to modern art, but only forced by it. Nor do I wish to impugn all music made with attention to "total organization," but only to dislodge the idea that what makes it legitimate is a philosophical theory—though such a theory may be needed in helping to understand the individual artistic success which alone would make it legitimate. It may be, given the velocity of our history, that the music and the theory of music illustrated in the recent work of Krenek is by now, five years later, already repudiated—not perhaps theoretically, but in fact, in the practice of those who constitute the musical world. What would this show? One may find that it shows such worries as have been expressed in this essay to be unfounded; that the fraudulent in art and the ideological in criticism will not defeat the practice of the real thing. At least they won't have this time; but that means that certain composers have in the meantime gone on writing, not only against the normal odds of art, but against the hope that the very concept of art will not be forgotten. That a few composers might, because of this distraction and discouragement, cease trying to write, is doubtless to be expected in a difficult period. But it is not unthinkable that next time all on whom the art relies will succumb to that distraction and discouragement. I do not absolutely deny, even in the face of powerful evidence, that in the end the truth will out. I insist merely that philosophy ought to help it out. Nor have I wished to suggest that the recognition of the "possibility of fraudulence" manifests itself as a permanent suspicion of all works giving themselves out as compositions or paintings or poems . . . . One *can* achieve unshakable justified faith in one's capacity to tell. I have wanted only to say that *that* is what one will have achieved. If someone supposes that that leaves us in a hopelessly irrational position, he is perhaps supposing a particular view of faith, and a limited horizon of hope.[5]

## X

I have spoken of the *necessities* of the problems faced by artists, of the *irreversibility* of the sequence of art styles, of the difficulties in a contemporary artist's continuing to *believe* in his work, or *mean* it. And I said it was the artist's need to maintain his own belief that forced him to give up—to the extent and in the way he has given up —the belief and response of his audience. This is reflected in literature as well, but differently. I do not mean, what I take to be obvious enough, that modern poetry often takes the making of poetry and the difficulties of poetry in the modern age, as its subject matter. What I have in mind is best exemplified in the modern theater. The fact that the language the literary artist uses does communicate directly with his audience—in ways the contemporary "languages" of painting and music do not—was earlier taken as an advantage to the literary artist. But it is also his liability. A writer like Samuel Beckett does *not* want what is communicated easily to be what he communicates—it is not what he means. So his effort is not to find belief from his audience, but to defeat it, so that his meaning *has* to be searched for. Similarly, modern dramatists do not *rely* on their audiences, but *deny* them. Suppose an audience is thought of as "those present whom the actors ignore." Then to stop ignoring them, to recognize them explicitly, speak *to* them, insist on the fact *that* this is acting and this is a theater, functions to remove the status of *audience* from "those out there who were ignored." Modern dramatists (e.g., Beckett, Genet, Brecht) can

---

[5] The addition of this paragraph is only the main, not the only, point at which a reading by the composer John Harbison caused modification or expansion of what I had written.

be distinguished by the various ways in which they deny the existences of audiences—as if they are saying: what is meant cannot be understood from that position.

But why not? Why, to raise the question in a more familiar form, can't one still write like Mozart? The question makes the obscurities and withdrawals and unappealingness of modern art seem *willful*— which is another *fact* of the experience of that art. But what is the answer to that question? One answer might be: Lots of people have written like Mozart, people whose names only libraries know; and Mozart wasn't one of them. Another answer might be: Beethoven wrote like Mozart, until he became Beethoven. Another: If Mozart were alive, he wouldn't either. Or even: the best composers do write as Mozart did (and as Bach and Beethoven and Brahms did), though not perhaps with his special fluency or lucidity. But by now that question is losing its grip, one is no longer sure what it is one was asking, nor whether these answers mean anything (which seems the appropriate consequence of looking for a simple relation between past and present). A final answer I have wanted to give is: No one *does* now write that way. But perhaps *somebody* does, living at the edge of an obscure wood, by candlelight, with a wig on. What would our response to him be? We wouldn't take him seriously as an artist? Nobody could mean such music now, be sincere in making it? And yet I've been insisting that we can no longer be sure that any artist is sincere—we haven't convention or technique or appeal to go on any longer: *anyone* could fake it. And this means that modern art, if and where it exists, *forces* the issue of sincerity, depriving the artist and his audience of every measure except absolute attention to one's experience and absolute honesty in expressing it. This is what I meant in saying that it lays bare the condition of art altogether. And of course it runs its own risks of failure, as art within established traditions does.

This will seem an unattractive critical situation to be left with. Don't we know that ". . . the goodness or badness of poetry has nothing to do with sincerity. . . . The worst love poetry of adolescents is the most sincere"? [6] But I am suggesting that we may not know what sincerity is (nor what adolescence is). The adolescent, I suppose it is assumed, has strong feelings, and perhaps some of them

[6] René Wellek, *A History of Modern Criticism*, Vol. II (New Haven: Yale University Press, 1955), p. 137.

can be described as feelings of sincerity, which, perhaps, he attaches to the words in his poetry. Does all that make the words, his utterance in the poem, sincere? Will he, for example, *stand by them*, later, when *those* feelings are gone? Suppose he does; that will not, of course, prove that his poetry is worthwhile, nor even that it is poetry. But I haven't suggested that sincerity proves anything in particular— it can prove madness or evil as well as purity or authenticity. What I have suggested is that it shows what kind of stake the stake in modern art is, that it helps explain why one's reactions to it can be so violent, why for the modern artist the difference between artistic success and failure can be so uncompromising. The task of the modern artist, as of the modern man, is to find something he can be sincere and serious in; something he can mean. And he may not at all.

Have my claims about the artist and his audience been based on hearsay, or real evidence, or really upon the work itself? But now the "work itself" becomes a heightened philosophical concept, not a neutral description. My claims do not rest upon works of art themselves, apart from their relations to how such works are made and the reasons for which they are made, and considering that some are sincere and some counterfeit. . . . But my claim is that to know such things is to know what a work of art is—they are, if one may say so, part of its grammar. And, of course, I may be taken in.

# *VIII*

# A Matter of Meaning It

## I

It is not surprising that Professors Beardsley and Margolis found what I had to say about modern art and modern philosophy obscure and, I take it, unsympathetic; I tried, in the opening section of my remarks, to give reasons why these subjects are liable to obscurity and unattractiveness—as it were, to make this fact itself a subject of philosophy. (In perhaps the way Hume suggests, in the Introduction to his *Dialogues on Natural Religion,* that the subject to follow is characterized by alternating obscurity and obviousness.) It is therefore the more surprising that they find me clear enough to agree in several points of interpretation and in one or two major proposals. (1) Both take it as a central motive of my paper to rule out certain developments within recent music as genuine art. (2) Both object to my insistence on the word "fraudulence," wishing some more neutral description. (3) Accepting the fact that objects of modern art create a problem for aesthetics, but taking the nature of that problem as known, each suggests an alternate line of solution, and in each case the solution is one which is, and is explicitly said to be, philosophically familiar: Beardsley's solution is to define a notion of art (i.e., music) broad enough to include the problematic objects; Margolis' is to regard the problem as another instance of "borderline cases" and therefore to

These rejoinders to Professors Beardsley and Margolis refer to their respective papers published in the Proceedings of the Oberlin Colloquium, *Art, Mind, and Religion* (Pittsburgh: University of Pittsburgh Press, 1967) , and are reprinted by permission of the publisher. Page references are to the Proceedings.

require the discovery of criteria for the "propriety" of treating the new music as art. (4) Both suggest that an obvious notion of organization or coherence will supply the (or a) determining ground for including objects under the new classification.

These are not my problems. Taking them in order:

1. I was not directly concerned to rule out or rule in any particular work as music, but to bring to attention the fact that this had become a problem in modern art and to suggest that it therefore ought to become a problem for philosophy. I do not think it is clear, and I found it of philosophical interest that it is not clear, what kind of problem modern art poses, nor what philosophical considerations might uncover it. But I am confident that the redefinition or extended application of the term "music" is not what is needed, for that leaves the behavior of composers and critics and audiences and the experience of the works themselves, old and new, incomprehensible—a problem has not been solved, but made invisible. Convinced that swans are white, and one day stopped by a black bird for all the world a swan, I have some freedom: "So I was wrong"; I learned something. "So there is a swan-like bird which is black"; but then I had better have a good reason for taking color to be so important. But in the present case it is as though there is something on the horizon which *for some reason* I insist on calling swans (and after all, it isn't as though I *knew* the reasons, or even had reasons, for calling the old ones swans), but which sometimes look and behave so differently that not only do I feel called on to justify *their* title, I feel called on to justify my hitherto unquestioned ability to recognize the old ones. How do I do it; what *is* it about them? Surely that graceful neck is essential—its melodic line, so to speak? But it may be that my experience of the new ones makes the old neck rather a distasteful feature sometimes, as though it were somehow arbitrary, as though the old ones now sometimes look *bent*.

2. Similarly, I was not directly concerned to condemn any given work as fraudulent, but to call attention to (what I took to be) the obvious but unappreciated *fact* that the experience of the modern is one which itself raises the question of fraudulence and genuineness (in something like the way I take the experience of momentary or extended irrelevance, and sudden relevance, to be characteristic of philosophy; the way the experience, and danger, of the distance or absence of God, and sudden closeness, is characteristic of modern

religion). It goes without saying that I may be wrong about this experience, or poor in characterizing it and sounding its significance. But if I am not wrong, then the problems it raises, or ought to raise, are not touched by suggesting that I am unjustly attributing motives to certain artists, nor by redefining terms in such a way that the attribution of fraudulence need not or cannot arise. For the experience itself has the form of attributing motives (I referred, for example, to the riots and inner violence which dog the history of the *avant garde*), and redefining some terms will not, or ought not to, make the experience go away.

3. What ought to make the experience go away? Further experience, or else nothing; entering the new world of these objects, understanding them not in theory but as objects of art, in the sense in which we have always, when we have ever, understood such objects.[1] This is the essential reason that redefinitions and borderline cases are irrelevant here. For the question raised for me about these new objects is exactly whether they are, and how they can be, *central*. If they are not, if I cannot in that way enter their world, I do not know what interest, if any at all, I would have in them. It *may* turn out to be one which would prompt me to think of them as borderline cases of art; or I might think of them as something which replaces (which replaces my interest in) works of art.

Not every object will raise this question of art, i.e., raise the question "What is art?" by raising the question "Is this, e.g., music?" Pop Art as a whole does not, and it is exactly part of its intention and ideology that it should not. For philosophy to scramble for definitions which accommodate these objects unproblematically as art—or art in a wide sense, or borderline cases of art—insures its irrelevance, taking seriously neither the claims such objects make (namely, that they are not art) nor the specialized amusements such objects can provide (e.g., a certain theatricality), nor the attitude they contain toward serious art (sc., that it is past); nor the despair under the fun, the nihilism under the comment, nor the cultural-philosophical confusion which makes such claims and fun and comment possible.

And not every new work which gives itself out as serious art will raise the question of art. Part of what I say in my paper is a function of the fact that, for me, Krenek's late work does not raise this ques-

---

[1] Certain consequences of "entering a new world" are drawn in "Aesthetic Problems of Modern Philosophy," which appears in this volume, pp. 84–86.

tion, and that, for example, Caro's sculpture does. It is not, in this context, important whether I am right or wrong about these particular cases; what is important here is what kind of issue this issue is, what I would be right or wrong about.

It is, first of all, an issue in which it is *up to me* (and, of course, up to you) whether an object does or does not count as evidence for any theory I am moved to offer; and "count as evidence" means "count as art at all." Both Beardsley and Margolis wish explicitly to separate the question of evaluation from the question of classification. Now I might define the problem of modernism as one in which the question of value comes first as well as last: to classify a modern work as art is already to have staked value, more starkly than the (later) decision concerning its goodness or badness. Your interest in Mozart is not likely to draw much attention—which is why such interests can be, so to speak, academic. But an interest in Webern or Stockhausen or Cage is, one might say, revealing, even sometimes suspicious. (A Christian might say that in such interests, and choices, the heart is revealed. This is what Tolstoy saw.) Philosophers sometimes speak of the phrase "work of art" as having an "honorific sense," as though that were a surprising or derivative fact about it, even one to be neutralized or ignored. But that works of art are valuable is analytically true of them; and that value is inescapable in human experience and conduct is one of the facts of life, and of art, which modern art lays bare.

Of course there is the continuous danger that the question will be begged, that theory and evidence become a closed and vicious circle. I do not insist that this is always the case, but merely that unless this problem is faced here no problem of the right kind can come to focus. For if everything counted as art which now offers itself as art, then questions about whether, for example, figurative content, or tonality, or heroic couplets are still viable resources for painters, composers, and poets would not only never have arisen, but would make no sense. When there was a tradition, everything which seemed to count did count. (And that is perhaps analytic of the notion of "tradition.") I say that Krenek's late work doesn't count, and that means that the way it is "organized" does not raise for me the question of how music may be organized. I say that Caro's steel sculptures count, and that raises for me the question of what sculpture is: I had —I take it everyone had—thought (assumed? imagined?)—but no one

word is going to be quite right, and that must itself require a philosophical account) that a piece of sculpture was something *worked*
(carved, chipped, polished, etc.); but Caro uses steel rods and beams
and sheets which he does not work (e.g., bend or twist) but rather, one
could say, *places*. I had thought that a piece of sculpture had the
coherence of a natural object, that it was what I wish to call spatially
closed or spatially continuous (or consisted of a group of objects of
such coherence); but a Caro may be open and discontinuous, one of
its parts not an outgrowth from another, nor even joined or connected with another so much as it is juxtaposed to it, or an inflection
from it. I had thought a piece of sculpture stood on a base (or
crouched in a pediment, etc.) and rose; but a Caro rests on the raw
ground and some do not so much rise as spread or reach or open. I
had heard that sculpture used to be painted, and took it as a matter
of fashion or taste that it no longer was (in spite of the reconstructed
praises of past glories, the idea of painted stone figures struck me as
ludicrous); Caro paints his pieces, but not only is this not an external
or additional fact about them, it creates objects about which I wish
to say they are not painted, or not *colored*: they have color not the
way, say, cabinets or walls do, but the way grass and soil do—the experience I recall is perhaps hit off by saying that Caro is not using
colored beams, rods, and sheets, but beams and rods and sheets of
color. It is almost as though the color helps de-materialize its supporting object. One might wish to say they are weightless, but that would
not mean that these massively heavy materials seem light, but, more
surprisingly, neither light nor heavy, resistant to the concept of
weight altogether—as they are resistant to the concept of size; they
seem neither large nor small. Similarly, they seem to be free of *texture,* so critical a parameter of other sculpture. They are no longer
*things.*[2] (Something similar seems to be true of the use of color in
recent painting: it is not merely that it no longer serves as the color
*of* something, nor that it is disembodied; but that the canvas we know
to underly it is no longer its *support*—the color is simply *there,* as the
canvas is. How it got there is only technically (one could say it is no
longer humanly) interesting; it is no longer *handled*.)

[2] In addition to the piece on Caro cited in note 4 of my opening paper, see also
Fried's catalogue essay for an exhibition of Caro's work at the Whitechapel Art Gallery,
London, September–October 1963; and Clement Greenberg's "The New Sculpture" and
"Modernist Sculpture, Its Pictorial Past," both in his *Art and Culture* (Boston: Beacon
Press, 1961).

The problem this raises for me is exactly not to decide whether this is art (I mean, sculpture), nor to find some definition of "sculpture" which makes the Caro pieces borderline cases of sculpture, or sculptures in some extended sense. The problem is that I am, so to speak, stuck with the knowledge that this is sculpture, in the same sense that any object is. The problem is that I no longer know what sculpture is, why I call *any* object, the most central or traditional, a piece of sculpture. How *can* objects made this way elicit the experience I had thought confined to objects made so differently? And that this is a matter of experience is what needs constant attention; nothing more, but nothing less, than that. Just as it needs constant admission that one's experience may be wrong, or misformed, or inattentive and inconstant.

This admission is more than a reaffirmation of the first fact about art, that it must be felt, not merely known—or, as I would rather put it, that it must be known for oneself. It is a statement of the fact of life—the metaphysical fact, one could say—that apart from one's experience of it there is nothing to *be* known about it, no way of knowing that what you know is relevant. For what else is there for me to rely on but my experience? It is only if I accept (my experience of) the Caro that I have to conclude that the art of sculpture does not (or does no longer) depend on figuration, on being worked, on spatial continuity, etc. Then what does it depend on? That is, again, the sort of issue which prompted me to say that modern art lays bare the condition of art in general. Or put it this way: That an object is "a piece of sculpture" is not (no longer) grammatically related to its "being sculptured," i.e., to its being the result of carving or chipping, etc., some material with some tool. Then we no longer know what kind of object a piece of sculpture (grammatically) is. That it is not a natural object is something we knew. But it also is not an artifact either—or if it is, it is one which defines no known craft. It is, one would like to say, a work of art. But what is it one will then be saying?

Two serious ambiguities in my initial paper become particularly relevant here:

*a*) Beardsley, with good reason, on several occasions is puzzled about whether I am addressing the question "Is this music?" or "Is this (music) art?". I was, and am, very uncertain about this important alternation; but I want to suggest what it is I am uncertain about and why I take it to be important.

There is this asymmetry between the questions: If there is a clear answer to the question, "Is this music (painting, sculpture . . .)?", then the question whether it is art is irrelevant, superfluous. If it is music then (analytically) it is art. That seems unprejudicial. But the negation does not: if it is not music then it is not art. But why does that seem prejudicial? Why couldn't we allow Pop Art, say, or Cage's evenings, or Happenings, to be entertainments of some kind without troubling about art? But we are troubled. Because for us, given the gradual self-definitions and self-liberations over the past century of the separate major arts we accept, Pop Art presents itself as, or as challenging, painting; Cage presents his work as, or as challenging the possibility of, music . . . . It would be enough to say that objects of Pop Art are not paintings or sculptures, that works of Cage and Krenek are not music—if we are clear what a painting is, what a piece of music is. But the trouble is that the genuine article—the music of Schoenberg and Webern, the sculpture of Caro, the painting of Morris Louis, the theatre of Brecht and Beckett—really does challenge the art of which it is the inheritor and voice. Each is, in a word, not merely modern, but modernist. Each, one could say, is trying to find the limits or essence of its own procedures. And this means that it is not clear a priori what counts, or will count, as a painting, or sculpture or musical composition . . . . So we haven't got clear criteria for determining whether a given object is or is not a painting, a sculpture . . . . But this is exactly what our whole discussion has prepared us for. The task of the modernist artist, as of the contemporary critic, is to find what it is his art finally depends upon; it doesn't matter that we haven't a priori criteria for defining a painting, what matters is that we realize that the criteria are something we must discover, discover in the continuity of painting itself. But my point now is that to discover this we need to discover what objects we *accept* as paintings, and why we so accept them. And to "accept something as a painting" is to "accept something as a work of art," i.e., as something carrying the intentions and consequences of art: the nature of the acceptance is altogether crucial. So the original questions "Is this music?" and "Is this art?" are not independent. The latter shows, we might say, the spirit in which the former is relevantly asked.

*b*) To say that the modern "lays bare" may suggest that there was something concealed in traditional art which hadn't, for some reason, been noticed, or that what the modern throws over—tonality, perspective, narration, the absent fourth wall, etc.—was something inessential to music, painting, poetry, and theater in earlier periods. These would be false suggestions.[3] For it is not that now we finally know the true condition of art; it is only that someone who does not question that condition has nothing, or not the essential thing, to go on in addressing the art of our period. And far from implying that we now know, for example, that music does not require tonality, nor painting figuration nor theater an audience of spectators, etc., exactly what I want to have accomplished is to make all such notions problematic, to force us to ask, for example, what the art was which as a matter of fact did require, or exploit, tonality, perspective, etc. Why did it? What made such things media of art? It may help to say that the notion of "modernism laying bare its art" is meant not as an interpretation of history (the history of an art), but as a description of the latest period of a history, a period in which each of the arts seems to be, even forced to be, drawing itself to its limits, purging itself of elements which can be foregone and which therefore seem arbitrary or extraneous—poetry wishing the abstraction and immediacy of lyricism; theater wishing freedom from entertainment and acting; music wishing escape from the rhythm or logic of the single body and its frame of emotion . . . . *Why* this has happened one would like to know, but for the moment what is relevant is that it has happened at a certain moment in history. For it was not always true of a given art that it sought to keep its medium pure, that it wished to assert its own limits, and therewith its independence of the other arts. Integrity could be assured without purity. So in saying that "we do not know what is and what is not essentially connected to the concept of music" I am not saying that what we do not know is which one or more phenomena are always essential to something's being music, but that we have yet to discover what at any given moment has been essential to our accepting something as music. As was said, this discovery is unnecessary as long as there is a tradition—when everything which is offered for acceptance is the real thing. But so far as the possibility of fraudulence is characteristic of the modern, then the need for a grounding of our acceptance becomes an issue for aesthetics. I think of it as a need for an answer to the question, What is a medium of art?

---

[3] Sources of these suggestions, and ways they are false, were brought out by Michael Fried in his course of lectures on Nineteenth Century French Painting, given at Harvard in the spring term of 1965–66.

Philosophers will sometimes say that sound is the medium of music, paint of painting, wood and stone of sculpture, words of literature. One has to find what problems have been thought to reach illumination in such remarks. What needs recognition is that wood or stone would not be a medium of sculpture *in the absence of the art of sculpture.* The home of the idea of a *medium* lies in the visual arts, and it used to be informative to know that a given medium is oil or gouache or tempera or dry point or marble . . . because each of these media had characteristic possibilities, an implied range of handling and result. The idea of a medium is not simply that of a physical material, but of a material-in-certain-characteristic-applications. Whether or not there is anything to be called, and any good purpose in calling anything, "the medium of music," there certainly are things to be called various media of music, namely the various ways in which various sources of sound (from and for the voice, the several instruments, the body, on different occasions) have characteristically been applied: the media are, for example, plain song, work song, the march, the fugue, the aria, dance forms, sonata form. It is the existence or discovery of such strains of convention that have made possible musical expression—presumably the role a medium was to serve. In music, the "form" (as in literature, the genre) is the medium. It is within these that composers have been able to speak and to intend to speak, performers to practice and to believe, audiences to attend and to know. Grant that these media no longer serve, as portraits, nudes, odes, etc., no longer serve, for speaking and believing and knowing. What now is a medium of music? If one wishes now to answer, "Sound. Sound itself," that will no longer be the neutral answer it seemed to be, said to distinguish music from, say, poetry or painting (whatever it means to "distinguish" things one would never have thought could be taken for one another); it will be one way of distinguishing (more or less tendentiously) music now from music in the tradition, and what it says is that there are no longer known structures which must be followed if one is to speak and be understood. The medium is to be discovered, or invented out of itself.

If these sketches and obscurities are of any use, they should help to locate, or isolate, the issue of Pop Art, which is really not central to the concerns of my paper. Left to itself it may have done no harm, its amusements may have remained clean. But it was not made to be left to itself, any more than pin ball games or practical jokes or starlets are; and in an artistic-philosophical-cultural situation in which mass magazines make the same news of it they make of serious art, and in which critics in elite magazines underwrite such adventures— finding new bases for aesthetics and a new future for art in every new and safe weirdness or attractiveness which catches on—it is worth saying: This is not painting; and it is not painting not because paint- ings *couldn't* look like that, but because serious painting doesn't; and it doesn't, not because serious painting is not forced to change, to explore its own foundations, even its own look; but because the *way* it changes—what will count as a relevant change—is determined by the commitment to painting as an *art,* in struggle with the history which makes it an art, continuing and countering the conventions and intentions and responses which comprise that history. It may be that the history of a given art has come to an end, a very few centuries after it has come to a head, and that nothing more can be said and meant in terms of that continuity and within those ambitions. It is as if the var- ious anti-art movements claim to *know* this has happened and to pro- vide us with distraction, or to substitute new gratifications for those well gone; while at the same time they claim the respect due only to those whose seriousness they cannot share; and they receive it, because of our frightened confusion. Whereas such claims, made from such a position, are no more to be honored than the failed fox's sour opinion about the grapes.

4. I have been saying that what the modern puts in question is not merely, so to speak, itself, but its tradition as a whole. Without allowing this to become problematic, one will, for example, suppose that "organization" of some more or less indefinite description, is essential to art. So I used Krenek and Caro as examples which I hoped would bring that supposition into question: If Krenek's work fails to be music, this proves not merely that "organization" is not a sufficient condition of art—which we ought to have learned from Beckmesser as well as from his progeny; it suggests that we do not know what to look for as organizing a piece of music, nor what the point of any particular organization is supposed to be. Since Caro's work succeeds in being sculpture, the received notion of organization pales in a more obvious way: I do not say that it has become com- pletely irrelevant but only that it is completely problematic. So far as "organization" just means "composition," his pieces have about the

same degree of organization as a three-legged stool. (Some will suppose that therefore a three-legged stool is a candidate for sculpture, and exhibit it. Well and good; look one over.) To say what "organization" means in reference to his work would be to say what organization consists in there.

## II

Whatever the distances between our philosophical and aesthetic sensibilities and tolerances, there are several further points at which it still seems to me reasonable to have hoped that what I wrote would have helped my commentators to some caution with their several certainties. Margolis makes me say, and say "angrily," that ". . . the new music 'expresses . . . contempt for the artistic process' " (p. 99); whereas what I said expressed this contempt was not "the new music," but two particular *theories* or apologies which are offered in defense of certain new music (supra p. 204). This slip is distressing, because the oblique and shifting relations between an art, and its criticism, and philosophy, is a major theme of the entire paper. Having summarized me, he begins his objections by (1) mentioning "the ideological battles which must be waged by artists *engagés,*" and (2) taking it as his "clue about the new electronic music that composers have dispensed with the keyboard by taking the entire range of sound (now technologically available for the first time) as their materials." He concedes (3) that "they have eliminated . . . notation and performance and improvisation in this regard," suggesting that they are "composing musical sculptures" (pp. 99–100). Taking these points in turn: (1) In what sense are composers and painters *engagés,* and why *must* ideological battles be waged by them? I suggested that composers, in obvious ways the least *engagés* of artists (in the normal, lately fashionable sense of that term), had become the most embattled artistically, and I took this as characteristic of the musical community now. To say, as if it is obvious, that artists "must" wage ideological battles, obscures the particular phenomenon I wanted to make surprising, that composers have come to feel compelled to defend their work in theoretical papers, a phenomenon I take, in turn, to be characteristic of the kind of work they are compelled to produce. It is, moreover, a phenomenon that has a recognizable and datable beginning in its modern form, with Wagner's writings in the middle of the nineteenth century. (2) To speak, as if in explanation, and with satisfaction, of "the entire range of sound now technologically available" is simply to accept the cant of one of the embattled positions, with no suggestion as to why that position has been opted for. (3) In *what* regard have notation, performance, and improvisation *not* been eliminated; and is this elimination of significance? When Margolis goes on to ask whether what is thereby "composed" may be called "musical sculptures," he astonishingly turns to the reader to find the answer, instead of giving his own; but since his phrase is baked up for the occasion, and since the only point in serving it would be to express an insight or temptation he has discovered in himself and therefore wishes us to test in ourselves, what can one conclude from his avoiding any response to it, but that there was nothing on his mind? So he has in fact given *no* suggestion about how this new access of the entire range of sound may or may not relate to music.

It may be true, as Beardsley says, that "Tolstoy at least knew what he was doing, for he was a radical aesthetic reformer, and understood very well that there is no more severe way to condemn works of art than to say that they are not even art at all" (p. 107). But one is not confident that Tolstoy's motives in his writings about art are justly seen when they are put as "condemning works of art"; for first, Tolstoy's point is that these works are not art, and second, he is condemning far more than putative works of art. Moreover, his condemnations seem mild compared to other ways in which art can be condemned, e.g., politically or religiously or simply through steady indifference—indeed, one of his motives, perhaps the most fundamental, was exactly to rescue genuine art (on anybody's view) from its condemnation to irrelevance, or to serving as morsels for the overstuffed, or as excitements for those no longer capable of feeling. Whatever Tolstoy understood very well, the denial that certain putative works of art are art at all is a criticism characteristic of, only available to criticism within, the modern period of art, beginning in the nineteenth century. Apart from Tolstoy and Nietzsche, other representative figures in this line would be Kierkegaard and Baudelaire, and Ruskin and Arnold.

## III

I had wanted to bring more data to the issues of intention and seriousness and sincerity, but Beardsley finds that the phenomena which I say force the issue of intention, instead finally lay it to rest (p. 106). Here we do seem flatly incomprehensible to one another. However intractable the issue has been, one is dragged back over it again, faced with the alternatives Beardsley proposes: what we are to notice in "music (narrowly speaking)" is, roughly, rhythm and/or melody (p. 107); and what we are to listen for in "music (broadly speaking)"—i.e., in that part of it which is not music (narrowly speaking)—are "any traces of musical worth" (p. 109). I find that I can imagine listening to almost anything (which is audible, or in motion) for some trace of musical worth—except precisely those works which I accept as *music* (unless the context is one in which I am convinced that a piece of music is for the most part without a trace of musical worth). "Musical worth" is explained as "patterns of inner relationship that give it shape, notable regional qualities that give it character" (p. 109). But one can find or produce things of that description virtually at will, e.g., with hand claps, feet taps, and the sound of spoons tinkling; I am not on such grounds moved to call them music, however entertaining the proceedings. (They may be *related* to music in various ways, e.g., the way a design, say of a room, may be related to some painting.) What is missing from the characterizations of both the narrow and the broad is the sense that the thing one is listening to, listening for, is the *point* of the piece. And to know its point is to know the answer to a sense of the question "Why is it as it is?" It *bears explanation,* not perhaps the way tides and depressions do, but the way remarks and actions do. And a question I meant to be raising in my paper was: Is there any reason other than philosophical possession which should prevent us from saying, what seems most natural to say, that such questions discover the artist's intention in a work? I gave a number of reasons for thinking that the philosophical prohibition against saying this is poorly or obscurely conceived, and others meant to show why it seems lucidly true, i.e., cases in which it is in fact right. The appeal to intention can *in fact* be inappropriate or distracting or evasive, as it can in moral contexts; no doubt it frequently is in some of the work of the literary historians and aestheticians opposed by the New Criticism. It is one irony of recent literary history that the New Criticism, with one motive fixed on preserving poetry from what it felt as the encroachment of science and logical positivism (repeating as an academic farce what the nineteenth century went through as a cultural tragedy), accepted undemurringly a view of intention established, or pictured, in that same philosophy—according to which an intention is some internal, prior mental event causally connected with outward effects, which remain the sole evidence for its having occurred.

This seems to underlie the following sort of remark: "Tolstoy's criteria of genuineness fail for well-known reasons—most decisively because the sincerity of the artist is seldom verifiable. Was Shakespeare sincere when he wrote *Macbeth* or Sonnet 73? Who can say?" (p. 106). Is that a rhetorical question? And does it mean, What difference does it make? But why ask it rhetorically? When I said that modern art forced the question of seriousness and intention and sincerity, I thought the implication clear enough that the issue was not *forced* in earlier art, and I suggested reasons for that: e.g., that conventions were deep enough to achieve conviction without private backing. If the question is a real one, what is the answer? Is it that *nobody* can say, because there is no verification available for any answer? But that assumes we know what "verification" would look like here. Beardsley refers to "well-known reasons" for the failure of such considerations. He may have in mind the sort of considerations pressed by him and W. K. Wimsatt in their well-known article, "The Intentional Fallacy":

> One must ask how a critic expects to get an answer to the question about intention. How is he to find out what the poet tried to do? If the poet succeeded in doing it, then the poem itself shows what he was trying to do. And if the poet did not succeed, then the poem is not adequate evidence, and the critic must go outside the poem—for evidence of an intention that did not become effective in the poem.[4]

It is still worth saying about such remarks that they appeal to a concept of intention as relevant to art which does not exist elsewhere: in, for example, the case of ordinary conduct, nothing is more *visible* than actions which are not meant, visible *in* the slip, the mistake, the accident, the inadvertence . . . , and by what follows (the embarrass-

---

[4] "The Intentional Fallacy," in W. K. Wimsatt, *The Verbal Icon* (Lexington: University of Kentucky Press, 1954; paperback, 1958, 1967), p. 4.

ment, confusion, remorse, apology, attempts to correct . . . ). Of
course we may not know what is happening in a given case: the boxer
who connects and wins may have meant to miss and throw the fight.
We may have to go outside the punch itself to find this out, but then
there is no question what kind of evidence will be relevant. Now,
how is it imagined we are to discover the artist's intention—when,
that is, we are told that there is no way inside the poem of verifying
it? Are we supposed to *ask* the poet, or interview someone who knows
him well? But the problem is: How is anything we learn in such ways
to be identified as the intention of *this* work?

I had suggested that a certain sense of the question "Why this?"
is essential to criticism, and that the "certain sense" is characterized
as one in which we are, or seem to be, asking about the artist's intention in the work. If this is correct, then these are plain facts, true
descriptions which depend on knowing what kind of objects poems
are and what kind of activity criticism is. The philosopher, hearing
such claims and descriptions, has his ancient choice: he can repudiate
them, on the ground that they *cannot* be true (because of his philosophical theory—in this case of what poems are and what intentions
are and what criticism is); or he can accept them as data for his
philosophical investigation, learning from them what it is his philosophizing must account for. Beardsley's procedure is the former, mine
the latter. According to Beardsley's, when a critic inquires about
intention, seriousness, sincerity, etc., he is forced outside the work.
My point is that he finds this true because of his idea of where an
intention is to be searched for, and because he has been reading
unhelpful critics. For the *fact* is that the correct sense of the question
"Why?" directs you further *into* the work. In saying that this, if true,
is a fact, I mean to be saying that it is no more than a fact; it is not an
*account* of objects of art, and intention, and criticism, which shows
the role of this fact in our dealings with art.

I said that it is not merely a bad picture of intention that makes
this seem false or contentious or paradoxical, it is also a bad picture
of what a poem is. It is the picture of a poem as more or less like a
physical object,[5] whereas the first fact of works of art is that they are

[5] "Judging a poem is like judging a pudding or a machine. One demands that it
work. It is only because an artifact works that we infer the intention of an artificer. 'A
poem should not mean but be.' A poem can *be* only through its *meaning*—since its
medium is words—yet it *is*, simply, *is*, in the sense that we have no excuse for inquiring
what part is intended or meant" (ibid., p. 4).

meant, meant to be understood.[6] A poem, whatever else it is, is an *utterance* (outer-ance). It is as true to say of poems that they are physical objects as to say of human actions that they are physical motions (though it is perfectly true that there would not be an action unless somebody moved, did something). But it is pointless to pursue this discussion in the absence of concrete instances of works and criticism to which each philosophy undertakes responsibility. So let me simply claim that apart from the recognition that one's subject, in art, is the intentionality of objects, one will appeal, in speaking of these objects, to sources of organization (rhyme schemes, scansion patterns, Baroque "structure," sonata "form," etc.) in ways which fail to tell why *this* thing is as it is, how it means what it does.

But of course I was claiming, in my paper, more than this. I was claiming that in modernist art the issue of the artist's intention, his seriousness and his sincerity, has taken on a more naked role in our acceptance of his works than in earlier periods. This is an empirical claim, depending on a view of the recent history of the arts and on my experience of individual works of that period. I discussed the concept of intention only long enough to try to head off the use of a philosophical theory which would prevent, or prejudice, an investigation of this claim. In this, I was evidently unsuccessful. So let me give one further suggestion about why, if the considerations I raised are relevant, they have not been confronted.

The New Critics' concentration on the poem itself, in a way which made the poet's intention or sincerity look irrelevant, had an immediate liability in their relative neglect of Romantic poets and their successors. (In itself, this is hardly surprising: particular poetic theories are directly responsive to *certain* poetic practice.) My claim can be put by saying that the practice of poetry alters in the nine-

---

[6] Someone will feel: "No. The first fact about works of art is that they are *sensuous*—their impact is immediate, not intellectual." There are times when that will be what needs emphasis, because that will be the thing we have forgotten. And I do not wish to deny what it means. But it only says why there is a problem. If words always supplied only information, if paintings were always diagrams or illustrations, if music were always the heightening of serious, or light, occasions; there would be no problem (or not the same problem) about whether, or how, the work is meant. Again, it should be considered that this emphasis on sensuousness is fully true only during certain moments in the arts, for example when pleasure is its motivation (when, say, gardening was still considered, as in Kant, one of the arts; and that motivation, in varying intensities, will no doubt continue in the major arts when gardens and gardening no longer serve it sufficiently). Still, if one wishes: The first question of aesthetics is: How does that (sensuous object) mean anything?

teenth and twentieth centuries, in such a way that the issues of intention and seriousness and sincerity are forced upon the reader by the
poem itself: the relation between author and audience alters (because
the relation between the author and his work alters, because the relation between art and the rest of culture alters . . . ). Specifically, the
practice of art—not merely the topic of art, but as it were the replacing or internalizing of its pervasive topic—becomes religious. When
Luther said, criticizing one form in which the sacraments had become
relics, "*All* our experience of life should be baptismal in character,"
he was voicing what would become a guiding ambition of Romanticism—when religious forms could no longer satisfy that ambition.
Baudelaire characterizes Romanticism as, among other things, intimacy and spirituality. This suggests why it is not merely the threat of
fraudulence and the necessity for trust which has become characteristic of the modern, but equally the reactions of disgust, embarrassment, impatience, partisanship, excitement without release, silence
without serenity. I say that such things, if I am right about them, are
just facts—facts of life, of art now. But it should also be said that they
are grammatical facts: they tell us what kind of object a modern
work of art is. It asks of us, not exactly *more* in the way of response,
but one which is more personal. It promises us, not the re-assembly
of community, but personal relationship unsponsored by that community; not the overcoming of our isolation, but the sharing of that
isolation—not to save the world out of love, but to save love for the
world, until it is responsive again. "Ah, love, let us be true to one
another . . . ." We are grateful for the offer, but also appalled by
it.

I say "we," and I will be asked "Who?" I will be told that it is
not Mr. Arnold speaking to us, but a mask of Arnold speaking to . . .
anyway not to us: we don't so much hear his words as overhear them.
That explains something. But it does not explain our responsibility
in overhearing, in *listening*: nor his in speaking, knowing he's over-
heard, and meaning to be. What it neglects is that we are to *accept*
the words, or refuse them; wish for them, or betray them. What is
called for is not merely our interest, nor our transport—these may
even serve as betrayals now. What is called for is our acknowledgment
that we are implicated, or our rejection of the implication. In dreams
begin responsibilities? In listening begins evasion.

Not that it is obvious how intention and sincerity and seriousness are to be established in art, any more than in religion or morality or love. But this is just what I have against the discussions I have read and heard on these topics; they are unreal in their confidence about what establishing an intention, or an attitude, would be like. A man asks me for a candlestick from the mantel and I bring it to him; he looks and says, "No. I meant the other one." Did he? Does his saying this establish his intention? Not in the absence of an understandable continuation. If he simply puts the thing on the floor beside him and I cannot imagine to what point, nor can I imagine what he may want to use it for later, nor can I see what its difference is from the one he rejected, I am not going to say that he *meant* this one rather than the other one. (Perhaps his intention was to demonstrate the completeness of my subservience, obeying pointless requests.) What the continuation will have to be, how it establishes the intention, will vary in range and complexity, with the context.

Take an example from the making of movies, which is relatively free of the ideologies and attitudes we have constructed for the major arts. On my interpretation of *La Strada,* it is a version of the story of Philomel: the Giulietta Masina figure is virtually speechless, she is rudely forced, she tells her change by playing the trumpet, one tune over and over which at the end fills the deserted beach and whose purity at last attacks her barbarous king. Suppose I want to find out whether Fellini intended an allusion to Philomel. If I ask him, and he affirms it, that may end any lingering doubts about its relevance. Suppose he denies it; will I believe him, take his word against my conviction that it is there? In fact, my conviction of the relevance is so strong here that, if I asked Fellini, I would not so much be looking for confirmation of my view as inquiring whether he had recognized this fact about his work. One may ask: "Doesn't this simply prove what those who deny the relevance of intention have always said? What is decisive is what is there, not what the artist intended, or said he intended." What this question proves is that a particular formulation of the problem of intention has been accepted. Because in what I have been urging, this alternative between "what is intended" and "what is there" is just what is being questioned. Intention is no more an efficient cause of an object of art than it is of a human action; in both cases it is a way of understanding the thing done, of describing what happens. "But you admit that Fellini may not have known, or may not find relevant, the connection with Philomel. And if he didn't

know, or doesn't see the relevance, surely he *can't* have intended it.
And yet it is there, or may be."

What is the relation between what you know (or knew) and
what you intend to be doing? It is obvious enough that not everything you know you are doing is something you are intending to be
doing (though it will also not be, except in odd circumstances, something you are doing unintentionally either). To take a stock example:
you know that firing a gun is making a lot of noise, but only in special
circumstances will making the noise be (count as) what it is you are
intending to do. But perhaps that is irrelevant: "It is still true that
anything you can be said to have intended or to be intending to do is
something you know you are doing. Either Fellini did or did not
know of the connection with the Philomel story. If he did not know
then it follows that he did not intend the connection. If he did know
then that connection may or may not have been intended by him.
In all these cases, what he knew and what he intended are irrelevant
to our response. It is what he has *done* that matters." But it is exactly
to find out what someone has done, what he is responsible for, that
one investigates his intentions. What does it mean to say "Making the
noise was not his intention"? What it comes to is that if asked what
he is doing he will not answer (or one will not describe him as)
"Making noise." That aspect of what he is doing is obvious, or irrelevant—there is no reason to call attention to it. But suppose there is.
There is a child asleep in that house; or terrified by noise; or the
noise is a signal of some kind. Suppose he hadn't known. Very well, it
can be pointed out to him; and now, should he go on firing the gun,
*what* he is doing will be differently described. We might say: his
intention will have altered. And yet he would be *doing* the same
thing? But the point is: when further relevances of what you are
doing, or have done, are pointed out, then you cannot disclaim them
by saying that it is not your intention to do those things but only the
thing you're concentrating on. "Unintentionally," "inadvertently,"
"thoughtlessly," etc., would not serve as excuses unless, having needed
the excuse, you stop doing the thing that keeps having these unintentional, inadvertent, thoughtless features.

"But doesn't this just show how different the artist's situation is?
There isn't going to be some obvious description like 'Firing a gun'
to describe what he's done, and even if there were, you couldn't *alter*
his intention (whatever that means) by pointing out the further rele-

vances of his work, because in looking for the artist's intention the point surely would not be to get him to stop doing what he is doing, or do something else; his intention is history, forever fixed—whatever it was, it has had *this* result—and the work it has created has consequences only in terms of that work itself. You say that if a man doesn't realize the concomitants of his action you can point them out; but before you point them out they were not known and hence cannot have been a part of *that* intention." The artist's situation is indeed different, but it doesn't follow that what we are interested in, being interested in his work, is not his intention (in the work).

Suppose Fellini hadn't thought of Philomel. How am I to imagine his negative response to my question—when, that is, I find that it doesn't matter what he says? Am I to imagine that he says, "No. I wasn't thinking of that," and there the matter drops? But one would not accept that even in so simple a case as the firing gun: he may not have thought of it before, but he had better think of it now. I am not aesthetically incompetent (any more than I am morally incompetent when I point out that a child is asleep or terrified); I know what kind of consideration is artistically relevant and what is not, as well as anyone else, though I may not be able to articulate this relevance as well as useful critics can, much less create the relevance in a work of art.

I say he had better think about it once I point out the connection; but obviously he may refuse to, and he *can* refuse because this is not a moral context, there is no new practical consequence forthcoming. But there are consequences: if he doesn't see the relevance, I am shaken in my trust in him as an artist. He may not care about that, but I do, and that is all I am concerned with here. Suppose he does acknowledge the relevance, but hadn't thought of it until it was pointed out to him. Wouldn't that in fact just show that he can't have intended it?  —So intention cannot be what secures the relevance of one's descriptions of a work.

Now the difference between the artist's case and the simple physical action becomes critical. Everything depends upon how the relevance is, or is not, acknowledged. Suppose he says, "Of course! That's just the feeling I had about my character when I was making the picture. Odd the story never occurred to me." Or: "How ironic. I had tried to translate that story into a modern setting several times with no success. Here, without realizing it, I actually did it." In such cases I am inclined to say that the relevance is intended. (Here, one will have to investigate ordinary cases in which, e.g., dissatisfied with the way you have put something—a phrase, or a vase—you are offered a new alternative and, accepting it, reply: "Yes, that's right. That's what I meant"—when, by hypothesis, *that* alternative had not occurred to you.) At a glance, one might take the second case ("without realizing it") as one of inadvertence rather than intention. But that would be true only if the allusion was one he hadn't wanted, doesn't want now. (In the land he has made, the artist is entitled to everything he wants, if it's there.) Nor am I prompted to add that the intention was *unconscious*. That may well describe certain cases, but its usefulness will have specifically to be made out. What would prompt it here is the idea that intentions must be *conscious*—the same idea which would prompt one to deny that Fellini can have intended the reference if it hadn't occurred to him at the time, if he hadn't been aware of it. But what is the origin of the idea that intentions must be conscious? It is not clear what that means, nor that it means anything at all, apart from a contrast with unconscious intentions; and it is not clear what that means.

Part of its origin is doubtless the fact that you can't be intending to do a thing if you don't *know* you're doing it, or rather don't know how what you are doing could have that consequence (if you didn't know about the child, you can't have intended to frighten it). But what does "knowing it" consist in? Certainly one can know a thing without bearing it in mind (fortunately—otherwise there wouldn't be room for much), or having it occur to you at regular intervals. It makes sense to say Fellini intended (that is to say, Fellini can have intended) the reference to Philomel if he knew the story and now sees its relevance to his own, whether or not the story and its relevance occurred to him at the time. (I do not say that under these conditions he did intend it; knowing is at best necessary, not sufficient for intention. Whether he did intend it depends on what he *did*, on the work itself.) This may still seem puzzling; it may still seem, for example, that no present or future relevation can show what an earlier intention was.

But why is this puzzling? Perhaps it has to do with our, for some reason, not being free to consider what "acknowledging an intention" is, or what "being shown relevance" is. Suppose the man had known about the child but had forgotten. Reminded, he is stunned, and quickly acknowledges his forgetfulness. Without that, or some similar, acknowledgment, the excuse/apology would not be acceptable—would not *be* an excuse or apology. Suppose he has conveniently forgotten; confronted, he may vehemently deny that he had known, or that it matters; or vehemently acknowledge that he had intended to wake or terrify the child. Vehemence here measures the distance between knowing a thing and having to acknowledge it. I imagined Fellini's acknowledgment of the relevance as coming with a sharp recognition, a sense of clarification. Otherwise, it is not an acknowledgment of something he intended or wanted. He might simply have been putting me off.

Perhaps the puzzlement comes from the feeling that it is not enough for him merely to have *known* the story; the knowledge must have been *active* in him, so to speak. And doesn't that mean he must have been aware of it? Two considerations now seem relevant:

1. It is not necessary for him in fact to have been aware of it; but it is necessary that he can *become* aware of it in a particular way. The man firing the gun can become aware of those further relevances only by being told them, or by further empirical exploration. But the artist becomes aware of them by bethinking himself of them; by, as it were, trying the intention on himself now. This difference is what one would expect. For there is no relevance to point out, in relation to a work of art, which the artist has not himself created. It is he who has put the child there and made it sleep or filled it with fear.

2. It is, or ought to be, obvious enough that an artist is a man who knows how to *do* something, to make something, that he spends his life trying to learn to do it better, by experience, practice, exercise, perception . . . . And as is familiar with any activity: you can be an expert at it (know how to do it well) without knowing (being aware of) what it is you do exactly; and certainly without being able to say how you do it. (There are obvious problems here. Can you know how to play the clarinet if you can't play the clarinet? You might know how—without being able to—well enough to teach someone to play. Only you won't, as part of your teaching, be able yourself to *demonstrate* the correct way. In certain cases one might wish to say that you couldn't *teach* someone how, but you could *tell* him how.) Suppose someone noticed that Babe Ruth, just before swinging at a pitch, bent his knees in a particular way. Obviously he may not be aware that he does this, but does it follow that it is not done inten-

tionally? If there is reason to believe that bending his knees is an essential part of what makes him good at batting—an explanation of how he does it—I find I want to say that he does it intentionally; he means to. I would not say this about the way he habitually tugs at his cap before gripping the bat, unless it were shown that this was connected with the way he then grips it—e.g., he has some secret substance in the bill of the cap, or it serves to fix his fingers in some special position. Nor would I say this about some action which hindered a performance—the way, for example, one of his team mates drops his shoulder as he swings; he may invariably do this, and be perfectly aware of it, and working hard to get over it: it is unintentional, he doesn't mean to. But all of this is hardly surprising: intending to do something is internally related to wanting something to happen,[7] and discovering an intention is a way of discovering an explanation. That one is locating intention is what accounts for the fact that a piece of criticism takes the form of an interpretation.

I do not wish to claim that everything we find in a work is something we have to be prepared to say the artist intended to put there. But I am claiming that our not being so prepared is not the inevitable state of affairs; rather, it must be exceptional (at least in successful works of art)—as exceptional as happy accidents, welcome inadvertencies, fortunate mistakes, pure luck.[8] Perhaps the actions of artists produce more such eventualities than other forms of human conduct (hence, the poet as dumb Bard, or wild child, and the function of the Muse). But then they are also fuller of intention (hence, the artist as genius, visionary).

Given certain continuations I may want to say: Fellini didn't intend the reference, but, being an artist he did something even

[7] This is one among several points at which acknowledgment is due G. E. M. Anscombe's *Intention* (Ithaca, N.Y.: Cornell University Press, 1957), a work which no one involved in this topic will safely neglect.

[8] The "must" in "must be exceptional" is a point of Transcendental Logic. It doesn't mean: Invariably, most of what is in the object is intended. It means: Our concept of a work of art is such that what is not intended in it has to be thought of, or explained, in contrast to intention, at the same level as intention, as the qualification of a human action. Of course not every portion of an interpretation will be directed simply to pointing out something which is there, i.e., something the artist may or may not have intended. Sometimes it will be directed toward helping us appreciate what has been pointed out. Sometimes this will involve evaluating the intention—e.g., as cheap, childish, courageous, perverse, willful; sometimes it will involve evaluating its execution, as, e.g., crude, brutal, thoughtless, inattentive; sometimes it will involve comparing the given work with another one whose intentions are different.

better; he re-discovered, or discovered for himself, in himself, the intention of that myth itself, the feelings and wants which originally produced it. Or I may simply say: So it wasn't intentional. I shall be surprised, perhaps led to go over his work again to discover whether I still find the connection as powerful as I did at first; perhaps it is merely a superficial coincidence, and blocks me from a more direct appreciation. But if I do still find it useful, I shall still use it in my reading of the film, not because his intention no longer guides me, but because what it does is exactly guide me (as it guided him). To say that works of art are intentional objects is not to say that each bit of them, as it were, is separately intended; any more than to say a human action is intentional is to say that each physical concomitant of it is separately intended—the noise, that grass crushed where I have stood, that branch broken by the bullet, my sharp intake of breath before the shot, and the eye-blink after . . . . But all these are things I have done, and any may become relevant. In tragedy, consequence altogether outstrips the creature's preview, and nature and society exact their price for a manageable world; in comedy, the price is born by nature and society themselves, smiling upon their creatures. In morality, our interest in intention, given the need to confront someone's conduct, is to localize his responsibility within the shift of events. In art, our interest in intention, given the fact that we are confronted by someone's work, is to locate ourselves in its shift of events. In all cases, the need is for coming to terms, for taking up the import of a human gesture. In all, I may use terms to describe what someone has done which he himself would not use, or may not know. (Here the problem of oblique contexts is explicitly relevant.) Whether what I say he has done is just or not just is something that will require justification, by further penetration into what has happened, what is there. What counts is what is *there*, says the philosopher who distrusts appeals to intention. Yes, but everything that is there is something a man has *done*.

Games are places where intention does not count, human activities in which intention need not generally be taken into account; because in games *what happens* is described solely in terms set by the game itself, because the consequences one is responsible for are limited a priori by the rules of the game. In morality, tracing an intention limits a man's responsibility; in art, it dilates it completely. The artist is responsible for everything that happens in his work—and not just in the sense that it is done, but in the sense that it is *meant*. It is a terrible responsibility; very few men have the gift and the patience and the singleness to shoulder it. But it is all the more terrible, when it *is* shouldered, not to appreciate it, to refuse to understand something meant so well.

I break off with one further way in which questioning the artist may work itself out. Instead of considering my inquiries with due solemnity, he may tell me to mind my business, or my manners; or deliberately mislead me. (So may his work. And of course by now the artist has dropped out anyway; it is his work we are interviewing.) What would this signify? Perhaps that he has said all he can, conveyed his intentions as fully as his powers allow, in the work itself— as if to say: "You want to spare yourself the difficulty of understanding me, but there is no way else to understand me; otherwise it would not have cost me such difficulty to make myself exactly understood." One might have been aware of that oneself, and not meant to be getting out of difficulty, but asking help to get in further. Why, in those circumstances, would the artist turn away? In *those* circumstances he might not. But then claiming to be in those circumstances is a large claim, and how does one justify it? Asking anyone about his intentions is asking whether he is meeting his responsibilities, asking an explanation of his conduct. And what gives one the right? In morality the right is given in one's relation to what has been done, or to the man who has done it. In art, it has to be earned, through the talent of understanding, the skill of commitment, and truthfulness to one's response—the ways the artist earned his initial right to our attention. If we have earned the right to question it, the object itself will answer; otherwise not. There is poetic justice.

# IX

# Knowing and Acknowledging

It is, I believe, generally assumed—certainly it is natural to assume—that the philosophical appeal to ordinary language constitutes some sort of immediate repudiation of traditional philosophy, in particular of that continuous strain or motive within traditional philosophy which is roughly characterizable as skepticism (a strain or motive which most clearly includes elements of Cartesianism and of British Empiricism). This formulation is vague enough, and the assumption I refer to, if I am right that it is there, is itself vague enough. It would be the latest in the long history of altering relations which philosophy, as it alters, will draw between itself and common sense or everyday belief or the experience of the ordinary man. And the specific terms of criticism in which one philosophy formulates its opposition to another philosophy or to everyday beliefs is as definitive of that philosophy as any of the theses it may produce. I wish in what follows to suggest that so far as the appeal to what we should ordinarily say is taken to provide an immediate repudiation of skepticism, that appeal is itself repudiated.

The usefulness, not to say the authority, of appeals to what we should ordinarily say, *as philosophical data*, depends upon their being met in independence of any particular philosophical position or theory. (This is, I take it, what the phrase "ordinary language" meant to its Oxford coiners: a view of words free of philosophical preoccupation.) It looks as if this is what is happening in appealing to ordinary language against skepticism: the skeptic has a particular philosophical view which positions his words oddly, whereas the ordinary language critic makes use only of what any unprejudiced man can see to be the straight truth. But this is partial, because it assumes that the skeptic need not be counted among those who can see that their words are in apparent conflict with what is ordinarily said and that he is not in full authority to settle, or account for, that conflict in ordinary terms.

The partiality of these ideas shows two ways: (1) They assume that the skeptic is for some reason less perfect a master of (say) English than his critic. Put this way, the assumption is patently incredible. But what else are we given to believe? That he misuses words or changes their meanings? (For no reason? Or out of perversity? Or guile?) Or that he cannot really mean what he says? (Because it is obviously not true?) But what reason is there to believe such claims? (2) When the skeptic repudiates something we would all say is the correct thing to say (for example, when he denies that I am certain that there is a table here or that I can see it) he immediately goes on to concede, for example, that "for practical purposes" I am certain and that "in a sense" I can see it (I see it "indirectly")—concessions which exactly register his knowledge that his conclusions are incompatible with what should ordinarily be said, and which leave what is ordinarily said quite intact, if somewhat abashed.

These concessions may themselves seem forced, or seem empty; but to show this you have to show that a master of English, who knows everything you know, has no real use for them. And how could this be shown? An essential step in showing it would be to convince the skeptic—that is, the skeptic in yourself—that you know what he takes his words to say. (Not exactly what he takes them to *mean*, as though they had for him some special or technical meaning.) Understanding from inside a view you are undertaking to criticize is sound enough practice whatever the issue. But in the philosophy which proceeds from ordinary language, understanding from inside is methodologically fundamental. Because the way you must rely upon yourself as a source of what is said when, demands that you grant full title to others as sources of that data—not out of politeness, but because the nature of the claim you make for yourself is repudiated without that acknowledgment: it is a claim that no one knows better than you whether and when a thing is said, and if this is not to be taken as a claim to expertise (a way of taking it which repudiates it) then it must be understood to mean that you know no better than others what you claim to know. With respect to the data of philosophy our positions are the same. This is scarcely a discovery of ordinary language philosophy; it is the latest confirmation of what the oracle said to Socrates. The virtue of proceeding from ordinary language is that it makes (or ought to make) this message inescapably present to us.

In particular, it provides the message with three methodological morals: (1) The appeal to ordinary language cannot directly repudiate the skeptic (or the traditional philosopher generally) by, for example, finding that what he says contradicts what we ordinarily say or by claiming that he cannot mean what he says: the former is no surprise to him and the latter is not obviously more than a piece of abuse. What the appeal can and ought directly to do is to display what the skeptic does or must mean, even how he can mean what he says. What other way is there to take him seriously? And if his critic has not taken him seriously, why should he listen to what he is told? He knows he is not understood. (2) This means that the appeal to what we should ordinarily say does not constitute a defense of ordinary beliefs or common sense. One could say: We can disagree in many of our beliefs, but that very disagreement implies that we agree in the use of the words which express those beliefs. (If the *words* meant something other than they seemed to mean, the skeptic would not even seem to conflict with ordinary beliefs when he says, for example, "I cannot know that another man is in pain because I cannot have his pain.") One could also say: The issues over which philosophers conflict with one another or with common sense are not "beliefs" which each has about the world. The *Investigations* has this: "I am not of the *opinion* that he has a soul" (p. 178). Nor am I of the opinion that there is a world, nor that the future will be like the past, etc. If I say that such ideas are the ground upon which any particular beliefs I may have about the world, or the others in it, are founded, this does not mean that I cannot find this ground to crack. (This is why the skeptic's knowledge, should we feel its power, is devastating: he is not challenging a particular belief or set of beliefs about, say, other minds; he is challenging the ground of our beliefs altogether, our power to believe at all.) Proceeding from what is ordinarily said puts a philosopher no closer to ordinary "beliefs" than to the "beliefs" or theses of any opposing philosophy, e.g., skepticism. In all cases his problem is to discover the specific plight of mind and circumstance within which a human being gives voice to his condition. Skepticism may not be sanity, but it cannot be harder to make sense of than insanity, nor perhaps easier, nor perhaps less revealing. And the first fact it reveals is that an appeal to what we should say is not the same as a piece of testimony on behalf of what we all believe. That the appeal sometimes presents itself as a piece of such testimony is what makes it natural to assume that the appeal is inherently anti-skeptical. But my interest in finding what I would say (in the way that is relevant to philosophizing) is not my interest in preserving my beliefs. (Of course I have not said what "in the way that is relevant to philosophizing" means. The point of these remarks is exactly that this requires investigation. The sentences which immediately precede this parenthesis might serve as beginning points in such an investigation.) My interest, it could be said, lies in finding out what my beliefs mean, and learning the particular ground they occupy. This is not the same as providing evidence for them. One could say it is a matter of making them evident. And my philosophical interest in making them evident is the same as my interest in making evident the beliefs of another man, or another philosophy. And I do not know what my interest in them would be, nor how I could make them evident, if I did not or could not share them. (3) It will seem that these remarks put the ordinary language critic at the mercy of his opposition— that a test of his criticism must be whether those to whom it is directed accept its truth, since they are as authoritative as he in evaluating the data upon which it will be based. And that is true. But what it means is not that the critic and his opposition must come to *agree* about certain propositions which until now they had disagreed about (for just as we do not *believe*, for example, that the world exists, so it would be empty to *agree* that it exists—you might as well *decide* that it exists). What this critic wants, or needs, is a possession of data and descriptions and diagnoses so clear and common that apart from them neither agreement nor disagreement would be possible—not as if the problem is for opposed positions to be reconciled, but for the halves of the mind to go back together. This ambition frequently comes to grief. But it provides the particular satisfaction, as well as the particular anguish, of a particular activity of philosophizing.

Two admirable articles have recently appeared which, it seems to me, harbor more or less definite ideas of the skeptic and share the sense that appeals to ordinary language constitute (what I have been calling) direct repudiations of skepticism concerning our knowledge of other minds.[1] In what follows I will use several passages from each as a way of exemplifying concretely several of the claims I have been making. These papers are congenial in their recognition that the skeptic's position needs accounting for if criticism against him is to be formidable. Both, however, are hasty in their conviction that this position has been correctly drawn, and to that extent their counter-assertions lack force. My object here is not to answer the questions, "What, or who, is the skeptic? What is the power of his position?"; it is an attempt to show why those questions are worth asking.

✳ ✳

The question of the privacy of pain, according to Professor Malcolm, is "the idea that it is impossible that two people should have (or feel) the *same* pain" (p. 138). Against this idea he cites Wittgenstein's remark: "In so far as it makes *sense* to say that my pain is the same as his, it is also possible for us both to have the same pain." The point here is that different kinds of objects have different criteria of identity. With a sensation—as with a color, style, disease, etc.—the criterion of identity, that in terms of which various instances count as *one*, is given by a description of it; with other objects—material objects, points?—the criterion may be identity of location.

Some philosophers might take this as a sufficient refutation of the skeptical idea that two people cannot have the same pain, so it is worth noticing that it is not. If, as it stands, it were a refutation, it must further be true that when an object's criterion of identity is a description, then we *only* count in terms of that description. But this also depends on the kind of object it is. To say we own the same car (that is, are partners) is to say that there is one car we own. (What makes it the same one is its physical integrity, so to speak.) To say we have the same car is to say that my car is the same as yours (both are 1952 MG-TD's). That they are the same means that they are not different, anyway not different *makes*. I do not know whether we will say they are different *cars*, but it cannot be denied that I have

---

[1] (1) Norman Malcolm, "The Privacy of Experience," in Avrum Stroll, ed. *Epistemology: New Essays in the Theory of Knowledge* (New York: Harper and Row, 1967), pp. 129–58. (2) John W. Cook, "Wittgenstein on Privacy," *The Philosophical Review*, Vol. LXXIV (1965), pp. 281–314; reprinted in G. Pitcher, ed. *Wittgenstein: The Philosophical Investigations* (New York: Doubleday Anchor Original, 1966). Page references to this article are according to its original occurrence.

mine and you have yours—that there are two. That the cars are counted as the same does not mean that there are not two of them. This may lead one to wonder: How can two things be the same thing? It may calm the wonder to be told: (1) where it makes sense to say that one thing is the same as another, it makes sense to say they are the same thing. It may flatly answer the wonder to be told: (2) there *aren't* two things, there is only one. This will be the answer with respect to colors or gaits, for example. If the color of that block fits the same description as the color of this block (say, #314 of the Universal Color Chips) then the color of the blocks is the same, period. If you ask, "But aren't there still two colors?", then unless you mean that one of them seems closer to #315 or #313, you don't know what "color" or "same" means, what *a* color is.

Which of these answers would one like to give to the question: How can two pains be one and the same pain? I think it is fair to say that Malcolm gives, or suggests, both answers, but it is not clear to me that this can coherently be done. Because the first answer seems clearly to imply that it also makes sense to say there are two pains, *two the same*; whereas the second answer denies flatly that it makes sense to say there are two at all. It seems that with pains, as with cars, but not with colors, we can say: In a sense there are two, but in a sense there is only one. And we see, or seem to see, what these senses are: philosophers have called them "qualitative identity" and "numerical identity." Malcolm therefore, wanting to deny that there is a good sense in which (descriptively) identical pains can be said to be *two,* properly undertakes to show that the notion of "numerical identity and difference" *has no application* to sensations. How is this made out?

"Given that the description of your image, feeling or emotion is the same as mine, there cannot be a *further* question as to whether yours is *different* from mine" (p. 144). But this can be said of our twin cars as well: they are not different. But there are two. *Why,* with respect to pains described the same, can there be no further question? Because "the same" *means* "descriptively the same"? Obviously it doesn't. Because "the same" *applied to pains* can only mean "descriptively the same"? But why shouldn't the skeptic at this point simply feel that this begs the question? Is there no further question because saying "the same" *settles* the question? But is this true? With cars the question *is* settled, in favor of two; with colors the question is also settled, in favor of one. How is it settled in the case of pain?

Malcolm finds (p. 142) that while "the temptation is great (indeed, overwhelming) to suppose that there is a sense of 'same sensation' in which two people *cannot* have the same," nevertheless "the case is really no different from that of styles, colors, opinions, and sudden thoughts." Sticking to color, how is this assimilation to be established? Or, what perhaps comes to the same, how can one share Malcolm's confidence that what the skeptic is expressing can only be "an overwhelming temptation" and cannot be an insight, or fact? Earlier Malcolm had said:

> Surface A and surface B have exactly the same color, i.e., they are "identical" or "indistinguishable" in color. Can there be a further question as to whether the color of A is numerically identical with the color of B? What would it mean? Given that the color of one area is indistinguishable from the color of another area, what more can be asked? Despite what we are tempted to think, there is not a sense of "same color" such that the color of one place *cannot* be the same as the color of another place. It is one of the most truistic of truisms that the very same shade of color can be many places at the same time (p. 141).

This seems to show how *different* colors are from, say, headaches. I can't offhand answer—offhand it means nothing to ask—whether the identically colored objects have numerically identical colors. But I *can* answer the question whether my headache is numerically identical with his. The answer is, Of course not! (though it's true we've compared notes and discovered that we suffer the same frightful headache, the one Dr. Ewig describes as part of Ewig's Syndrome). I may not like the question, or quite see its point, but it seems I have to answer as I answered—"have to answer" in the sense that if I do not the skeptic would seem justified in feeling that I was *avoiding* the answer, avoiding the truth. Whereas in the case of color, I simply and truly *have no answer*. "Despite what we are tempted to think . . ." Malcolm says. But I do not find that I am a bit tempted to think that there is some sense of "same color" such that the color of one object *cannot* be the same as the color of another.

What Malcolm's assimilation of pain to color shows is solely that color and pain are alike in this respect: both are counted or identified in terms of descriptions. But in this respect both of them are also like 1952 MG-TD's. Colors cannot be counted in any other way, but it is not *plain* that pains cannot be counted any other way. If pressed at this point I find I would say that in this respect pains are more like objects than like colors. We may both have Dr. Ewig's Syndrome, with its headache, but I have mine and you have yours, I express or suppress mine, and you yours. If we are both given identical blue headbands, then while I have my headband and you have yours, I don't have my blue and you yours. There *could* be a blue which was my blue (one I alone know how to mix, or characteristically wear), but it would be different from your blue (if you had one); that's the point of saying "my" here, the point of associating it with me in particular—though you may copy or adopt it. But if a headache is (described as) my headache, the point of associating it with me is not necessarily to distinguish it from yours. It is not generally important whether it is different from yours, if you happen to have one; though we may try to determine whether we hurt in the same place, or as much, perhaps because that will help diagnose its cause, but perhaps because misery loves company. There is as much or as little point in associating it with me as there is point in showing that I have one. "My headache is worse" is as much an *expression* of the headache as "I have a headache" is. And it is striking that the point of locating *exactly* where the child hurts, while it is in part, or first, to see what needs to be done, is also, and often wholly, to be able to sympathize more relevantly. One could say: Our interest in pain is different from our interest in color. The fundamental importance of someone's having pain is *that* he has it; and the nature of that importance—namely, that he is suffering, that he requires *attention*—is what makes it important to know where the pain is, and how severe and what kind it is (among a very few kinds, e.g., throbbing, dull, sharp, searing, flashing . . .). These are the ways we have of identifying pains; and so you can say, if you like, that if one pain gets identified by these criteria with the same results as another does (same place, same degree, same kind) then it is the same pain. But it also seems to me not *quite* right, or these criteria of identity are not quite enough, to make fully intelligible saying "the same."

These criteria are meant to show, to the extent possible, that the two pains (I mean, this man's pain and that man's pain) are physically identical (or indistinguishable); but exact physical similarity is not in every case enough to establish the application of "(descriptively) the same." (Physical integrity is sufficient in the case of re-identifying an object as the same one you saw yesterday, or used when you were there last year. . . .) Unless there is a *standard* description of an object in terms of which specific features are antecedently established as securing the application of the description, and thereby securing that various instances count as the same, then "(descriptively) the same" is not fully justified. And generally: physical identity (that is, empirical indistinguishability) is neither sufficient nor necessary to justify "(descriptively) the same." It is not sufficient: for two peas in a pod may be empirically indistinguishable (apart from their difference of location, on a particular occasion) but that would not lead us to say that the peas are one and the same (unless, perhaps, they are together being contrasted with a third pea of a different variety). It is not necessary: for if there *is* some standard description (or some striking feature in terms of which a description is constructed) which secures the application of "(descriptively) the same" to each of two instances, then we tolerate an indefinitely wide physical discrepancy between the instances. My MG-TD may be badly battered and yours freshly hammered out and repainted, but we still have the same car; my headache may be causing a twitch in my eyelid, or go with a mild nausea, but if both meet Dr. Ewig's criteria then we have the same headache. (Perhaps these considerations explain why Wittgenstein says merely "*in so far as* it makes sense to say my pain is the same as his . . ."; he does not say that it always makes sense, nor even that it ever does fully.) We could say: Our normal interest in saying "descriptively the same" is the interest in the standards in terms of which instances are counted the same (e.g., an interest in their cost or consequences or treatment or the taste they express), not an interest in their physical identity (which comes up when the point is, for example, to *match* objects, in order to get one of the right weight or color, or determine one of the right proportion . . .). So it looks as if, whether or not the skeptic has falsely taken "numerical identity or difference" to be applicable to sensations, the philosopher opposing skepticism is led to apply "descriptively the same" apart from its normal criteria—as though he has no real use for the concept (except to refute the skeptic).

The skeptic comes up with his scary conclusion—that we can't know what another person is feeling because we can't have the same feeling, feel his pain, feel it the way he feels it—and we are shocked;

we must refute him, he would make it impossible ever to be attended to in the right way. But he doesn't *begin* with a shock. He begins with a full appreciation of the decisively significant facts that I may be suffering when no one else is, and that no one (else) may know (or care?); and that others may be suffering and I not know, which is equally appalling. But then something happens, and instead of pursuing the significance of these facts, he is enmeshed—so it may seem —in questions of whether we can have the same suffering, one another's suffering. But whether or not one senses that the issue has become deflected in the course of his investigation, his motivation in it is still stronger, even more comprehensible, than that of the anti-skeptic. I mean: it is clear why the skeptic has to consider whether we can feel (have) the (same) experience another person feels (has). He has, or seems to himself to have, discovered that unless we can share or swap feelings, we can't know what that person is experiencing (if anything). I do not say this is a perfectly unobjectionable idea, but I am far from confident that I know what is objectionable about it. And I am confident that if I *have to consider* the question "Can I have the same feeling he does?", consider it seriously, not knowing as it were what the answer *must* be, then the honest answer must be, No. Let me be as clear as I can: it may turn out that the question is badly conceived, and that the honest answer collects merely an illusion of honesty and provides only the illusion of an answer. But I do not see that this has been *shown*. It is *assumed*, I think it is clear, that the skeptic *cannot* be serious, that he has discovered nothing which his words are trying, perhaps slightly forced, to convey. But what justification is there for such assumptions? That his conclusion conflicts with common sense? He knows that, and he accounts for it. That in practical situations he does not practice his skepticism? He knows that, and he accounts for it. That there is a sense in which we *can* have the same feeling? He knows that, too: that is exactly *why* he says that we do not have *literally* the same, *numerically* the same, feeling—conceding as it were that we have descriptively the same. Now again, he may here have been pushed into a distorted utterance, contracted the illusion of a discovery. But this cannot be shown by insisting that we do or can have the same.

To offer that as an answer to the skeptic (and what other reason is there for *insisting* upon it?) is fatal. It is (1), as was said, inaccurate; or, where accurate, disappointingly limited. It is (2) empty, because the skeptic's use of the qualification "literally or numerically" means exactly that he is not denying that the feelings may be descriptively the same. This accounts for the way (3) the skeptic's supposed discovery is *stronger* than the anti-skeptic's supposed fact (which appears as a fact, even an arbitrary fact, about language); because the obvious fact that we can (or can be said to) have the same is *undercut* by the discovery that we cannot have literally or numerically the same. (His discovery makes our ordinary use of "the same" seem a *façon de parler*, and makes the ordinary language philosopher's *appeal* to this use seem willful ignorance or superficiality.) The underlying reason for this is that the skeptic's problem, unlike the anti-skeptic's, is directed to what I spoke of earlier as our natural interest in the occurrence of pain, namely, *that* a given man has it. It reveals (4) that the anti-skeptic's motivation is at least as questionable as the skeptic's. For what is at stake for the anti-skeptic in insisting that we *can* have the same? Suppose we *can*, now, have the same (descriptively the same, the same in the sense in which it makes sense to say "the same") pain as anyone else can have—say a headache localized over the right eye. Does *he* have this particular pain? Granted that he can, does he? Can we know here and now that he does? And faced with that question, *my* pain is obviously irrelevant (it may even make it harder for me to find out whether he has the pain). Someone may even be led now to suppose that, apart from my pain, I need (a replica of) his in order to know whether he has it. And we don't know how to grant *that*. If this is the way things are, we don't know whether he has the pain or not; we never can.

But of course it will be objected: "You make it seem that being unable to imagine having (or to grant that we may have) literally or numerically the same pain as he has (i.e., have his pain) describes a real or intelligible experience. But it is a complete confusion; there is nothing we need or need to grant. You have tolerated the idea of 'numerical or literal identity,' but that is what is incoherent. There is no such thing to grant; the wish for it is a wish for nothing; not a real wish." But why isn't this hysterical? What I have said is this: To meet the skeptic by saying that we *can* have the same feeling, fails; in failing, it perpetuates the idea that whether we have the same feeling is *relevant* to whether we can know what another is feeling; but if this is taken as relevant, it is discovered that the sense in which we can have the same feeling is insufficient for knowing whether another person feels what I feel, or feels anything at all.

A gap has (apparently) been revealed which must be closed if we are to know whether another is in pain, a gap described in terms of "having numerically or literally the same pain he has."

If this is not perfectly intelligible, it is not perfectly unintelligible either. (That is the trouble with skepticism; and the skeptic has an explanation of it. For example, he may speak of knowing something which he cannot believe.) To say it is completely unintelligible is something which has to be made out, and it is not clear what making it out will have to consist in. The *words* aren't unintelligible. (If, as I began by arguing, comparing the skeptic's words with their everyday use does not automatically show that he means nothing, but rather shows what he *must* mean, or *does* mean, then the question is, (how) can he? It is a *question*.) One wants to say: What it *envisions* is unintelligible. But *what* is envisioned which is unintelligible? It looks as if to make out that it is unintelligible you have to do exactly what the person who claims to envision it has to do —say what is envisioned. But it is exactly your point that this cannot be done. Does your inability prove your point, or defeat it? If you take it to prove your point, what you are assuming is that your inability has, so to speak, the same significance as the skeptic's—that is, you assume that if what he envisions is intelligible he has to be able to say what it is; or rather, you assume that the fact that he can't means that he can't show it to be intelligible. But there will seem to him to be *this* asymmetry between his inability and yours: he doesn't need to show its intelligibility—because, perhaps, he knows he means the words, they have *that* much intelligibility, and it doesn't matter that they do not describe an envisionable state of affairs; they are the only (they are the *right*) words for meeting the situation he has found himself in. (If not, so much the worse for his words.) Whereas you *do* need to show its unintelligibility, since, so to speak, you have no other use for the words than that. What you then need to do is show that *he* has no real use for them either, that their intelligibility is illusory, that he can't *really* mean them, that he has merely the *impression* of saying something.[2] How is this to be done?

Take a different case. At a certain point in his investigation, a

<hr>

[2] The last of these diagnoses is Cook's (cf. pp. 294, 300). Because a number of my remarks—including the whole of the paragraph to which this note is attached—are prompted by reservations about specific diagnoses Cook elaborates (another central one concerns the "supposed literal sense" of sentences or statements—cf. pp. 296–97), I should say explicitly that I do not regard my remarks as overturning those diagnoses, and certainly not as exhausting their interest.

traditional epistemologist will say: You can't see the back of the object, nor its inside, so all you see, at most, is the front surface. Is this unintelligible? Suppose one tries to make this out as follows: "*What* can't I do? I don't know what it would be like if I *could* see the back half while standing in front of it! It's as if you envision a situation in which seeing an object would be having one's sight penetrate through an infinite layer of surfaces. That is what is not intelligible. And until you make that intelligible, it makes no sense to say I can't do it." But is that true? And doesn't it seem to increase the hysteria it wishes to oppose? And why can't the skeptic here simply feel: "You don't understand what I mean. My words are intelligible, it's obvious what they mean, and your suggestion of a situation which cannot be envisioned just shows you don't understand. Your idea simply indicates that you have no use for those words, and the reason you have no use for them is that you do not appreciate what I have discovered." The anti-skeptic will now want to show the skeptic that he sees no real problem either, has no real use for the words either. But how? Presumably by finding out what the source of the apparent intelligibility is, what gives the impression of meaning something; in a word, by diagnosis. —But we know the source of the intelligibility: the words themselves, the fact that *they* are intelligible, i.e., that in some contexts they carry full meaning. "You can't see the back half, so you don't know it's red all over"—there is no trouble finding a practical context in which that is a fact (namely, one in which it is of practical importance that the object be (say) red all over and in which you cannot in fact see the part not facing you). And now comes the objection: The skeptic uses a form of words that makes perfect sense in certain contexts and then applies it to a case in which it makes no sense. He takes a context in which the back half of an object is in fact hidden from view and uses that as the model for seeing objects generally.

The problem with this objection is that it cuts two ways: it does show that the skeptic is shifting contexts, but it also shows why what he says *is intelligible*. (If not fully, still not fully not.) That these words are not ordinarily used in such contexts doesn't mean they can't naturally be given application in them. (Using language depends on this ability to give application in new contexts.) Whether his words mean what they say here, or only produce in him the impression of a meaning, depends on whether they have been given application. And it doesn't seem obvious that an object can't (and even oughtn't to) be taken to be something whose front ineluctably conceals its back. This is, of course, not all the skeptic wants. He wants us to see the rightness, the inevitability of his application; and given that, his conclusion comes fast. But it is *no* argument against his application to say that if he is allowed it an unwelcome conclusion follows.

Similarly with "we cannot have literally or numerically the same feeling as another." Malcolm says that "If the distinction between 'the same' and 'numerically the same' *were* to be given an application to sensations, then we should have to *make up* criteria for it" (p. 145). He takes the case of the Siamese twins with a common hand and notes our conflict in deciding whether to call a pain in that hand one pain or two. But we don't need the common hand to bring out this conflict. If each of us has the pain (caused, say, by a hammer blow) in the same place on our left hands (say, under the nail of the thumb), then asked "Are there one or two pains?" we will be pulled in the same directions as in the case of the Siamese twins. This may mean that such a case is not of the right kind for giving the distinction its application. It might even be that what produced the Siamese twins as the right kind of case is a particular picture of what "having numerically the same pain" would be, if so to speak it had a use— a picture in which the pain is located in numerically the same place. But is this the right, or a necessary, picture?

Take a case adapted from that of the Corsican Brothers, one of whom, call him Second, suffers everything which happens to his brother First. Whip First and Second writhes with him (not in sympathy, *seeing* what's happening; but even miles away, not knowing what is happening). Add to this the fact that Second never suffers unless First does: whip Second himself and he doesn't feel it. I assume further that there is no physical trauma produced in Second by what First undergoes. What I wish the example to create is the sense that Second feels pain because First *feels* it—so that, for example, if First is anaesthetized, Second equally feels nothing. Therefore it is crucial to the example that First be something we treat as a living body. (It is not unimaginable that it be a dummy or a doll which has some peculiar causal connection with Second. But that would not be a case of "feeling because another feels it.")   —I think one finds that the usual philosophical remark to the effect that "Any pain one feels will be one's own" is, though said to be logically necessary, simply false here. Second *has* no pain of his own; he has only First's pain. And doesn't it describe this situation to say: His pain is not just descriptively the same as First's, it is numerically the same?

So here we have a pain in *this* body and a pain in *that* body and it is numerically the same pain, literally the same. The thing which looked unintelligible, was so, only given a certain picture. What has happened to make the situation intelligible is this: while we still have pain in two bodies, we no longer have, so to speak, two *owners* of pain. That is, the pain in Second's body is not Second's pain. (This is not a case of "feeling pain in another's body.") It is not clear whether Second will express his pain by saying "I am in pain" or "He (First) is in pain"; nor whether he will locate the pain in his leg *on* his leg or on First's. What is significant is that he can do either. Which he will do will depend on the point of expressing and locating the pain in a given context. It is not that he is in doubt whether he (or, for that matter, First) is in pain; but that expressing and locating pain can be said to have a different point than they now have. (His pain won't be relieved unless you attend to First; but he may nevertheless be comforted if you attend to him (Second).)

Does this give the skeptic what he took to be necessary in order to know that another is in pain? Surely it cannot be denied that Second *knows* that First is in pain, knows what he feels, and knows it *because* he feels it, because he *has* that pain?

The skeptic, on this realization of his wish, has got more than he bargained for. Let us ask: Does First know what Second feels, that Second is in pain? I think one will be pulled in opposite directions. One of them will be: Since they have numerically the same pain, First *must* know. But another will be: What *can* First know other than his own pain? That's the *only* pain he has. That it is the only pain *Second* has is perhaps irrelevant here; for even if one insists that Second is feeling something separate from First, and that First's feeling tells him that, First's feeling, as it were, drowns it out. Every pain First feels is *his*. (This now means something in contrast to Second, none of whose feelings are his.) First knows *what* Second feels (and when and where he is feeling it)—but so can we know those things. I would like to say that First's knowledge of Second's pain—if based on his own pain—is somehow too intellectual to be called "knowledge that Second is in pain"; he indeed has, I feel like saying, a model of Second's pain, but the primary fact for him is that *he* feels it, as if there is no way around it to appreciate the individuality of Second's pain (though First may sympathize, in moments of saintliness or calm, with Second's *position* with respect to him). If First's knowledge is not based on his own pain, then he knows, or fails to know, the way anyone would. The numerical identity of his pain with Second's is unusable for just the thing for which it seemed indispensable. The skeptic's wish is granted, but it does not—or ought not to—satisfy him.

Nor does it—nor ought it to—satisfy him in the case of Second's knowing First's pain. Here what emerges is not so much that the wish is insufficient as that it is a wish for the wrong thing. We admitted that Second has not only numerically the same pain as First, but has First's pain, and that he knows First is in pain on the basis of his having it. But I find that while it may not wholly be wrong to say "Second knows First is in pain," this again is not what *we* mean by "knowing someone is in pain." Not because I (in Second's position) do not know that the pain I have is *his*, had by him (First). (That was true of the case in which I gave myself descriptively the same pain; and perhaps it is true of First's position.) It is rather that *his* pain no longer contrasts with *my* pain, his has no further content, so to speak; "his pain" no longer differentiates what he feels from what I feel, him from me; he is not *other* in the relevant sense. I said that in the former case (First knowing Second) First's knowledge is "too intellectual"; even though he has the same pain as Second, he still has to "infer" (or remember?) that Second is in pain. So the phenomenological pang in having to say that knowing another mind is a matter of inference—something shared by the skeptic and the anti-skeptic—remains after we have granted what seemed to be lacking in our knowledge of the other. In the latter case (Second knowing First), Second's knowledge is "too immediate"; his "having" First's pain is, one might say, an effect of that pain, not a response to it—a different phenomenological pang. But how shall we understand this wish for a *response* to my expressions (of pain, of any region of the mind)? Does it suggest that our concept of my knowledge of another is bound up with the concept of my freedom, an independence from the other, from all others—which I may or may not act upon? What is this "knowing a person"?

* *

What does it mean to say, "I know he is in pain," and how does that differ from saying, "I know I am in pain"? It will perhaps be thought that I should have asked these questions before submitting to the skeptic's wish to "know another's pain the way he does," because that wish can be shown to be incoherent quite directly, namely by showing that one does not *know* one's own pain at all, or, as it may be put, that the statement "I know I am in pain" is senseless. So the whole idea that he knows something I do not know is senseless.

I claimed earlier that the attempt to answer the skeptic's denial that two people can have the same pain, by the head-on assertion that they *can*, puts the anti-skeptic in a weaker position than the skeptic; where "weaker" means "weaker in conviction or motivation" and "no better in faithfulness to what we all believe"—so that our ordinary beliefs seem subject either to open repudiation or to faint-hearted defense. Something similar is happening here.

At some stage the skeptic is going to be impressed by the fact that my knowledge of others depends upon their *expressing themselves*, in word and conduct. That is surely an essential fact to be impressed by. And then he realizes that the other may not in fact express himself, or that his expression may be falsified (deliberately or in some other way); and that again is undeniable. It follows that in such a case I would not know what is going on in the other. So the skeptic adds, supposing himself to express that fact, "But still *he* knows." And if *now* the anti-skeptic digs in his heels, he must seem to the skeptic simply perverse. The only obvious reason for digging in one's heels here is that in another moment it will turn out that *I* can *never* know; and we don't want that. So again, if that is the reason, then the skeptic must suppose that you are just avoiding the truth. There is a fact there to be recorded. The skeptic records it by saying "He knows what he is feeling." There is, I take it, no suggestion that the skeptic can't speak English as well as another man, so why assume that he is mis-speaking here? Because that *isn't* what the words "He knows he's in pain" record? Two questions arise: (1) What *does* record that fact? And (2) What does "He knows he's in pain" record? The anti-skeptic goes on to answer the second of these questions, but the skeptic will not be much impressed; it will seem like quibbling about words. Because *his* fact needs recording, and until you can show what records it you have no grip against his conviction that, whatever else "He knows he's in pain" records, it also records this fact. This is another way of saying what I meant by calling the anti-skeptic's position weaker: the skeptic has a fact which needs noticing and recording; the anti-skeptic has no fact of his own to compete with that, he has only some words to think about, and his words keep looking like they *deny the facts*.

"I know I am in pain" is senseless, Malcolm says. Well, the skeptic realizes that *something* is odd about it, but since he needs it he diagnoses why it seems odd (e.g., it is so trivially true as not to be worth saying—except to someone trivial enough to deny it) and then goes on using it. If the anti-skeptic is to penetrate this defense, it can't be enough to show that it is odd, even very odd, or that the skeptic's diagnosis of its oddness is wrong. He has to show that its oddness prevents it from recording that fact. Is that what showing that it is "senseless" accomplishes?

How is its senselessness made out? Malcolm argues that the "I know" in "I know I'm in pain" "cannot do any of its normal jobs" (p. 148). He cites three normal jobs: claiming grounds, authority, and privileged position. But are there no other relevant functions of "I know"? Here are three more: (1) There is "I know New York (Sanskrit, the signs of the Zodiac, Garbo, myself)." To know in such cases is to have become acquainted with, or to have learned, or got the hang of. (2) There is, again, "I know I am a nuisance," "I know I am being childish," "I know I am late." To (say you) know in these cases is to admit, confess, *acknowledge*. (3) There is, again, the use of "I know" to *agree* or confirm what has been said, or to say I *already* knew.   —Can it be shown that none of these additional uses exemplifies a (the) relevant use of "I know" in "I know I'm in pain"? They are not obviously irrelevant. So what accounts for Malcolm's having taken the uses of "I know" he cites as alone relevant, suggesting that if it has a genuine use with respect to first person present tense statements about pain, it must be one of these?

The uses Malcolm cites are ones connected with the idea of certainty; in them "I know" contrasts with "I believe"; all claim that one is in a position to know, and someone who uses them competently must be prepared to document his claim. It is true that "I know I'm in pain" hasn't the function of claiming certainty. Professor Cook puts this by saying that it is not an "expression of certainty" (p. 287). We might put it by saying, "I know I'm in pain" does not mean "I'm certain I'm in pain"—there is no condition short of certainty which the claim to certainty would be excluding. Cook allows *a* use of "I know I'm in pain" (Malcolm allows a similar use of "I know I have a toothache"), one related to the final use of "I know" I added to Malcolm's three, the one in which I *agree*. But this use is not, as Cook correctly and usefully says, an expression of certainty; it is an expression of *exasperation* (p. 285); and the implication is that this use is not going to help the argument that I know something which no one else can know. —It is worth noticing that it is not *because* it is an expression of exasperation that it *can't* be an expression of certainty (i.e., senseless as an expression of certainty). "I *know* Washington never told a lie" expresses certainty; and it *also* can express exasperation (say in a context in which you go on refusing to believe me; or one in which you tell *me* about George Washington, as if it's news, when it was I who told you). Its exasperation does not compete, so to speak, with its other potentialities of expression.

It is obvious enough, but unremarked, that "I know I'm in pain" (containing as its assertible factor "I am in pain") is an *expression of pain* (accepting Wittgenstein's view that "I am in pain" is such an expression). It may also be an expression of exasperation. And it has the form ("I know I . . .") of an *acknowledgment* (the second use of "I know" which I added to Malcolm's three). As an acknowledgment (admission, confession) it is perfectly intelligible. It won't be one which is used very often, perhaps; it requires a context in which, for some reason, I wish to conceal my pain—say because to admit it would be shameful, or would look like an excuse —and the person to whom I say "I know I . . ." here is trying to get me to admit it.

Does *this* use of "I know I'm in pain" also repudiate the skeptic's argument, i.e, does it fail to record his fact? What he wanted to say was "Only *he* knows whether he's in pain; I do not know." One is fully entitled to say "Only he can acknowledge his pain; I can't"; and it can be said with exasperation (which would not prevent it from being true) and as an expression of certainty. It is not, it seems, in fact what the skeptic does say; he says that the other alone *knows*, not that the other alone *can acknowledge*. But what is the difference? It isn't as if being in a position to acknowledge something is *weaker* than being in a position to know it. On the contrary: from my acknowledging that I am late it follows that I know I'm late (which is what my words say); but from my knowing I am late, it does not follow that I acknowledge I'm late—otherwise, human relationships would be altogether other than they are. One could say: Acknowledgment goes beyond knowledge. (Goes beyond not, so to speak, in the order of knowledge, but in its requirement that I *do* something or reveal something on the basis of that knowledge.)

Is it, then, a suppressed premise of the skeptic's that "If he can acknowledge he's in pain then he knows whether he is in pain"? And would we deny this premise?   —"Still, this does not alter the fact that if he says 'I know I'm in pain' he will not be expressing certainty, and *this* is what the skeptic needs."   —Perhaps he will not be expressing *certainty*; but why can one not say, what his words say, that he is expressing *knowledge*? And isn't *that* what the skeptic needs? But then, if the philosopher really stuck to the idea of another person's failing to *acknowledge* his experiences, he would never become a skeptic; that is, the philosopher's fact would simply be the ordinary fact that sometimes we just do not know the experiences of others: they often, even more often than not, conceal them. This does not lead to his unleashed conclusion that we can *never* know, that the feelings of another are ineluctably concealed from us because we can not *have* them.

Maybe the situation is like this: the fact that another person may now be in pain yet not acknowledge that he is in pain, is the same as, or seems to entail, the fact that he now knows that he is in pain; and this turns into the (imagined?) fact—or is read as the (imagined) fact—that he is now *certain* that he is in pain. And from *this* point, the rest of the argument is forced upon us, seems undeniable: How does he know (what is his certainty based on)? Because he feels (has) it (the fact that he feels (has) it). But obviously I can't feel it, I can't have the same feeling he has, his feeling; so I can never be certain another person is in pain. Moreover, even if he tells me, he might only be feigning, etc., etc.

This argument may be incoherent, or have incoherent presuppositions; but it does not *begin* incoherently, and it is not clear, once begun, that any given step is avoidable. Any formidable criticism, I take it, must be as compelling as the argument itself is. I have suggested in particular that neither of two criticisms are strong enough to place much confidence in: neither "We *can* have the same pain" (which denies the truth of one of the steps) nor "The form of words 'I know I am in pain' is senseless, as an expression of certainty" (which takes a presupposition to be incoherent). Our choice seems to be this: either we accept the anti-skeptic's *analysis* of the several statements made by the skeptic, which explain why they make no sense, or are false; or we hold on to the obvious facts which they seem to record, and conclude that the offered analysis cannot be correct, has not followed the argument.

✳ ✳

The head-on effort to defeat skepticism allows us to think we have explanations where in fact we lack them. More important, in fighting the skeptic too close in, as it were, the anti-skeptic takes over—or encourages—the major condition of the skeptic's argument, viz., that the problem of knowledge about other minds is the problem of certainty. At the same time, he neglects the fundamental insight of the skeptic by trying single-mindedly to prove its non-existence —the insight, as I wish to put it, that *certainty is not enough*. What I mean can perhaps be brought out this way: In concentrating on the skeptic's apparently impossible demands (and neglecting what may be the insight which produces those demands) the anti-skeptic concentrates on the first-person half of the problem of other minds, to the neglect of the third person, as though half believing the skeptic's repudiation of the third person. When he does consider that person, it is in contrast to the first person, and largely only to the extent of saying that such statements as "I know (am certain) he is in pain," "I doubt whether he is in pain" *make sense* as opposed to their first person analogues (cf. Malcolm, p. 146). Obviously they do make sense in this opposition—that is, as expressions of certainty. But in *this* sense they raise no special problems about our knowledge: sometimes we are certain, sometimes we know we are not; and on various obvious grounds—we heard it over the radio, or someone told us, or we went upstairs and saw for ourselves, or we heard him cry out, or we saw opened medicine bottles on his night table, etc. But there *are* special problems about our knowledge of another; *exactly the problems the skeptic sees*. And these problems can be said to invoke a special concept of knowledge, or region of the concept of knowledge, one which is not a function of certainty. This region has been pointed to in noticing that a first person acknowledgment of pain is not an expression of certainty but an expression of pain, that is, an exhibiting of the *object* of knowledge. There is an analogue to this shift in the case of third person utterances about pain.

I said: Third person utterances about sensations—where they express certainty—raise no special problems about our knowledge of others. I could also have said: They are not *basic* to the problem of other minds, the way "I see it" is basic to establishing claims to know the external world. The gamekeeper may have told me, or I figured it out for myself, or I have noticed footprints in the sand—but unless I see (or sense) the bittern in the garden, the basic way of knowing has not been forthcoming, and when it comes it takes precedence: unless somebody has actually witnessed the thing, the whole structure of reports may collapse. (It is exactly when *my* witnessing of the thing, under the best possible conditions, does (seem to) collapse that I know the entire structure of reports about the external world collapses.) Similarly, unless there is someone who knows (there is a way of knowing) at first hand, or directly, that another person is in pain, the whole structure of reports about another is left up in the air.  —But there *is* someone who knows, there is a position which is totally different from mine in the matter of knowing whether he is in pain, different not only in being better (as if certain factors in my position were increased in accuracy or range) but in being decisive, making the best position I can be in seem second hand: namely, *his* position. I do not mean to insist upon the validity of this idea of "position," but phenomenologically, as a datum, it seems to me undeniable. I think everyone recognizes the experience which goes with it, that it is some terrible or fortunate fact, at once contingent and necessary, that *I* am not in that position; the skeptic merely comes to concentrate upon it. And it is not obviously invalid.

Cook offers this repudiation of such an idea: the idea that I cannot know another's feeling because I cannot *have* that feeling

> . . . makes out the difference between first- and third-person sensation statements to rest on a matter of circumstance (like being unable to see my neighbor's crocuses), whereas Wittgenstein has made us realize that the difference resides in the language game itself. The difference does not rest on some circumstance, and therefore . . . [the idea] which purports to name such a circumstance with the

words "being unable to feel another's sensations", is inherently confused (p. 291).

Why is "being unable to feel another's sensation" not a circumstance? Because, I take it, it is not something that can coherently be imagined to be other than it is; it does not describe an *inability* of ours, but a general fact of (human) nature. (This is, one assumes, the force of saying "the difference resides in the language game itself".) But why can't a general fact of nature be thought of, accurately, as a circumstance, a permanent circumstance? The circumstance is, I feel like saying, *him*. The problem, that is, may be that the formulation "inability to feel" tries but fails to capture my experience of separation from others. This does not make it inherently confused but, one might say, much too weak—as though words are in themselves too weak to record this fact. If the skeptic does not recognize this failure of (his) words, then *this* is the correct criticism of him here (though we do not yet know how serious a criticism it is). But to apply an inaccurate term of criticism to him (to say of him, falsely, that his idea is inherently confused) further deflects the truth to which he is responding.

What wishes to express itself as an "inability" might vanish if I could become clear what my *abilities* are in this domain and in this way make clear what it seems to me they are insufficient to accomplish. It may look as if that is just what the analogy of the neighbor's crocuses makes clear, that I am regarding my inability to enter my neighbor's mind as something like an inability to enter his garden; only, as it were, it is a permanent inability, the garden is sealed or charmed out of reach. And then, shown this, I am to realize that this is a bad analogy and to conclude that there is nothing I cannot do.　—But *is* this my impression, when, that is, I am under the impression that there is something I cannot know about my neighbor? And why should I conclude that it is wrong—as the expression of an impression, for which words are too weak anyway? (For it isn't as if the *words* "enter into the minds of others" are themselves senseless. It is only a way of *taking* the words, a "picture" of their application, that is being called senseless; and it looks as if the senseless way of taking them is expressed by the analogy of entering a garden. But that is the question: *Is* that the way they are, or need to be, taken? And isn't there a way of taking "enter his garden" which makes it a correct (figurative) description of what I do when I enter his mind?) I would express my feeling, rather, simply as one of inability; that is, one of being *powerless*. And I do not see that I have to accept the question, "Powerless to do *what*?"; any more than if I sometimes express a particular sense of being defenseless or dependent I have to specify, in order to substantiate the validity of this feeling, what it is I am defenseless against or dependent upon. Of course I do not claim that the sense of powerlessness is to be taken at face value, as though it itself, so to speak, shows what it is I am powerless to do; on the contrary, it is my point that it does not claim to do this. The feeling needs accounting for, as dependence and defenselessness do. And it is not clear a priori that in accounting for it one will not be contributing to an investigation of our knowledge of other minds. What is certain is that a false or forced account of it will not show it to be irrelevant to such an investigation.

Adapting another remark from the *Philosophical Investigations*, we might say: We know what the word "know" means, and we know what the words "a pain" mean, so we think we must know—or it must be obvious—what the combination "knowing a pain" means. Here the skeptic does seem impressed by a particular picture: a man's knowing his pain is something he is doing continuously (the eye turned inward and staring); which makes it unlike any other familiar kind of knowing. One feels here like saying to the skeptic: What is continuous is the sensation itself, and saying that a man *knows* this sensation adds nothing to saying that the sensation is *there*. But is that true? What it adds is the fact that the sensation is not *here*, that it is not continuous in me, so that even if I can be said to know he is in pain, I do not know it continuously, hence not the way he knows it. You may wish to say that "knowing continuously" is not *knowing* at all. But this has yet to be made out—for no one has denied that he can be *said* to know he is in pain (as a joke, for example); and if he knows then mustn't he know continuously? And the picture has at least this significance: it shows something of the inaccuracy of the neighbor's garden as a diagnosis of our impressions. For that analogy captures the impression that I am sealed *out*; but it fails to capture the impression (or fact) of the way in which *he* is sealed *in*. He is not in a position to walk in that garden as he pleases, notice the blooms when he chooses: he is *impaled* upon his knowledge.

The skeptic may not record that fact accurately, and he will come to the point of saying that we do not know this. But *this* is what we do not know, according to his picture (if my filling in of that picture is right as far as it goes). And this seems to me to be the right picture; and it is not false to say we do not know what it pictures. For what it pictures is the fact that behavior is *expressive* of mind; and this is not something we know, but a way we *treat* "behavior." The skeptic in effect goes on to say that we have no *reason* to treat behavior in this way. And is that false?   —But what he turns out to mean is that behavior is one thing, the experience which "causes" or is "associated" with it is something else. That is, he stops treating behavior as expressive of mind, scoops mind out of it. My point, however, is not to trace out the full extent of the skeptic's motivations; it is merely to deny that they, and what they lead him to, are senseless; or rather, to show that what he wants to know—namely, what it is we go on in the idea that behavior is expressive—is the right thing to want to know.

I take the philosophical problem of privacy, therefore, not to be one of finding (or denying) a "sense" of "same" in which two persons can (or cannot) have the same experience, but one of learning why it is that something which from one point of view looks like a common occurrence (that we frequently have the same experiences—say looking together at a view of mountains, or diving into the same cold lake, or hearing a car horn stuck; and that we frequently do not have the same experiences—say at a movie, or learning the results of an election, or hearing your child cry) from another point of view looks impossible, almost inexpressible (that I have your experiences, that I *be* you). What is it I cannot do? Since I have suggested that this question is a real one (i.e., that the sense of "cannot" here is real), and since nevertheless I have suggested that the question has no answer (on the ground that the words "cannot have his feeling" are "too weak" for the experience they wish to convey), I would need, in accounting for these facts, to provide a characterization of this sense of incapacity *and* provide the reason for our insistence upon putting it into words. I find that, at the start of this experience, I do not want to give voice to it (or do not see what voice to give it) but only to point (to others, or rather to the fact, or the being, of others) and to gesture towards my self. Only what is there to point to or gesture towards, since everything I know you know? It shows;

everything in our world shows it. But I am filled with this feeling—of our separateness, let us say—and I want you to have it too. So I give voice to it. And then my powerlessness presents itself as ignorance—a metaphysical finitude as an intellectual lack. (Reverse Faust, I take the bargain of supernatural ignorance.)

Consider, finally, how *special* the use of "I know he is in pain" is as an expression of certainty. Almost as special as the use of "I know I'm in pain" as an expression of exasperation. (And of course "I know he's in pain" is very likely to *be* an expression of exasperation.) To bring out *how* special the expression of certainty is, consider the other non-first person always (so far as I know) neglected in these discussions, the second person: "I know you are in pain." I said that the reason "I know I am in pain" is not an expression of certainty is that it is an expression of pain—it is an exhibiting of the object about which someone (else) may be certain. I might say here that the reason "I know you are in pain" is not an expression of certainty is that it is a response to this exhibiting; it is an expression of *sympathy*. ("I know what you're going through"; "I've done all I can"; "The serum is being flown in by special plane.")

But why is sympathy expressed in this way? Because your suffering makes a *claim* upon me. It is not enough that I *know* (am certain) that you suffer—I must do or reveal something (whatever can be done). In a word, I must *acknowledge* it, otherwise I do not know what "(your or his) being in pain" means. Is. (This is "acknowledging it *to* you." There is also something to be called "acknowledging it *for* you"; for example, I know you want it known, and that you are determined not to make it known, so I tell. Of course I do not acknowledge it the way you do; I do not acknowledge it *by expressing pain*.) But obviously sympathy may not be forthcoming. So when I say that "We must acknowledge another's suffering, and we do that by responding to a claim upon our sympathy," I do not mean that we always in fact *have* sympathy, nor that we always ought to have it. The claim of suffering may go unanswered. We may feel lots of things—sympathy, *Schadenfreude*, nothing. If one says that this is a *failure* to acknowledge another's suffering, surely this would not mean that we fail, in such cases, to *know* that he is suffering? It may or may not. The point, however, is that the concept of acknowledgment is evidenced equally by its failure as by its success. It is not a description of a given response but a category in terms of which a given response is evaluated. (It is the sort of concept Heidegger calls an *existentiale*.) A "failure to know" might just mean a piece of ignorance, an absence of something, a blank. A "failure to acknowledge" is the presence of something, a confusion, an indifference, a callousness, an exhaustion, a coldness. Spiritual emptiness is not a blank. —Just as, to say that behavior is expressive is not to say that the man impaled upon his sensation must express it in his behavior; it is to say that in order not to express it he must *suppress* the behavior, or twist it. And if he twists it far or often enough, he may lose possession of the region of the mind which that behavior is expressing.

This may seem clearly false, for if I am in pain how could I lose possession of that knowledge, whatever I do to my behavior? The specialness in the example of pain, always a matter waiting to become problematic in these discussions, may be easiest to overlook here. Let me conclude, therefore, with a word about this, marking a direction investigation might take. Three features of the concept of pain seem immediately relevant: (1) It is a phenomenon fully transparent to consciousness. (2) It is expressed by more or less definite forms of behavior. (3) It presents a case in which the distinction between the inner and the outer seems easy to draw. It is obvious enough that such features are useful to the skeptic's line of thought. The first feature secures intuitiveness for his remark that "even though *I* can't know, *he* knows"; the second eases the idea that there is a *clear* lack which may prevent my knowing, namely the absence of that definite behavior, and simultaneously undermines any standing which his *words* might naturally have in my knowing him; the third enables whatever stability the skeptical conclusion has. (A phenomenon such as envy, or the sense of loss, or working on a jigsaw puzzle, or a ringing in the ears, would lack one or another of these features. But it would be hasty to conclude that the skeptic had chosen his example just in order to illustrate his prior conclusions. It may be, rather, that the example is produced by the problem he takes himself to see, forced upon him by intellectual honesty and phenomenological scrupulousness; and then he reads off his conclusions from that necessary example.) Elsewhere, the first feature is what Wittgenstein is going on in remarking that "It can't be said of me at all (except perhaps as a joke) that I *know* I am in pain"; the second encourages the idea that Wittgensteinian criteria are exclusively behavioral; combined with this, the third creates the impression that he is a behaviorist. (He isn't a skeptic, so what else can he be?)

Of course Wittgenstein often denies that a particular feeling or experience is decisive for the application of a concept to others (or to oneself). Never, however, to deny the importance—much less deny the existence (whatever that would mean)—of the inner, but to bring to light false ideas of what is "inner." Similarly, he often speaks of criteria as consisting in what someone "says and does"; but rarely does he speak of someone's *behavior*. We are sometimes interested in an incongruence between feeling and its expression, but then we are perhaps interested in how someone *acts*; if his *behavior* (e.g., his deportment) is in question, that is not necessarily because his feeling is obscure—on the contrary, it may be obvious—but because it is incongruent with the place he is in. We are often interested in explaining someone's behavior; but we can hardly in general do this by appealing to *those* feelings (the ones expressed by the behavior in question), since what we may have been asking for is precisely an explanation for his feeling that way. We know (it is obvious) that dolls do not have feelings; but it should be no less obvious that dolls also do not exhibit behavior. Whether robots exhibit (creaturely) behavior (forms of *life*) is as much a problem—is perhaps the same problem—as whether they "have" "consciousness." —But if "behavior" and "consciousness" go together, in their presence and in their absence, how do "outer" and "inner" come apart?

We don't know whether the mind is best represented by the phenomenon of pain, or by that of envy, or by working on a jigsaw puzzle, or by a ringing in the ears. A natural fact underlying the philosophical problem of privacy is that the individual will take *certain* among his experiences to represent his *own* mind—certain particular sins or shames or surprises of joy—and then take his mind (his self) to be unknown so far as *those* experiences are unknown. (This is an inveterate tendency in adolescence, and in other troubles. But it is inherent at any time.) There is a natural problem of *making* such experiences known, not merely because behavior as a whole may seem irrelevant (or too dumb, or gross) at such times, but because one hasn't forms of words at one's command to release those feelings, and hasn't anyone else whose interest in helping to find the words one trusts. (Someone would have to *have* these feelings to know what I feel.) Here is a source of our gratitude to poetry. And this sense of unknownness is a competitor of the sense of childish fear as an explanation for our idea, and need, of God. —And why should the mind be less dense and empty and mazed and pocked and clotted—and why less a whole—than the world is? At least we can say that in the case of some mental phenomena, when you have twisted or covered your expressions far or long enough, or haven't yet found the words which give the phenomenon expression, I may know better than you how it is with you. I may respond even to the fact of your separateness from me (not to mention mine from you) more immediately than you.

To know you are in pain is to acknowledge it, or to withhold the acknowledgment. —I know your pain the way you do.

# X

# The Avoidance of Love

## A READING OF *KING LEAR*

A common way to remember the history of writing about Shakespeare is to say that until Bradley's *Shakespearean Tragedy* appeared in 1904, and culminating there, its main tradition had concentrated on Shakespeare's characters, while in recent generations emphasis has fallen on general patterns of meaning, systems of image or metaphor or symbol now taking the brunt of significance. Like most intellectual maps, this one is not only crude but fails worst in locating the figures one would like best to reach: Can Coleridge or Bradley really be understood as interested in characters *rather than* in the words of the play; or are the writings of Empson or G. Wilson Knight well used in saying that they are interested in what is happening in the words *rather than* what is happening in the speakers of the words? It is, however, equally easy and unhelpful to say that both ends of the tradition have been interested *both* in characters *and* in their words, first because this suggests that there are two things each end is interested in, whereas both would or should insist that they are interested only in one thing, the plays themselves; second, because there is clearly a shift in emphasis within that tradition, and a way of remarking that shift is to say that it moves away from studies of character into studies of words, and because such a shift raises problems of

Citations to the text of *King Lear* are from K. Muir, ed. (Cambridge: Harvard University Press, 1952, Arden Edition).

history and of criticism which ought not to be muffled in handy accommodations.

A full description, let alone explanation, of the history of Shakespearean criticism would be part of a full description of Western cultural history since the Renaissance. Failing that, one can still notice that the simply described shift from character to words is implicated in various more or less primitive theories whose hold on contemporary scholars is yet to be traced. For suppose we ask *why* such a shift has occurred. Immediately this becomes two questions: What has discouraged attention from investigations of character? What, apart from this, has specifically motivated an absorbing attention to words? I think that one reason a critic may shun direct contact with characters is that he has been made to believe or assume, by some philosophy or other, that characters are not people, that what can be known about people cannot be known about characters, and in particular that psychology is either not appropriate to the study of these fictional beings or that psychology is the province of psychologists and not to be ventured from the armchairs of literary studies. But is any of this more than the merest assumption; unexamined principles which are part of current academic fashion? For what is the relevant psychology? Of course, to account for the behavior of characters one is going to apply predicates like "is in pain," "is ironic," "is jealous," "is thinking of . . ." to them. But does that require psychological expertise? No more than to apply these predicates to one's acquaintances. One reason a critic is drawn to words is, immediately, that attention to characters has often in fact been given apart from attention to the specific words granted them, so it looks as if attention to character is a distraction from the only, or the final, evidence there is for a reading of a literary work, namely the words themselves. But it is then unclear what the words are to be used as evidence for. For a correct interpretation? But what would an interpretation then be of? It often emerges that the evidence provided by the words is to support something called the symbolic structure or the pattern of something or other in the piece. But such concepts are bits of further theories which escape any support the mere presence of words can provide. Moreover, there is more than one procedure which could count as "attending to words themselves." (Just as there is more than one way of expressing "faithfulness to a text.") The New Critics encouraged attention to the ambiguities, patternings, tensions of words; the picture is of a (more or less hidden) structure of which the individual words are parts. Another mode of attention to the particular words themselves is directed to the voice which says them, and through that to the phenomenology of the straits of mind in which only those words said in that order will suffice; here the picture is of a spiritual instant or passage for which only these words discover release, in which they mean deeply not because they mean many things but because they mean one thing completely. This is not necessarily a matter of better or worse but of different modes or needs of poetry.

It seems reasonable to suppose that the success of the New Criticism in the academic study of literature is a function of the way it is *teachable*: you can train someone to read complex poems with sufficient complexity, there is always something to say about them. But it is not clear what would count as training someone to read a lyric. You will have to demonstrate how it rests in the voice, or hauls at it, and you perhaps will not be able to do that without undergoing the spiritual instant or passage for which it discovers release (that is, unable to say what it means without meaning it then and there); and you may or may not be able to do that during a given morning's class, and either eventuality is likely to be inopportune in that place.

The most curious feature of the shift and conflict between character criticism and verbal analysis is that it should have taken place at all. How could any serious critic ever have forgotten that to care about a specific character is to care about the utterly specific words he says when and as he says them; or that we care about the utterly specific words of a play because certain men and women are having to give voice to them? Yet apparently both frequently happen. Evidently what is to be remembered here is difficult to remember, or difficult to do—like attending with utter specificity to the person now before you, or to yourself. It has been common enough to complain of the overinterpretation a critic may be led to, or may have recourse to; the problem, however, is to show us where and why and how to bring an interpretation to a close. (This is no easier than, perhaps no different from, discovering when and how to stop philosophizing. Wittgenstein congratulated himself for having made this possible, saying that in this discovery philosophy is given peace (*Investigations*, §133).)

My purpose here is not to urge that in reading Shakespeare's plays one put words back into the characters speaking them, and replace characters from our possession back into their words. The point is rather to learn something about what prevents these commendable activities from taking place. It is a matter of learning what it is one uses as data for one's assertions about such works, what kinds of appeal one in fact finds convincing. I should like to add that identical problems arise in considering the phenomenon of ordinary language philosophy: there the problem is also raised of determining the data from which philosophy proceeds and to which it appeals, and specifically the issue is one of placing the words and experiences with which philosophers have always begun in alignment with human beings in particular circumstances who can be imagined to be having those experiences and saying and meaning those words. This is all that "ordinary" in the phrase "ordinary language philosophy" means, or ought to mean. It does not refer to particular words of wide use, nor to particular sorts of men. It reminds us that whatever words are said and meant are said and meant by particular men, and that to understand what they (the words) mean you must understand what they (whoever is using them) mean, and that sometimes men do not see what they mean, that usually they cannot say what they mean, that for various reasons they may not know what they mean, and that when they are forced to recognize this they feel they do not, and perhaps cannot, mean anything, and they are struck dumb. (Here it is worth investigating the fact that the formula "He said . . ." can introduce either indirect discourse or direct quotation. One might feel: Indirect discourse doesn't literally report what someone *said*, it says what he *meant*. Then why do we say "He said . . ." rather than "He meant . . .", an equally common formula, but used for other purposes? Perhaps the reason is that what is said *is* normally what is meant, even that what is said is necessarily normally what is meant—if there is to be language. Not more than normally, however, because there are any number of (specific) ways in which and occasions on which one's words do not say what one means. Because the connection between using a word and meaning what it says is not inevitable or automatic, one may wish to call it a matter of convention. But then one must not suppose that it is a convention we would know how to forgo. It is not a matter of convenience or ritual, unless having language is a convenience or unless thinking and speaking are rituals.) If philosophy sometimes looks as if it wishes nothing more than to strike us dumb, then it should not be overlooked that philosophy also claims to know only what an ordinary man can know, and that we are liable to silence so produced only because we have already spoken, hence thought, hence justified and excused, hence philosophized, and are hence always liable not merely to say more than we know (a favorite worry of modern philosophy) but to speak above the conscience at the back of our words, deaf to our meaning. A philosopher like Austin, it is true, concentrates on examples whose meaning can be brought out by appealing to widely shared, or easily imaginable, circumstances (once he has given directions for imagining them)—circumstances, roughly, that Wittgenstein refers to as one of "our language games." But Wittgenstein is also concerned with forms of words whose meaning cannot be elicited in this way—words we sometimes have it at heart to say but whose meaning is not secured by appealing to the way they are ordinarily (commonly) used, because there is no ordinary use of them, in that sense. It is not, therefore, that I mean something *other* than those words would ordinarily mean, but rather that what they mean, and whether they mean anything, depends solely upon whether I am using them so as to make my meaning. (An instance cited by Wittgenstein is Luther's remark that "Faith resides under the left nipple.") In general, Part II of the *Philosophical Investigations* moves into this region of meaning. It is a region habitually occupied by poetry.

*King Lear* is particularly useful as a source for investigating the question of critical data and for assessing some causes of critical disagreement because there are a number of traditional cruxes in this play for which any critic is likely to feel compelled to provide his own solution. Some important ones are these: How are we to understand Lear's motivation in his opening scene? How Cordelia's? Is Gloucester's blinding dramatically justified? What is the relation between the Lear plot and the Gloucester sub-plot? What happens to the Fool? Why does Edgar delay before revealing himself to his father? Why does Gloucester set out for Dover? Why does France not return with Cordelia? Why must Cordelia die?

In the first half of this essay I offer a reading of the play sticking as continuously to the text as I can—that is, avoiding theorizing about the data I provide for my assertions, appealing to any considerations which, in conscience, convince me of their correctness—in the course of which the traditional cruxes are either answered or altered. Then, in the second half, I ask why it is, if what I say is correct, that critics have failed to see it. This precipitates somewhat extended speculations about the difficulties in the perception of such drama as *King Lear* presents, and I do not expect, even if my reading were accepted, that these speculations will find very immediate assent, nor even very readily be found relevant. But since whatever critical discoveries I can claim to have made hardly result from unheard of information, full conviction in them awaits a convincing account of what has kept them covered.

## I

In a fine paper published a few years ago, Professor Paul Alpers notes the tendency of modern critics to treat metaphors or symbols rather than the characters and actions of Shakespeare's plays as primary data in understanding them, and undertakes to disconfirm a leading interpretation of the symbolic sort which exactly depends upon a neglect, even a denial, of the humanness of the play's characters.[1] If I begin by finding fault with his reading, I put him first to acknowledge my indebtedness to his work. His animus is polemical and in the end this animus betrays him. For he fails to account for the truth to which that leading interpretation is responding, and in his concern to insist that the characters of the play are human beings confronting one another, he fails to characterize them as specific persons. He begins by assembling quotations from several commentators which together comprise the view he wishes to correct—the view of the "sight pattern":

> In *King Lear* an unusual amount of imagery drawn from vision and the eyes prompts us to apprehend a symbolism of sight and blindness having its culmination in Gloucester's tragedy. . . . The blinding

---

[1] *"King Lear* and the Theory of the Sight Pattern," in R. Brower and R. Poirier, eds. *In Defense of Reading* (New York: E. P. Dutton and Co., 1963), pp. 133–52.

of Gloucester might well be gratuitous melodrama but for its being imbedded in a field of meanings centered in the concept of *seeing*. This sight pattern relentlessly brings into the play the problem of seeing and what is always implied is that the problem is one of insight. . . . It is commonly recognized that just as Lear finds "reason in madness" so Gloucester learns to "see" in his blindness. . . . The whole play is built on this double paradox.[2]

But when Alpers looks to the text for evidence for this theory he discovers that there is none. Acts of vision and references to eyes are notably present, but their function is not to symbolize moral insight; rather, they insist upon the ordinary, literal uses of eyes: to express feeling, to weep, and to recognize others. Unquestionably there is truth in this. But the evidence for Alpers' view is not perfectly clear and his concepts are not accurately explored in terms of the events of the play. The acts of vision named in the lines he cites are those of giving *looks* and of *staring*, and the function of these acts is exactly *not* to express feeling, or else to express cruel feeling. Why? Because the power of the eyes to see is being used in isolation from their capacity to weep, which seems the most literal use of them to express feeling.

Alpers' dominant insistence upon the third ordinary use of the eyes, their role in recognizing others, counters common readings of the two moments of recognition central to the "sight pattern": Gloucester's recognition of Edgar's innocence and Lear's recognition of Cordelia. "The crucial issue is not insight, but recognition" (Alpers, p. 149): Gloucester is not enabled to "see" because he is blinded, the truth is heaped upon him from Regan's luxuriant cruelty; Cordelia need not be viewed symbolically, the infinite poignance of her reconciliation with Lear is sufficiently accounted for by his literal recognition of her.   —But then it becomes incomprehensible why or how these children have *not* been recognized by these parents; they had not become literally invisible. They are in each case banished, disowned, sent out of sight. And the question remains: What makes it possible for them to be *received* again?

    [2] Alpers gives the references for the elements of his quotation as follows: J. I. M. Stewart, *Character and Motive in Shakespeare* (New York: Longmans, Green and Co., 1949), pp. 20–21; R. B. Heilman, *This Great Stage* (Baton Rouge: Louisiana State University Press, 1948), p. 25; L. C. Knights, *Some Shakespearean Themes* (London: Chatto and Windus, 1959), p. 107; *King Lear*, ed. K. Muir (Cambridge: Harvard University Press, 1952, Arden edition), lx.

In each case, there is a condition necessary in order that the recognition take place: Gloucester and Lear must each first recognize himself, and allow himself to be recognized, revealed to another. In Gloucester, the recognition comes at once, on hearing Regan's news:

> O my follies! Then Edgar was abused.
> Kind Gods, forgive me that, and prosper him!
>
> <div align="right">(<i>III, vii,</i> 90–91)</div>

In each of these two lines he puts his recognition of himself first. Lear's self-revelation comes harder, but when it comes it has the same form:

> Do not laugh at me;<br>For, as I am a man, I think this lady<br>To be my child Cordelia.
>
> <div align="right">(<i>IV, vii,</i> 68–70)</div>

He refers to himself three times, then "my child" recognizes her simultaneously with revealing himself (as her father). Self-recognition is, phenomenologically, a form of insight; and it is because of its necessity in recognizing others that critics have felt its presence here.[3]

Lear does not attain his insight until the end of the fourth Act, and when he does it is climactic. This suggests that Lear's dominating motivation to this point, from the time things go wrong in the opening scene, is *to avoid being recognized*. The isolation and avoidance of eyes is what the obsessive sight imagery of the play underlines. This is the clue I want to follow first in reading out the play.

If the blinding is unnecessary for Gloucester's true seeing of Edgar, why is Gloucester blinded? Alpers' suggestion, in line with his emphasis on the literal presence of eyes, is that because the eyes are physically the most precious and most vulnerable of human organs, the physical assault on them best dramatizes man's capacity for

---

[3] This of course is not to say that such critics have correctly interpreted this feeling of insight, and it does not touch Alpers' claim that such critics have in particular interpreted "moral insight" as "the perception of moral truths"; nor, finally does it weaken Alpers' view of such an interpretation as moralizing, hence evading, the significance of (this) tragedy. I am not, that is, regarding Alpers and the critics with whom, on this point, he is at odds, as providing alternative readings of the play, between which I am choosing or adjudicating. Their relation is more complex. Another way of seeing this is to recognize that Alpers does not deny the presence of a controlling "sight pattern" in *King Lear*, but he transforms the significance of this pattern.

cruelty. But if the symbolic interpretation seems hysterical, this explanation seems overcasual, and in any case does not follow the words. Critics who have looked for a *meaning* in the blinding have been looking for the right thing. But they have been looking for an aesthetic meaning or justification; looking too high, as it were. It is aesthetically justified (it is "not an irrelevant horror" (Muir, p. lx)) just because it is morally, spiritually justified, in a way which directly relates the eyes to their power to see.

GLOU.                          . . . but I shall see
     The winged vengeance overtake such children.
CORN. See't shalt thou never. . . .
                                                  (*III, vii,* 64–66)

And then Cornwall puts out one of Gloucester's eyes. A servant interposes, wounding Cornwall; then Regan stabs the servant from behind, and his dying words, meant to console or establish connection with Gloucester, ironically recall Cornwall to his interrupted work:

FIRST SERV. O! I am slain. My Lord, you have one eye left
     To see some mischief on him. Oh!               *Dies.*
CORN. Lest it see more, prevent it. Out, vile jelly!
                                                  (*III, vii,* 80–82)

Of course the idea of punishment by plucking out eyes has been implanted earlier, by Lear and by Goneril and most recently by Gloucester himself, and their suggestions implicate all of them spiritually in Cornwall's deed. But Cornwall himself twice gives the immediate cause of his deed, once for each eye: to prevent Gloucester from seeing, and in particular to prevent him from seeing *him.* That this scene embodies the most open expression of cruelty is true enough; and true that it suggests the limitlessness of cruelty, once it is given its way—that it will find its way to the most precious objects. It is also true that the scene is symbolic, but what it symbolizes is a function of what it means. The physical cruelty symbolizes (or instances) the psychic cruelty which pervades the play; but what this particular act of cruelty means is that cruelty cannot bear to be seen. It literalizes evil's ancient love of darkness.

This relates the blinding to Cornwall's needs; but it is also related to necessities of Gloucester's character. It has an aptness which takes on symbolic value, the horrible aptness of retribution. (It is not merely literary critics who look for meaning in suffering, attempting to rationalize it. Civilizations have always done it, in their myths and laws; men do it in their dreams and fears of vengeance. They learned to do it from Gods.) For Gloucester has a fault, not particularly egregious, in fact common as dirt, but in a tragic accumulation in which society disgorges itself upon itself, it shows clearly enough; and I cannot understand his immediate and complete acquiescence in the fate which has befallen him (his acknowledgment of his folly, his acceptance of Edgar's innocence, and his wish for forgiveness all take just twenty syllables) without supposing that it strikes him as a retribution, forcing him to an insight about his life as a whole. Not, however, necessarily a true insight. He has revealed his fault in the opening speeches of the play, in which he tells Kent of his *shame*. (That shame is the subject of those speeches is emphasized by Coleridge; but he concentrates, appropriately enough, on *Edmund's* shame.) He says that now he is "braz'd to it," that is, used to admitting that he has fathered a bastard, and also perhaps carrying the original sense of soldered fast to it. He recognizes the moral claim upon himself, as he says twice, to "acknowledge" his bastard; but all this means to him is that he acknowledge that he has a bastard for a son. He does not acknowledge *him*, as a son or a person, with *his* feelings of illegitimacy and being cast out. *That* is something Gloucester ought to be ashamed of; his shame is itself more shameful than his one piece of licentiousness. This is one of the inconveniences of shame, that it is generally inaccurate, attaches to the wrong thing.

In case these remarks should seem inappropriate in view of the moment at which Shakespeare wrote, and someone wishes at this stage to appeal to the conventions of Elizabethan theater according to which a Bastard is an evil character, hence undeserving of the audience's sympathy, and thereby suggest that it is unthinkable that Gloucester should feel anything other than a locker room embarrassment at what has sprung from him, then I should ask that two points be borne in mind: (1) It is a particular man, call him Shakespeare, we are dealing with, and while it is doubtless true that a knowledge of the conventions he inherited is indispensable to the full understanding of his work, the idea that these conventions supply him with solutions to his artistic purposes, rather than problems or media within which those purposes are worked out, is as sensible as supposing that one has explained why a particular couple have decided to divorce by saying that divorce is a social form. (There are, of course, proper occasions for explanations of that kind; for example, an explanation of why separation is not the same as divorce.) Shakespeare's plays are conventional in the way that their language is grammatical, in the way that a football game satisfies the rules of football: one has to know them to understand what is happening, but consulting them will not tell you who plays or speaks well and who mechanically, nor why a given remark or a particular play was made *here,* nor who won and who lost. You have to know something more for that, and you have to look. (2) At the moment at which *King Lear* was written, Sir Robert Filmer was an adolescent. It is hard not to suppose that when this eldest son and pillar of society wrote his defense of patriarchal society, and consequently of primogeniture, he was talking about something which had been problematic since his youth and something which needed his defense in 1630 because it was by then becoming openly questioned.⁴ But this is perfectly clear from Edmund's opening soliloquy. The idea that Shakespeare favored primogeniture, or supposed that only a bastard would question it, is one which must come from a source beyond Shakespeare's words. In that soliloquy Edmund rails equally against his treatment as a bastard and as a younger son—as if to ask why a younger son should be treated like a bastard. Both social institutions seem to him arbitrary and unnatural. And nothing in the play shows him to be wrong—certainly not the behavior of Lear's legitimate older daughters, nor of Regan's lawful husband, nor of legitimate King Lear, who goes through an abdication without abdicating, and whose last legitimate act is to banish love and service from his realm. When Shakespeare writes a revenge tragedy, it is *Hamlet*; and when he presents us with a Bastard, legitimacy as a whole is thrown into question.

That Gloucester still feels shame about his son is shown not just by his descriptions of himself, but also by the fact that Edmund ". . . hath been out nine years, and away he shall again" (*I, i, 32*), and by the fact that Gloucester has to joke about him: joking is a familiar specific for brazening out shame, calling enlarged attention to the thing you do not want naturally noticed. (Hence the comedian sports disfigurement.) But if the failure to recognize others is a fail-

---

⁴ See the Introduction by Peter Laslett to his edition of Filmer's *Patriarcha* (Oxford: Basil Blackwell, 1949).

ure to let others recognize you, a fear of what is revealed to them, an avoidance of their eyes, then it is exactly shame which is the cause of his withholding of recognition. (It is not simply his legal treatment that Edmund is railing against.) For shame is the specific discomfort produced by the sense of being looked at, the avoidance of the sight of others is the reflex it produces. Guilt is different; there the reflex is to avoid discovery. As long as no one *knows* what you have done, you are safe; or your conscience will press you to confess it and accept punishment. Under shame, what must be covered up is not your deed, but yourself. It is a more primitive emotion than guilt, as inescapable as the possession of a body, the first object of shame. —Gloucester suffers the same punishment he inflicts: in his respectability, he avoided eyes; when respectability falls away and the disreputable come into power, his eyes are avoided. In the fear of Gloucester's poor eyes there is the promise that cruelty can be overcome, and instruction about how it can be overcome. That is the content which justifies the scene of his blinding, aesthetically, psychologically, morally.

This raises again the question of the relation between the Gloucester sub-plot and the Lear plot. The traditional views seem on the whole to take one of two lines: Gloucester's fate parallels Lear's in order that it become more universal (because Gloucester is an ordinary man, not a distant King, or because in happening to more than one it may happen to any); or more concrete (since Gloucester suffers physically what Lear suffers psychically). Such suggestions are not wrong, but they leave out of account the specific climactic moment at which the sub-plot surfaces and Lear and Gloucester face one another.

> EDGAR. I would not take this from report; it is,
> And my heart breaks at it.
>
> *(IV, vi,* 142–143)

I have felt that, but more particularly I have felt an obscurer terror at this moment than at any other in the play. The considerations so far introduced begin, I think, to explain the source of that feeling.

Two questions immediately arise about that confrontation: (1) This is the scene in which Lear's madness is first broken through; in the next scene he is reassembling his sanity. Both the breaking through and the reassembling are manifested by his *recognizing* someone, and my first question is: Why is it Gloucester whom Lear is first able to recognize from his madness, and in recognizing whom his sanity begins to return? (2) *What* does Lear see when he recognizes Gloucester? What is he confronted by?

1. Given our notion that recognizing a person depends upon allowing oneself to be recognized by him, the question becomes: Why is it Gloucester whose recognition Lear is first able to bear? The obvious answer is: Because Gloucester is blind. Therefore one can be, can only be, *recognized by him without being seen*, without having to bear eyes upon oneself.

Leading up to Lear's acknowledgment ("I know thee well enough . . .") there is that insane flight of exchanges about Gloucester's eyes; it is the only active cruelty given to Lear by Shakespeare, apart from his behavior in the abdication scene. But here it seems uncaused, deliberate cruelty inflicted for its own sake upon Gloucester's eyes.

GLOU.                                Dost thou know me?
LEAR. I remember thine eyes well enough. Dost thou squiny at me?
No, do thy worst, blind Cupid; I'll not love.
Read thou this challenge; mark but the penning of it.
                                  (*IV, vi,* 137–140)

(This last line, by the way, and Gloucester's response to it, seems a clear enough reference to Gloucester's reading of Edmund's letter, carrying here the suggestion that he was blind then.)

GLOU. Were all thy letters suns [sons?], I could not see.
LEAR. Read.
GLOU. What! with the case of eyes?
LEAR. Oh, ho! are you there with me? No eyes in your head, nor no money in your purse? Your eyes are in a heavy case, your purse in a light: yet you see how this world goes.
GLOU. I see it feelingly.
LEAR. What! art mad? A man may see how this world goes with no eyes. . . .

            ·         ·         ·

                           Get thee glass eyes;
And, like a scurvy politician, seem
To see the things thou dost not. . . .
                   (*IV, vi,* 141–151; 172–174)

Lear is picking at Gloucester's eyes, as if to make sure they are really gone. When he is sure, he recognizes him:

> If thou wilt weep my fortunes, take my eyes;
> I know thee well enough; thy name is Gloucester. . . .
>
> $(IV, vi, 178–179)$

(Here "take my eyes" can be read as a crazy consolation: your eyes wouldn't have done you any good anyway in this case; you would need to see what I have seen to weep my fortunes; I would give up my eyes not to have seen it.)

This picking spiritually relates Lear to Cornwall's and Regan's act in first blinding Gloucester, for Lear does what he does for the same reason they do—in order not to be seen by this man, whom he has brought harm. (Lear exits from this scene running. From what? From "A Gentleman, with Attendants." His first words to them are: "No rescue? What! A prisoner?" But those questions had interrupted the Gentleman's opening words to him, "Your most dear daughter—". Lear runs not because in his madness he cannot distinguish friends from enemies but because he knows that recognition of himself is imminent. Even madness is no rescue.)

2. This leads to the second question about the scene: What is Lear confronted by in acknowledging Gloucester? It is easy to say: Lear is confronted here with the direct consequences of his conduct, of his covering up in rage and madness, of his having given up authority and kingdom for the wrong motives, to the wrong people; and he is for the first time confronting himself. What is difficult is to show that this is not merely or vaguely symbolic, and that it is not merely an access of knowledge which Lear undergoes. Gloucester has by now become not just a figure "parallel" to Lear, but Lear's double; he does not merely represent Lear, but is psychically identical with him. So that what comes to the surface in this meeting is not a related story, but Lear's submerged mind. This, it seems to me, is what gives the scene its particular terror, and gives to the characters what neither could have alone. In this fusion of plots and identities, we have the great image, the double or mirror image, of everyman who has gone to every length to avoid himself, caught at the moment of coming upon himself face to face. (Against this, "take my eyes" strikes psychotic power.)

The identity is established at the end of the blinding scene, by Regan:

> Go thrust him out at gates, and let him smell
> His way to Dover.
>
> *(III, vii, 92–93)*

It is by now commonly appreciated that Gloucester had, when that scene began, no plans for going to Dover. Interpreters have accounted for this discrepancy by suggesting that Shakespeare simply wanted all his characters present at Dover for the climax, adding that the repeated question "Wherefore to Dover?" may have put that destination in Gloucester's mind, which has been kicked out of shape. But this interprets the wrong thing, for it overlooks the more obvious, anyway the first, discrepancy. The question is why *Regan* assumes that he is going to Dover. (Her husband, for example, does not: "Turn out that eyeless villain.") We may wish here to appeal to those drummed "Dover's" to explain her mind, and to suppose that she associates that name with the gathering of all her enemies. But the essential fact is that the name is primarily caught to the image of her father. In her mind, the man she is sending on his way to Dover is the man she *knows* is sent on his way to Dover: in her paroxysms of cruelty, she imagines that she has just participated in blinding her father.

And Gloucester apparently thinks so too, for he then, otherwise inexplicably, sets out for Dover. "Otherwise inexplicably": for it is *no* explanation to say that "the case-histories of suicides contain stranger obsessive characteristics than this" (Muir, xlix). There is no reason, at this stage—other than our cultural advantage in having read the play before—to assume that Gloucester is planning suicide. He sets out for Dover because he is *sent* there: by himself, in sending Lear, in whose identity he is now submerged; and by the thrust of Regan's evil and confusion. But he has no *reason* to go there, not even some inexplicable wish to commit suicide there. At the beginning of the plan to go to Dover he says "I have no way" *(IV, i, 18)*. It is only at the end of that scene that he mentions Dover *cliff (IV, i, 73)*. One can, of course, explain that he had been thinking of the cliff all along. But what the text suggests is that, rather than taking a plan for suicide as our explanation for his insistence on using Dover cliff, we ought to see his thought of the cliff, and consequently of suicide, as *his* explanation of his otherwise mysterious mission to Dover. Better suicide than no reason at all.

When Shakespeare's lapses in plot construction are noticed, critics who know that he is nevertheless the greatest of the bards undertake to excuse him, or to justify the lapse by the great beauty of its surroundings. A familiar excuse is that the lapse will in any case not be noticed in performance. No doubt there are lapses of this kind, and no doubt they can sometimes be covered by such excuses. But it ought also to occur to us that what looks like a lapse is sometimes meant, and that our failure to notice the lapse is just that, our failure. This is what has happened to us in the present scene. We "do not notice" Regan's confusion of identity because we share it, and in failing to understand Gloucester's blanked condition (or rather, in insisting upon understanding it from our point of view) we are doing what the characters in the play are seen to do: we avoid him. And so we are implicated in the failures we are witnessing, we share the responsibility for tragedy.

This is further confirmed in another outstanding lapse, or crux —Gloucester's appearance, led by an old man, to Edgar-Tom. The question, as generally asked, is: Why does Edgar wait, on seeing his father blind, and hearing that his father knows his mistake, before revealing himself to him? The answers which suggest themselves to that question are sophisticated, not the thing itself. For example: Edgar wants to clear himself in the eyes of the world before revealing himself. (But he could still let his *father* know. Anyway, he does tell his father before he goes to challenge Edmund.) Edgar "wants to impose a penance on his father, and to guarantee the genuineness and permanence of the repentance" (Muir, 1). (This seems to me psychologically fantastic; it suggests that the first thing which occurs to Edgar on seeing his father blinded is to exact some further punishment. Or else it makes Edgar into a monster of righteousness; whereas he is merely self-righteous.) Edgar wants to cure his father of his desire to commit suicide. (But *revealing himself* would seem the surest and most immediate way to do that.) And so on. My dissatisfaction with these answers is not that they are psychological explanations, but that they are explanations of the wrong thing, produced by the wrong question: Why does Edgar *delay*? "Delay" implies he is going to later. But we do not *know* (at this stage) that he will; we do not so much as know that he intends to. In terms of our reading of the play so far, we are alerted to the fact that what Edgar does is most directly described as *avoiding recognition*. *That* is what we want an explanation for.

And first, this action bears the same meaning, or has the same consequences, it always has in this play: mutilating cruelty. This is explicit in one of Gloucester's first utterances after the blinding, led into Edgar's presence:

> Oh! dear son Edgar,
> The food of thy abused father's wrath;
> Might I but live to see thee in my touch,
> I'd say I had eyes again.
>
> (*IV, i,* 21–24)

So Edgar's avoidance of Gloucester's recognition precisely deprives Gloucester of his eyes again. This links him, as Lear was and will be linked, to Cornwall and the sphere of open evil.

This reading also has consequences for our experience of two subsequent events of the play.

1. In a play in which, as has often been said, each of the characters is either very good or very bad, this revelation of Edgar's capacity for cruelty—and the *same* cruelty as that of the evil characters—shows how radically implicated good is in evil; in a play of disguises, how often they are disguised. And Edgar is the ruler at the end of the play, Lear's successor, the man who must, in Albany's charge, "the gor'd state sustain." (A very equivocal charge, containing no assurance that its body may be nursed back to health; but simply nursed.) If good is to grow anywhere in this state, it must recognize, and face, its continuity with, its location within a maze of evil. Edgar's is the most Christian sensibility in the play, as Edmund's is the most Machiavellian. If the Machiavellian fails in the end, he very nearly succeeds; and if the Christian succeeds, his success is deeply compromised.

2. To hold to the fact that Edgar is avoiding recognition makes better sense to me of that grotesque guiding of Gloucester up no hill to no cliff to no suicide than any other account I know. The special

quality of this scene, with its purest outbreak of grotesquerie, has been recognized at least since Wilson Knight's essay of 1930.[5] But to regard it as *symbolic* of the play's emphasis on the grotesque misses what makes it so grotesque, and fails to account for the fact that Edgar and Gloucester find themselves in this condition. It is grotesque because it is so *literal* a consequence of avoiding the facts. It is not the emblem of the Lear universe, but an instance of what has led its minds to their present state: there are no lengths to which we may not go in order to avoid being revealed, even to those we love and are loved by. Or rather, especially to those we love and are loved by: to other people it is *easy* not to be known. That grotesque walk is not full of promise for our lives. It is not, for example, a picture of mankind making its way up Purgatory;[6] for Gloucester's character is not purified by it, but extirpated. It shows what people will *have* to say and try to mean to one another when they are incapable of acknowledging to one another what they have to acknowledge. To fill this scene with nourishing, profound meaning is to see it from Edgar's point of view; that is, to avoid what is there. Edgar is Ahab, trying to harpoon the meaning of his life into something external to it; and we believe him, and serve him. He is Hedda Gabler, with her ugly demand for beauty. In the fanciful, childish deceit of his plan, he is Tom Sawyer in the last chapters of *Huckleberry Finn*, enveloping Jim's prison with symbols of escape, instead of opening the door.

If one wishes a psychological explanation for Edgar's behavior, the question to be answered is: Why does Edgar avoid his father's recognition? Two answers suggest themselves. (1) He is himself ashamed and guilty. He was as gullible as his father was to Edmund's "invention." He failed to confront his father, to trust his love, exactly as his father had failed him. He is as responsible for his father's blinding as his father is. He wants to make it up to his father before asking for his recognition—to make it up instead of repenting, acknowledging; he wants to *do* something instead of stopping and seeing. So he goes on doing the very thing which needs making up for. (2) He cannot bear the fact that his father is incapable, impotent, maimed.

---

[5] *"King Lear* and the Comedy of the Grotesque," one of the studies comprising *The Wheel of Fire*, originally published by Oxford University Press, 1930; published in the fifth revised edition by Meridian Books, Inc., New York, 1957.
[6] Suggested by R. W. Chambers, *King Lear*, 1940; cited by Muir, p. l.

He wants his father still to be a father, powerful, so that *he* can remain a child. For otherwise they are simply two human beings in need of one another, and it is not usual for parents and children to manage that transformation, becoming for one another nothing more, but nothing less, than unaccommodated men. That is what Lear took Edgar to be, but that was a mad, ironic compliment; to become natural again, men need to do more than remove their clothes; for they can also cover up their embarrassment by nakedness. Men have their inventions, their accommodations.

We learn in the course of Edgar's tale, after his successful duel with Edmund, when it was that he brought himself to allow his father to recognize him:

> Never—O fault!—revealed myself unto him
> Until some half-hour past, when I was arm'd. . . .
> (V, iii, 192–193)

*Armed*, and with the old man all but seeped away, he feels safe enough to give his father vision again and bear his recognition. As sons fear, and half wish, it is fatal. Now he will never know whether, had he challenged recognition when recognition was denied, at home, both of them could have survived it. That Edgar is so close to the thing love demands contributes to the grotesque air of the late scenes with his father.[7] Love does maintain itself under betrayal; it does allow, and forward, its object's wish to find the edge of its own existence; it does not shrink from recognition that its object is headed for, or has survived, radical change, with its attendant destructions— which is the way love knows that a betrayal is ended, and is why it provides the context for new innocence. But Edgar does not know that love which has such power also has the power to kill, and, in going to the lengths he takes it, must be capable of absolute scrupulousness. It cannot lead, it can only accompany, past the point it has been, and it must feel that point. It is Edgar's self-assurance here which mocks his Christian thoroughness.

✳ ✳

We now have elements with which to begin an analysis of the most controversial of the *Lear* problems, the nature of Lear's motiva-

---

[7] The passage from this sentence to the end of the paragraph was added as the result of a conversation with Rose Mary Harbison.

tion in his opening (abdication) scene. The usual interpretations follow one of three main lines: Lear is senile; Lear is puerile; Lear is not to be understood in natural terms, for the whole scene has a fairy tale or ritualistic character which simply must be accepted as the premise from which the tragedy is derived. Arguments ensue, in each case, about whether Shakespeare is justified in what he is asking his audience to accept. My hypothesis will be that Lear's behavior in this scene is explained by—the tragedy begins because of—the same motivation which manipulates the tragedy throughout its course, from the scene which precedes the abdication, through the storm, blinding, evaded reconciliations, to the final moments: by the attempt to avoid recognition, the shame of exposure, the threat of self-revelation.

Shame, first of all, is the right kind of candidate to serve as motive, because it is the emotion whose effect is most precipitate and out of proportion to its cause, which is just the rhythm of the *King Lear* plot as a whole. And with this hypothesis we need not assume that Lear is either incomprehensible or stupid or congenitally arbitrary and inflexible and extreme in his conduct. Shame itself is exactly arbitrary, inflexible and extreme in its effect. It is familiar to find that what mortifies one person seems wholly unimportant to another: think of being ashamed of one's origins, one's accent, one's ignorance, one's skin, one's clothes, one's legs or teeth. . . . It is the most isolating of feelings, the most comprehensible perhaps in idea, but the most incomprehensible or incommunicable in fact. Shame, I've said, is the most primitive, the most private, of emotions; but it is also the most primitive of *social* responses. With the discovery of the individual, whether in Paradise or in the Renaissance, there is the simultaneous discovery of the isolation of the individual; his presence to himself, but simultaneously to *others*. Moreover, shame is felt not only toward one's own actions and one's own being, but toward the actions and the being of those with whom one is identified —fathers, daughters, wives . . . , the beings whose self-revelations reveal oneself. Families, any objects of one's love and commitment, ought to be the places where shame is overcome (hence happy families are all alike); but they are also the place of its deepest manufacture, and one is then hostage to that power, or fugitive.   —L. B. Campbell, in *Shakespeare's Tragic Heroes*,[8] collects valuable examples of

---

[8] New York: Barnes and Noble, Inc., 1966; the quotation which follows is from pp. 181–182 of this edition. The book was first published in 1930 by the Cambridge University Press.

Renaissance "doctrine," and sorts them perspicuously around Shakespeare's topics. But she follows a typical assumption of such investigations—that if Shakespeare's work is to be illuminated by these contemporary doctrines, he must illustrate them. For example:

> It must be evident, then, that there was in Shakespeare's day an old and firmly founded philosophy of anger, finding its sources in ancient medicine and ancient philosophy and in the mediaeval makings-over of those ancient sources as well. According to this philosophy, pride or self-esteem is the condition in which anger takes its rise, vengeance becomes its immediate object, and some slight, real or imagined, is its cause. Anger is folly; anger brings shame in its train. The sequence of passions is pride, anger, revenge, and unless madness clouds the reason altogether, shame.

But in *King Lear* shame comes first, and brings rage and folly in its train. Lear is not maddened because he had been wrathful, but because his shame brought his wrath upon the wrong object. It is not the fact of his anger but the irony of it, specifically and above all the *injustice* of it, which devours him.

That Lear is ashamed, or afraid of being shamed by a revelation, seems to be the Fool's understanding of his behavior. It is agreed that the Fool keeps the truth present to Lear's mind, but it should be stressed that the characteristic mode of the Fool's presentation is *ridicule*—the circumstance most specifically feared by shame (as accusation and discovery are most feared by guilt). Part of the exquisite pain of this Fool's comedy is that in riddling Lear with the truth of his condition he increases the very cause of that condition, as though shame should finally grow ashamed of itself, and stop. The other part of this pain is that it is the therapy prescribed by love itself. We know that since Cordelia's absence "the fool hath much pin'd away" (*I, iv,* 78), and it is generally assumed that this is due to his love for Cordelia. That need not be denied, but it should be obvious that it is directly due to his love for Lear; to his having to see the condition in Lear which his love is impotent to prevent, the condition moreover which his love has helped to cause, the precise condition therefore which his love is unable to comfort, since its touch wounds. This is why the Fool dies or disappears; from the terrible relevance, and the horrible irrelevance, of his only passion. This is the point of his connection with Cordelia, as will emerge.

I call Lear's shame a hypothesis, and what I have to say here will

perhaps be hard to make convincing. But primarily it depends upon
not imposing the traditional interpretations upon the opening events.
Lear is puerile? Lear senile? But the man who speaks Lear's words is
in possession, if not fully in command, of a powerful, ranging mind;
and its eclipse into madness only confirms its intelligence, not just
because what he says in his madness is the work of a marked intelligence, but because the nature of his madness, his melancholy and
antic disposition, its incessant invention, is the sign, in fact and in
Renaissance thought, of genius; an option of escape open only to
minds of the highest reach. How then can we understand such a mind
seriously to believe that what Goneril and Regan are offering in that
opening scene is love, proof of his value to them; and to believe that
Cordelia is withholding love? We cannot so understand it, and so all
the critics are right to regard Lear in this scene as psychologically
incomprehensible, or as requiring a psychological make-up—*if* that is,
we assume that Lear believes in Goneril and Regan and not in
Cordelia. But we needn't assume that he believes anything of the
kind.

We imagine that Lear *must* be wildly abused (blind, puerile,
and the rest) because the thing works out so badly. But it doesn't
*begin* badly, and it is far from incomprehensible conduct. It is, in
fact, quite ordinary. A parent is bribing love out of his children; two
of them accept the bribe, and despise him for it; the third shrinks
from the attempt, as though from violation. Only this is a king, this
bribe is the last he will be able to offer; everything in his life, and in
the life of his state, depends upon its success. We need not assume that
he does not know his two older daughters, and that they are giving
him false coin in return for his real bribes, though perhaps like most
parents he is willing not to notice it. But more than this: there is
reason to assume that the open possibility—or the open fact—that
they are *not* offering true love is exactly what he wants. Trouble
breaks out only with Cordelia's "Nothing," and her broken resolution
to be silent.  —What does he want, and what is the meaning of the
trouble which then breaks out?

Go back to the confrontation scene with Gloucester:

If thou wilt weep my fortunes, take my eyes.

The obvious rhetoric of those words is that of an appeal, or a bargain. But it is also warning, and a command: If you weep for me, the

same thing will happen to me that happened to you; do not let me see what you are weeping for. Given the whole scene, with its concentrated efforts at warding off Gloucester, that line says explicitly what it is Lear is warding off: Gloucester's sympathy, his love. And earlier:

> GLOU. O! Let me kiss that hand.
> LEAR. Let me wipe it first, it smells of mortality.
>
> *(IV, vi, 134–135)*

Mortality, the hand without rings of power on it, cannot be lovable. He feels unworthy of love when the reality of lost power comes over him. That is what his plan was to have avoided by exchanging his fortune for his love at one swap. He cannot bear love when he has no reason to be loved, perhaps because of the helplessness, the passiveness which that implies, which some take for impotence. And he wards it off for the reason for which people do ward off being loved, because it presents itself to them as a demand:

> LEAR. No. Do thy worst, blind Cupid; I'll not love.
>
> *(IV, vi, 139)*

Gloucester's presence strikes Lear as the demand for love; he knows he is being offered love; he tries to deny the offer by imagining that he has been solicited (this is the relevance of "blind Cupid" as the sign of a brothel); and he doesn't want to pay for it, for he may get it, and may not, and either is intolerable. Besides, he has recently done just that, paid his all for love. The long fantasy of his which precedes this line ("Let copulation thrive" . . . . "There is the sulphurous pit—burning, scalding, stench, consumption . . .") contains his most sustained expression of disgust with sexuality (ll. 116ff.)—as though furiously telling himself that what was wrong with his plan was not the debasement of love his bargain entailed, but the fact that love itself is inherently debased and so unworthy from the beginning of the bargain he had made for it. That is a maddening thought; but still more comforting than the truth. For some spirits, to be loved knowing you cannot return that love, is the most radical of psychic tortures.

✳ ✳

This is the way I understand that opening scene with the three daughters. Lear knows it is a bribe he offers, and—part of him anyway—wants exactly what a bribe can buy: (1) false love; and (2) a public expression of love. That is: he wants something he does not have to return *in kind,* something which a division of his property fully pays for. And he wants to *look* like a loved man—for the sake of the subjects, as it were. He is perfectly happy with his little plan, until Cordelia speaks. Happy not because he is blind, but because he is getting what he wants, his plan is working. Cordelia is alarming precisely because he *knows* she is offering the real thing, offering something a more opulent third of his kingdom cannot, must not, repay; putting a claim upon him he cannot face. She threatens to expose both his plan for returning false love with no love, and expose the necessity for that plan—his terror of being loved, of needing love.

Reacting to over-sentimental or over-Christian interpretations of her character, efforts have been made to implicate her in the tragedy's source, convicting her of a willfulness and hardness kin to that later shown by her sisters. But her complicity is both less and more than such an interpretation envisages. That interpretation depends, first of all, upon taking her later speeches in the scene (after the appearance of France and Burgundy) as simply uncovering what was in her mind and heart from the beginning. But why? Her first utterance is the aside:

What shall Cordelia speak? Love, and be silent.

This, presumably, has been understood as indicating her decision to refuse her father's demand. But it needn't be. She asks herself what she can say; there is no necessity for taking the question to be rhetorical. She wants to obey her father's wishes (anyway, there is no reason to think otherwise at this stage, or at any other); but how? She sees from Goneril's speech and Lear's acceptance of it what it is he wants, and she would provide it if she could. But to pretend publicly to love, where you do not love, is easy; to pretend to love, where you really do love, is not obviously possible. She hits on the first solution to her dilemma: Love, and be silent. That is, love *by being* silent. That will do what he seems to want, it will avoid the expression of love, keep it secret. She is his joy; she knows it and he knows it. Surely that is enough? Then Regan speaks, and following that Cordelia's second utterance, again aside:

> Then poor Cordelia!
> And yet not so; since I am sure my love's
> More ponderous than my tongue.
>
> $(I, i, 76-78)$

Presumably, in line with the idea of a defiant Cordelia, this is to be interpreted as a re-affirmation of her decision not to speak. But again, it needn't be. After Lear's acceptance of Regan's characteristic out-stripping (she has no ideas of her own, her special vileness is always to increase the measure of pain others are prepared to inflict; her mind is itself a lynch mob) Cordelia may realize that she will *have* to say something. "More ponderous than my tongue" suggests that she *is* going to move it, not that it is immovable—which would make it more ponderous than her love. And this produces her second groping for an exit from the dilemma: to speak, but making her love seem less than it is, out of love. Her tongue will move, and obediently, but against her condition—then poor Cordelia, making light of her love. And yet *she* knows the truth. Surely that is enough?

But when the moment comes, she is speechless: "Nothing my lord." I do not deny that this can be read defiantly, as can the following "You have begot me, bred me, lov'd me" speech. She is outraged, violated, confused, so young; Lear is torturing her, claiming her devotion, which she wants to give, but forcing her to help him betray (or not to betray) it, to falsify it publicly. (Lear's ambiguity here, want-ing at once to open and to close her mouth, further shows the ordinariness of the scene, its verisimilitude to common parental love, swinging between absorption and rejection of its offspring, between encouragement to a rebellion they failed to make, and punishment for it.) It may be that with Lear's active violation, she snaps; her resentment provides her with words, and she levels her abdication of love at her traitorous, shameless father:

> Happily, when I shall wed,
> That lord whose hand must take my plight shall carry
> Half my love with him . . . .
>
> $(I, i, 100-102)$

The trouble is, the words are too calm, too cold for the kind of sharp rage and hatred real love can produce. She is never in possession of her situation, "her voice was ever soft, gentle and low" (*V, iii,* 272–273), she is young, and "least" (*I, i,* 83). (This notation of her stature and of the quality of her voice is unique in the play. The idea of a defiant *small* girl seems grotesque, as an idea of Cordelia.) All her words are words of love; to love is all she knows how to do. That is her problem, and at the cause of the tragedy of King Lear.

I imagine the scene this way: the older daughters' speeches are public, set; they should not be said to Lear, but to the court, sparing themselves his eyes and him theirs. They are not monsters first, but ladies. He is content. Then Cordelia says to him, away from the court, in confused appeal to their accustomed intimacy, "Nothing"— don't force me, I don't know what you want, there is nothing I can say, to speak what you want I must not speak. But he is alarmed at the appeal and tries to cover it up, keeping up the front, and says, speaking to her and to the court, as if the ceremony is still in full effect: "Nothing will come of nothing; speak again." (*Hysterica passio* is already stirring.) Again she says *to him:* "Unhappy that I am, I cannot heave my heart into my mouth"—not the heart which loves him, that always has been present in her voice; but the heart which is shuddering with confusion, with wanting to do the impossible, the heart which is now in her throat. But to no avail. Then the next line would be her first attempt to obey him by speaking publicly: "I love your Majesty according to my bond; no more no less"—not stinting, not telling *him* the truth (what is the true *amount* of love this loving young girl knows to measure with her bond?), not refusing him, but still trying to conceal her love, to lighten its full measure. Then her father's brutally public, and perhaps still publicly considerate, "How, how, Cordelia! Mend your speech a little, lest you may mar your fortunes." So she tries again to divide her kingdom (". . . that lord whose hand must take my plight shall carry half my love with him . . ."). Why should she wish to shame him publicly? He has shamed himself and everyone knows it. She is trying to conceal him; and to do that she cuts herself in two. (In the end, he faces what she has done here: "Upon such sacrifices, my Cordelia. . . ." Lear cannot, at that late moment, be thinking of prison as a sacrifice. I imagine him there partly remembering this first scene, and the first of Cordelia's sacrifices—of love to convention.)

After this speech, said in suppression, confusion, abandonment, she is shattered, by her failure and by Lear's viciousness to her. Her sisters speak again only when they are left alone, to plan. Cordelia revives and speaks after France enters and has begun to speak *for* her:

> Sure, her offence
> Must be of such unnatural degree
> That monsters it, or your fore-vouch'd affection
> Fall into taint; which to believe of her,
> Must be a faith that reason without miracle
> Should never plant in me.

(I, i, 218–223)

France's love shows him the truth. Tainted love is the answer, love dyed—not decayed or corrupted exactly; Lear's love is still alive, but expressed as, colored over with, hate. Cordelia finds her voice again, protected in France's love, and she uses it to change the subject, still protecting Lear from discovery.

A reflection of what Cordelia now must feel is given by one's rush of gratitude toward France, one's almost wild relief as he speaks his beautiful trust. She does not ask her father to relent, but only to give France some explanation. Not the right explanation: What has "that glib and oily art" got to do with it? That is what her sisters needed, because their task was easy: to dissemble. Convention perfectly suits these ladies. But she lets it go at that—he hates me because I would not flatter him. The truth is, she *could* not flatter; not because she was too proud or too principled, though these might have been the reasons, for a different character; but because nothing she could have done would have *been* flattery—at best it would have been *dissembled flattery*. There is no convention for doing what Cordelia was asked to do. It is not that Goneril and Regan have taken the words out of her mouth, but that here she cannot say them, because for her they are true ("Dearer than eye-sight, space and liberty . . ."). She is not disgusted by her sister's flattery (it's nothing new); but heart-broken at hearing the words she wishes she were in a position to say. So she is sent, and taken, away. Or half of her leaves; the other half remains, in Lear's mind, in Kent's service, and in the Fool's love.

(I spoke just now of "one's" gratitude and relief toward France. I was remembering my feeling at a production given by students at Berkeley during 1946 in which France—a small part, singled out by Granville-Barker as particularly requiring an actor of authority and distinction—was given his full sensitivity and manliness, a combination notably otherwise absent from the play, as mature womanliness is. The validity of such feelings as touchstones of the accuracy of a reading of the play, and which feelings one is to trust and which not, ought to be discussed problems of criticism.)

✴ ✴

It may be felt that I have forced this scene too far in order to fit it to my reading, that too many directions have to be provided to its acting in order to keep the motivation smooth. Certainly I have gone into more detail of this kind here than elsewhere, and I should perhaps say why. It is, first of all, the scene in which the problem of performance, or the performability, of this play comes to a head, or to its first head. Moreover, various interpretations offered of this scene are direct functions of attempts to *visualize* its progress; as though a critic's conviction about the greatness or weakness of the scene is a direct function of the success or unsuccess with which he has been able to imagine it concretely. Critics will invariably dwell on the motivations of Lear and Cordelia in this scene as a problem, even while taking their motivation later either as more or less obvious or for some other reason wanting no special description; and in particular, the motives or traits of character attributed to them here will typically be ones which have an immediate visual implication, ones in which, as it were, a psychological trait and its physical expression most nearly coalesce: at random, Lear is described as irascible (Schüking), arrogant, choleric, overbearing (Schlegel), Cordelia as shy, reluctant (Schüking), sullen, prideful (Coleridge), obstinate (Muir). This impulse seems to me correct, and honest: it is one thing to say that Cordelia's behavior in the opening scene is not inconsistent with her behavior when she reappears, but another to *show* its consistency. This is what I have wanted to test in visualizing her behavior in that scene. But it is merely a test, it proves nothing about my reading, except its actability; or rather, a performance on these lines would, or would not, prove that. And that is a further problem of aesthetics— to chart the relations between a text (or score), an analysis or interpretation of it, and a performance in terms of that analysis or interpretation.

The problem is not, as it is often put, that no performance is ideal, because this suggests we have some clear idea of what an ideal performance would be, perhaps an idea of it as embodying all true interpretations, every resonance of the text struck under analysis. But this is no more possible, or comprehensible, than an experiment which is to verify every implication of a theory. (Then what makes a theory convincing?) Performances are actions, and the imitations of actions. As with any action, a performance cannot contain the totality of a human life—though one action can have a particularly summary or revelatory quality, and another will occur at a crossroads, and another will spin tangentially to the life and circumstances which call it out, or rub irrelevantly or mechanically against another. Some have no meaning for us at all, others have more resonance than they can express—as a resultant force answers to forces not visible in the one direction it selects. (Then what makes action bearable, or comprehensible?) I cannot at will give my past expression, though every gesture expresses it, and each elation and headache; my character is its epitome, as if the present were a pantomime of ghostly selections. What is necessary to a performance is what is necessary to action in the present, that it have its autonomy, and that it be in character, or out, and that it have a specific context and motive. Even if everything I have said about Cordelia is true, it needn't be registered explicitly in the way that first scene is played—there may, for example, be merit in stylizing it drastically. Only there will be no effort to present us with a sullen or prideful or defiant girl who reappears, with nothing intervening to change her, as the purest arch of love.

Nor, of course, has my rendering of the first scene been meant to bring out all the motivations or forces which cross there. For example, it might be argued that part of Lear's strategy is exactly to put Cordelia into the position of being denied her dowry, so that he will not lose her in marriage; if so, it half worked, and required the magnanimity of France to turn it aside. Again, nothing has been said of the theme of politics which begins here and pervades the action. Not just the familiar Shakespearean theme which opens the interplay between the public and private lives of the public creature, but the particularity of the theme in this play, which is about the interpenetration and confusion of politics with love; something which, in modern societies, is equally the fate of private creatures—whether in the form of divided loyalties, or of one's relation to the State, or, more pervasively, in the new forms love and patriotism themselves take: love wielding itself in gestures of power, power extending itself with claims of love. *Phèdre* is perhaps the greatest play concentrated to this theme of the body politic, and of the body, torn by the privacy of love; as it is closest to *King Lear* in its knowledge of shame as the experience of unacceptable love. And Machiavelli's knowledge of the world is present; not just in his attitudes of realism and cynicism, but in his experience of the condition to which these attitudes are appropriate—in which the inner and outer worlds have become totally disconnected, and man's life is all public, among strangers, seen only from outside. Luther saw the same thing at the same time, but from inside. For some, like Edmund, this is liberating knowledge, lending capacity for action. It is what Lear wants to abdicate from. For what Lear is doing in that first scene is trading power for love (pure power for mixed love); this is what his opening speech explicitly says. He imagines that this will prevent future strife now; but he is being counselled by his impotence, which is not the result of his bad decision, but produces it: he feels powerless to *appoint* his successor, recognized as the ultimate test of authority. The consequence is that politics becomes private, and so vanishes, with power left to serve hatred.

✳ ✳

The final scene opens with Lear and Cordelia repeating or completing their actions in their opening scene; again Lear abdicates, and again Cordelia loves and is silent. Its readers have for centuries wanted to find consolation in this end: heavy opinion sanctioned Tate's Hollywood ending throughout the eighteenth century, which resurrects Cordelia; and in our time, scorning such vulgarity, the same impulse fastidiously digs itself deeper and produces redemption for Lear in Cordelia's figuring of transcendent love. But Dr. Johnson is surely right, more honest and more responsive: Cordelia's death is so shocking that we would avoid it if we could—*if* we have responded to it. And so the question, since her death is restored to us, is forced upon us: Why does she die? And this is not answered by asking, What does her death mean? (cp: Christ died to save sinners); but by answering, What killed her? (cp: Christ was killed by us, because his news was unendurable).

Lear's opening speech of this final scene is not the correction but the repetition of his strategy in the first scene, or a new tactic designed to win the old game; and it is equally disastrous.

CORD. Shall we not see these daughters and these sisters?
LEAR. No, no, no, no! . . .

$$(V, iii, 7-8)$$

He cannot finally face the thing he has done; and this means what it always does, that he cannot bear being seen. He is anxious to go off to prison, with Cordelia; his love now is in the open—that much circumstance has done for him; but it remains imperative that it be confined, out of sight. (Neither Lear nor Cordelia, presumably, knows that the soldier in command is Gloucester's son; they feel unknown.) He is still ashamed, and the fantasy expressed in this speech ("We two alone will sing like birds i' the cage") is the same fantasy he brings on the stage with him in the first scene, the thwarting of which causes his maddened destructiveness. There Cordelia had offered him the marriage pledge ("Obey you, love you, and most honor you"), and she has shared his fantasy fully enough to wish to heal political strife with a kiss (or perhaps it is just the commonest fantasy of women):

CORD.                                         Restoration hang
        Thy medicine on my lips. . . .

$$(IV, vii, 26-27)$$

(But after such abdication, what restoration? The next time we hear the words "hang" and "medicine," they announce death.) This gesture is as fabulous as anything in the opening scene. Now, at the end, Lear returns her pledge with his lover's song, his invitation to voyage (". . . so we'll live, and pray, and sing, and tell old tales, and laugh . . ."). The fantasy of this speech is as full of detail as a day dream, and it is clearly a happy dream for Lear. He has found at the end a way to have what he has wanted from the beginning. His tone is not: we will love *even though* we are in prison; but: because we are hidden together we can love. He has come to accept his love, not by making room in the world for it, but by denying its relevance to the world. He does not renounce the world in going to prison, but flees from it, to earthly pleasure. The astonishing image of "God's spies" (V, iii, 17) stays beyond me, but in part it contains the final emphasis upon looking without being seen; and it cites an intimacy which requires no reciprocity with real men. Like Gloucester toward Dover, Lear anticipates God's call. He is not experiencing reconciliation with a daughter, but partnership in a mystic marriage.

If so, it cannot be, as is often suggested, that when he says

Upon such sacrifices, my Cordelia,
The Gods themselves throw incense.

(*V, iii*, 20–21)

he is thinking simply of going to prison with Cordelia as a sacrifice. It seems rather that, the lines coming immediately after his love song, it is their love itself which has the meaning of sacrifice. As though the ideas of love and of death are interlocked in his mind— and in particular of death as a payment or placation for the granting of love. His own death, because acknowledging love still presents itself to him as an annihilation of himself. And her death, because now that he admits her love, he must admit, what he knew from the beginning, that he is impotent to sustain it. This is the other of Cordelia's sacrifices—of love to secrecy.

Edmund's death reinforces the juncture of these ideas, for it is death which releases his capacity for love. It is this release which permits his final act:

. . . some good I mean to do
Despite of mine own nature. Quickly send . . .

(*V, iii*, 243–244)

What has released him? Partly, of course, the presence of his own death; but that in itself need not have worked this way. Primarily it is the fact that all who have loved him, or claimed love for him, are dead. He has eagerly prompted Edgar to tell the tale of their father's death; his reaction upon hearing of Goneril's and Regan's deaths is as to a solution to impossible, or illegitimate, love: "All three now marry in an instant"; and his immediate reaction upon seeing their dead bodies is: "Yet Edmund was belov'd." *That* is what he wanted to know, and he can acknowledge it now, when it cannot be returned, now that its claim is dead. In his following speech he means well for the first time.

It can be said that what Lear is ashamed of is not his need for love and his inability to return it, but of the *nature* of his love for Cordelia. It is too far from plain love of father for daughter. Even if we resist seeing in it the love of lovers, it is at least incompatible with the idea of her having any (other) lover. There is a moment, beyond the words, when this comes to the surface of the action. It is the moment Lear is waking from his madness, no longer incapable of seeing the world, but still not strong enough to protect his thoughts: "Methinks I should know you and know this man . . ." (*IV, vii,* 64). I take it "this man" is generally felt to refer to Kent (disguised as Caius), for there is clearly no reason to suppose Lear knows the Doctor, the only other man present. Certainly this is plausible; but in fact Lear never does acknowledge Kent, as he does his child Cordelia.[9] And after this recognition he goes on to ask, "Am I in France?" This question irresistibly (to me) suggests that the man he thinks he should know is the man he expects to be with his daughter, her husband. This would be unmistakable if he directs his "this man" to the Doctor, taking him for, but not able to make him out as,

---

[9] Professor Jonas Barish—to whom I am indebted for other suggestions about this essay as well as the present one—has pointed out to me that in my eagerness to solve all the *King Lear* problems I have neglected trying an account of Kent's plan in delaying making himself known ("Yet to be known shortens my made intent" (*IV, vii,* 9)). This omission is particularly important because Kent's is the one delay that causes no harm to others, hence it provides an internal measure of those harms. I do not understand his "dear cause" (*IV, iii,* 52), but I think the specialness of Kent's delay has to do with these facts: (1) It never prevents his perfect faithfulness to his duties of service; these do not require—Kent does not permit them to require—personal recognition in order to be performed. This sense of the finitude of the demands placed upon Kent, hence of the harm and of the good he can perform, is a function of his complete absorption into his social office, in turn a function of his being the only principal character in the play (apart from the Fool) who does not appear as the member of a *family.* (2) He does not delay revealing himself to Cordelia, only (presumably) to Lear. A reason for that would be that since the King has banished him it is up to the King to reinstate him; he will not presume on his old rank. (3) If his plan goes beyond finding some way, or just waiting, for Lear to recognize him first (not out of pride but out of right) then perhaps it is made irrelevant by finding Lear again only in his terminal state, or perhaps it always consisted only in doing what he tries to do there, find an opportunity to tell Lear about Caius and ask for pardon. It may be wondered that we do not feel Lear's fragmentary recognitions of Kent to leave something undone, nor Kent's hopeless attempts to hold Lear's attention to be crude intrusions, but rather to amplify a sadness already amplified past sensing. This may be accounted for partly by Kent's pure expression of the special poignance of the servant's office, requiring a life centered in another life, exhausted in loyalty and in silent witnessing (a silence Kent broke and Lear must mend); partly by the fact that Cordelia has fully recognized him: "To be acknowledg'd, Madam, is o'er-paid" (*IV, vii,* 4); partly by the fact that when his master Lear is dead, it is his master who calls him, and his last words are those of obedience.

France. He finds out it is not, and the next time we see him he is pressing off to prison with his child, and there is no further thought of her husband. It is a standing complaint that Shakespeare's explanation of France's absence is perfunctory. It is more puzzling that Lear himself never refers to him, not even when he is depriving him of her forever. Either France has ceased to exist for Lear, or it is importantly from him that he wishes to reach the shelter of prison.

I do not wish to suggest that "avoidance of love" and "avoidance of a particular kind of love" are alternative hypotheses about this play. On the contrary, they seem to me to interpret one another. Avoidance of love is always, or always begins as, an avoidance of a particular kind of love: men do not just naturally not love, they learn not to. And our lives begin by having to accept under the name of love whatever closeness is offered, and by then having to forgo its object. And the avoidance of a particular love, or the acceptance of it, will spread to every other; every love, in acceptance or rejection, is mirrored in every other. It is part of the miracle of the vision in *King Lear* to bring this before us, so that we do not care whether the *kind* of love felt between these two is forbidden according to man's lights. We care whether love is or is not altogether forbidden to man, whether we may not altogether be incapable of it, of admitting it into our world. We wonder whether we may always go mad between the equal efforts and terrors at once of rejecting and of accepting love. The soul torn between them, the body feels torn (producing a set of images accepted since Caroline Spurgeon's *Shakespeare's Imagery* as central to *King Lear*), and the solution to this insoluble condition is to wish for the tearing apart of the world.

Lear wishes to escape into prison for another old reason—because he is unwilling to be seen to weep.

> The good years shall devour them, flesh and fell,
> Ere they shall make us weep: we'll see 'em starved first.
> (*V, iii*, 24–25)

See them shalt thou never. And in the end he still avoids Cordelia. He sees that she is weeping after his love song ("Wipe thine eyes"). But why is she in tears? Why does Lear think she is? Lear imagines that she is crying for the reasons that he is on the verge of tears—the old reasons, the sense of impotence, shame, loss. But *her* reasons for tears do not occur to him, that she sees him as he is, as he was, that he is unable to take his last chance; that he, at the farthest edge of life, must again sacrifice her, again abdicate his responsibilities; and that he cannot know what he asks. And yet, seeing that, it is for him that she is cast down. Upon such knowledge the Gods themselves throw incense.

It is as though her response here is her knowledge of the end of the play; she alone has the capacity of compassion Lear will need when we next see him, with Cordelia dead in his arms: "Howl, howl, howl! O! you are men of stones." (Cp. the line and a half Dante gives to Ugolino, facing his doomed sons, a fragment shored by Arnold: "I did not weep, I so turned to stone within. They wept. . . .") Again he begins to speak by turning on those at hand: "A plague upon you, murderers, traitors all!" But then the tremendous knowledge is released: "I might have saved her. . . ." From the beginning, and through each moment until they are led to prison, he might have saved her, had he done what every love requires, put himself aside long enough to see through to her, and be seen through. I do not mean that it is clear that he could, at the end, have done what Edmund feared (". . . pluck the common bosom on his side, And turn our impress'd lances in our eyes . . ."); but it is not clear that he could not. And even if he had not succeeded, her death would not be on his hands. In his last speech, "No, no, no, no" becomes "No, no, no life!" His need, or his interpretation of his need, becomes her sentence. This is what is unbearable. Or bearable only out of the capacity of Cordelia. If we are to weep her fortunes we must take her eyes.

✳ ✳

Is this a Christian play? The question is very equivocal. When it is answered affirmatively, Cordelia is viewed as a Christ figure whose love redeems nature and transfigures Lear. So far as this is intelligible to me, I find it false both to the experience of the play and to the fact that it *is* a play. *King Lear* is not illustrated theology (anyway, which theology is thought to be illustrated, what understanding of atonement, redemption, etc., is thought to be figured?), and nature and Lear are not touched, but run out. If Cordelia exemplifies Christ, it is at the moment of Crucifixion, not Resurrection. But the moment of his death is the moment that Christ resembles us, finally takes the human condition fully into himself. (This is why every figure reaching the absolute point of rejection starts becoming a figure of Christ. And perhaps why it is so important to the Christ story that it begins with birth and infancy.) It is in his *acceptance* of this condition that we are to resemble him. If Cordelia resembles Christ, it is by having become fully human, by knowing her separateness, by knowing the deafness of miracles, by accepting the unacceptability of her love, and by nevertheless maintaining her love and the whole knowledge it brings. One can say she "redeems nature" (*IV, vi,* 207), but this means nothing miraculous, only that she shows nature not to be the cause of evil—there is no cause in nature which makes these hard hearts, and no cause outside either. The cause is the heart itself, the having of a heart, in a world made heartless. Lear is the cause. Murderers, traitors *all*.

Another way, the play can be said to be Christian—not because it shows us redemption—it does not; but because it throws our redemption into *question*, and leaves it up to us. But there is no suggestion that we can take it up only through Christ. On the contrary, there is reason to take this drama as an alternative to the Christian one. In the first place, Christianity, like every other vision of the play, is not opted for, but tested. Specifically, as was said earlier, in Edgar's conduct; more generally, in its suggestion that all appeals to Gods are distractions or excuses, because the imagination uses them to wish for complete, for final solutions, when what is needed is at hand, or nowhere. But isn't this what Christ meant? And isn't this what Lear fails to see in wishing to be God's spy before he is God's subject? Cordelia is further proof of this: her grace is shown by the absence in her of any unearthly experiences; she is the only good character whose attention is wholly on earth, on the person nearest her. It is during the storm that Lear's mind clouds most and floods with philosophy; when it clears, Cordelia is present.

These considerations take us back to the set of ideas which see Lear as having arrived, in the course of the storm, at the naked human condition—as if the storm was the granting of his prayer to "feel what wretches feel." It may seem that I have denied this in underlining Lear's cruelty to Gloucester and in placing him at the cause of Cordelia's death, because it may feel as if I am blaming Lear for his behavior here.[10] And what room is there for blame? Is he to blame for being human? For being subject to a cosmic anxiety and to fantasies which enclose him from perfect compassion? Certainly blame is inappropriate, for certainly I do not claim to know what *else* Lear might do. And yet I cannot deny that my pain at Lear's actions is not overcome by my knowledge of his own suffering. I might describe my experience of him here as one of unplaceable blame, blame no one can be asked to bear and no one is in a position to level—like blaming heaven. That does not seem to me inappropriate as an experience of tragedy, of what it is for which tragedy provides catharsis. (Neither Kent nor Cordelia requires tragedy for purification, the one preceding the other transcending personal morality.) What I am denying is that to say Lear becomes simply a man is to say that he achieves the unaccommodated human condition. The ambiguities here stand out in Empson's suggestion of Lear as scapegoat and outcast.[11] This cannot be wrong, but it can be made too much of, or the wrong thing. We do not want the extremity of Lear's suffering to have gone for nothing, or for too little, so we may imagine that it has made him capable of envisioning ours. But as the storm is ending he is merely humanly a scapegoat, as any man is on the wrong end of injustice; and no more an outcast than any man out of favor. Only at his finish does his suffering measure the worst that can happen to a man, and there not because he is a scapegoat

[10] In a detailed and very useful set of comments on an earlier draft of this essay, Professor Alpers mentions this as a possible response to what I had written; and it was his suggestion of Empson's appeal to the scapegoat idea as offering a truer response to Lear's condition which sent me back to Empson's essay. It was as an effort to do justice to Alpers' reaction that I have included the ensuing discussion of scapegoats in *King Lear*. Beyond this, I have altered or expanded several other passages in the light of his comments, for all of which I am grateful.

[11] "Fool in Lear," in *The Structure of Complex Words* (Ann Arbor: The University of Michigan Press, 1967, Ann Arbor Paperback), pp. 145, 157. Because of Empson's espousal of it, Orwell's essay on Lear may be mentioned here ("Lear, Tolstoy and the Fool," reprinted from *Shooting an Elephant and Other Essays* in F. Kermode, ed., *Four Centuries of Shakespearean Criticism* (New York: Avon Books, 1965), pp. 514–31). It is, perhaps, of the nature of Orwell's piece that one finds oneself remembering the feel of its moral passion and honesty and the clarity of its hold on the idea of *renunciation* as the subject of the play, without being able oneself to produce Orwell's, or one's own, evidence for the idea in the play—except that the meaning of the entire opening and the sense of its consequences, assume, as it were, a self-evidence within the light of that idea. It is probably as good a notation of the subject as one word could give, and Orwell's writing, here as elsewhere, is exemplary of a correct way in which the moral sensibility, distrusting higher ambitions, exercises its right to judge an imperfect world, never exempting itself from that world.

but because he has made a scapegoat of his love. But that Cordelia is Lear's scapegoat is compatible with Lear's being ours. And seeing him as a scapegoat is not incompatible with seeing him as avoiding love—on the contrary, it is this which shows what his connection with us is, the act for which he bears total, sacrificial consequences. If this play contains scapegoats, it is also about scapegoats, about what it is which creates scapegoats and about the cost of creating them. To insist upon Lear as scapegoat is apt to thin our sense of this general condition in his world; and this again would put us in his position—not *seeing* it from his point of view (maintaining ours), but accepting his point of view, hence denying the other characters, and using the occasion not to feel for him (and them) but to sympathize with ourselves.

All the good characters are exiled, cast out—Cordelia and Kent initially, Edgar at the beginning and Lear at the end of Act II, Gloucester at the end of Act III. But there is from the opening lines a literal social outcast of another kind, the Bastard, the central evil character. A play which has the power of transforming Kings into Fools equally has the power of overlapping Kings and Bastards—the naked human condition is more than any man bargains for. Empson finds Lear's "most distinct expression of the scapegoat idea" in the lines

> None does offend, none; I say none. I'll able 'em:
> Take that of me, my friend, who have the power
> To seal the accuser's lips.
>
> (*IV, vi,* 170–172)

Empson reads: "The royal prerogative has become the power of the outcast to deal directly on behalf of mankind . . . ." I do not question the presence of this feeling, but it is equivocal. For what is the nature of this new, direct power of sealing lips? The problem is not just that "None does offend, none; I say none . . ." protests too much, as though Lear can't quite believe it. The problem is that Edmund also deals with men to seal their lips, and he can directly, even elatedly, use this human power because he is an outcast, because judgment has *already* been passed upon him. That is the justice of his position. And he could express himself in the words "None does offend . . .". He would mean, as in his second soliloquy (*I, ii,* 124–

140), that all are equally evil and evasive, hence no man is in a position from which to judge offense in others.

What would this prove, except that the Devil can quote scripture? But that is proof enough if it proves that the greatest truths are nothing, mean harm or help or nothing, apart from their application in the individual case. We see (do we see?) how Edmund's meaning repudiates the Gospels: he is not speaking on behalf of mankind, but on his own; and he is not forgoing judgment, but escaping it by making it indiscriminate, cynicizing it. Then do we see how Lear's mind, in its rage at injustice, is different from Edmund's? For Lear too has a private use for this indiscriminate condemnation of the world. Suppose we see in the progress of Lear's madness a recapitulation of the history of civilization or of consciousness: from the breaking up of familial bonds and the release of offenses which destroy the social cosmos (III, iv), through the fragile replacement of revenge by the institution of legal justice (III, vi), to the corruption of justice itself and the breaking up of civil bonds (IV, vi). In raging with each of these stages in turn, Lear's mind gusts to a calm as the storm calms, drawing even with the world as it goes. (This is why, adapting Empson's beautiful and compassionate perception, Lear at this point removes his boots, at home again in the world.) If he is an outcast, every man is, whose society is in rags about him; if he is a scapegoat, every man is, under the general shiftings of blame and in the inaccuracy of justice. Lear has not arrived at the human condition he saw imaged in poor naked Tom (the sight which tipped him from world-destroying rage into world-creating madness); but one could say he now has this choice open to him. He finds himself a man; so far he has abdicated. But he has not yet chosen his mortality, to be one man among others; so far he is not at one, atonement is not complete. He has come to terms with Goneril and Regan, with filial ingratitude; he has come back from the way he *knew* madness lies. But he has not come to terms with parental insatiability (which he denounced in his "barbarous Scythian" speech (I, i, 116), and which Gloucester renounces in "the food of thy abused father's wrath" (IV, i, 22)). He has not come back to Cordelia. And he does not.

Evidence for this in this scene is not solely that his "None does offend" is said still stranded in madness (nor even in the possible hint of power in the fact that he does not just take off his boots but imagines them removed for him, as by a servant) but in the content of his ensuing sermon ("I will preach to thee"):

> When we are born, we cry that we are come
> To this great stage of fools.
>
> *(IV, vi,* 184–185)

This is a sermon, presumably, because it interprets the well-known text of tears with which each human life begins. But, as Empson puts it, "the babies cannot be supposed to know all this about human affairs." I think Lear is there feeling like a child, after the rebirth of his senses (children do naturally "wawl and cry" at injustice); and feeling that the world is an unnatural habitat for man; and feeling it is unnatural because it is a stage. Perhaps it is a stage because its actors are seen by heaven, perhaps because they are seen by one another. Either way, it is Lear (not, for example Gloucester, Lear's congregation) who sees it there as a stage. But why a stage of fools? There will be as many answers as there are meanings of "fool." But the point around which all the answers will turn is that it is when, and because, he sees the world as a stage that he sees it peopled with fools, with distortions of men, with natural scapegoats, among whom human relationship does not arise. Then who is in a position to level this vision at the world? Not, of course, that it is invalid—no one could deny it. The catch is that there is no one to assert it—without asserting himself a fool. The world-accusing Fool, like the world-accusing Liar, suffers a Paradox. Which is why "the praise of Folly" must mean "Folly's praise." (To say that the theatricalization of others turns them to scapegoats is a way of putting the central idea of Part II of this essay.)

But if the sense in which, or way in which, Lear has become a scapegoat is not special about him, he can be said to be special there in his *feeling* that he is a scapegoat and in his universal casting of the world with scapegoats. This is an essential connection between him and Gloucester's family: Gloucester is in fact turned out of society, and while he is not left feeling that society has made a scapegoat of him, he has made scapegoats of his sons, deprived each of his birth-right, the one by nature and custom, the other by decree. Each reciprocates by casting his father out, in each case by a stratagem, though the one apparently acts out of hatred, the other apparently out of love; and each of the brothers makes a scapegoat of the other, the one by nature and custom, the other by design. Like Edgar, Lear casts himself in the role of scapegoat, and then others suffer for it; like Edmund, he finds himself the natural fool of Fortune, a customary scapegoat, and then kill, kill, kill, kill, kill, kill (cf. *IV, vi,* 189)—the mind clawing at itself for a hold. These nests of doublings (and in no play is Shakespeare's familiar doubling of themes so relentless, becoming something like the medium of the drama itself, or its vision of the world) suggest that the dramatic point of Shakespeare's doublings is not so much to amplify or universalize a theme as to focus or individuate it, and in particular to show the freedom under each character's possession of his character. Each way of responding to one's foolishness is tested by every other; each way of accepting one's having been cast out is tested by every other; that Gloucester is not driven mad by filial ingratitude (though he is no stranger to the possibility: his very openness in looking at it ("I'll tell thee, friend, I am almost mad myself" (*III, iv,* 169–170) makes him a sensitive touchstone of normalcy in this) means that there is no necessary route Lear's spirit has followed. One will want to object that from the fact that a route is not necessary to Gloucester it does not follow that it is not necessary to Lear. But that is the point. To find out why it is necessary one has to discover who Lear is, what *he* finds necessary, his specific spins of need and choice. His tragedy is that he has to find out too, and that he cannot rest with less than an answer. "Who is it that can tell me who I am?" (*I, iv,* 238). At the first rebuff in his new condition, Lear is forced to the old tragic question. And the Fool lets out his astonishing knowledge: "Lear's shadow." At this point Lear either does not hear, or he thinks the Fool has *told* him who he is, and takes it, as it seems easy to take it, to mean roughly that he is in reduced circumstances. It would be somewhat harder to take if he heard the suggestion of *shade* under "shadow." But the truth may still be harder to be told, harder than anything that can just be told.

Suppose the Fool has precisely answered Lear's question, which is only characteristic of him. Then his reply means: Lear's shadow can tell you who you are. If this is heard, it will mean that the answer to Lear's question is held in the inescapable Lear which is now obscure and obscuring, and in the inescapable Lear which is projected upon the world, and that Lear is double and has a double. And then this play reflects another long curve of feeling about doubling, describing an emphasis other than my recent suggestion that it haunts the characters with their freedom. In the present guise it taunts the characters with their lack of wholeness, their separation from themselves, by loss or denial or opposition. (In Montaigne: "We are, I know not how, double in ourselves, so that what we believe we disbelieve, and cannot rid ourselves of what we condemn." [12] By the time of Heine's *Doppelgänger* ("Still ist die Nacht . . ."), the self is split from its past and from its own feeling, however intimately present both may be.) But in either way, either by putting freedom or by putting integrity into question, doubling sets a task, of discovery, of acknowledgment. And both ways are supported in the moment Lear faces Gloucester and confuses identities with him.

If on a given experience of the play one is caught by the reference to adultery and then to "Gloucester's bastard son" which launch Lear's long tirade against the foulness of nature and of man's justice, one may find that absent member of the Gloucester family presiding over Lear's mind here. For Lear's disgust with sexual nature is not far from Edmund's early manic praise of it, especially in their joint sense of the world as alive in its pursuit; and Edmund's stinging sensitivity to the illegitimacy of society's "legitimacy" prefigures Lear's knowledge of the injustice of society's "justice." If, therefore, we are to see in this play, in Miss Welsford's fine phrase, the investing of the King with motley, then in this scene we may see the King standing up for bastards—an illegitimate King in an unlawful world. (Edmund had tossed off a prayer for bastards, and perhaps there is a suggestion that the problem with prayers is not that few are answered but that *all* are, one way or another.) As the doublings reflect one another, each character projecting some more or less eccentric angle to a common theme, one glimpses the possibility of a common human nature which each, in his own way, fails to achieve; or perhaps glimpses the idea that its gradual achievement is the admission of reflection in oneself of every theme a man exhibits. As Christ receives reflection in every form of human scapegoat, every way in which one man bears the brunt of another's distortion and rejection. For us the reflection is brightest in Cordelia, because of her acceptance, perhaps because she

[12] Auden uses this as the epigraph to *The Double Man*; I have not yet found its context.

is hanged; it is present, on familiar grounds, in the mysteries of the
Fool. I cannot help feeling it, if grossly, in the figure of the Bastard
son. I do not press this. Yet it makes us reflect that evil is not wrong
when it thinks of itself as good, for at those times it recaptures a
craving for goodness, an experience of its own innocence which the
world rejects.

✳ ✳

There is hope in this play, and it is not in heaven. It lies in the
significance of its two most hideous moments: Gloucester's blinding
and Cordelia's death. In Gloucester's history we found hope, because
while his weakness has left him open to the uses of evil, evil *has* to
turn upon him because it cannot bear him to witness. As long as that
is true, evil does not have *free* sway over the world. In Cordelia's
death there is hope, because it shows the Gods more just—more than
we had hoped or wished: Lear's prayer is answered again in this. The
Gods are, in Edgar's wonderful idea, clear. Cordelia's death means
that *every* falsehood, every refusal of acknowledgment, will be
tracked down. In the realm of the spirit, Kierkegaard says, there is
absolute justice. Fortunately, because if all we had to go on were the
way the world goes, we would lose the concept of justice altogether;
and then human life would become unbearable. Kant banked the immortality of the soul on the fact that in *this* world goodness and happiness are unaligned—a condition which, if never righted, is incompatible with moral sanity, and hence with the existence of God. But
immortality is not necessary for the soul's satisfaction. What is necessary is its own coherence, its ability to judge a world in which evil is
successful and the good are doomed; and in particular its knowledge
that while injustice may flourish, it cannot rest content. This, I take
it, is what Plato's *Republic* is about. And it is an old theme of
tragedy.

Its companion theme is that our actions have consequences
which outrun our best, and worst, intentions. The drama of *King
Lear* not merely embodies this theme, it comments on it, even
deepens it. For what it shows is that the *reason* consequences furiously hunt us down is not merely that we are half-blind, and unfortunate, but that we go on doing the thing which produced these
consequences in the first place. What we need is not rebirth, or salvation, but the courage, or plain prudence, to see and to stop. To

abdicate. But what do we need in order to do that? It would be salvation.

## II

These last remarks come from a response not so much to the content of the play as to its form. It is a drama not about the given condition in which the soul finds itself (in relation to Gods or to earth) but about the soul, as Schopenhauer puts the vision of Kant, as the provider of the given, of the conditions under which Gods and earth can appear. It is an enactment not of fate but of responsibility, including the responsibility for fate. However this is finally to be put, its reception demands a particular kind of perception.

What I have in mind can best be brought out in the following way. Suppose that what I have said about why Gloucester is blinded, why he goes to Dover, why he tries suicide, why Edgar avoids his recognition, why he reveals himself when he does, what produces Edmund's attempt to undo his sentence upon Lear and Cordelia, why Gloucester is the first person Lear recognizes, why Cordelia weeps after Lear's imprisoned fantasy, etc. etc.—suppose my answers are true. The problem is then unavoidable: How can critics not have seen them? For it is not that the answers I take to be correct are *recherché*; one needn't have the learning of Bradley or Chambers, or the secrets of Empson, or the discrimination of Johnson, or the passion of Coleridge or Keats, to arrive at them. Their difficulty is of a different kind, an opposite kind.

It is the difficulty of seeing the obvious, something which for some reason is always underestimated, habitually perhaps but not solely by critics, even when the art which hosts them is devoted to that seeing, and the artist set against that underestimation. What *seems* obvious is traced out by the invisible powers of fashion, which offers us reasons whose convenience is almost irresistible. (If this is something we know, it is also something we equally underestimate.) The examples which emerge as most pressing are these: When the well-made play shows us what drama is we say that Shakespeare is poor at plotting, and since we know he is great we excuse him, and then we cross our minds and say that the defects will not be noticed in the heat of performance. When scruples and exercises of New

Criticism tell us what poems are, we say that Shakespeare's plays are poems and therefore structures of meaning, and in this way account for their densities, assuring ourselves that even if we do not or cannot perceive them in a given moment they nevertheless have their effect. When we are made to know that Shakespeare lived in Shakespeare's age and so dealt in his age's understandings and conventions, we can forget that it is Shakespeare demanding of us; and so *his* Bastard slumps back into "the" Bastard of his age, from which he had pointedly lifted it. In some cases (typically in the first kind of example) psychology is invoked to take up the moral or aesthetic slack, in other cases (typically in the last kind of example), and doubtless in response to its earlier misuse, psychology is said to be irrelevant. And in all cases the drama is missed, our perception of it blanked.

* *

I pause here to indicate why I am not trying unduly to blur the immodest or melodramatic quality of the claims I have made: that quality will itself be serviceable if it provides further data for investigating the act of criticism.[13] I am assuming, that is, that criticism is inherently immodest and melodramatic—not merely from its temptations to uninstructive superiority and to presumptuous fellow feeling (with audience or artist) but from the logic of its claims, in particular from two of its elements: (1) A critical position will finally rest upon calling a claim *obvious*; (2) a critical discovery will present itself as the *whole* truth of a work, a provision of its total meaning. Taken in familiar ways, these claims seem easily disconfirmable. How can a claim be obvious if not everyone finds it obvious? (And there is always someone who does not—maybe the critic himself won't tomorrow.) And how can a claim to total meaning be correct when so much is left out? (And there is always something.) But if critical judgments are felt to be refuted on *such* grounds, they are not merely intolerant but a little idiotic. (That is the implied claim of such refutations. I don't say it is never justified.) But suppose we hold on to the intolerance and hold off the idiocy for a moment. Then we have to ask: How could serious men habitually make such *vulnerable*

[13] The facts of intolerance, expressed as part of an examination of their causes and reasons, particularly of the starkness of their appearance in the criticism of modern arts, is the content of Michael Fried's contribution to *Art Criticism in the Sixties* (New York: October House, Inc., 1967), four papers that comprised a symposium held at Brandeis University in May, 1966.

s? (Meaning, perhaps, claims so *obviously* false?) But suppose ___ is another way of taking them; that is, suppose our familiar ways of taking them are what make them seem a bit simple. What are these ways? They take a claim to obviousness as a claim to certainty, and they take the claim to totality as a claim to exhaustiveness. The first of these ways is deeply implicated in the history of modern epistemology, and its effect has been to distrust conviction rather than to investigate the concept of the obvious. (Wittgenstein's later philosophy can be thought of as investigations of obviousness.) The second of these ways expresses the exclusiveness of a lived world, instanced by the mutual offense and the interminable and glancing criticisms of opposed philosophies, and its effect has been to distrust exclusiveness or to attempt exhaustiveness rather than to investigate the concept of totality. It is in the nature of both of these sources of intolerance to appear to be private; because in both one at best has nothing to go on but oneself. (A fashionable liberalism has difficulty telling the difference between seriousness and bigotry. A suggestion of the difference is that the bigot is never isolated. A more ambitious connoisseur will number the differences between seriousness and madness.) This is why a critical discovery is often accompanied by a peculiar exhilaration and why recognition of a critical lapse is accompanied by its peculiar chagrin. One will want to know how (and whether) these emotions differ from the general relish of victory and the general anguish at defeat—say, in science. I do not say that in every case there are differences, but I point to the different ways in which concepts such as "discovery," "advance," "talent," "professional," "insight," "depth," "competition," "influence," etc. are, or may be, applied in criticism and in science—the different shapes of the arenas in which victory and defeat are determined. It seems difference enough that one imagines a major scientific insight occurring to a man along with an impulse to race into the streets with it, out of relief and out of the happy knowledge that it is of relevance to his townsmen; whereas the joy in a major critical insight may be unshareable if one lacks the friends, and even not need to be spoken (while perhaps hoping that another will find it for himself). This must go with the fact that the topics of criticism are not objects but works, things which are *already* spoken. And if arrogance is inherent in criticism (and therefore where not in the Humanities?), then humility is no less painful a task there than anywhere else. Nor is it surprising that the specific elements of arrogance afflict both criticism and philosophy: if philosophy can be thought of as the world of a particular culture brought to consciousness of itself, then one mode of criticism (call it philosophical criticism) can be thought of as the world of a particular work brought to consciousness of itself.

✳ ✳

That the perceptions of an age are formed and disturbed by ghostly fashions is scarcely news. And the difficulties of maturing past them are not the difficulties I am primarily interested in here; they are not peculiar to our failure to confront such drama as *King Lear* unearths. This failure has to do with the mode of this drama itself. Indeed, if my reading of it is correct, the drama is exactly about this difficulty. The difficulty lies in a refusal, a refusal expressed as a failure to acknowledge. (That this is a refusal, something each character is *doing* and is going on doing, is what makes these events add up to tragedy rather than to melodrama—in which what you fail to see is simply something out of sight; or to a scene of natural catastrophe—in which what you fail to prevent is simply beyond prediction or reach.) But isn't this at most the difficulty of the characters in the play? What has this got to do with our difficulties in "appreciating this mode of drama," whatever that turns out to mean?

I have more than once suggested that in failing to see what the true position of a character is, in a given moment, we are exactly put in his condition, and thereby implicated in the tragedy. How? Obviously we are not, as Edgar is, standing in Gloucester's presence; we can neither delay nor not delay, avoid nor not avoid, revealing ourselves to him. If, therefore, my suggestion makes sense, there must be an answer to the question: *What* connects us with Edgar when we accept his conduct in the scenes with his father? What is the point or mechanism of this identification? And the answer to this question is the answer to the question: What is the medium of this drama, how does it do its work upon us? My reading of *King Lear* will have fully served its purpose if it provides data from which an unprejudicial description of its "work" can be composed. One such description would be this: The medium is one which keeps all significance continuously before our senses, so that when it comes over us that we have missed it, this discovery will reveal our ignorance to have been willful, complicitous, a refusal to see. This is a fact of my experience in reading the play (it is not a fact of my experience in seeing the play, which may say something either about its performability or about the performances I have seen of it, or about the nature of performance generally). It is different from the experience of comprehending meanings in a complex poem or the experience of finding the sense of a lyric. These are associated with a thrill of recognition, an access of intimacy, not with a particular sense of exposure. The progress from ignorance to exposure, I mean the treatment of an ignorance which is not to be cured by information (because it is not caused by a lack of information) outlines one motive to philosophy; this is a reason for calling Shakespeare's theater one of philosophical drama. (A test of this would be to consider that the experience of these discoveries—or their proper organ—is as of memory. What precedes certain discoveries is a necessity to *return* to a work, in fact or in memory, as to unfinished business. And this may be neutral as between re-reading and re-seeing. Then one recalls that one sense of philosophy takes memory as its organ of knowledge. An outstanding question is then: What sends us back to a piece or a passage?—as though it is not finished with us. In the opening pages of *Biographia Literaria*, Coleridge takes as his first measure of the worth of a poem the fact that we return to it. Knowing that not just any way of returning will constitute such a measure (say, one in order to prepare for tomorrow's lesson, or to look up an illustration for a thing one already knows), he adds that the return is to be made "with the greatest pleasure." But he is not there concerned to characterize the nature of this pleasure, nor our need of it. The trouble with speaking of this returning as a *remembering* is that it provides access to something we haven't first known and then *forgotten*. Suppose we say that the experience is one of *having to remember*. Then one thinks of Wordsworth's rehearsal (in Book VIII of the *Prelude*) of the motive, and resolution, to know of good and evil, "not as for the mind's delight but for her safety"—the feminine cast registering the mind's need for protection, but the masculine drift showing knowledge that such safety is not achieved through protection, but in action. Evidently Wordsworth is not speaking merely of his past, but of the motive, and resolution, to write—write poetry of such ambitions as the poem he is now writing, and thus give to action the body of the past joined with the soul of the present. And why should the need that sends us back to art be disconnected from the necessity upon which the artist goes for it?)

* *

A structural strategy in *King Lear* brings this out another way. The abdication scene has always been known to be extraordinary, and a familiar justification of it has been that we, as spectators, simply must accept it as the initial condition of the dramatic events and then attend to its consequences. Of course we can do this, or something like it: In a certain context someone says, "Once upon a time there was an old King who had three daughters. Two were very cruel, but the youngest, who was very good and beautiful, was her father's favorite. . . ." So people sometimes say that *King Lear* opens as a fairy tale opens. But it doesn't. It is not narrated, and the first characters we see are two old courtiers discussing the event of the day. The element of fairy tale then appears, centered in other characters, against whose mode of reality the opening figures we have met stand as measures and witnesses, here and hereafter, thus at once heightening and confining the unreal or unseen power we may respond to as a "fairy tale character," focussing it upon the figure of Lear and suggesting it to be something whose sudden changes befall ordinary human beings. If the drama is taken to show the tragic consequences of this initial condition, it should simultaneously be taken to show, what fairy tales have always known, the lengths there are to go in order to remove a spell; the purity, above all the faithfulness it requires. In Shakespeare's world this was still visible only in extraordinary events. By the time of the worlds of Ibsen and Chekhov, after fairy tales had been collected and shelved, the spell finds its life in our ordinary lives: nothing can break the one without breaking the other. I have pointed to other explicit moments of magic in the play, Cordelia's kiss and Lear's song to her. The moral of such moments extends back to the abdication scene: there is no problem of *accepting* them; on the contrary, they are—well, magical.

The idea that the abdication scene strains belief suggests a careful ignorance of the quick routes taken in one's own rages and jealousies and brutalities. Obviously what makes it believable is not an overwhelming tenderness (*that* temptation is yet to come); what is apparently irresistible is recourse to some interpretation which deadens awareness of the ordinary, the civilized violence escaping from it (recourses such as "ritualistic," "fairy tale," "an old crochety tyrant," "an archaic setting"). This uncovers what I meant by the structural strategy of the play's opening scene: we *do* accept its events as they come to light; anyway we sit through them, and we accommodate ourselves to them one way or another; after which, as a consequence of which, we have to accept less obviously extraordinary events as unquestionable workings out of a bad beginning. To speak of this as a strategy may suggest that Shakespeare intended it to have this effect; and do I want to make such a claim? But why not? A critic who strains at this claim will allow himself to swallow the notion that Shakespeare counted on the fact that he was only using an old story whose initial improbabilities he needn't be responsible for. Maybe. Only this raises, and makes unwelcome, urgent questions: Why does he use *this* story? What does he see in it? Why *show* the abdication rather than begin with various accounts of it? Whereas all I need as evidence for saying that Shakespeare intended the strategy of our accepting it (that is, all the claim comes to) is that he put it there and we do accept it, if in confusion. If further explanation is required, then I have equally clear facts to appeal to: what we witness is simultaneously confirmed by the rest of the audience, if the work is successful (this cognitive function of audience is, so far as I know, unremarked, but it seems to me as evident as the contagion and power of laughter an audience can generate, or the enthusiasm it inspires in a public utterance); again, we are helped by the initial verisimilitude in the characters of Kent and Gloucester; and helped further in seeing that no one present on the stage *accepts* Lear's behavior—all who speak (save one) find it extraordinary. So should we. But also ordinary. And a strategy whose point is to break up our sense of the ordinary (which is not the same as a strategy whose point is to present us with spectacularly extraordinary events) also has claim to be called philosophical: this is perhaps why an essential response in both philosophy and tragedy is that of wonder. (Later versions of this strategy are Marxian and Kierkegaardian dialectic, which dramatize both the historical contingency in states we had hitherto accepted as inevitable and the necessity in states we had hitherto thought passing.)

Having lost the power to distinguish the acceptable from the questionable, do we nevertheless still know right from wrong? Whatever the gaudy distractions of Christianizing in reading Shakespeare's plays, it serves him better than the stinting distractions of moralizing. Many critics seem to know quite well what is good for Lear and what he ought not to have done.[14] But suppose we are merely scrupulous and compassionate enough to recognize that any of this is what we do not know, or anyway that the characters themselves know every bit as much in that line as we do. (If not, then again it is not tragedy which has been revealed.) The form of problem we face is: Why *can't* they do or see something? What power has taken them over? For the *content* of Lear's conflict is not tragic, I mean the public conflict—he need not, for example, choose either to sacrifice his daughter or the lives of his subjects. Here the well-known experience of *inevitability* in a tragic sequence comes to attention. But to what shall we attribute it? Not, in all conscience, and after Bradley, to Fate or character or some over-riding classical passion—not merely because we can no longer attach old weight to these words, but because, immediately, they do not account for the particular lie of events in the plots Shakespeare selects for tragedy. And more important, they are directly false to our experience, which is, for all their hidden manipulation, by circumstance or passion, that these figures are radically and continuously *free*, operating under their own power, at every moment choosing their destruction. Kant tells us that man lives in two worlds, in one of which he is free and in the other determined. It is as if in a theater these two worlds are faced off against one another, in their intimacy and their mutual inaccessibility. The audience is free—of the circumstance and passion of the characters, but that freedom cannot reach the arena in which it could become effective. The actors are determined—not because their words and actions are dictated and their future sealed, but because, if the dramatist has really peopled a world, his characters are exercising all the freedom at their command, and specifically failing to. Specifically; not exercising or ceding it once for all. They are, in a word, men; and our liabilities in responding to them are nothing other than our liabilities in responding to any man—rejection, brutality, sentimentality, indifference, the relief and the terror in finding courage, the ironies of human wishes.

It was not wrong to read the sense of inevitability in terms of a

---

[14] This is the attitude that Alpers' study is meant most directly to discourage.

chain of cause and effect; what was wrong, what became insufficient to explain our lives, was to read this chain as if its first link lay in the past, and hence as if the present were the scene of its ineluctable effects, in the face of which we must learn suffering. With Kant (because with Luther) and then Hegel and Nietzsche, not to say Freud, we became responsible for the meaning of the suffering itself, indeed for the very fact that the world is to be comprehended under the rule of causation at all. What has become inevitable is the fact of endless causation itself, together with the fact of incessant freedom. And what has become the tragic fact is that we cannot or will not tell which is which. When tragedy leapt from inevitability, we had been taken into the confidence of the tale, hints of the characters' ignorance of their fate were laid ("dramatic irony"). The awe in experiencing it was like the awe in suddenly falling into the force of nature or of crowds or in watching a building collapse. We are not in Shakespeare's confidence. Now tragedy grows from the fortunes we choose to interpret, to accept, as inevitable, and we have no more hints of ignorance than the characters have. Edmund sees something like this (in his early soliloquy, ". . . we make guilty of our disasters the sun, the moon, and stars . . ."), but, being Edmund, he finds it comic. And no play can show more instances and ranges than *King Lear* in which God's name and motive are taken in vain. The past cannot now be clarified as Teiresias clarified it (that would now be a relief, however terrible its terms) for the present is not clear or strong enough to believe such predictions. It is only about *others* that prophecy commands our attention. (Hence, for example, the vogue of Game Theory, and the fashion of looking for the "cause" of historical events.) But the seer is not needed. Nothing we can know or need to know is unknown.

✳ ✳

"Surely," it will be said, "whatever all this is supposed to mean, it is not relevant to our relation with those figures up there, it applies at best to their relations with one another, or to ours with one another. You forget this is theater; that they are characters up there, not persons; that their existence is fictional; that it is not up to us to confront them morally, actually enter their lives." How might I forget this? By becoming like the child who screams at Red Riding Hood the truth of her situation? But I don't scream out, any longer;

that is just a matter of getting older and learning how to behave. (Though of course "just a matter" does not mean that it is not profound learning. It is as profound as learning not to wet the bed, and I can do that in my sleep. If I couldn't, the learning wouldn't yet have amounted to much.) What am I to remember, and what good would it do if I did? I know people are annoyed by what seems feigned innocence, and with a final mustering of patience they tell me that I am to remember that I am in a theater. And how do I do that? How do I remember something there is no obvious way for me to forget? ("Don't forget where you are" is not meant to inform me of the place I am in, but calls to my attention a more or less distracted or obsessive piece of behavior which I immediately know to be unacceptable there—like smoking in church.) Am I to remember to be entertained? But suppose I am not; why should I be? Am I to remember that I am not responsible for those people up there? Presumably this is not a way of saying that they are none of my business or that they have not been made real for me by their creator. But what else is it a way of saying? Am I to remember that I do not have to confront them, give them my warnings or advice or compassion? But I am confronting them (unless my head or heart is lowered, in fear or boredom) and I *have* this advice or warning or compassion or anxiety; if you haven't, you don't see what I see. But I cannot *offer* it to them or *share* it with them. That is true; they cannot hear my screams. But that is something else; that is something I do not have to remember, something I know as I know that I cannot choose the content of my dreams or suffer my daughter's pain or alter my father's childhood.

So the question arises: Why do I choose to subject myself to this suffering? Why do I deliberately confront a situation which fills me with a pity and terror I know are ineffective? Two familiar lines of answer have been drawn to such a question. One of them looks to the use to be made of these feelings in the aesthetic context, their (cathartic) effect upon *me*; the other denies that it is real pity and terror that I feel, but rather some aesthetic (more or less distant) counterpart of them. Whatever their respective merits and obscurities, both answers pass the sense of the question which is troubling me, which is brought out by asking: How do I know I am to *do* nothing, confronted by such events? The answer, "Because it is an aesthetic context" is no answer, partly because no one knows what an aesthetic context is, partly because, if it means anything, a factor of its meaning is "a context in which I am to do nothing"; which is the trouble.

But my object here is not a theory of tragedy. It is simply to suggest, staying within the evidence of the reading I have given of one play, how this mode of drama works upon us and what mode of perception it asks of us. For I feel confident not only that this play works upon us differently from other modes of theater, but that it is dramatic in a way, or at a depth, foreign to what we have come to expect in a theater, even that it is essentially dramatic in a way our theater and perception does not fathom. These are scarcely new thoughts, but no statement of them I know has seemed to me to get out clearly enough what this sense of drama is. Doubtless only someone who shares this sense will credit or consider the few suggestions I can make about it here.

✳ ✳

Clearly, as we are always told, its particular dramatic effect is a function of the fact that its words are poetry. Sometimes Shakespeare's plays are said to be poems, but obviously they are not poems; they are made in a medium which knows how to use poetry dramatically. It is an accomplishment of the same magnitude, even of the same kind, as the discovery of perspective in painting and of tonality in music—and, apparently, just as irretrievable, for artistic purposes now. The question is: How does the medium function which uses poetry in this way?

It is not uncommon to find Shakespeare's plays compared to music, but in the instances I have seen, this comparison rests upon more or less superficial features of music, for example, on its balance of themes, its recurrences, shifts of mood, climaxes—in a word, on its theatrical properties. But music is, or was, dramatic in a more fundamental sense, or it became so when it no longer expanded festivals or enabled dancing or accompanied songs, but achieved its own dramatic autonomy, worked out its progress in its own terms. Perhaps this begins with Monteverdi (born three years after Shakespeare), but in any case it is secured only with the establishment of tonality and has its climax in the development of sonata form. The essence of the quality I have in mind has to do with the notion of *development*: not, as in early sonata forms, merely with an isolated section in which fragments of earlier material are recolored and reassembled, but with the process, preeminent in late Beethoven and Brahms, in which the earlier is metamorphosed into new stabilities, culminating in a work like the *Hammerklavier* Sonata, in which *all* later material can be said to be "contained" in the rising and falling interval of a third in the opening two bars. The question I wish to raise here is: How is music made this way to be perceived? *What* are we to perceive in order to understand and respond to what is said? Obviously not, in the example alluded to, merely or primarily the rising and falling thirds. I will say that the quality we are to perceive is one of *directed motion,* controlled by relations of keys, by rate of alteration, and by length and articulation of phrases. We do not know where this motion can stop and we do not understand why it has begun here, so we do not know where we stand nor why we are there. The drama consists in following this out and in finding out what it takes to follow this out.

The specific comparison with Shakespeare's drama has to do with the two most obvious facts about what is required in following this music: first, that one hears its directedness; second, that one hears only what is happening now.

The critical element appears to be that of directedness, because obviously all music, and all language and all conduct, shares the property that not everything of significance is perceptible now. And yet there is the decisive difference between waiting for a sentence in prose or conversation to end and attending to a line of poetry or a tonal phrase, a difference suggested by such facts as these: in conversation, a remark which begins a certain way can normally have only one of a definite set of endings; we know why a remark has begun as it has or we can find out why in obvious ways; and the remark will come to an end of its own accord, what counts as an end is given in the language; so if, for example, we *hang* on these words, that is not because of something happening in these words before us now. It is as if dramatic poetry and tonal music, forgoing these givens, are made to imitate the simplest facts of life: that life is lived in time, that there is a now at which everything that happens happens, and a now at which for each man everything stops happening, and that what has happened is not here and now, and that what might have happened then and there will never happen then and there, and that what will happen is not here and now and yet may be settled by what is happening here and now in a way we cannot know or will not see here and now. The perception or attitude demanded in following this drama is one which demands a continuous attention to what is happening at each here and now, as if everything of significance is happening at this moment, while each thing that happens turns a leaf of time. I think of it as an experience of *continuous presentness*. Its demands are as rigorous as those of any spiritual exercise—to let the past go and to let the future take its time; so that we not allow the past to determine the meaning of what is now happening (something else may have come of it) and that we not anticipate what will come of what has come. Not that anything is possible (though it is) but that we do not know what is, and is not, next.

✳ ✳

Epistemology will demonstrate that we cannot know, cannot be certain of, the future; but we don't believe it. We anticipate, and so we are always wrong. Even when what we anticipate comes to pass we get the wrong idea of our powers and of what our safety depends upon, for we imagine that we *knew* this would happen, and take it either as an occasion for congratulations or for punishments, of ourselves or others. Instead of acting as we can and remaining equal to the consequences. (Here one might consider the implication of the fact that you say "I knew it!" with sharp relief or sudden anguish, and that of course it does not mean that in fact you were fully apprized of a particular outcome. It means, roughly, that "something told you," something you wish you had harkened to. And while that is no doubt true, the frame of mind in which you express it, by saying in that particular way that you *knew*, assures that you will not harken. Because it reveals a frame of mind in which you had tried, and are going on trying now, to alchemize a guess or a hope or a suspicion into a certainty, a *pry* into the future rather than an intimation of conscience.)

Nietzsche thought the metaphysical consolation of tragedy was lost when Socrates set *knowing* as the crown of human activity. And it is a little alarming, from within the conviction that the medium of drama which Shakespeare perfected also ended with him, to think again that Bacon and Galileo and Descartes were contemporary with those events. We will hardly say that it was *because* of the development of the new science and the establishing of epistemology as the monitor of philosophical inquiry that Shakespeare's mode of tragedy disappeared. But it may be that the loss of presentness—which is what the disappearance of that mode of tragedy means—is what works us into the idea that we can save our lives by knowing them. This seems to be the message both of the new epistemology and of Shakespeare's tragedy themselves.

In the unbroken tradition of epistemology since Descartes and Locke (radically questioned from within itself only in our period), the concept of knowledge (of the world) disengages from its connections with matters of information and skill and learning, and becomes fixed to the concept of certainty alone, and in particular to a certainty provided by the (by my) senses. At some early point in epistemological investigations, the world normally present to us (the world in whose existence, as it is typically put, we "believe") is brought into question and vanishes, whereupon all connection with a world is found to hang upon what can be said to be "present to the senses"; and that turns out, shockingly, not to be the world. It is at this point that the doubter finds himself cast into skepticism, turning the existence of the external world into a problem. Kant called it a scandal to philosophy and committed his genius to putting a stop to it, but it remains active in the conflicts between traditional philosophers and their ordinary language critics, and it inhabits the void of comprehension between continental ontology and Anglo-American analysis as a whole. Its relevance to us at the moment is only this: The skeptic does not gleefully and mindlessly forgo the world we share, or thought we shared; he is neither the knave Austin took him to be, nor the fool the pragmatists took him for, nor the simpleton he seems to men of culture and of the world. He forgoes the world for just the reason that the world is important, that it is the scene and stage of connection with the present: he finds that it vanishes exactly with the effort to *make* it present. If this makes him unsuccessful, that is because the presentness achieved by certainty of the senses cannot compensate for the presentness which had been elaborated through our old absorption in the world. But the wish for genuine connection is there, and there was a time when the effort, however hysterical, to assure epistemological presentness was the best expression of seriousness about our relation to the world, the expression of an awareness that presentness was threatened, gone. If epistemology wished to make knowing a substitute for that fact, that is scarcely foolish or knavish, and scarcely some simple mistake. It is, in fact, one way to describe the tragedy *King Lear* records.

For its characters, having for whatever reason to forgo presentness to their worlds, extend that disruption in their knowing of it (Lear and Edmund knowing they cannot be loved, Regan knowing the destination of Gloucester, Edgar knowing he is contemned and has to win acceptance). But how do we stop? How do we learn that what we need is not more knowledge but the willingness to forgo knowing? For this sounds to us as though we are being asked to abandon reason for irrationality (for we know what these are and we know these are alternatives), or to trade knowledge for superstition (for we know when conviction is the one and when it is the other —the thing the superstitious always take for granted). This is why we think skepticism must mean that we cannot know the world exists, and hence that perhaps there isn't one (a conclusion some profess to admire and others to fear). Whereas what skepticism suggests is that since we cannot know the world exists, its presentness to us cannot be a function of knowing. The world is to be *accepted*; as the presentness of other minds is not to be known, but acknowledged. But what is this "acceptance," which caves in at a doubt? And where do we get the idea that there is something we cannot do (e.g., prove that the world exists)? For this is why we take Kant to have said that there are things we cannot know; whereas what he said is that something cannot be known—*and* cannot coherently be doubted either, for example, that there is a world and that we are free. When Luther said we cannot know God but must have faith, it is clear enough that the inability he speaks of is a logical one: there is not some comprehensible activity we cannot perform, and equally not some incomprehensible activity we cannot perform. Our relation to God is that of parties to a testament (or refusers of it); and Luther's logical point is that you do not accept a promise by knowing something about the promisor. How, if this is the case, we become confused about it clearly requires explanation, and the cure will be sufficiently drastic —crucifying the intellect. But perhaps no less explanation is required to understand why we have the idea that knowing the world exists is to be understood as an instance of knowing that a particular object exists (only, so to speak, an enormously large one, the largest). Yet this idea is shared by all traditional epistemologists.[15] (Its method-ological expression is the investigation of our knowledge of the external world by an investigation of a claim that a particular object exists.) Nor is it surprising that it is the intellect which, still bloody from its victories, remains to be humbled if the truth here is to emerge. Reason seems able to overthrow the deification of everything but itself. To imagine that what is therefore required of us is a new rage of irrationality would be about as intelligent as to imagine that because heaven rejects the prideful man what it craves is a monkey. For the point of forgoing knowledge is, of course, to know.

To overcome knowing is a task Lear shares with Othello and Macbeth and Hamlet, one crazed by knowledge he can neither test nor reject, one haunted by knowledge whose authority he cannot impeach, one cursed by knowledge he cannot share. Lear abdicates sanity for the usual reason: it is his way not to know what he knows, or to know only what he knows. At the end, recovered to the world, he still cannot give up knowledge, the knowledge that he is captured, lost, receiving just punishment, and so he does again the thing for which he will now irrecoverably be punished. It is the thing we do not know that can save us. (This is what fairy tales told, when third sons collected or comforted abandoned things and hags. It is what

[15] A particularly brilliant occurrence of it runs through Hume's *Dialogues on Natural Religion*: It is the essential assumption of Cleanthes (the new believer) which Philo (the new skeptic) does not question, and I suppose that one or other of them, or both together, pretty well exhaust Hume's discoveries in this region. Freed from this assumption, the *experience* of design or purpose in the world (which Cleanthes always begins with and comes back to, and which Philo confirms) has a completely different force. It is no longer a modest surmise about a particular object, for which there is no good evidence (none against, but none for); but rather, being a natural and *inescapable* response, it has, in terms of Hume's own philosophizing, the same claim to reveal the world as our experience of causation (or of objecthood) has. —This is essentially the view of Hume's *Dialogues* that I have presented in my classes over a number of years. In the spring of 1967 I began studying and teaching the writings of Heidegger, and the discussion of the concepts of *world* and *worldhood* near the beginning of *Being and Time* seem to me not only intuitively clear against this background, but to represent the beginnings of a formidable phenomenological investigation of a phase of empiricism, indeed of traditional epistemology altogether. Part II of this essay bears marks of that reading, notably in the transition from the concept of being in someone's *presence* to that of being in his *present* (e.g., p. 337); but the ideas do not derive from that reading, and my understanding of Heidegger's work is still too raw for me to wish to claim support from it.

I am not unaware of the desperate obscurity of these remarks about traditional epistemology, both in this note and in the section of this essay from which it is suspended. That is the point at which my reliance on my doctoral thesis (cited in the Acknowledgments) is most sustained.

theology knew as grace. Ignorance of it is the damnation of Faust, the one piece of knowledge he could not bargain for.)

In addition to the notions of continuous presentness and of the attempt to overcome knowledge, I have sometimes wanted to speak of the *reality of time* as a way of hitting off the experience of this mode of drama. At each moment, until their last, the future of each character in *King Lear* is open; and in the end each closes it, except for Cordelia, who chooses, out of love, to let it close. This is not the way time is conceived in other dramaturgy. In *Phèdre*, time is frozen, as place is; the action is transfixed by the lucidity which arrays itself against the truth, absorbing its brilliance, and the lucidity which supervenes as truth breaks through. In Ibsen, time is molded to fit the moments at which drama, carefully prepared, explodes into the action. It depends for its effect not on the fact of time but upon the feats of timing, upon something's happening at the right, or the wrong, time. One slip and it is melodrama; but then one slip and Racine is oratory. In *Phèdre* we are placed unprotected under heaven, examined by an unblinking light. In *Hedda Gabler,* we watch and wait, unable to avert our eyes, as if from an accident or an argument rising at the next table in a restaurant, or a figure standing on the ledge of a skyscraper. In *King Lear* we are differently implicated, placed into a world not obviously unlike ours (as Racine's is, whose terrain we could not occupy) nor obviously like ours (as Ibsen's is, in whose rooms and rhythms we are, or recently were, at home), and somehow participating in the proceedings—not listening, not watching, not overhearing, almost as if dreaming it, with words and gestures carrying significance of that power and privacy and obscurity; and yet participating, as at a funeral or marriage or inauguration, confirming something; it could not happen without us. It is not a dispute or a story, but history happening, and we are living through it; later we may discover what it means, when we discover what a life means.

✳ ✳

In each case the first task of the dramatist is to gather us and then to silence and immobilize us. Or say that it is the poster which has gathered us and the dimming house-lights which silence us. Then the first task of the dramatist is to reward this disruption, to show that this very extraordinary behavior, sitting in a crowd in the dark, is very sane. It is here that we step past the carry of Dr. Johnson's words. He is right in dismissing—anyway, in denying—the idea that we need to have what happens in a theater made credible, and right to find that such a demand proceeds from a false idea that otherwise what happens in a theater is incredible, and right to say that our response to the events on a stage is neither to credit nor to discredit them: we know we are in a theater. But then he does not stop to ask, What is it that we then know? What is a theater? Why are we there? —anyway, not for longer than it takes to answer, ". . . the spectators . . . come to hear a certain number of lines recited with just gesture and elegant modulation." It is not clear to me how seriously this straight-faced remark is meant. Its rhetoric may be that of the academic's put-down of the enthusiast. (Listeners come to an opera to hear a certain number of tunes sung with just pitch and elegant phrasing. Spectators at a football game go to see a certain number of gigantic men attack one another for the possession of a bag of air.) Or it may be that *Garrick's* gestures and modulations were worth assembling for. Or it may be that the London theaters of that time typically provided an experience of expert recitation. What seems clear enough is that the theater was not important to Johnson; that a certain provision of inside entertainment was sufficient to justify the expense of an evening there. But if the point is entertainment, then his difficult acquaintance Hume had re-raised a question which needs attention: Why should such matters provide entertainment? Hume's even more difficult acquaintance Rousseau, for whom the theater was important, re-raised the next question: What is the good of such entertainment?

What is the state of mind in which we find the events in a theater neither credible nor incredible? The usual joke is about the Southern yokel who rushes to the stage to save Desdemona from the black man. What is the joke? That he doesn't know how to behave in a theater? That would be plausible here, in a way it would not be plausible in accounting for, or dealing with, the child screaming at Red Riding Hood, or the man lighting a cigarette in church. It treats him like the visitor who drinks from the finger bowl. That fun depends upon the anxious giggle at seeing our customs from a distance, letting them show for a moment in their arbitrariness. We have no trouble understanding what his mistake has been, and the glimpse of arbitrariness is beneficial because the custom justifies itself again: we see the point of having the finger bowl and so (apart from threats to symbol and caste) it doesn't matter that there are other ways of keeping clean, it is enough that this is our way. But what mistake has the yokel in the theater made, and what is *our* way? He thinks someone is strangling someone. —But that is true; Othello is strangling Desdemona. — Come on, come on; you know, he thinks that very man is putting out the light of that very woman right now. —Yes, and that is exactly what is happening. —You're not amusing. The point is that he thinks something is really happening, whereas nothing is really happening. It's play acting. The woman will rise again to die another night. —That is what I thought was meant, what I was impatiently being asked to accede to. The trouble is that I really do not understand what I am being asked, and of course I am suggesting that you do not know either. You tell me that that woman will rise again, but I know that she will not, that she is dead and has died and will again die, die dead, die with a lie on her lips, damned with love. You can say there are two women, Mrs. Siddons and Desdemona, both of whom are mortal, but only one of whom is dying in front of our eyes. But what you have produced is two names. Not all the pointing in the world to *that* woman will distinguish the one woman from the other. The trouble can be put two ways; or, there are two troubles and they pull opposite ways: you can't point to one without pointing to the other; and you can't point to both at the same time. Which just means that *pointing* here has become an incoherent activity. Do you wish to say that Mrs. Siddons has not died, or does not die? These are not incomprehensible remarks, but the first implies that she had been in danger and the second suggests that she is not scheduled for death. At least our positions would then be distinguishable, if incomprehensible. I mean, the intentions with which we go to the theater are equally incomprehensible. You go, according to what has so far come out, in order to find that Mrs. Siddons is not dead; I go to watch Desdemona die. I don't particularly enjoy the comparison, for while I do not share your tastes they seem harmless enough, where mine are very suspect.

The case of the yokel has its anxieties. How do we imagine we might correct him?—that is, *what* mistake do we suppose him to have made? If we grant him the concept of play-acting, then we will tell him that this is an instance of it: "They are only acting; it isn't real." But we may not be perfectly happy to have had to say that. Not that we doubt that it is true. If the thing *were* real. . . . But somehow we had *accepted* its non-factuality, it made it possible for there to have been a play. When we say it, in assurance, it comes out as an empirical assertion. Doubtless it has a very high degree of probability, anyway there is no reason to think that Mrs. Siddons is in danger; though of course it is not logically absurd to suppose otherwise. —But now our philosophical repressions are getting out of control. This isn't at all what we meant to be saying. Beforehand, her danger was absolutely out of the question, we did not have to rule it out in order to go on enjoying the proceedings. We do not *have* to now either, and yet the empirical and the transcendental are not as clearly separate as, so to speak, we thought they were. "They are only pretending" is something we typically say to children, in reassurance; and it is no happier a thing to say in that context, and no truer. The point of saying it there is not to focus them on the play, but to help bring them out of it. It is not an instructive remark, but an emergency measure. If the child cannot be brought out of the play by working through the content of the play itself, he should not have been subjected to it in the first place.

Neither credible nor incredible: that ought to mean that the concept of credibility is inappropriate altogether. The trouble is, it is inappropriate to real conduct as well, most of the time. That couple over there, drinking coffee, talking, laughing. Do I believe they are just passing the time of day, or testing out the field for a flirtation, or something else? In usual cases, not one thing or another; I neither believe nor disbelieve. Suppose the man suddenly puts his hands to the throat of the woman. Do I believe or disbelieve that he is going to throttle her? The time for that question, as soon as it comes to the point, is already passed. The question is: What, if anything, do I do? What I believe hangs on what I do or do not do and on how I react to what I do or do not do. And whether something or nothing, there will be consequences. At the opening of the play it is fully true that I neither believe nor disbelieve. But I am something, perplexed, anxious. . . . Much later, the warrior asks his wife if she has said her prayers. Do I believe he will go through with it? I know he will, it is a certainty fixed forever; but I hope against hope he will come to his senses; I appeal to him, in silent shouts. Then he puts his hands on her throat. The question is: What, if anything, do I do? I do nothing; that is a certainty fixed forever. And it has its consequences.

*Why* do I do nothing? Because they are only pretending? That would be a reason not to do anything if it were true of the couple over there, who just a moment ago were drinking coffee, laughing. There it is a reason because it tells me something I did not know. Here, in the theater, what does it tell me? It is an excuse, whistling in the dark; and it is false. Othello is not pretending. Garrick is not pretending, any more than a puppet in that part would be pretending. I know everything, and yet the question arises: Why do I sit there? And the honest answer has to be: There is nothing I can do. Why not?

If the yokel is not granted the concept of play-acting, you will not be able to correct him, and that has its own anxiety; not just that of recognizing that people may be wholly different from oneself, but in making us question the inevitability of our own concept of acting, its lucidity to ourselves. You may then have to restrain him and remove him from the theater; you may even have to go so far as to stop the play. *That* is something we can do; and its very extremity shows how little is in our power. For that farthest extremity has not touched Othello, he has vanished; it has merely interrupted an evening's work. Quiet the house, pick up the thread again, and Othello will reappear, as near and as deaf to us as ever. —The transcendental and the empirical crossing; possibilities shudder from it.

The little joke on the yokel is familiar enough of its kind. The big joke, and not just on the yokel, is his idea that *if* the thing were in fact happening he would be able to stop it, be equal to his chivalry. It is fun to contemplate his choices. Will he reason with Othello? (After Iago has destroyed his reason.) Tell him the truth? (Which the person who loves him has been doing over and over.) Threaten him, cross swords with him? (That, one would like to see.) —There is nothing and we know there is nothing we can do. Tragedy is meant to make sense of that condition.

It is said by Dr. Johnson, and felt by Tom Jones' friend Partridge, that what we credit in a tragedy is a possibility, a recognition that if we were in such circumstances we would feel and act as those characters do. But I do not consider it a very live possibility that I will find myself an exotic warrior, having won the heart of a young high-born girl by the power of my past and my capacity for poetry, then learning that she is faithless. And if I did find myself in that position I haven't any idea what I would feel or do. —That is not what is meant? Then what is? That I sense the possibility that I will feel impotent to prevent the object I have set my soul on, and won, from breaking it; that it is possible that I will trust someone who wishes me harm; that I can become murderous with jealousy and know chaos when my imagination has been fired and then gutted and the sense of all possibility has come to an end? But I know, more or less, these things now; and if I did not, I would not know what possibility I am to envision as presented by this play.

✳ ✳

It may seem perverse or superficial or plain false to insist that we *confront* the figures on a stage. It may seem perverse: because it is so obvious what is meant in saying we do *not* confront them, namely, that they are characters in a play. The trouble with this objection is its assumption that it is obvious what kind of existence characters in a play have, and obvious what our relation to them is, obvious why we are present. Either what I have been saying makes these assumptions less comfortable, or I have failed to do what I wished to do. It may seem superficial: because saying that we "confront" them seems just a fancy way of saying that we *see* them, and nobody would care to deny that. The trouble is that we no more merely see these characters than we merely see people involved elsewhere in our lives—or, if we do merely see them that shows a specific response to the claim they make upon us, a specific form of acknowledgment; for example, rejection. It may seem plain false: because we can no more confront a character in a play than we can confront any fictitious being.

The trouble is, there they are. The plain fact, the only plain fact, is that we do not *go up* to them, even that we cannot.   —"Obviously not. Their existence is fictional."   —Meaning what? That they are not real? Meaning what? That they are not to be met with in space and time? This means they are not in nature. (That is, as Leibniz puts it, they are not objects to which one of *every* pair of opposite predicates truly applies—e.g., that one or the other of them has children or has not, ate breakfast or did not. But no such pair can be ruled out in advance of coming to know a character; and more is true of him than we take in at a glance, or in a generation of glances. And more that we are responsible for knowing. Call him our creation, but then say that creation is an exhausting business. It would not be creation from nothing, but from everything—that is, from a totality, the world of the words.) And neither is God in nature, neither are square roots, neither is the spirit of the age or the correct tempo of the Great Fugue. But if these things do not exist, that is not because they are not in nature. And there have so far always been certain people who have known how to find each of them. Calling the existence of Lear and others "fictional" is incoherent (if understandable) when used as an explanation of their existence, or as a denial of their existence. It is, rather, the name of a problem: _What is the existence of a character on the stage_, what kind of (grammatical) entity is this? We know several of its features:

1. A character is not, and cannot become, aware of us. Darkened, indoor theaters dramatize the fact that the audience is invisible. A theater whose house lights were left on (a possibility suggested, for other reasons, by Brecht) might dramatize the equally significant fact that we are also inaudible to them, and immovable (that is, at a _fixed_ distance from them). I will say: We are not in their presence.

2. They are in our presence. This means, again, not simply that we are seeing and hearing them, but that we are acknowledging them (or specifically failing to). Whether or not we acknowledge others is not a matter of choice, any more than accepting the presence of the world is a matter of choosing to see or not to see it. Some persons sometimes are capable of certain blindnesses or deafnesses toward others; but, for example, avoidance of the presence of others is not blindness or deafness to their claim upon us; it is as conclusive an acknowledgment that they are present as murdering them would be. Tragedy shows that we are responsible for the death of others even when we have not murdered them, and even when we have not manslaughtered them innocently. As though what we have come to regard as our normal existence is itself poisoning.

But doesn't the fact that we do not or cannot go up to them just mean that we do not or cannot acknowledge them? One may feel like saying here: The acknowledgment cannot be _completed_. But this does not mean that acknowledging is impossible in a theater. Rather it shows what acknowledging, in a theater, is. And acknowledging in a theater shows what acknowledgment in actuality is. For what is the difference between tragedy in a theater and tragedy in actuality? In both, people in pain are in our presence. But in actuality acknowledgment _is_ incomplete, in actuality there is no acknowledgment, unless we put ourselves in their presence, reveal ourselves to them. We may find that the point of tragedy in a theater is exactly relief from this necessity, a respite within which to prepare for this necessity, to clean out the pity and terror which stand in the way of acknowledgment outside. ("Outside of here it is death"—maybe Hamm the actor has the theater in mind.)

3. How is acknowledgment expressed; that is, how do we put ourselves in another's presence? In terms which have so far come out, we can say: By revealing ourselves, by allowing ourselves to be seen. When we do not, when we keep ourselves in the dark, the consequence is that we convert the other into a character and make the world a stage for him. There is fictional existence with a vengeance, and there is the theatricality which theater such as *King Lear* must overcome, is meant to overcome, shows the tragedy in failing to overcome.[16] The conditions of theater literalize the conditions we exact for existence outside—hiddenness, silence, isolation—hence make that existence plain. Theater does not expect us simply to stop theatricalizing; it knows that we can theatricalize its condi-

---

[16] That the place of art is now pervasively threatened by the production of objects whose hold upon us is theatrical, and that serious modernist art survives only in its ability to defeat theater, are companion subjects of Michael Fried's "Art and Objecthood" (*Artforum*, Volume V, No. 10, June, 1967, pp. 12–23). It is, among other things, the most useful and enlightening explanation of the tastes and ambitions of the fashionable modern sensibility I know of. Its conjunction with what I am saying in this essay (even to the point of specific concepts, most notably that of "presentness") is more exact than can be made clear in a summary, and will be obvious to anyone reading it. I take this opportunity to list other of Fried's recent writings which develop the notions and connections of modernism and seriousness and theatricality, but which I have not had occasion to cite specifically: "Shape as Form: Frank Stella's New Paintings," *Artforum*, Volume V, No. 3, November, 1966, pp. 18–27; "The Achievement of Morris Louis," *Artforum*, Volume V, No. 6, February, 1967, pp. 34–40 (the material of this essay is incorporated in Fried's forthcoming book on Louis, to be published by Harry N. Abrams, Inc.); "New Work by Anthony Caro," *Artforum*, Volume V, No. 6, February, 1967, pp. 46–47; "Jules Olitski," introductory essay to the catalogue of an exhibition of Olitski's work at the Corcoran Gallery, Washington, D.C., April–June, 1967; "Two Sculptures by Anthony Caro," *Artforum*, Volume VI, No. 6, February 1968, pp. 24–25. Because Fried's work is an instance of what I called "philosophical criticism" (p. 313), let me make explicit the fact that this title is not confined to such pieces as "Art and Objecthood" nor to those on Stella and on Olitski, all of which are intensely theoretical or speculative; it applies equally to the two short pieces on Caro, each of which just consists of uninterrupted descriptions (in the first case of four, in the second case of two) of Caro's sculptures. Moreover, this writing would not be "philosophical" in the relevant sense if it did not essentially contain, or imply, descriptions of that sort. Not, of course, that I suppose my having spoken of "bringing the world of a particular work to consciousness of itself" (ibid.), will convey what sorts of descriptions these are, to anyone who has not felt them. To characterize them further would involve investigations of such phenomena as "attending to the words themselves" and "faithfulness to a text."

we can theatricalize any others. But in giving us a place within which our hiddenness and silence and separation are accounted for, it gives us a chance to stop.

When we had the idea that acknowledgment must be incomplete in a theater, it was as if we felt *prevented* from approaching the figures to whom we respond. But we are not prevented; we merely in fact, or in convention, do not. Acknowledgment is complete without that; that is the beauty of theater. It is right to think that in a theater *something* is omitted which must be made good outside. But what is omitted is not the claim upon us, and what would make good the omission is not necessarily approaching the other. For approaching him outside does not satisfy the claim, apart from making ourselves present. (Works without faith.) Then what expresses acknowledgment in a theater? What plays the role there that revealing ourselves plays outside? That is, what counts as putting ourselves into a character's presence? I take this to be the same as the question I asked at the beginning of this discussion: What is the mechanism of our identification with a character? We know we cannot approach him, and not because it is not done but because nothing would count as doing it. Put another way, they and we do not occupy the same space; there is no path from my location to his. (We could also say: there is no distance between us, as there is none between me and a figure in my dream, and none, or no one, between me and my image in a mirror.) We do, however, occupy the same time.

And the time is always now; time is measured solely by what is now happening to them, for what they are doing now is all that is happening. The time is of course not necessarily *the* present—that is up to the playwright. But the time presented, whether the present or the past, is this moment, at which an arrival is awaited, in which a decision is made or left unmade, at which the past erupts into the present, in which reason or emotion fail. . . . The novel also comprises these moments, but only as having happened—not necessarily *in* the past; that is up to the novelist. —But doesn't this amount only to saying that novels are narrated and that the natural sound of narration is the past tense? Whereas plays have no narrator. —What does it mean to say they "have no narrator," as though having one is the normal state of affairs? One may feel: the lack of a narrator means that we confront the characters more directly, without interposed descriptions or explanations. But then couldn't it equally be said that, free of the necessity to describe or explain, the dramatist is free to leave his characters more opaque?

Here I want to emphasize that no character in a play *could* (is, logically, in a position from which to) narrate its events. This can be seen various ways:

1. No mere character, no mere human being, commands the absolute credibility of a narrator. When he (who?) writes: "He lay flat on the brown, pine-needled floor of the forest, his chin on his folded arms, and high overhead the wind blew in the tops of the pine trees," there is no doubt possible that there is a forest here and that its floor is pine-needled and brown, and that a man is lying flat on it. No character commands this credibility of assertion, not because he may not be as honest as a man can be, but because he is an actor; that is, what he is doing or suffering is part of what is happening; he is fixed in the present. The problem is not so much that he cannot, so to speak, see *over* the present, but that he cannot insert a break in it; if he narrates, then *that* is what he is doing, that has become what is now happening. But a narrator cannot, I feel like saying, make anything happen; that is one source of his credibility. (The use of so-called "first person narrative" cedes absolute credibility, but then *this* narrator is not so much a character of the events he describes as he is the antagonist of the reader. We will have to return to this.)

2. This comes out if we notice the two points in *King Lear* at which Shakespeare provides a character with a narration: the Gentleman's account to Kent concerning Cordelia's reception of his letters (*IV, iii*, 12–33) and Edgar's late account of his father's death (*V, iii*, 181–218). As one would expect of any narration by one character to another, these speeches have the effect of interrupting the action, but the difference is that the Gentleman speaks when Shakespeare has interrupted the action for him (or when the events are themselves paused, as for breath); whereas Edgar takes it upon himself to interrupt the action, and as with every other action in this play, Shakespeare tallies its cost. This act of narration occurs within the same continuity of causation and freedom and responsibility as every other act of the play. For it emerges that this long tale has provided the time within which Edmund's writ on the life of Lear and on Cordelia could be executed. Edgar's choice to narrate then and there

is as significant as the content of his narration, and his responsibility for this choice is expressed by the fact that his narration (unlike the Gentleman's) is first person. This further suggests why one may feel that a "first person narrative" is not a narrative; or rather, why the more a first person account takes on the formal properties of a narrative, a tale, the more suspicious the account becomes. For a first person account is, after all, a confession; and the man who has something to confess has something to conceal. And the man who has the word "I" at his disposal has the quickest device for concealing himself. And the man who makes a tale with this word is either distracted from the necessity of authenticating his use of it, or he is admitting that he cannot provide its authentication by himself, and so appealing for relief. We have had occasion to notice moments in Edgar's narration which show that he remains concealed to himself throughout his revelations. The third person narrator, being deprived of self-reference, cannot conceal himself; that is to say, he has no self, and therefore nothing, to conceal. This is another source of his credibility. Then what is the motive for telling us these things? Which really means: What is ours in listening to it?

Philosophy which proceeds from ordinary language is proceeding from the fact *that* a thing is said; that it is (or can be) said (in certain circumstances) is as significant as what it says; its being said then and there is as determinative of what it says as the meanings of its individual words are. This thought can sometimes bring to attention the extraordinary *look* of philosophical writing. The form of, say, Descartes' *Meditations* is that of a first person narrative: "Nevertheless, I must remember that I am a man, and that consequently I am accustomed to sleep and in my dreams to imagine the same things that lunatics imagine when awake, or sometimes things which are even less plausible." But one realizes that there is no particular person the narrative is about (if, that is, one had realized that it looks as if there were some particular person it is about and that if there is not there ought to be some good reason why it sets out to look as if there were), and that its motive, like the motive of a lyric poem, is absolute veracity. And someone whose motive is absolute veracity is likely to be very hard to understand.

3. Accounts which are simultaneous with the events they describe—which are written or spoken in the present tense—are, for instance, reports or announcements; reporters and announcers are

people who tell you what *is* happening. There is room, so to speak, for their activity because they are in a position to know something *we* do not know. But here, in a theater, there is no such position. We are present at what is happening.

* *

I will say: We are not in, and cannot put ourselves in, the presence of the characters; but we are in, or can put ourselves in, their *present*. It is in making their present ours, their moments as they occur, that we complete our acknowledgment of them. But this requires making their present *theirs*. And that requires us to face not only the porousness of our knowledge (of, for example, the motives of their actions and the consequences they care about) but the repudiation of our perception altogether. This is what a historian has to face in knowing the past: the epistemology of other minds is the same as the metaphysics of other times and places. Those who have felt that the past has to be *made* relevant to the present fall into the typical error of parents and children—taking difference from each other to threaten, or promise, severance from one another. But we are severed; in denying that, one gives up not only knowledge of the position of others but the means of locating one's own. In failing to find the character's present we fail to make *him* present. Then he is indeed a fictitious creature, a figment of my imagination, like all the other people in my life whom I find I have failed to know, have known wrong. How terribly difficult this is to stop doing is indexed by the all but inescapable temptation to think of the past in terms of theater. (For a while I kept a list of the times I read that some past war or revolution was a great drama or that some historical figure was a tragic character on the stage of history. But the list got too long.) As if we were spectators of the past. But from what position are we imagining that we can see it? One there, or one here? The problem is sometimes said to be that we have our own perspective, and hence that we see only from an angle. But that is the same impulse to theatricality, now speaking with a scientific accent. (If bias or prejudice is the issue, then a man has his ordinary moral obligation to get over it.) For there is no *place* from which we can see the past. Our position is to be discovered, and this is done in the painful way it is always done, in piecing it out totally. That the self, to be known truly, must be known in its totality, and that this is practical, is the teaching, in their various ways, of Hegel, of Nietzsche, and of Freud.

If the suggestion is right that the "completion of acknowledgment" requires self-revelation, then making the characters present must be a form of, or require, self-revelation. Then what is revealed? Not something about me personally. Who my Gloucester is, and where my Dover is, what my shame attaches to, and what love I have exiled in order to remain in control of my shrinking kingdom—these are still my secrets. But perhaps I am better prepared for the necessity to give them up, freed of pity for myself and terror at myself. What I reveal is what I share with everyone else present with me at what is happening: that I am hidden and silent and fixed. In a word, that there is a point at which I am helpless before the acting and the suffering of others. But I know the true point of my helplessness only if I have acknowledged totally the fact and the true cause of their suffering. Otherwise I am not emptied of help, but withholding of it. Tragedy arises from the confusion of these states. Catharsis, if that is the question, is a matter of purging attachment from everything but the present, from pity for the past and terror of the future. My immobility, my transfixing, rightly attained, is expressed by that sense of awe, always recognized as the response to tragedy.[17] In another word, what is revealed is my separateness from what is happening to them; that I am I, and here. It is only in this perception of them as separate from me that I make them present. That I make them *other,* and face them.

And the point of my presence at these events is to join in confirming this separateness. Confirming it as neither a blessing nor a curse, but a fact, the fact of having one life—not one rather than two, but this one rather than any other. I cannot confirm it alone. Rather, it is the nature of this tragedy that its actors have to confirm their separateness alone, through isolation, the denial of others. What is purged is my difference from others, in everything but separateness.

Their fate, up there, out there, is that they must act, they are in the arena in which action is ineluctable. My freedom is that I am

---

[17] Here I may mention J. V. Cunningham's *Woe or Wonder: The Emotional Effect of Shakespearean Tragedy* (Denver: University of Denver Press, 1951), a work I have more than once had on my mind in thinking of these topics, less for particular detail than for its continuous sense that the effect of tragedy is specific to it, hence part of its logic.

not now in the arena. Everything which can be done is being done. The present in which action is alone possible is fully occupied. It is not that my space is different from theirs but that I have no space within which I can move. It is not that my time is different from theirs but that I have no present apart from theirs. The time in which that hint is laid, in which that knowledge is fixed, in which those fingers grip that throat, is all the time I have. There is no time in which to stop it. At his play, Claudius knows this; which makes him an ideal auditor of serious drama. Only he was unlucky enough to have seen the play after he had actually acted out the consequences of its, and of his, condition: so it caught his conscience instead of scouring it.

Now I can give one answer to the question: Why do I do nothing, faced with tragic events? If I do nothing because I am distracted by the pleasures of witnessing this folly, or out of my knowledge of the proprieties of the place I am in, or because I think there will be some more appropriate time in which to act, or because I feel helpless to un-do events of such proportion, then I continue my sponsorship of evil in the world, its sway waiting upon these forms of inaction. I exit running. But if I do nothing because there is nothing to do, where that means that I have given over the time and space in which action is mine and consequently that I am in awe before the fact that I cannot do and suffer what it is another's to do and suffer, then I confirm the final fact of our separateness. And that is the unity of our condition.

The only essential difference between them and me is that they are there and I am not. And to empty ourselves of all other difference can be confirmed in the presence of an audience, of the community, because every difference established between us, other than separateness, is established by the community—that is, by us, in obedience to the community. It is by responding to this knowledge that the community keeps itself in touch with nature. (With Being, I would say, if I knew how.) If C. L. Barber is right (in *Shakespeare's Festive Comedy*) in finding that the point of comedy is to put society back in touch with nature, then this is one ground on which comedy and tragedy stand together. Comedy is fun because it can purge us of the unnatural and of the merely natural by laughing at us and singing to us and dancing for us, and by making us laugh and sing and dance. The tragedy is that comedy has its limits. This is part of the sadness within comedy; the emptiness after a long laugh. Join hands here as we may, one of the hands is mine and the other is yours.

Fortune, in this light, is an instrument of tragedy not because it turns, and turns outside of us. (This is about what Kent thinks of it—"Fortune, good night; smile once more; turn thy wheel" (*II, ii,* 173); and Edgar—". . . made tame to Fortune's blows" (*IV, vi,* 222).) This idea can prompt caution, or feed the wish for vengeance, or inspire a pretty and noble renunciation. Noble Kent is sincere, but Edgar is not; as he is voicing his view of Fortune he is waiting for his chance. That he has altered himself in disguising himself becomes revelatory of his character; as it is revelatory of Kent that his disguise does not alter him, he remains the faithful servant through all. Fortune, in the light of this play, is tragic because it is *mine*; not because it wheels but because each man takes his place upon its wheel. This is what I take Edmund and Lear to discover. Edmund, as he is fallen, and with his life over, is waiting his chance to do some good; and he says "The wheel is come full circle; I am here" (*V, iii,* 174). That "I am here"—imitating Abraham's response when God calls his name (Genesis 22:1)—is the natural expression of the knowledge that my life is mine, the ultimate piece of fortune. That is what I understand Lear's huge lines of revelation to mean: ". . . I am bound upon a wheel of fire . . ." (*IV, vii,* 46–47). His tears scald not because his fortunes are low but because he feels them to be his; all the isolated thrusts of rejection, the arbitrary cuts of ingratitude, the loyalties which shamed and the loves which flayed, the curses flung vile and infinite and sterile against the breaking of his state, these all now make sense, they make the sense his life makes, fortune no longer comes from outside, his life is whole, like a wheel which turns. It is here he takes his life wholly upon himself. So his succeeding lines show his sense of rebirth. That one has to die in order to become reborn is one tragic fact; that one's wholeness deprives others of their life is another; that one's love becomes incompatible with one's life and kills the thing it loves is another. Lear is reborn, but into his old self. That is no longer just tragic, it suggests that tragedy itself has become ineffective, out-worn, because now even death does not overcome our difference. Here again, Gloucester's life amplifies Lear's. For it is one thing, and tragic, that we can learn only through suffering. It is something else that we have nothing to learn from it.

Tragedy is not about the fact that all men are mortal (though perhaps it is about the fact that mortals go to any lengths to avoid that knowledge). Every death is about that fact, and attendance at a tragedy is not a substitute for attendance at a funeral. (We need one another's presence for more than one reason.) A tragedy is about a *particular* death, or set of deaths, and specifically about a death which is neither natural or accidental. The death is *inflicted* (as in suicide or homicide) and it is a punishment or an expiation (like an execution or a sacrifice). But if the death is inflicted, it *need* not have happened. So a radical contingency haunts every story of tragedy. Yet no one *knows* that it could have been prevented because no one knows what would have prevented it. By the time we see these events, or any others whose tragedy shows, the maze of character and circumstance is unchartable. Of course if Othello had not met Iago, if Lear had not developed his plan of division, if Macbeth had not listened to his wife. . . . But could these contingencies have been prevented? If one is assured they could have been, one is forgetting who these characters are. For if, for example, Othello hadn't met Iago he would have created another, his magnetism would have selected him and the magic of his union would have inspired him. So a radical necessity haunts every story of tragedy. It is the enveloping of contingency and necessity by one another, the entropy of their mixture, which produces events we call tragic. Or rather, it is why the death which ends a tragedy strikes one as *inexplicable*: necessary, but we do not know why; avoidable, but we do not know how; wrapped in meaning, but the meaning has not come out, and so wrapped in mystery. This is clearest in the case of Lear, where critics differ over whether he dies from grief or (illusory) joy. But it is equally true of Shakespeare's other tragic heroes: we know from the witches well before Macbeth dies that his death will be mysterious, satisfying (in its efforts to evade) a prophecy; Hamlet knows that his death will remain mysterious, because now that it is time he has no time to tell his story, and he knows that Horatio, whom out of friendship he commissions to tell it, does not understand it; Othello dies upon a kiss, and it is as though he dies *from* it. Of course we may in each case determine upon a cause of death; but the cause does not explain *why* they die. And the question is raised.

It is not then answered. There is no answer, of the kind we think there is. No answer outside of us. Edgar's closing lines have tempted some into looking there for a summary of the play's meaning: "Speak what we feel, not what we ought to say." But at the beginning Lear and Cordelia spoke what they felt, anyway certainly not what they ought to have said. And so it began. These plays begin as mysteriously as they end, with a crazy ritual, some witches, a ghost, an incomprehensible petulant accusation and denial. And they begin and end this way for the same reason, to maintain us in a present.

At the beginning there is no reason why things have come to this pass, nothing an exposition could clarify. It is a crossroads, they are there. There is danger in the truth that everything which happens is "contained" in these openings. For this postulate of "organic form," the dominant postulate of modern analysis both in poetry and in music, may suggest that what succeeds the presence of the opening is all that *could* have succeeded it. Whereas what succeeds it is one working out of its content.   —This is still misleading, for what does "its content" mean? What succeeds the opening is . . . a succession from it. What goes on to happen is not inevitable; but anything that goes on to happen inevitably bears marks of what has gone before. What has gone before was not inevitable, but when it has happened its marks are inevitable. What the idea of "organic structure" omits is the necessity of action, the fact of succession. "The content" of the opening means *nothing* until it is brought out; we could say there is no content until it is brought out. And when it all comes out and is brought to a close its content is not exhausted. We could say, it has infinite content: but what this comes to is that we have stopped pursuing it (or it us), that we have been shown that a stop can be *made*. Of course the artist sees more deeply into the possibilities of succession than we do—so we often praise his faculty of invention; but he also sees more poignantly what does not succeed—and we do not often enough sense his power of silence; and he must also bring whatever happens to a close—but we are rarely grateful enough for his mastery of form, as if we took this mastery to be the observation of formalities (in order that we may anticipate) rather than the formation of the observable (in order that we may see).

At the close of these successions we are still in a present, it is another crossroads. *King Lear, Othello,* and *Hamlet* close with promises of words and understanding to come; as if to say, what has happened has stopped but it has not come to an end, we have yet to come to terms with what has happened, we do not know where it will end. *Macbeth* closes not with promises of further words, but just with promises, a hurried string of them, as if to get out of the range of Macbeth's eyes, there in his head; as if those present know, but do not care now to linger over the knowledge, that there are still witches unaccounted for. It is at such inopportune moments that we are cast into the arena of action again, crossroads again beneath our feet. Because the actors have stopped, we are freed to act again; but also compelled to. Our hiddenness, our silence, and our placement are now our choices.

One last word, in this light, about a pair of familiar topics in discussions of tragedy. Why are princes (or the high born) the subjects of tragedy? Why is high tragedy no longer, apparently, an available artistic option? Everything said, in my hearing, about the appropriateness of the high born is right enough: they show most dramatically a downfall, which tragedy comments upon; the life of an entire community is staked in their fortunes; they rationalize the use of elevated style, in particular, of poetry. To this list I would add two simple, or geometrical, features of the prince: (1) The state of which he is head, as befits the medieval universe, is closed. The extremest consequences attending on his life and death, however extensive and however high their cost, are finite, run a certain course —so long, that is, as the state survives. However far his life and death have entered his subjects, each has a position from which to assess its effects, and pay for them. (2) His life and death are the largest in his state, hence easiest to see matched or lost to one another; and since his legitimate succession is the only promise of continued life to his state, his death has to be accounted for. When the closed world burst into the infinite universe, consequences became fully unlimited and untraceable. (Lear suffers even this. His bursting is the sign that the play itself, and tragedy as a whole, has burst its bounds. I have had occasion to notice that when the King confuses abdication, not only does he drain himself of authority, he saps his institutions of authority altogether. Then ceremony is mere ceremony. So at the end no convention has the force to oppose force, of arms or of feeling; no shared form of life controls vengeance nor shapes passion. Tragedy was the price of justice, in a disordered world. In a world without the hope of justice, no price is right.)

Now we are surrounded by inexplicable pain and death, no death is more mysterious or portentous than others, because every death which is not the fruit of a long life is now unaccounted for, since we cannot or will not account for it: not just because, taking local examples, we no longer know why a society may put its own people to death for breaking its rules, nor when it may intervene with death in a foreign place, nor because highway deaths need not happen, nor because the pollution of our air and water has become deliberate, nor because poverty has become inflicted—but because we do not know our position with respect to such things. We are present at these events, and no one is present without making something happen; everything which is happening is happening to me, and I do not know what is happening. I do not know that my helplessness is limited only by my separateness, because I do not know which fortune is mine and which is yours. The world did not become sad; it was always sad. Tragedy has moved into the world, and with it the world becomes theatrical.

Classical tragedies were always national, so perhaps it is not surprising that nations have become tragic. And of the great modern nations which have undergone tragedy, through inexplicable loss of past or loss of future or self-defeat of promise, in none is tragedy so intertwined with its history and its identity as in America. It is cast with uncanny perfection for its role, partly because its power is so awe-inspiring, partly because its self-destruction is so heartbreaking. It had a mythical beginning, still visible, if ambiguous, to itself and to its audience: before there was Russia, there was Russia; before there was France and England, there was France and England; but before there was America there was no America. America was *discovered*, and what was discovered was not a place, one among others, but a setting, the backdrop of a destiny. It began as theater. Its Revolution, unlike the English and French and Russian Revolutions, was not a civil war; it was fought against outsiders, its point was not reform but independence. And its Civil War was not a revolution; the oppressed did not rise, and the point was not the overthrow of a form of government but secession and union, the point was its identity. And neither of these points was settled, nor has either been lost, through defeat or through loss of empire or change of political constitution. So its knowledge is of indefeasible power and constancy. But its fantasies are those of impotence, because it remains at the mercy of its past, because its present is continuously ridiculed by the fantastic promise of its origin and its possibility, and because it has never been assured that it will survive. Since it had a birth, it may die. It feels mortal. And it wishes proof not merely of its continuance but of its existence, a fact it has never been able to take for granted. Therefore its need for love is insatiable. It has surely been given more love than any other nation: its history, until yesterday, is one in which outsiders have been drawn to it and in which insiders are hoarse from their expressions of devotion to it. Those who voice politically radical wishes for this country may forget the radical hopes it holds for itself, and not know that the hatred of America by its intellectuals is only their own version of patriotism. It is the need for love as proof of its existence which makes it so frighteningly destructive, enraged by ingratitude and by attention to its promises rather than to its promise, and which makes it incapable of seeing that it is destructive and frightening. It imagines its evils to come from outside. So it feels watched, isolated in its mounting of waters, denying its shame with mechanical lungs of pride, calling its wrath upon the wrong objects.

It has gone on for a long time, it is maddened now, the love it has had it has squandered too often, its young no longer naturally feel it; its past is in its streets, ungrateful for the fact that a hundred years ago it tore itself apart in order not to be divided; half of it believes the war it is now fighting is taking place twenty-five years ago, when it was still young and it was right that it was opposing tyranny. People say it is isolationist, but so obviously it is not isolationist: since it asserted its existence in a war of secession and asserted its identity in a war against secession it has never been able to bear its separateness. *Union* is what it wanted. And it has never felt that union has been achieved. Hence its terror of dissent, which does not threaten its power but its integrity. So it is killing itself and killing another country in order not to admit its helplessness in the face of suffering, in order not to acknowledge its separateness. So it does not know what its true helplessness is. People say it is imperialist and colonialist, but it knows that it wants nothing more. It was told, as if in a prophecy, that no country is evil which is not imperialist or colonialist. So it turns toward tyranny, to prove its virtue. It is *the* anti-Marxist country, in which production and possession are unreal and consciousness of appreciation and of its promise is the only value. The Yankee is as unpractical as the Cavalier, his action as metaphysical as his greatest literature. Yet what needs doing, could he see his and his world's true need, he could do, no one else so capable of it or so ready for it. He *could*. It's a free country. But it will take a change of consciousness. So phenomenology becomes politics.

✳ ✳

Since we are ineluctably actors in what is happening, nothing can be present to us to which we are not present. Of course we can still know, more than ever, what is going on. But then we always could, more or less. What we do not now know is what there is to acknowledge, what it is I am to make present, what I am to make myself present to. I know there is inexplicable pain and death everywhere, and now if I ask myself why I do nothing the answer must be, I choose not to. That is, doing nothing is no longer something which has a place insured by ceremony; it is the thing I am doing. And it requires the same energy, the same expense of cunning and avoidance, that tragic activity used to have to itself. Tragedy, could it now be written, would not show us that we *are* helpless—it never did, and we are not. It would show us, what it always did, why we (as audience) are helpless. Classically, the reason was that pain and death were in our presence when we were not in theirs. Now the reason is that we absent ourselves from them. Earlier, the members of the audience revealed only their common difference from the actors. Now each man is revealed privately, for there is no audience, apart from each man's making himself an audience; what is revealed is that there is no community, no identity of condition, but that each man has his reasons, good or bad, for choosing not to act. After a tragedy now, should one be written, the members of the audience would not see one another measured against nature again, but ranged against it, as if nature has been wiped out and the circle of social and historical arbitrariness is now complete. The point of reason, the thing that made it seem worth deifying, was not simply that it provided God-like power, but that it could serve to rationalize and hence to minimize distress. But the consequences of its uses, since no one is responsible for them—that is, no one more than anyone else—is that it has made everything require an answer, and only I have the answer;

that is, no one has it if I have not. And if I have not, I am guilty; and if I have, and do not act upon it, I am guilty. What we forgot, when we deified reason, was not that reason is incompatible with feeling, but that knowledge requires acknowledgment. (The withdrawals and approaches of God can be looked upon as tracing the history of our attempts to overtake and absorb acknowledgment by knowledge; God would be the name of that impossibility.) Either you have to be *very* careful what you know—keep it superficial or keep it away from the self and one's society and history and away from art and from heaven—or else in order not to acknowledge what you have learned you will have to stifle or baffle feeling, stunt the self. This is why, in the visions of Marx and of Kierkegaard, reason and philosophy must be made to end.

In such circumstances, a purpose of tragedy remains unchanged: to make us practical, capable of acting. It used to do that by showing us the natural limitations of action. Now its work is not to purge us of pity and terror, but to make us capable of feeling them again, and this means showing us that there is a place to act upon them. This does not mean that tragedy now must become political. Because first, it was always political, always about the incompatibility between a particular love and a particular social arrangement for love. Because second, and more specifically, we no longer know what is and is not a political act, what may or may not have recognizable political consequences. That, for example, editorials and public denunciations of a government now have consequences which are accommodated by that government is something we have grown accustomed to. And we have known since Agamemnon that the child of a king may be sacrificed by its parent for the success of the state. But we had hardly expected, what now is apparently coming to be the case, that the ordinary citizen's ordinary faithfulness to his children may become a radical political act. We have known, anyway since eighteenth-century France and nineteenth-century America and Russia that high art can be motivated by a thirst for social change. But in an age in which the organs of news, in the very totality and talent of their coverage, become distractions from what is happening, presenting everything happening as overwhelmingly present, like events in old theater—in such an age the intention to serious art can itself become a political act: not because it can label the poison in public words, purify the dialect of the tribe—perhaps it can't, for all words now are public and there is no known tribe; but because it is the intention to make an object which bears one's conviction and which might bring another to himself; it is an attestation of faith that action remains mine to perform or withhold, of knowledge that the world of fashion and loss and joylessness is not all there is and is powerless if I do not give it power; it provides, apart from the good man, what evidence there is of things unseen, and is the region in which absolute virtue is, and is all that is, rewarded. Such knowledge is good for the soul. It is also good for the society which still likes to see virtue rewarded; it is destructive to the society which has lost the habit of virtue. We could also say: We no longer know what is and is not news, what is and is not a significant fact of our present history, what is and is not relevant to one's life. The newspaper tells me that everything is relevant, but I cannot really accept that because it would mean that I do not have one life, to which some things are relevant and some not. I cannot really deny it either because I do not know why things happen as they do and why I am not responsible for any or all of it. And so to the extent that I still have feeling to contend with, it is a generalized guilt, which only confirms my paralysis; or else I convert the disasters and sensations reported to me into topics of conversation, for mutual entertainment, which in turn irritates the guilt.

One function of tragedy would be to show me that this view of the world is itself chosen, and theatrical. It would show that events are still specific, that guilt will alter itself or puff itself out of shape, in order to deny debt for the specific deed for which one is responsible, that the stakes of action and inaction are what they always were, that monsters of evil are only men, that the good in the world is what good men do, that at every moment there is a present passing me by and that the reason it passes me by is the old reason, that I am not present to it. In *King Lear*, we miss presentness through anticipation, we miss the present moment by sweet knowledge of moments to come or bitter knowledge of moments past. Now we miss presentness through blindness to the fact that the space and time we are in are specific, supposing our space to be infinite and our time void, losing ourselves in space, avoided by time.

If a tragedy would not know how to look, which could bring presentness back, still it knows something: it knows that this ignorance is shared by all modernist arts, each driving into itself to maintain the conviction it has always inspired, to reaffirm the value which men have always placed upon it. It knows that, to make us practical, our status as audience will have to be defeated, because the theater no longer provides a respite from action, but one more deed of inaction, hence it knows that theater must be defeated, inside and out. It knows that we do not have to be goaded into action, but, being actors, to be given occasion to stop—in our case, to stop choosing silence and hiddenness and paralysis, or else to choose them in favor of ourselves. It knows that this requires that we reveal ourselves and that, as always, this is not occasioned by showing me that something happening is relevant to me—that is inescapably the case—but by showing me something to which I am relevant, or irrelevant. Oedipus and Lear could learn this by learning what, within the wheeling of events, they are affected by and what they are causing. Their tragic fact was that they could find who they were only by finding themselves at the cause of tragedy. They are heroic because they care completely who they are; they are tragic because what they find is incompatible with their existence. Our tragic fact is that we find ourselves at the cause of tragedy, but without finding ourselves.

We have, as tragic figures do, to go back to beginnings, either to un-do or to be undone, or to do again the thing which has caused tragedy, as though at some point in the past history is stuck, and time marks time there waiting to be released. Lear causes tragedy when his fast intent to shake all cares pushes his final care into the open. In normal periods, tragic acts are skirted by one's cares remaining superficial enough or mutually compatible enough for them not to suffer naked exposure. In the typical situation of tragic heroes, time and space converge to a point at which an ultimate care is exposed and action must be taken which impales one's life upon the founding care of that life—that in the loss of which chaos is come, in the loss of which all is but toys, in the loss of which there is nothing and nothing to come, and disgust with the self, natural enough at any time, becomes overwhelming. Death, so caused, may be mysterious, but what founds these lives is clear enough: the capacity to love, the strength to found a life upon a love. That the love becomes incompatible with that life is tragic, but that it is maintained until the end is heroic. People capable of such love could have removed mountains; instead it has caved in upon them. One moral of such events is obvious: if you would avoid tragedy, avoid love; if you cannot avoid love, avoid integrity; if you cannot avoid integrity, avoid the world; if you cannot avoid the world, destroy it. Our tragedy differs from this classical chain not in its conclusion but in the fact that the conclusion has been reached without passing through love, in the fact that no love seems worth founding one's life upon, or that society—and therefore I myself—can allow no context in which love, for anything but itself, can be expressed. In such a situation it can look as if the state is the villain and all its men and women merely victims. But that picture is only a further extension of the theatricality which causes it. Our problem is that society can no longer hear its own screams. Our problem, in getting back to beginnings, will not be to find the thing we have always cared about, but to discover whether we have it in us always to care about something.

The classical environment of tragedy was the extraordinary and the unnatural, and it is tempting, now that things have changed, to say that the environment of tragedy has become the ordinary and the natural. Except that we no longer know what is ordinary and natural, and hence no longer know what is tragic and what is not (so it is not surprising that tragedies are not written). We could say that just this amnesia is our tragedy. Except that it is not amnesia and it is not necessarily bad—for it is not as if we knew or could remember a state of society in which the ordinary was the natural state of affairs. All we know is, at one time a state of affairs was *accepted* by those trained to it as natural. (From which it does not follow that all such states of affairs are good, nor even that those born to the manner found it good.) That itself may seem cause enough for envy. Yet we know no less about our own state of affairs. Except that we also know our reversals of fortune can come about through *any* change: it no longer requires the killing of kings; the heaving of past into present; a forest of enemies advancing. Our ghostly commissions are unnoticeable; perhaps they are only the half-hearted among our parents' wishes, which they would have been half-proud to see us decline and which we only half-know have been executed. Reversal can also come with a shift in what we accept as natural, as in those odd moments throughout which, as in successful prayer, we really know, say, that a black man is a man like any other; that our child or parent is a person like any other, entitled to and cursed by the same separateness as any other; that the good opinion of people we do not care about is humiliating to care about and that the bad opinion of people we do care about may be humiliating to care about too much. At such moments the way we live appears unnatural, the world we have chosen becomes extraordinary and unnecessary, the death lingering for us seems unnatural, as though we have chosen to die as we have chosen to live, for nothing. If that is theatrical, it is equally theatrical to *look for something* for which to live or die. There are only the old things, and they are at hand, or nowhere. Then how, in space and out of time, shall we make ourselves present to them?

Hamlet dies before an audience, harping on the audience present to him, and his consciousness of himself is immortalized by his consciousness of them. That is not an option for us, not merely because we cannot command an audience, since no one's position is relevantly different from mine; but because, since no one's position is relevantly different from mine, to convert others into an audience is to further the very sense of isolation which makes us wish for an audience. Its treatment of this fact is what makes *King Lear* so threatening, together with its consequent questioning of what we accept as natural and legitimate and necessary. The cost of an ordinary life and death, of insisting upon one's one life, and avoiding one's own cares, has become the same as the cost of the old large lives and deaths, requires the same lucidity and exacts the same obscurity and suffering. This is what Lear knows for the moment before his madness; it is the edge Gloucester's blinding has led him to. Immediately after Lear's prayer (*III, iv,* 28–36), he gives himself up to the tempest in his mind and to the storm which is to destroy the world; Gloucester's thoughts, just after his prayer (*IV, i,* 66–71), turn to Dover and its cliff. That is, successful prayer is prayer for the strength to change, it is the beginning of change, and change presents itself as the dying of the self and hence the ending of the world. The cause of tragedy is that we would rather murder the world than permit it to expose us to change. Our threat is that this has become a common option; our tragedy is that it does not seem to us that we are taking it. We think *others* are taking it, though they are not relevantly different from ourselves. Lear and Gloucester are not tragic because they are isolated, singled out for suffering, but because they had covered their true isolation (the identity of their condition with the condition of other men) within hiddenness, silence, and position; the ways people do. It is the enormity of this plain fact which accompanies the overthrow of Lear's mind, and we honor him for it.

But we will not abdicate. As though this was *his* answer, while ours will come later, on another occasion, from outside. And it does look, after the death of kings and out of the ironies of revolutions and in the putrefactions of God, as if our trouble is that there used to be answers and now there are not. The case is rather that there used not to be an unlimited question and now there is. "Human reason has this peculiar fate that in one species of its knowledge it is burdened by questions which, as prescribed by the very nature of reason itself, it is not able to ignore, but which, as transcending all its powers, it is not able to answer." (Preface to the first edition of the *Critique of Pure Reason*, opening sentence.) Hegel and Marx, as we know, found this fate not in human reason but in human history. Hegel then denied the distinction between them, Marx thought they could at last be distinguished. Hegel thought both were finished, Marx thought both could now begin. The world whistles over them. We cannot hear them.

\* \*

If it is right to relate the drama in *King Lear* to the drama in music, then it should not surprise us that this source of drama disappeared from theater, for it has more recently disappeared from music as well—anyway, disappeared as something that can be taken for granted. The comparison between Shakespearean theater and tonal music is not a mere analogy, but it is not an explanation either. For it is not as if we know so well how we listen to this music that we can apply our knowledge there to the theater. On the contrary, it seems to me equally illuminating, and perhaps even closer to an explanation, to say that, when we understand, we listen to the music most familiar to us in the way we follow lines and actions in that medium which makes poetry drama. In my experience, this kind of listening is no longer fully possible with the disappearance of tonality —perhaps it is this continuous presentness which we miss most in the difficulties of post-tonal music, more than its lack of tunes and harmony and pulse rhythm. It would, I believe, be possible to study the work of serious composers of the past two generations or so, and certainly those now at work, in terms of the ways in which they avoid, and attempt to reclaim, its history of drama. This suggests that faithfulness now to the art of music is not expressed by an effort, as it may be put, to find modes or organization based upon sound itself (a form of words which may describe all music, or none at all) but to discover what it is about sounds in succession which at any time has allowed them to be heard as presentness.

Nietzsche began writing by calling for the rebirth of tragedy from the spirit of music. But that had already happened, as drama lost the use of poetry and turned to music. What Nietzsche heard in Wagner was something else—the death, and the call for the death, of music and of drama and hence of society, as they had been known.

# THEMATIC INDEX

# Thematic Index

This listing is not meant to be exhaustive, nor rigidly selective. It is supposed to be useful, both as a guide to concerns which go over the edges of the individual essays, and as suggestions of lines of further development.

# INDEX OF NAMES

# Index of Names